CHARIOTS AND OTHER WHEELED VEHICLES

IN ITALY BEFORE THE ROMAN EMPIRE

J. H. Crouwel

Oxbow Books
Oxford and Oakville

Published by
Oxbow Books, Oxford, UK

ISBN 978-1-84217-467-8

A CIP record for this book is available from the British Library

This book is available direct from

Oxbow Books, Oxford, UK
(Phone: 01865-241249; Fax: 01865-794449)

and

The David Brown Book Company
PO Box 511, Oakville, CT 06779, USA
(Phone: 860-945-9329; Fax: 860-945-9468)

or from our website

www.oxbowbooks.com

Library of Congress Cataloging-in-Publication Data

Crouwel, J. H.
Chariots and other wheeled vehicles in Italy before the Roman empire / J.H. Crouwel. -- 1st [edition].
    pages cm
Includes bibliographical references and index.
ISBN 978-1-84217-467-8
1. Chariots--Italy--History. 2. Carriages and carts--Italy--History. 3. Italy--Antiquities. I. Title.
TS2010.C75 2012
932'.014--dc23
                            2012011367

Cover: Small-scale chariot model (J. Spruytte)

Printed in Wales by
Gomer Press, Llandysul, Wales

In memory of Ann Brown and Mary Littauer

Contents

Acknowledgements

During the preparation of this study I have profited greatly from the help of five people: Mrs M. A. Littauer read early drafts of much of the text, generously sharing her ideas with me and improving the English in the years before her death in December 2005; my sister-in-law G. Skyte-Bradshaw also gave much help with the English; Mrs G. Jurriaans-Helle carefully and critically read the manuscript; Dr J. Morel prepared several drawings, bringing his exemplary skill and patience to bear on this time-consuming task; Dr A. Emiliozzi discussed with me the results of her remarkable work on the remains of actual vehicles from ancient Italy and their reconstruction, in the context of the exhibition in Viterbo organized by her in 1997.

In addition, I am most grateful to all those others who have helped with information and advice of various kinds, supplied photographs or gave permission to reproduce illustrations, or allowed me to study material under their care: G. Brownrigg, Professor H. A. G. Brijder, Dr J. P. Crielaard, Dr A. Curci, Dr A. De Santis, Dr M. Diepeveen-Jansen, Dr T. Doorewaard, Professor M. Gnade, R. Hurford, Dr M. van Leusen, M. Lucassen, Dr P. Lulof, Dr E. Macnamara, I. Mantel, Dr L. B. van der Meer, Dr J. R. Mertens, Professor E. M. Moormann, Dr C. W. Neeft, Dr A. J. Nijboer, Professor F. Quesada Sanz, M. de Reuver, A. Spruytte, Dr J. Swaddling, Dr D. J. Waarsenburg and J. Zhang. Special thanks are due to J. Eerbeek and A. Dekker for invaluable help with the preparation of the text and illustrations.

This study is dedicated to the memory of Mrs Ann Brown who generously passed on to me her extensive documentation of chariots in Italy before the Roman Empire, and of Mary Littauer, with whom I collaborated on the subject of ancient wheeled vehicles and riding for so many years.

Amsterdam/Castricum, June 2011

Preface

This study presents evidence for transport by wheeled vehicle in Italy before the Roman Imperial period, the beginning of which is often thought to be marked by Augustus's conquest of Egypt in 30 BC.

There are three categories of wheeled vehicle documented for the period under study. One is the chariot, a fast, usually horse-drawn conveyance with two spoked wheels, designed to carry one or more persons, who normally remained standing. The others are the cart, also a two-wheeler but designed to carry a stable load, i.e. goods or seated passengers, and the four-wheeled wagon. (These and other more technical terms, marked in the text by *q.v.*, are explained in the Glossary, below.)

The sources of information currently available are extensive. They include many figured documents, most of them two-dimensional, such as architectural terracottas, stone reliefs, vase and wall paintings. There are also bronze and terracotta models in the round, mostly small. In addition, remains of actual vehicles, in a few cases accompanied by their harness teams, have been identified from various tombs. The wooden parts of the vehicle have usually decayed but metal elements are preserved, though not often *in situ*. There are also numerous metal bridle bits, as well as other horse gear; most of the latter were used with chariot teams, though some may have belonged to ridden horses.

The varied archaeological sources that will be discussed primarily relate to the cultures of central and northern Italy. The material mostly ranges in date from the eighth and seventh centuries BC onwards, while some actual wheels and horse bits go back to the second millennium BC. The mainly figured documents from the sphere of the Greek colonies in southern Italy and Sicily – the areas often referred to as *Magna Graecia* – will be used with caution and mainly for comparative purposes. This is because the chariots represented there, from the later seventh century BC onwards, are usually of distinct (mainland) Greek type. Our figured evidence in general often poses the question of how to distinguish between vehicles that were actually used in Italy and those deriving from Greek or oriental artistic models.

Apart from the archaeological sources, textual information relating to the vehicles that were in use during the period under study may be found in Greek and Roman texts.

Serious interest in wheeled vehicles in Italy prior to the Roman Imperial period was first recorded in E. Nachod's *Der Rennwagen bei den Italiker und ihren Nachbarn*, published in 1909 as one of a series of doctoral dissertations on chariots in the ancient world supervised by F. Studnizcka at the University of Leipzig.

Chariot representations from central Italy were considered in studies of terracotta revetment plaques from temples or other public buildings in central Italy by E. D. van Buren (1921), A. Andrén (1939–1940 and 1974) and Å. Åkerström (1954).

Evidence for chariot racing yielded by these and other figured documents was fruitfully discussed by R. C. Bronson in 1965 (see also 1956). The 1960s also saw the publication of F. W. von Hase's corpus of surviving metal horse bits of the early centuries of the first millennium BC (1969).

A major contribution to the subject of wheeled vehicles was made by E. Woytowitsch in *Die Wagen der Bronze- und frühen Eisenzeit in Italien* (1978). This book brought together and described in detail many of the actual vehicle remains, as well as illustrating a variety of representations.[1] In the same year

---

[1] Included are also various objects and representations that are not directly relevant to our subject. These include bronze wheeled cauldrons, and many imported Greek vases (see our p. 26, note 111 and p. 90, note 15).

O. Cornaggio Castigioni and G. Calegari published an extensive article on remains of actual disk and cross-bar wheels from northern Italy.

The possible military use of chariots was discussed by Ch. Saulnier (1980) and P. E. Stary (especially 1980 and 1981a). Wheeled vehicles and their use received detailed attention in U. Höckmann's study of the bronzes from the so-called Tomba dei Bronzi at Castel San Mariano in Umbria (1982). In the 1980s also appeared studies by L. Galeotti (1986–1988) of aspects of the construction of chariots and carts, and by Bartoloni and C. Grottanelli (1984, reprinted in 1989) on their functions and social significance. Chariots and roads featured in contributions to *Stradi degli Etruschi* (1985). Important also is W. Weber's brief survey of vehicles in Italy before and during the Roman Empire (1986; see also 1978), as well as sections on Italy in S. Piggott's masterly overview of wheeled vehicles in prehistoric Europe (1983, 86, 97f., 130f., 178–84, 190–3). Vehicles from Italy were also considered in contributions by C. F. E. Pare and others to a collective work on the actual wagons of the Hallstatt period north of the Alps (*Vierrädrige Wagen* 1987), and again in Pare's exhaustive study of 1992, *Wagons and Wagon Graves of the Early Iron Age in Central Europe*.

The 1990s saw the publication of important studies by L. Nebelsick (1992) of foreign influences on chariots in Italy, and by G. Bartoloni (1993) of the social functions of the vehicles. A brief discussion of chariot construction by H. Hayen (1991) and an overview of their material remains by F. Cordano (1994) also appeared.

Chariots, their material remains and/or representations, together with actual horse bits and other gear, featured prominently in several temporary exhibitions and the accompanying catalogues: see especially *Etrusker in der Toskana* (Hamburg 1987), *Die Welt der Etrusker* (Berlin 1990), *La grande Roma dei Tarquini* (Rome 1990), *Antichità dall'Umbria* (New York 1991), *Principi etruschi fra Mediterranea ed Europa* (Bologna 2000) and *Gli Etruschi* (Venice 2000). Some of these catalogues, along with other recent publications (Boitani 1983; 1985; 1987; Boitani and Aureli 1988; Emiliozzi 1988; 1991; 1992; 1996), described (reconstructions of) actual chariots and carts, from both old and recent excavations.

The more recent literature on the subject is dominated by the book accompanying an exhibition which was entirely devoted to the subject of wheeled vehicles, *Carri da guerra e principi etruschi* (Viterbo, Ancona and Rome 1997–2000). This exhibition, organized by A. Emiliozzi, brought together for the first time several specially-made, full-scale reconstructions of actual vehicles. The contributions by various scholars to the book present a wealth of information on, and (re-) interpretation of, chariots and other types of vehicle in different parts of ancient Italy (see especially Colonna 1997; Emiliozzi 1997; Cerchiae, Golucci Pescatori and D.'Hardy 1997; Camerin 1997a). The appended catalogue of vehicular remains ('*Repertorio del carri proveniente della peninsola italiana*'), compiled by N. Camerin and Emiliozzi, is invaluable, its 280 entries hugely expanding on Woytowitsch's survey of 1978.

The literature of the early twenty-first century includes more work by Emiliozzi (2000; 2001a; 2001b; 2004; 2004–5; 2006; Emiliozzi, Moscati and Santoro 2007, 150–4), observations and additional bibliography by G. Bartoloni (2003, 170–92), and a reappraisal of the vehicular remains from the Tomba dei Bronzi at Castel Mariano by S. Bruni (2002). Vehicular remains, along with horse bits and other gear, were also considered in studies on the Tomba del Trono at Verucchio in Emilia Romagna (P. von Eles and others in *Guerriero e sacerdote* 2002), the Tomba del Tridente at Vetulonia in Toscana (Cygielman and Pagnoni 2006) and a tomb at Capena in Lazio (Sommella Mura 2004–5). Other such remains, from Marche (the region of ancient Picenum), were described in recent exhibition catalogues (*Eroi e regine* 2001; *Museo Civico Archeologico ('F. Savini') Teramo* 2006; *Potere e splendore* 2008). Of note is also C. Scheffer's article on chariot racing (2003). The vehicle burials and social functions of chariots, carts and wagons were discussed by P. Amann (2000, 66–75).

Most recently, chariots (and carts) were discussed in N. A. Winter's magisterial study of all known terracotta revetment plaques of the sixth–fifth century from central Italy (2009). The social functions of chariots and other wheeled vehicles were discussed anew by C. Riva (2010, especially 95–107). Chariots also figured prominently in the full publication of one temple with such plaques, *Il tempio arcaico di Caprifico di Torrecchio* (see Lubtchansky 2010; Lulof 2010a; 2010b). This book also contained my own first brief account of chariots (in central) Italy (Crouwel 2010; see also Crouwel 2006).

The above overview shows that chariots and other types of wheeled vehicle in Italy before the Roman Empire have received a fair deal of attention over the years. As yet, however, there is no systematic study along the lines of my two previous works on vehicles in ancient Greece (Crouwel 1981 and 1992). In particular, comparative material from Greece and further east, as well as from Europe north of the Alps, can help towards a better understanding of the vehicles of Italy and the ways in which they were used.

It remains to outline the organization of this study. A glossary of technical terms, with some drawings for clarity's sake, is followed by a chapter (Chapter I) describing the evidence for roads and for the animals that were used in draught. Then follows a detailed account of chariots (Chapter II). These vehicles are discussed according to their constituent parts (body, axle, wheels and traction system), the ways in which their draught teams were harnessed and controlled, and the use to which the chariots were put. The other types of vehicle – carts and wagons – are next treated in similar fashion (Chapters III and IV). Chapter V looks at the history of wheeled vehicles in Italy before the Roman Imperial period. It traces local, Italic characteristics and possible foreign influences, and assesses the relative importance of the different kinds of wheeled vehicle and of other means of land transport – by pack and riding animal. In Appendices 1 and 2 the wheeled vehicles depicted in so-called Situla Art of northern Italian and Alpine regions, and 'the Celtic chariot' are discussed.

The study as a whole is concerned chiefly with technical matters, as were my earlier ones of wheeled vehicles in Greece. The available Latin and Greek textual evidence is used with caution. A detailed study of the social and economic implications of the various wheeled vehicles is not attempted, mainly in view of the paucity of explicit information available for the period under consideration.

In this book, regions and ancient place names in Italy are usually referred to by their modern Italian names. When referring to individual tombs, the Italian names rather than their English translations are used.

Chronological Table

Note. All dates are BC, unless stated otherwise. The relative and absolute chronologies adopted here are simplified and all dates are approximate. My main, recent source is Gleba 2008 (1–3 with table 1). It is well known that the absolute chronology of the Late Bronze Age and Iron Age (traditionally *c.* 1350/1300–750/700) in central and northern Italy is in a state of flux. The question is whether the conventional dates, which are used in this study, have to be raised by 25 or more years.[2]

Neolithic	6000–2800
Chalcolithic	2800–2300
Early Bronze Age	2300–1700
Middle Bronze Age	1700–1350
Late Bronze Age	1350–1000
Early Iron Age	1000–750/700
Orientalizing	750/700–600
Archaic	600–475/450
Classical	475/450–300
Hellenistic	300–30

---

[2] See especially Pacciarelli 2000 and the expert contributions to *Oriente e occidente* (2005); Fulminante 2009 (fig. 15.10).

Glossary of technical terms

This glossary duplicates earlier ones to a large extent (Crouwel 1992, 14–17; Littauer and Crouwel 2002, xv–xx). Where possible, cross references to drawings in the main text (Figs 2–5, pp. xiii–xx) are given.

Axle	(Figs 4–5). A rod passing beneath the vehicle floor, the wheels revolving on it or it revolving with the wheels; in antiquity, always of wood.
Axle brackets	(Fig. 4). Elements fastened to the floor frame of a cart, in order to accommodate a revolving axle.
Backing element	An element of harness that transmits the backward (as opposed to the usual forward) movement of the draught animals to the vehicle, at the same time preventing them from backing out of harness.
Biga	A two-horse chariot.
Bit	(Fig. 3). Bridle element for control of the horse by the mouth; composed of mouthpiece and cheekpieces – the latter often erroneously called *psalia* in the literature.
Blinkers	Elements attached to the cheekstraps of the headstall.
Body or box	(Fig. 2). Used here to designate the floor and siding of a vehicle.
Breaststrap	The harness element that passes around the breast and is attached at either end to the dorsal yoke.
Bridle	Means of controlling the horse by the head, composed of a headstall, with or without a bit, and reins.
Browband	(Fig. 2). Headstall strap running across the forehead.
Canon	Mouthpiece of a metal bit, or each single element of a composed ('jointed') mouthpiece.
Cart	(Fig. 4). Always two-wheeled, but with wheels of any construction; used for carrying stable loads, i.e. goods or seated passengers.

	A-frame cart	Cart with the two side timbers running forward to join just before the yoke, giving the whole frame the shape of a capital A.
	Y-poled cart	Cart with the two side timbers bent inwards and brought together a short distance in front of the body, to run contiguously out to the yoke (see also *Y-pole*).

Cavalry	The term may only be properly applied to mounted troops when these are trained to the degree where they can function with precision *as a unit* – not only advancing on command but changing gaits, turning, deploying and reassembling in their proper positions in the ranks.
Chariot	(Fig. 2). A light, fast, two-wheeled, usually horse-drawn vehicle with spoked wheels; used for warfare, racing and ceremonial purposes. Its crew usually stood.
Cheekpieces	(Fig. 3). Two paired elements of a bit, lying at the corners of the horse's lips. Attached to the headstall by cheekstraps, the cheekpieces held the mouthpiece in place, and might also exert pressure on the outside of the horse's lower jaw.
Cheekstraps	(Figs 2–3). Side straps of the headstall, attached to the cheekpieces of the bit and serving to hold them in place.

Crownpiece	Part of the headstall going from side to side over the crown or poll of the horse's head, as continuation of the cheekstraps.
Draught bar or *pole axle*	(Figs 4–5). Part of the fore carriage of a wagon, allowing the draught pole or pole axle to articulate vertically.
Draught pole	(Figs 2, 4–5). The wooden element that connects the vehicle to the yoke.
Felloe	(Fig. 2). The rim of a wheel, into which the outer ends of the spokes are mortised.
Fore carriage	(Fig. 5). Part of a wagon's undercarriage, formed by the pivoting front axle and the kingpin, the draught bar or pole axle, the two traction arms or hounds, and the slide bar.
Frontlet	(also called nosepiece or chamfron). Protective or decorative element lying over the forehead and nasal bone of a horse.
Gauge	See *wheel track.*
Girth	(Fig. 2). The strap passing from side to side under the belly of a draught animal and attached to the yoke ends; in antiquity often acting as a backing element.
Goad	Pointed rod, for prodding.
Half noseband	See *noseband.*
Halter	A simple headstall, used for leading an animal or for tying it up by the head.
Harness	The aggregate of straps that attach an animal to the traction elements of a vehicle. In antiquity especially a breaststrap or neckstrap and a girth or backing element.
	Shaft harness Harness to attach a single animal between a pair of poles which are connected to the vehicle.
Headstall	Part of the bridle, made of straps or rope and designed to hold a controlling bit or noseband in place. It comprises a crownpiece, cheekstraps, a throatlash, sometimes a browband and a noseband.
Hub	See *nave.*
Kingpin	(Fig. 5). Vertical bolt, passing through the centre of the front axle and the forward end of the perch or wagon pole, allowing the wagon's front axle to swivel.
Linch pin	(Fig. 2). A toggle pin passing through the axle end to prevent the wheels from slipping off.
Lock	The amount of turn the front axle and its support structure of a wagon can achieve.
Mouthpiece	(Fig. 3). The part of the bit lying mainly inside the horse's mouth. Composed of one or more canons, it is accordingly called single and solid or 'jointed'.
Nave or *hub*	(Fig. 2). The inner cylindrical element of a wheel, in which the inner ends of the spokes are secured and through which the axle passes.
Nave hoop	A band, usually of metal, encircling one or both ends of the nave to prevent it from splitting.
Neckstrap	(Fig. 2). The strap passing around the neck of each horse and attached at either end to the neck yoke or yoke saddle. Its purpose is to hold the yoke in place.
Noseband	One of the straps of the headstall. It usually encircles the nose and jaw but, in the form of a half noseband, may run across the nose from cheekstrap to cheekstrap.
Outrigger or *trace horse*	In teams of three or four horses abreast (*trigae* and *quadrigae*), a horse not directly under the yoke, but connected more loosely with the vehicle.
Perch or *wagon pole*	(Fig. 5). Central bar, often Y-shaped, connecting the front and rear axles of a wagon; together, the perch and axles form the undercarriage.
Pole brace(s)	(Fig. 4). Element(s) helping to connect the draught pole to the vehicle.
Pole horse or *polar*	One of the two horses that flank the draught pole and are under yoke.
Pole-end support	Thong running back from the forward end of the draught pole to the chariot's body.
Poll	The crown of the horse's head.
Quadriga	A four-horse chariot.

Reins	(Fig. 2). Straps running back from the bit to the driver's hands.
Slide bar	(Fig. 5). Part of the forecarriage of a wagon's *undercarriage*, allowing the perch or wagon pole to slide over it when the front axle pivots.
Spoke	The radial timber of a wheel, connected with the nave at one end and with the felloe at the other.
Terret	Ring through which reins pass; in antiquity terrets were fastened to the draught pole or yoke, or to a harness element on the animal's back.
Throatlash	The strap or thong passing under the throat or rear of the jaw from cheekstrap to cheekstrap and securing the headstall.
Trace	Strap or thong running back from a trace horse or outrigger to the chariot body.
Trace horse	See *outrigger*.
Traction arms or *hounds*	(Fig. 5). Parts of the fore carriage of a wagon's undercarriage.
Tread	The running surface of a wheel of any type.
Triga	A three-horse chariot.
Tyre	(Fig. 2). An outer element of the wheel, protecting the tread of the felloe; in antiquity of metal, rawhide or wood. It also helped to consolidate the wheel.
Undercarriage	(Fig. 5). The fore carriage, the rear axle and the connecting perch or wagon pole, supporting the wagon's body.
Wagon	Four-wheeled, usually relatively heavy vehicle.
Wheel	*Cross-bar wheel*. Wheel with a diametric bar, through which the axle passes. Lighter 'cross-bars' run at right angles to the central bar, between it and the felloe.
	Disk wheel (Fig. 4). Wheel of solid appearance, made of one piece of wood or of several – then called 'composite disk'.
	Spoked wheel (Fig. 2). Wheel composed of a nave or hub, spokes and felloe, often with a tyre.
Wheel track or gauge	The distance between the centres of the treads of the two wheels of a vehicle.
Withers	The most prominent area of an equid's or a bovid's spine, formed by the vertebral processes and located between the shoulder blades. The height of an equid is measured from the ground to the highest point of the withers.
Yoke	Wooden element running across the neck or back of two or more animals and connecting them with the draught pole(s).
	Dorsal yoke Yoke resting on the animals' back, just behind the withers.
	Neck yoke (Figs 2–3). Yoke resting on the animals' neck, ahead of the withers.
Yoke braces	Two leather thongs branching out from the draught pole and running to either arm of the yoke, to prevent the latter from swivelling on the pole.
Yoke peg	Wooden peg passing through the yoke and draught pole, near the latter's forward end.
Yoke saddles	Wooden elements for adapting the yoke to the conformation of equids. Of inverted Y shape, their handle was lashed to the yoke and their 'legs' lay along the animal's shoulders.
Yoke-saddle pad	A piece of leather or fabric, lying beneath the 'legs' of a yoke saddle.
Y-pole	On two-wheelers, composite draught pole, formed of two poles, one coming from each side of the two-wheeled vehicle, bent inwards and brought together a short distance ahead of the body, to run contiguously out to the yoke. On four-wheelers, single pole forking just in front of the vehicle body, its prongs attached rigidly, or to a draught bar or pole axle so as to allow the draught pole to articulate vertically.

Figure 1. Map of Italy, showing regions and places mentioned in the text

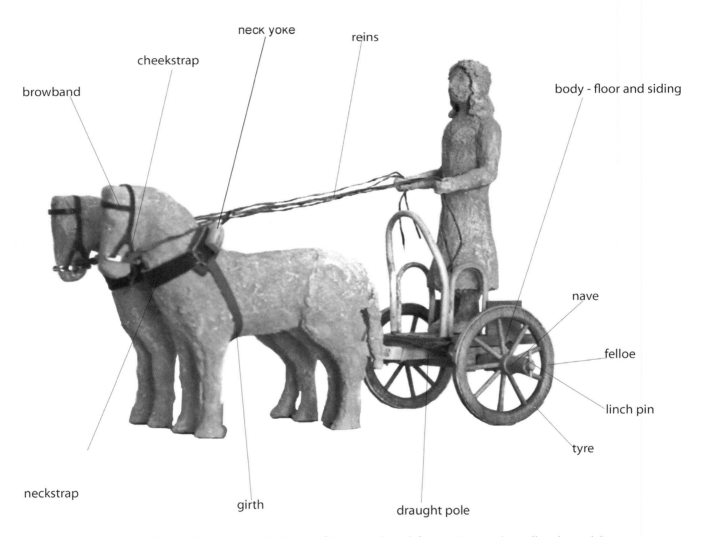

neck yoke

reins

cheekstrap

browband

body - floor and siding

nave

felloe

linch pin

tyre

neckstrap

girth

draught pole

Figure 2. Terminology: harnessed chariot of Type I (adapted from J. Spruytte's small-scale model)

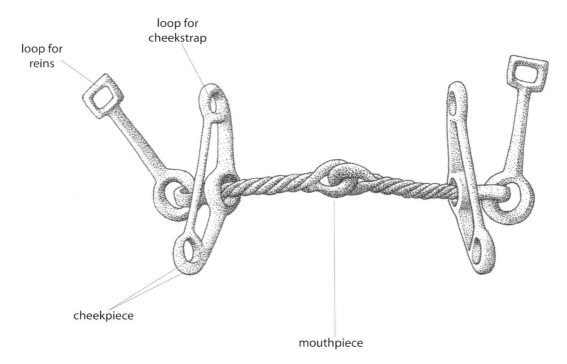

Figure 3. Terminology: bronze horse bit from Bologna, Benacci Caprara cemetery, tomb 938. Bologna, Museo Civico (adapted from Von Hase 1969, pl. 12, no. 134)

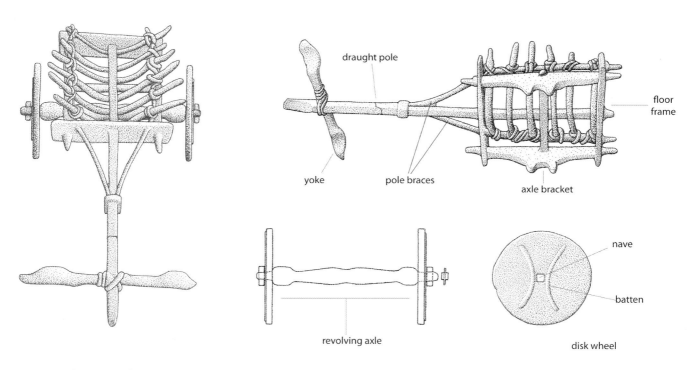

Figure 4. Terminology: bronze model of unharnessed cart from Bolsena. Rome, Museo Nazionale di Villa Giulia 56097 (adapted from Woytowitsch 1978, pls 38–39, no. 168)

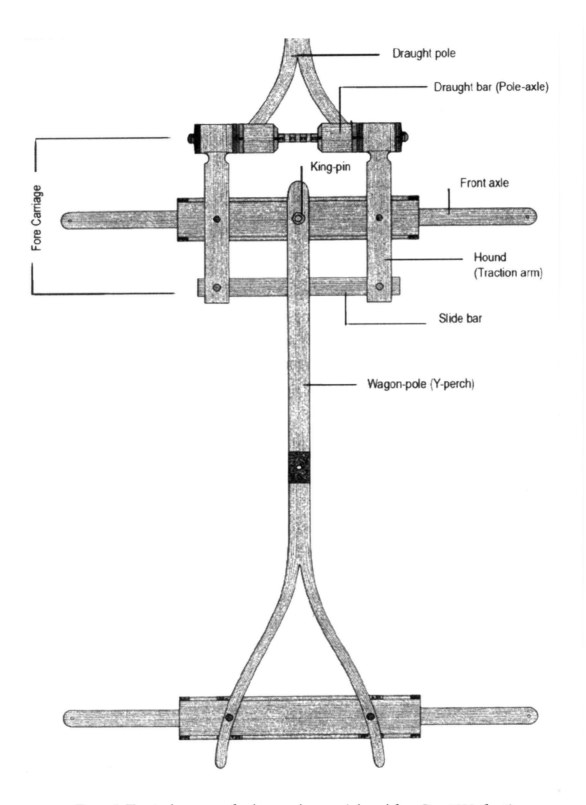

Figure 5. Terminology: part of unharnessed wagon (adapted from Pare 1992, fig. 1)

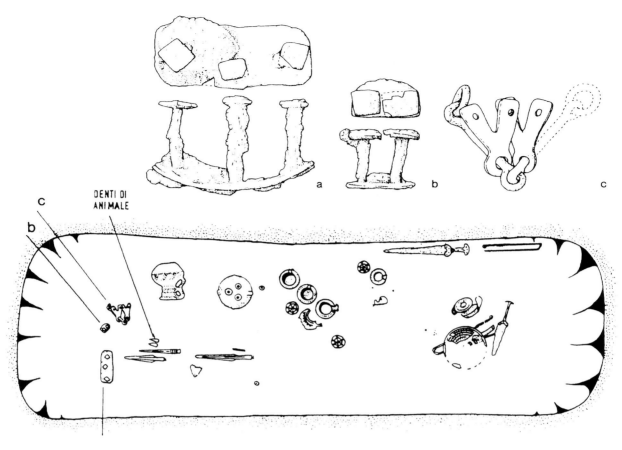

Figure 6. Veii, Quattro Fontanili cemetery, tomb EE 10 B: plan, fragments of iron tyre (a, b), horse bit (c) and horse teeth (after Nebelsick 1992, fig. 7).

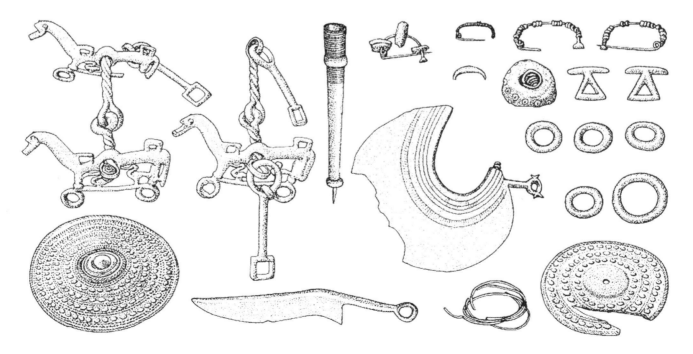

Figure 7. Inventory of Bologna, Benacci Caprara cemetery, tomb 34 (after Von Hase 1969, fig. 5A)

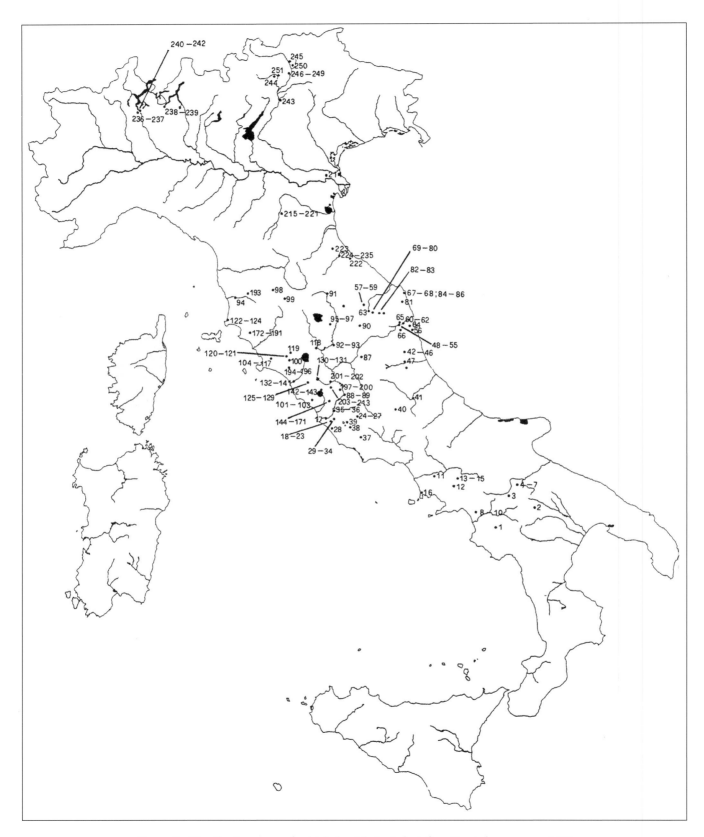

Figure 8. Distribution map of vehicle burials in Italy (after *Carri da guerra*, p. 310)

CHAPTER I

Background to the Enquiry

1. Terrain and roads

The Italian peninsula offers a great variety of landscape forms, ranging from extensive plains – as in the Po valley in the north and in much of the south – and coastal lowlands to hill country and the rugged Apennine mountain range. In many cases, abrupt changes from one landform to another can be observed.[1] While the open and level areas would be conducive to transport by wheeled vehicle, the broken topography of the hills and mountains favours movement on foot or on the back of animals. Pedestrians and animals carrying people or goods needed only simple tracks or paths – in other words, ungraded and unpaved lines of communication. These could be fairly narrow and steep, allowing a shorter, more direct route than would be possible for wheeled vehicles. The latter, if they were not to be restricted to the open and level country, needed wider roads, gently graded to avoid abrupt rises and drops in height and with a minimum of hair-pin bends for negotiating the steeper slopes. For vehicles to negotiate broken terrain, particularly strong and durable construction would often be necessary.[2]

Physical evidence for roads – and streets – capable of taking wheeled vehicles and dating to the time before the Roman Empire has been claimed for different parts of Italy.[3] When reviewing the existing surface remains two basic questions must be asked. The first is whether the postulated (stretch of) road was really designed for wheeled vehicles and not for pedestrians, mounts or pack animals. Although the latter, strictly speaking, needed only tracks or paths, we know that the Via Appia and other well-known, all-weather Roman 'highways' were built primarily to facilitate the movement of troops marching on foot (see below).

Having identified a road as designed for – or at least used by – wheeled transport, an identification helped by the presence of wheelruts in combination with a level road surface of a certain minimum width,[4] we face the second question of how to decide when exactly such a road was built. It is well known that roads of the Roman Empire period were often built over a pre-existing road surface. Here again several factors must be taken into consideration which, preferably in combination with each other, help to provide an answer. The type of construction of any given road, which may or may not be characteristic of one particular period, is important in this respect, as is dating material, especially pottery, used in the making of the road. Furthermore, the location of the road in relation to habitation sites, sanctuaries, tombs or quarries of a particular period may assist in determining when it could have been most useful.

Well-laid and paved roads suitable for wheeled traffic first become visible in different parts of central Italy in the sixth century BC. Such roads required considerable investment of manpower as well as a high degree of organization and technical skills. Good examples are yielded by recent excavations at

---

[1] See a.o. *Italy. Geographical Handbook Series B.R.* 517, vols 1–4 (Mason, K. ed.). Oxford (Naval Intelligence Division) 1944–5; Barker and Rassmussen 1998, ch. 1 (particularly bearing on ancient Etruria and adjacent areas).

[2] See Crouwel 1981, 29; 1992, 21.

[3] For a fairly recent overview, see Quilici 1997; see also Quilici 1988 and 1992.

[4] For the distinction between vehicular and non-vehicular built roads, see also French 1993 (who adopted a standard width of 6.25 m for a 'highway', i.e. a two-lane vehicular road).

Satricum in Lazio, where a succession of roads connected the lower settlement with the acropolis and its sanctuary of the goddess Mater Matuta.[5] One excavated stretch of road consisted of two parallel stone walls or kerbs, *c.* 5–6 m apart, with different layers of filling material between, the latter topped by successive relayings of pavements of shunks of tufa (volcanic rock) and/or pebbles. The evidence at Satricum, dating to the later sixth and early fifth centuries, also includes one wheelrut, a drainage system and side-walks for pedestrians. Other sites in Lazio have produced evidence in excavation for similar but narrower paved roads. These roads, 2 m to 4.40–4.70 m in width, remained in use from the sixth century until Roman Republican times or later.[6]

In Lazio a very wide (over 10 m) stone-paved road, again with a raised kerb, ran from the major site of Cerveteri to its harbour Pyrgi. Excavations have shown that this road, with its side walls and drainage facilities, was used from the sixth century until the Roman Imperial period.[7] Remains of another road, 4 m wide and with side walls, have been excavated at Acquarossa in southern Toscana.[8]

Over the years, sustained fieldwork in this part of central Italy has revealed successive road-systems linking important habitation and sanctuary sites and probably going back to the seventh and sixth centuries.[9] The roads, which may radiate from such centres as Cerveteri and Veii and often ran along the crests of long, narrow ridges, were of different and less sophisticated construction than the later Roman ones in the same area or elsewhere. One frequently found feature is the deep cuttings in the soft volcanic rock which carried the mostly unpaved roads from the valley-bottoms up to the ridges above on a gradient thought suitable for wheeled traffic. Some of these roads reveal wheelruts, indicating a wheel track (*q.v.*) of *c.* 1.30 m.[10] Wheelruts are also still visible in the Banditaccia cemetery at Cerveteri, where they are usually attributed to hearses going to and from the elaborate tombs built in the seventh and sixth centuries.[11]

It is well known from physical remains and textual sources that the Romans – in Republican and Imperial times – built and maintained a wide range of roads serving a variety of purposes. The military highways are the best documented. These radiated from the city of Rome in different directions and helped the Romans to expand and consolidate their rule throughout Italy and, later, to other parts of their empire.[12] There is textual information that the Via Appia, the first major link with the south, was planned by the censor Appius Claudius Caecus in 312. Originally running as far as Capua (present-day Santa Maria Capua Vetere) in Campania, it was subsequently extended all the way to the harbour of Brindisi in Puglia on the Adriatic coast, the road covering a distance of some 550 km.[13]

The Via Appia and other 'highways' were built and maintained by the state, primarily to provide a firm

---

[5] Gnade 2002, 7–23; also 1997, 94–7; 2006 and 2007; Maaskant-Kleibrink 1992, 18–28 (she attributes the earliest road remains to the Orientalizing period, i.e. the seventh century); also Quilici 1997, 76 and fig. 3.

[6] Acqua Acetosa Laurentina on the periphery of Rome (Quilici 1992, 19f. and fig. 1; 1997, 75 and fig. 2), Tor de'Cenci (Quilici 1992, 20f. and fig. 2) and Tor Bella Monaca (Quilici 1992, 22f. and figs 5–8); see also Gnade 2002, 23–9.

[7] Quilici 1989, 461 and fig. 3.2–6; Gnade 2002, 18.

[8] Quilici 1997, 78 and fig. 4; Gnade 2002, 19.

[9] See especially Ward Perkins 1962; Quilici 1989; 1992; 1997, 76–82; also a.o. Frederiksen and Ward Perkins 1957; *Strade degli Etruschi* (contributions by M. Cristofani, G. Nardi and S. Moscati); Ward Perkins 1957; Nardi 1989; Barker and Rassmussen 1998, 172f.

[10] Quilici 1992, 20 and n. 10; also a.o. Haynes 2000, fig. 116.

[11] See a.o. Quilici 1997, 80; Moretti and Maetzke 1970, pl. 33; *Stradi degli Etruschi* fig. 23; Macnamara 1990, fig. 12. For the tombs and their dating, see Prayon 1975, especially 175f. According to U. Höckmann (1982, 31 n. 204), the distance between the ruts indicates a wheel track of 1.42 m. Wheelruts can also be observed near Tuscania; see Barker and Rassmussen 1998, 172 and fig. 65.

[12] The literature on Roman (carriageable) roads is vast. A selection: Pekáry 1968; Roth 1979, 214–17; Chevallier 1976; Von Hagen 1978 (for wheelruts, see pls 1 and 51); Radke 1981; Gualandi 1990; Adam 1994, 276–90; Caselli 1994; White 1994, 93–100; Villa 1995; Esch 1997; Barker and Rassmussen 1998, 23f., 267f.; Staccioli 2003. Of great importance are the monographs in the series *Atlante tematico di topografa romana* (Quilici, L. and Quilici Gigli, S. eds), of which so far volumes 1–3 have appeared (1992, 1993, 1996). Much relevant information and discussion can also be found in Laurence 1999 and Van Tilburg 2007.

[13] Livy 9.29.5 and 10.23.12. Livy 10.47.4 records the paving of the Via Appia in the Rome area in 293. For the building of the Via Appia and its impact, see especially Laurence 1999, 13–24.

footing for soldiers marching in all sorts of weather conditions and to enable them to move as quickly and directly as possible. These long-distance Roman roads, like other roads in Italy and elsewhere in the Empire, came to be used for other transport and communication as well, and they quickly acquired a key economic importance. Their principal purpose was to afford rapid transit; the 'highways' followed, whenever possible, a straight course, avoiding bends or detours. When necessary, they made use of rock cuttings, arched bridges, viaducts or even tunnels. The roads varied in width, on average 3–8 m, and often had their sides marked by kerbstones, as had earlier roads (see above), and they were lined with drainage channels. The carefully made roadbed was topped with a surface of gravel or pebbles or, where traffic was particularly heavy, by blocks of volcanic stone. Although not primarily designed for these kinds of traffic, the Roman Republican and Imperial roads were suitable also for transport on animal back as well as by wheeled vehicle. The latter use is confirmed by the occasional presence of wheelruts and by textual references. For instance, the poet Horace tells of his journey in 38 or 37, as a member of a state mission, by wheeled vehicle from Rome to Brindisi along the Via Appia.[14]

The existence of carriageable roads in Italy before the time of the Roman Empire can be inferred also from the evidence of wheeled vehicles that is presented by actual remains and figured documents. Admittedly, the ornate two- and four-wheeled carriages that were buried in various tombs probably did not circulate widely but were only used at ceremonial occasions. In the written sources we read that people – mainly women, grandees and priests – went from one place to another by vehicle, and on journeys in and around Rome during the Republic and later (see Chapter III.7). Interestingly, at various times laws were promulgated or rescinded to restrict the use of vehicles in the city, so as to avoid congestion. It may be noted that such explicit physical evidence as wheelruts for the use of wheeled vehicles in Roman cities can be seen in the streets of Pompeii.[15]

Other texts mention the use of vehicles for agricultural purposes on country estates in Republican and Imperial times, implying the existence of carrigeable roads linking these and other types of sites. There are usually no physical traces left of these roads.[16]

Turning now to the types of vehicles used on the roads and streets, we will see below (Chapter II.7) that chariots in Italy – before and during the Roman Empire – were mostly used in ceremonies and for racing, and so did not need many roads. Thus the carriageable roads were used by other vehicles, namely carts and wagons. There is evidence to show that these functioned mainly in civilian transport, carrying people as well as farm produce, building materials or other commodities over shorter or longer distances, and as part of the military baggage train.[17]

2. Draught animals

Horses

The horse appears to have been introduced into Italy as a domesticated animal in the third millennium BC. Apart from horse bones among animal refuse from settlement sites in central and northern Italy, there is an almost complete skeleton from Le Cerquete-Fianello not far from Rome. The animal, an adult male standing *c.* 1.35 m at the withers, was found together with two dogs as part of a ritual deposition.[18]

---

[14] *Satires* 1.5 (vehicles called *redae*); see Casson 1974, 194–6; Kolb 2000, 37–9.

[15] For the streets with wheelruts at Pompeii, see especially Tsujimura 1991; Poehler 2006. Remains of actual vehicles are known from buildings in this city; see Maiuri 1932, 191–8 and nn. 122–3; Röring 1954, 2 n. 4, 69f.

[16] Laurence 1998, especially 138–43; 1999, 59–62.

[17] For the movement of people by wheeled vehicle on Roman roads and streets, see a.o. Casson 1974, chapters 10–12; Bender 1978; Black 1995; Giebel 1999, 131–214; Laurence 1999, especially 82f.; Kolb 2000; Van Tilburg 2005, 59–72; 2007, especially 41–84. For the transport of goods by vehicle, see our p. 88 and notes 127–128.

[18] See Curci and Tagliacozzo 1995 and 1998; also De Grossi Mazzorin 1994, 147 (list of sites); 1996, 181–218 (especially 183–5); De Grossi

Horse bones continue to be represented, always in small numbers, among domestic refuse of the second millennium and later in different parts of Italy.[19]

Osteological information on horses used in draught becomes available in the first millennium BC from a few tombs containing chariot burials. The poorly-preserved skeletons of two horses from a sixth century tomb at Ischia di Castro near Viterbo in Toscana have been identified as 5 or 6 year olds, one of them standing *c.* 1.23–1.25 m at the withers.[20] The animals were found lying in identical positions, one ahead of the other, in the narrow entrance corridor to the tomb. One horse still had the iron mouthpiece of a bridle bit in its mouth, and the two clearly formed the harness team of the ornate chariot that was buried in the tomb chamber.

Remains of another pair of horses have been discovered at the San Cerbone cemetery of Populonia in Toscana. The iron-bitted animals, *c.* 10 year olds, may have stood 1.33 m and 1.35 m at the withers. Together with a decorated chariot, they had been placed in a specially dug pit outside a tomb of the early fifth century.[21]

Four horses along with four bridle bits have been reported from the entrance corridor of a tomb in the Rollo necropolis at Vulci, also in Toscana. The animals apparently formed a team, arranged on either side of the draught pole of a chariot. The tomb has been dated to *c.* 550–540.[22] Other horse remains have been reported from cemeteries in Toscana and other parts of central Italy, including at Vulci, Populonia and Capua (modern Santa Maria di Capua Vetere), but not in association with vehicle burials.[23] There are also very brief references to horse bones and teeth from warrior tombs with vehicular remains from Veii in Lazio. One of these, Quattro Fontanili tomb EE 10 B, has been dated as early as 760–730 (Fig. 6).[24] Very recently (2008), two and three horse skeletons respectively were discovered during resumed excavations in the Lippi cemetery at Verucchio in Emilia Romagna. This large cemetery was used in the earlier part of the first millennium.[25]

Horse burials are also attested at Bologna in the north. They include a recent find of two horses in the Via Belli cemetery which was used in the eighth and seventh centuries. The animals were clearly a draught team, as they had bronze bits in their mouth. According to a brief report, a bronze spearhead was 'placed on the neck of one of the horses at throat level; it is likely that this was the weapon used to sacrifice the animals.'[26]

Other horse burials are known from Padua and elsewhere in the north-eastern part of Italy, presently

Mazzorin, Riedel and Tagliacozzo 1998.

[19] See a.o. De Grossi Mazzorin 1994, 145–8; 1995, 176; De Grossi Mazzorin and Riedel 1997, 478 (and bibliography); De Grossi Mazzorin, Riedel and Tagliacozzo 1998; Azzaroli 1972, especially 287–93, 296; 1979; Gejvall 1967, 267, 271; 1982, 68; Lepiksaar 1975, 78; Barker 1976, 297, 305f.; Bökönyi 1991, 219; Cardarelli 1993, 391; Curci and Tagliacozza 1995 (fig. 18: distribution map of sites); Barker and Rassmussen 1998, 185; *Carri di guerra* 257 (B. Wilkins); Cardarelli 1992, 391; also Lubtchansky 2005, 32–6.

[20] *Carri da guerra* 203–205 and pl. xx: 4 (F. Boitani), 320 (Repertorio no. 100); Boitani 1985, 217; Azzaroli 1972, 297–9 and pls 52–6; 1975, 86–9; 1980, 290; 1989, 1439f. and pl. II. For the chariot, see our p. 8 and note 2.

[21] De Agostino 1957, 14, 16 and fig. 12 (sketch plan); Azzaroli 1972, 299–303; 1975, 85f.; 1989, 1439f.; *Carri da guerra* 322 (Repertorio no. 122). For the chariot, see our p. 20 and note 67.

[22] Emiliozzi 1996, 337; *Carri da guerra* 329 (Repertorio no. 196). For a later dating, *c.* 450, based on decorated bronzes from the tomb, see Colonna 1996, 349.

[23] De Agostino 1957, 16; L. Milani in *Notizie degli scavi di antichità* (Serie 5) 1908, 216f., and Minto 1922, 185 (Populonia, San Cerbone cemetery; two horses found together with metal gear; see our p. 41 and note 226); Nunzio 1984, 514 and pl. 90b (two horses found together in a 'Samnite' cemetery at Curti, Capua); see also Lubtchansky 2005, 36.

[24] Quattro Fontanili cemetery, tomb EE 10 B; see A. Cavalotti-Batchvarova in *Notizie degli scavi di antichità* (Serie 8) 21 (1967), 138–46, nos 27 (horse teeth), 23 (iron horse bit) and 24 (fragments of iron nailed-on wheel tyre) and fig. 35; *Carri da guerra* 325 (Repertorio no. 159). For the date of this tomb, see Guidi 1993, 76, 89f. (Veii phase IIB); Bartolini 2003, 171. Picazzano cemetery, Tomba di Guerriero; see *Carri da guerra* 325 (Repertorio no. 155).

[25] Gleba 2008–9, 107 and fig. 3 (Lippi tomb 65).

[26] Gleba 2008–9, 106. See also Pincelli and Morigo Govi 1975, 462 and 469 (horse remains from tombs 760 and 770 in the San Vitale cemetery).

known as the province of Veneto. These burials mostly range in date from the sixth to the second century.[27] One horse, from the Canal del Piàvego cemetery at Padua, was described as *c.* 12 years old and as being stockier than the draught horses mentioned above.[28]

Of particular interest is the discovery of no fewer than 27 buried horses in the cemetery known as Le Brustolade at Altino, not far from Venice.[29] The horse burials are reported as dating from *c.* 450 to the third century. The animals are 12–15 years old and include mostly stallions, but also two mares and one possible gelding. The animals were found either singly or in twos or threes, which has led to the suggestion that some of them were used in draught. In a few cases, horses were accompanied by a bronze or iron bit or other metal gear.[30] This recalls the burial of a horse, again with a bit and other metal trappings, at Santa Lucia di Tolmino.[31] Bones belonging to 20 horses were found in fourth century contexts at the Fornace santuary, also at Altino.[32]

All these horses, as well as those represented among domestic refuse, fall within the 'medium large pony' category of today's western classification, the dividing line between these and 'large ponies' being a height of 1.47 m at the withers. In this the Italian animals compare well with the chariot horses of ancient Greece and the Near East: all are distinctly small by modern standards.[33] The same is true of the horses of the Hallstatt and La Tène periods in Europe north of the Alps.[34]

The three horses found in a tomb of the third century belonging to the Canal Bianco cemetery of Adria on the Veneto coast were distinctly larger and more robust. The animals were less than 10 years old and stood 1.50–1.55 m at the withers.[35] Two of these horses had iron bits in their mouths and were found yoked to a vehicle; the third horse had a bronze bit.[36] It may be noted that local inscriptions and ancient Greek authors repeatedly refer to Venetic horses.[37] This breed must ultimately derive from that region.

Another rather large – 1.49 m at the withers – and robust horse is the 16 year old stallion from a necropolis at Pantanello near Metaponto in southern Italy. The animal was buried on its own, possibly in the late fourth–early third century, and is thought to have been brought as a mount from the eastern Mediterranean.[38] It may be noted that the horses of the Roman Imperial period mostly ranged from 1.35 m to 1.50 m.[39]

The figured documents convey some idea of the physical appearance of horses in Italy before the Roman Empire. The same type of animal seems to have been used in driving and riding. Chariot horses

---

[27] For brief overviews, see Zampieri 1994, 44; Gambacurta and Tirelli 1996, 72f.; De Grossi Mazzorin, Riedel and Tagliacozzo 1988, 88.

[28] Azzaroli 1980; Riedel 1982; Scarfí and Tombolani 1985, 56f.; De Grossi Mazzarin, Riedel and Tagliacozzi 1998, 88.

[29] See especially Riedel 1982; Scarfí and Tombolani 56f.; Gambacurta and Tirelli 1996; Gambacurta 2003.

[30] See II.6 and p. 48 and note 257.

[31] Marchesetti 1993, 189, 269f. and pl. 30: 1 and 8.

[32] See especially Fiore, Salerno and Tagliacozzo 2003.

[33] Littauer and Crouwel 1979, 57, 82; Crouwel 1981, 33; 1992, 24.

[34] See Koch, J. K. 2006, 22f.; Dular 2007, 743f. (information supplied by S. Bökönyi).

[35] Azzaroli 1975, 93f; 1996, 83–5; Zampieri 1994, 44 with n. 28.

[36] From tomb 115. See a.o. Fogolari 1940, 440f. and pl. 43:2; Barfield 1971, pl. 67; Fogolari and Scarfí 1976, 73f. and pls 44–5 (with bibl.); Frey 1968, 318; 1976, 173f. and figs 1–2; Gambacurta and Tirelli 1996, 73; Camerin 1997, 44; *Carri da guerra* 331 (Repertorio no. 214); Gambacurta 2003, 96f., 99. For the paired bits, see our p. 48 and note 257. The curb-type bit associated with the single horse indicates a mount rather than a chariot's trace horse (q.v.), for which see our p. 48 and note 259.

[37] Marinetti 2003 (inscriptions). Anderson 1961, 36–8; Azzaroli 1980, 293; De Grossi Mazzorin, Riedel and Taglicozzo 1998, 88; Gambacurta 2003, 98 (literary texts).

[38] Carter 1998, 131, 135f., 143f. and fig. 2a–b (skeleton from tomb 316, studied by S. Bökönyi), see also 133–40 (other single horse burials, some of them accompanied by a metal bit, and horse remains among domestic refuse from different sites in southern Italy, ranging in date from the sixth to the early third centuries); also Lubtchansky 2005, 35. *Cf.* the horse, standing only 0.95–1.10 m and with a bit in its mouth, from a disturbed tomb of the seventh century at Pollenza in Marche (G. De Marinis in *Potere e splendore* 234–5).

[39] Junkelmann 1990, 39–43 (most of the skeletal evidence comes from outside Italy. The three horses from the villa complex of emperor Tiberius at Sperlonga had a height at the withers of 1.30–1.35 m, 1.40–1.45 m and 1.45–1.50 m respectively.

and mounts are quite often depicted as stallions. Piebald horses are sometimes shown in Etruscan black-figure vase painting.[40] There is no evidence for special treatment of the forelock or mane. The tails are left long, those of the large-scale terracotta team of two winged horses from the fourth century pediment of the Ara della Regia temple at Tarquinia being bound near the upper end (Pl. 68).[41]

Mules

As in Greece, the equids seen pulling carts in figured documents of the sixth century and later are often distinguished from the horses, so common in chariot traction, by their long ears (Pls 109, 114–115). These animals may be identified as mules – the infertile offspring of a jack-ass and a mare.[42] Mules, strong and durable as they are, frequently appear as draught (and pack) animals in ancient and more recent cultures. Their use with carts or wagons, is also well attested in Latin and Greek texts.[43] In other cart representations from Italy the animals look like horses rather than mules (Pls 106–108, 110, 112–113), while in yet others the rendering is too imprecise or fragmentary to allow a firm distinction to be made.

A pair of equids, recently found in a pit at Sirolo (ancient Numana) in Marche, have been briefly described as horses or as being more likely mules. The animals were both over 20 years old, standing 1.17–1.28 m at the withers. The pit was clearly associated with a rich female burial in a tomb of the late sixth century. The contents of this so-called Tomba della Principessa included two vehicles – a chariot and a cart.[44]

Bovids

The use of bovids for pulling wheeled vehicles is explicitly documented only once – by an Etruscan bronze cart model from Civltà Castellana (ancient *Falerii Veteres*)(Pl. 89).[45] For comparison, there is a similar dearth of representations of bovid-drawn vehicles in ancient Greece.[46] On the other hand, Latin and Greek texts refer to bovids (surely oxen, i.e. castrated bulls) in connection with carts and/or wagons transporting bulky or heavy commodities.[47] Thus we may assume ox-draught for the cart with its superstructure suitable for hay or other farm produce, represented by another Etruscan bronze model, from Bolsena (Pl. 88).[48] Figured documents and texts attest to the use of similar bovine draught teams with ploughs in ancient Italy and Greece.[49]

---

[40] See p. 9 and note 8 (the Amphiaraus Amphora from Vulci). Piebald horses are also illustrated in fourth century tomb paintings from Paestum in Campania; see Pontrandolfo and Rouveret 1992, ills p. 144: 1–2 (Andriuolo, tomb 48).

[41] Height of slab 1.15 m. See a.o. *Gli Etruschi di Tarquinia* cat. no. 903; Moscati, S. 1987, pl. 213; Sprenger and Bartoloni 1990, pl. 211; Barker and Rassmussen 1998, fig. 109.

[42] For ass bones among animal refuse, see a.o. Lepiksaar 1975, 78 (Luni sul Mignone); Gejvall 1982, 68 (Acquarossa); Bökönyi 1991, 219–23 (Tortoreto-Fortellezza on the central Adriatic coast, in contexts of the tenth–fifth centuries); Placidi 1978, 270f. (Torrionaccio in Lazio); also Spivey and Stoddart 1990, 65; Barker and Rassmussen 1998, 185 (Toscana).

[43] *DarSag* III.2, *s.v. mulus*; *RE s.v.* Esel, Maultier und Maulesel; White 1970, 294–6, 300f., also 293f. (ass); Toynbee 1973, 176, 185–92, and particularly Laurence 1999, 123–35 (Roman textual and figured sources); Hyland 1990, 72, 231–5; Crouwel 1992, 25 (Greece); Adams, J. N. 1993; Coulston 2001, 109f., 112f., 115 (pack and draught mules depicted on the Column of emperor Trajan in Rome); Chandezon 2005, 208–10, 212f.

[44] *Carri da guerra* 319 (Repertorio no. 86: I Pini cemetery, Circolo 1, tomb 4), 234 and figs 6–7 (pit with equids, described by M. Landolfi), 254–9 (bone report by B. Wilkins). For the vehicles, see our p. 70 and note 4.

[45] Richter 1915, 167f. *s.v.* nos 412–15 and ill. (reportedly found in a tomb, together with bronze figurines of bovids, goats and pigs and a model plough); Rostovtzeff 1957, 20 *s.v.* pl. II: 2–4; Woytowitsch 1978, no. 280 and pl. 39.

[46] Crouwel 1992, 26.

[47] Toynbee 1973, 152, 161f, and White 1970, 281f. (Roman Italy); Crouwel 1992, 26 (Greece).

[48] See Paribeni 1928, 340–3 and fig. 1 (the model was found together with a model axe and knife, all three regarded as votive offerings); Woytowitsch 1978, no. 168 and pls 38–9; Piggott 1983, 191f.; Pisani Sartorio 1988, 61f. and figs 65–6 (reconstruction); Crouwel 1992, 79 and pl. 31: 1; *Les Étrusques et l'Europe* no. 125; *Gli Etruschi* ill. p. 76.

[49] For ploughs, see bronze models from Arezzo (Cristofani 1985, fig. 54; *Les Étrusques et l'Europe*, no. 123; *Gli Etruschi* no. 16) and Castellana (*Falerii Veteres*). Richter 1915, 168 *s.v.* nos 412–15 with ill.; from same find complex as our bronze cart model, our note 45 and Pl. 89). See also

Other animals

Winged horses, side by side with wingless ones, are first depicted pulling chariots in the sixth century, for instance on several of the moulded terracotta revetment plaques century from different sites in central Italy (Pls 70–71, 73,[50] and on an ivory plaque from Tarquinia (Pl. 58).[51] There is also the fourth century terracotta team of winged horses pulling an otherwise lost chariot from Tarquinia (see above). Winged horses, which are seen in the same role on funerary stelae from Bologna and on various other figured documents from different parts of Italy, derive from Greek iconography (Pl. 61).[52]

A supernatural setting is also apparent in other figured documents. These include sixth century Etruscan gold rings illustrating chariots – and carts – drawn by teams composed of sphinxes and stags (Pl. 102).[53] There is also an ivory carving on a lid of *c.* 600 from Marzabotto in Toscana, representing a chariot pulled by two panthers and two horses (Pl. 33).[54]

Of note are also the draught animals in scenes set in the Underworld. In a tomb painting dating to the later fourth century from Sarteano in Toscana, the chariot is driven by a female demon and pulled by a team consisting of two lions and two griffins.[55] Paired griffins are seen pulling the chariot of Persephone in two fourth century red-figure vase paintings from Orvieto.[56]

---

the plough groups among the decoration of a well-known bronze wheeled stand of the eighth century from tomb 2 of the Olmo Bello cemetery at Bisenzio in Toscana (Woytowitsch 1978, no. 127 and pl. 24; Torelli 1996, 360–3 and figs 49–50; M. Menichetti in *Roma. Romolo, Remo*, 228f.; *Gli Etruschi* cat. no. 14; Cherici 2005, 129–37; Pacciarelli 2002, 301–8, 312–15). Miniature bronze models of ploughs and yokes are known from the Genio militare deposit at Talamone (ancient Telamon) in Toscana, dating to *c.* 150–100; see *Les Étrusques et l'Europe* nos 126–30. Remains of actual wooden ploughs and a yoke have been found at the Early Bronze Age sites of Lavagnone and Fiavé-Carera 5 and 7 in northern Italy; see Peroni 1983; 1984; 1987, 200, 236, 350f., 353–5 and figs 98–9, 170–3 and pls 40–1, 61; Randsborg 1991, 119 and fig. 11; Cardarelli 1993, 388. For (ox-drawn) ploughs and ploughing in Italy, see a.o. White 1970, 174–8, 281f.; 1984, 59f.; Toynbee 1973, 152; Kolendo 1980, especially ch. 3; Bassi and Forni 1988 (including more recent times); Barker and Rassmussen 1998, 189f. and fig. 72 (present-day Etruria); Carafi 2000. For ploughs and ploughing in Greece, see a.o. Crouwel 1992, 97f.; Burford 1993, 120–7.

[50] See p. 10 and notes 16–17 (plaques of the Rome-Caprifico and Veii-Rome-Velletri types, as well as plaques from Palestrina).

[51] Huls 1957, no. 67; Brendel 1995, 180 and fig. 117; *Gli Etruschi* no. 120; Martelli 2001, 167 and fig. 5.

[52] For the Bologna stelae, showing chariot horses with and without wings, see p. 63. See also a.o. Etruscan gold rings: Boardman 1967, nos B II 3 and B II 4 and pl. 2; no. B IV 2 and pl. 4 (also Richter 1968, no. 719). For teams of winged horses in Greek art, see Lacroix 1974, 81–5; Schauenburg 1957; Crouwel 1992, 26; Mertens-Horn 1992, 20–22 (examples from southern Italy, including terracotta plaques from Metaponto, San Biagio, see fig. 1 – our Pl. 75 – and pl. 1).

[53] Chariot teams: Boardman 1967, nos B II 7 (also Richter 1968, no. 720) and B II 8 and pl. 2. Cart teams: Boardman 1967, nos B II 10 (also Richter 1968, no. 718) and B I 11 (also Richter 1968, no. 717).

[54] Gentili 1978; *Civiltà degli Etruschi* cat. no. 3.118; *La formazione della città in Emilia Romagna* 129 no. 1a–c and fig. 83 (G. Bermond Montanari); Colonna 1987, 17 and fig. 3.

[55] Pianacce cemetery, Tomba della Quadriga Infernale; see Minetti 2005, 138f., 144f. and pls 25, 29, 30c; 2006, 25–44 and figs 23, 25–6, 29; also 2007; Steingräber 2009, 215, 218 and ill. p. 216f.

[56] Twin neck-amphora of the Vanth Group; see Beazley 1947, 170, (neck-amphorae nos 4–5); Capelletti 1992, nos 61–2; Bonami 2006, 526f. and fig. 3: middle and bottom.

CHAPTER II

Chariots

Knowledge of the existence, construction and functions of this kind of two-wheeled vehicle comes from actual remains, mostly from funerary contexts of the eighth–sixth century, and from representations, mainly two-dimensional and in profile, ranging from the seventh century onwards.

As noted in the general introduction, the wooden parts of the actual vehicles have usually completely decayed. In rare cases, such as that of a chariot from a seventh century tomb at Vulci in Toscana, bits of wood have survived to help reconstruct the original vehicle.[1] Even more exceptional is a sixth century burial at Ischia di Castro in the same region, where enough survived of the wooden parts of the chariot for a plaster cast of it to be made.[2] More often the presence of chariots – or, for that matter, carts or wagons – is based on surviving metal parts. The latter were rarely found in *situ*. In these cases the identification of the type of vehicle and, if possible, its (partial) reconstruction, is based on the presence or absence of certain metal elements thought to be typical of one type of vehicle but not of others.

1. Types and body

Four or five types of chariot can be identified – chiefly on the basis of differences in the siding of the vehicle body, in conjunction with the shape of the floor plan. For this reason type and body are treated under the same heading.[3] As we shall see, by no means all vehicles attested by surviving metal parts or illustrated in figured documents can be grouped under clear-cut types.

Chariot Type I

The best documented type has a rounded profile, with a narrow U-shaped floor plan and a siding consisting of three or five parts of unequal height. The most detailed information is supplied by the partly or entirely bronze-sheathed chariots from rich tombs of the seventh and sixth centuries in Toscana, Umbria and Lazio. The same type may be assumed for several other, less well preserved chariots associated with burials ranging from the later eight to the sixth century (Pls 1–10).

Many figured documents of the later seventh–fifth centuries from the same and other regions in central Italy show this type of chariot, the earliest representation being fragments of an unprovenanced Bucchero jug (Pl. 50).[4] The figured documents include two models in the round. One of these crowns the ivory lid of a pyxis of *c.* 600 from Marzabotto in Toscana (Pl. 33).[5] The other is an incompletely

---

[1] Woytowitsch 1978, no. 34 and pls 6–7; Emiliozzi 1992, 99–102 and figs 18–20; *Carri da guerra* 329 (Repertorio no. 195), 139–45 (A.M. Sgubini Moretti on the tomb and its finds), 145–8 (A. Emiliozzi on the chariot), 152f. (G. F. Priori on the wood of the chariot) and figs 10–20 and pls 3–5; *Gli Etruschi* cat. no. 81; *Signori di Maremma* cat. no. 1.120.

[2] Woytowitsch 1978, no. 36 and pl. 4; Boitani 1985 (with notes on the restoration by P. Aureli); 1987; Boitani and Aureli 1988, 127f. and pls 53–6; *Carri da guerra* 320 (Repertorio no. 100 *s.v.* Castro), 203–6 and fig. 1 and pls 20–1 (F. Boitani); *Civiltà degli Etruschi* cat. no. 9.11; *Gli Etruschi* cat. no. 75.

[3] For earlier classifications, see Nachod 1909; Nebelsick 1992, 103–10.

[4] Camporeale 1991, 82 and pl. 67b–c; 1993, no. 1 and fig. 1.

[5] See p. 7 and note 54.

preserved terracotta model from a tomb at Pitigliano, also in Toscana and presumably dating to the sixth century.[6] The two-dimensional, profile representations of Type I chariots are mainly sixth century Etruscan and include tomb paintings (Pls 34–6),[7] black-figure vase paintings (Pls 40–45),[8] pottery with roller-stamp decoration (so-called Impressed Red Ware),[9] engraved gold finger rings,[10] a bronze cauldron from Capua known as the Lebes Barone,[11] and bronze sheathings with repoussé decoration (Pl. 55).[12] Chariots of Type I also appear in reliefs on Etruscan stone tomb-markers (known as cippi) of the early fifth century,[13] and on a stone sarcophagus from Cerveteri, sometimes assigned to the later fifth century but more likely dating to *c.* 350–320 (Pl. 63).[14] Finally, there are also many representations of this type of chariot on relief-moulded and originally brightly painted terracotta revetment plaques of the sixth

[6] Pellegrini 1903, 273 and fig. 7; Hencken 1968, 129, 536, 582 and fig. 493c; Woytowitsch 1978, no. 163 and pl. 33; Egg and Pare 1995, cat. no. 3 and pl. I: top.

[7] **Tarquinia**: see Steingräber 1985, no. 47 (our Pl. 34. Tomba delle Bighe; see also Brendel 1995, 266–8, fig. 182; *Malerei der Etrusker* no. 16), no. 65 (Tomba Francesca Giustiniani = Tomba dell due Bighe; see also Stenico 1963, pls 43, 45), no. 82 (Tomba del Letto Funebre), no. 83 (Tomba del Maestro delle Olimpiadi), no. 92 and colour pls 123–4 (= no. 53. Our Pl. 35. Tomba delle Olimpiadi; see also Bartoccini, Lerici and Moretti 1959). **Chiusi**: see Steingräber 1985, no. 15 (Tomba del Colle Casuccini; see also Stenico 1963, pls 41–2; Brendel 1995, 277f., fig. 194; *Malerei der Etrusker* no. XVIII; *L'archeologia racconta* no. 63), no. 17 (Tomba di Montollo), no. 22 (our pl. 36) (Tomba di Poggio al Moro = Tomba Dei or Grotta delle Monache), no. 25 (Tomba della Scimmia; see also *Malerei der Etrusker* no. XVI). The incompletely preserved chariot depicted in the Tomba della Quadriga Infernale at Sarteano (see our p. 7 and note 55) may also be of Type I.

[8] **Neck-amphora** by the Amphiaraus Painter, the so-called Amphiaraus Amphora, from Vulci (our Pl. 40): see Dohrn 1937, no. 134; 1966, especially 113f., 133, 135 and ill. 26; Åkerström 1954, 196–9 and figs 9–11; Hampe and Simon 1964, pl. 7: 3; 1967, 69–71, 76 and pl. 32: 2; Hannestad 1976, 54 no. 1 and pl. 3 (*cf.* 55 no. 9 = Bastianelli 1940, 365 and pl. 28:1–2: a jug by the same painter, with – worn – chariots possibly of similar type); Woytowitsch 1978, no. 238 and pl. 45. **Neck-amphora**, name piece of the Painter of Berlin Amphora 2154, from Vulci (our Pl. 41): see Beazley 1947, 17f.; Bronson 1966, 24–8 and pls 5–9; *Die Welt der Etrusker. Archäologische Denkmäler* no. B 5.29. **Neck amphora** by same painter, also from Vulci: see Beazley 1947, 17f.; Bronson 1966, 28–34 and pls 10–13; Brendel 1995, 198 and fig. 132. **Neck-amphora** by the Painter of Vatican 238 (our Pl. 42): see Dohrn 1938, 286f. and pl. 53: 3; Beazley 1947, 16 no. 5; Spivey 1987, 43 no. 1; Drukker 1988, 24–7 and figs 3–4. **Neck-amphora** by the Micali Painter (our Pl. 45): see Moltesen 1982; *La ceramica degli Etruschi* no. 127; Spivey 1987, 29 no. 190; *Un artista etrusco* no. 18. **Hydria**, close to the Micali Painter but not by his own hand: see Fairbanks 1928, no. 573; Spivey 1987, 31. **Neck-amphora** by the Paris Painter, from Cerveteri, Banditaccia cemetery: see Dohrn 1966, 132f. and ills 24–5; Hannestad 1974, 46 no. 16; Hampe and Simon 1967, 76; *Un artista etrusco* 29 and fig. 37. **Neck-amphora** by the Paris Painter (our Pl. 43): see Hampe and Simon 1964, pls 2: 1, 3: 1, pl. 4; 1967, 68–98 and pl. 35: 2; 1971; Dohrn 1966, 125–45 and ills 21–2 (considered to be a fake); Hampe and Simon 1971, no. 70; *CVA* Heidelberg 2, pls 55–6; Mingazzini 1973; Hannestad 1974, 46 no. 18. **Neck-amphora** by the Tityos Painter: see Hampe and Simon 1964, pls 9–10; Dohrn 1966, especially 113–25 and ills 1–3; Hannestad 1976, 56 no. 15; Reusser *et al.* 1988, no. E 73. **Jug(?)** by the Tityos Painter (our Pl. 44): see *AA*, 1904, 60 and fig. 1; Dohrn 1937, no. 123; Grünhagen 1948, 60 and fig. 1; Hannestad 1976, 59 no. 37 and pls 20–21a. Also a **hydria** of so-called Polledrara Ware, probably from the Isis Tomb in the Polledrara cemetery at Vulci: see Smith, C. 1894, 206–12 with pl. 6 (a chariot of our Type II seems to be shown on the opposite side, pl. 7); Krauskopf 1974, 10–13; Menichetti 1984, 65–7 and figs 37–8.

[9] Camporeale 1972, 70–2 (fregio XXI); 1993, no. 15; also a.o. Ridgway, F.R. 1986, 284 no. 5 with fig. 5a–b. In other cases the type of chariot depicted remains uncertain, see a.o. Scalia 1968, nos 157–8 and fig. 7b, nos 270–2 and fig. 11d.

[10] See Boardman 1967, nos B II 3 and pl. 2, II 4 and pl. 2 (also Woytowitsch 1978, no. 219B and pl. 45), B II.6, B II 7 and pl. 2 (also Richter 1968, no. 720; Woytowitsch 1978, no. 216 and pl. 45), B II 8 and pl. 2, B II 12, B II 13 and pl. 2, B II 14 and pl. 3 (also Richter 1968, no. 716; Woytowitsch 1978, no. 217 and pl. 45), B II 15 (also Richter 1968, no. 721), B IV 2 and pl. 4 (also Richter 1968, no. 719; Woytowitsch 1978, no. 215 and pl. 45), and probably B III 1 and pl. 4). See also Woytowitsch 1978, no. 219A and pl. 45.

[11] See a.o. Haynes 1965b, 16f. and fig. 1; Thuillier 1976, and 1985, 152f.; Woytowitsch 1978, no. 227A and pl. 45; Capuis 1995, 168–72 and pl. 27.

[12] **Decoration of bronze sheathing** of one side of the body of the Monteleone chariot (see p. 13, note 34): see Woytowitsch 1978, no. 231 and pls 8 and 14; *Antichità dall'Umbria a New York* ills pp. 111–12; Brendel 1995, 149 and fig. 99; *Carri da guerra* pls 12, 17. **Decorated sheet bronze fragments** from the Tomba dei Bronzi at Castel San Mariano (see p. 14, note 35): see Petersen 1894, 308 no. 53: a–b, fig. 14; Woytowitsch 1978, no. 74 with pl. 8; Höckmann 1982, 36–8 and figs 19–20, pl. 15: 7. Also the incompletely preserved vehicle among the sheet-bronze decoration of another actual chariot from the same tomb; see Hampe and Simon 1964, pl. 20 and *Beilage*; Woytowitsch 1978, no. 73 and pl. 8; Höckmann 1982, 42–4 and fig. 25 and pl. 30 (from 'Streitwagen II'). For the actual chariot, which was possibly of our Type V, see our p. 24 and note 95.

[13] See especially Jannot 1984, no. C,I,8 and fig. 172 (also Paribeni 1938, no. 118; Brendel 1978, 280 and fig. 197; Sprenger and Bartoloni 1990, pl. 166, middle; *Gli Etruschi* cat. no. 261), no. C,II,22 and fig. 265 (also Paribeni 1938, no. 128; *L'archeologia racconta* no. 57), no. C,III,14 and fig. 345 no. D,II,4 and fig. 539 (also Paribeni 1938, no. 119). Other scenes are too fragmentary to shed light on the chariot type; see Jannot 1984, no. C,II,24 and fig. 268, no. C,II,33 and fig. 286, no. C,III,14 and fig. 345. See also Paribeni 1938, no. 130; Moltesen 1982, 70 and fig. 17; Thuillier 1997a (is the relief carving ancient in this case?). A chariot of Type I is also depicted on an unprovenanced, contemporary house-shaped urn of stone; see Pryce 1931, no. D 10; Jannot 1984, no. A',3 and fig. 84.

[14] From Cerveteri, Banditaccia cemetery (our Pl. 63); see especially Herbig 1952, no. 83 and pls 1–2; Helbig 1963, no. 612; Höckmann 1982, 153; Schäfer 1989, 37 and pl. 5:2; Holliday 1990, 76, 78 and fig. 1; Sprenger and Bartoloni 1990, pls 202–3; Brendel 1995, 323–5 and fig. 246; Massa Pairault 1996, 151f. with ills; Van der Meer 2008, 68–71 no. *H83* and figs 35, 37.

century. These were used to decorate and protect the wooden roofs of temples and other public buildings at sites in different parts of central Italy.[15] Among the plaques showing chariots, those belonging to the Veii-Rome-Velletri decorative roofing system of *c.* 530 (so named because identical moulds were used at these three sites)[16] and its variant called the Rome-Caprifico system of *c.* 520 present particularly well preserved chariot representations (Pls 70–71).[17] It has recently been proposed that these plaques were made in the same workshop, which was situated in Veii or, more likely, Rome.[18] Well preserved chariot representations are also seen revetment plaques of *c.* 510–500 from Palestrina (ancient Praeneste) (Pl. 73)[19] and on others dating to *c.* 530 from an unknown site.[20]

Considering the material evidence for Type I chariots first, the earliest well documented instance may be a vehicle that was buried along with a pair of metal horse bits in tomb 15 of the Via Pontina cemetery at Castel di Decima in Lazio (Pl. 1).[21] This rich warrior tomb dates to the later eighth century. The recent reconstruction – on paper – of the chariot includes a U-shaped floor with a thong flooring, and a railwork siding consisting of a series of six rails extending along the front and sides (Pl. 1a). The reconstruction seems to owe much to two much better preserved chariots of the seventh century, from Vulci and Populonia in Toscana, except for the front rail which is formed from two rather than one hoop rising above the side rails. The reconstruction of a two-part front rail is apparently based on the finding in the tomb of a series of loop-shaped metal fittings (Pl. 1b). These are thought to have served as the fastening of thongs that kept leather screening material in the lower parts of a corresponding number of siding rails in place.[22] In the reconstruction drawing, a pair of small tubular metal elements with one end sharply curving inwards are tentatively placed at the forward ends of two side rails (Pl. 1a, c). Their proposed interpretation – as attachments for the single reins or traces (*q.v.*) of the two extra horses or outriggers (*q.v.*) of a four-horse team – is unlikely. Castel di Decima tomb 15 contained not four but two metal bridle bits (Pl. 1d),[23] suggesting a two-horse harness team. Evidence for *quadrigae* is anyway limited as regards central and northern Italy before the Roman Imperial period, *bigae* and *trigae* being much more common (see Chapter II.5). Rather, the small tubular elements anticipate the pair of metal ones found with some other chariot burials of the seventh–sixth centuries at Castel di Decima and other sites (see below, *s.v.* chariot Type IV). The two seventh century chariots mentioned above,

---

[15] Many of the plaques showing Type I chariots were included in Andrén 1939–40 and 1974. For more recent finds and discussion, see especially various contributions to *La grande Roma* and *Deliciae Fictiles* I, II and III. See now Winter, N. A. 2009, chs 4–5 and index *s.v.* chariot, chariot procession, chariot race, charioteer.

[16] See especially Andrén 1939–40, 409f. nos 1–2 with pl. 126: 442–3; *La grande Roma* nos 4.1.11–15, 5.1.28–32, 8.6.11–16, 10.1–2; Winter, N. A. 2009, 311–24, 328, 330, 333f., 351–5, 362–4, 366–70, 392f., 580f. nos 5.A.1.a–b and f, 5.D.1.a and c, 5.D.2.a and c, 5.D.3.a and c with ills 5.1.1–2, 5.9.1, 5.13.1–2, 5.14.2, 5.15.2 and figs 5.1–2, 5.15, 5.18, 5.20–21, 5.23 (and ills of Roofs 5–2 to 5–7).

[17] See especially Brown, A. C. 1974; De Reuver 1997; *La grande Roma* nos 4.1.24–26, 5.1.32 and 9.6.76; Lubtchansky 2006; Lulof 2006; Winter, N. A. 2009, 311, 313, 323–4, 330f., 351–3, 355, 358–60, 368f., 392f., 581 nos 5.A.1.b, 5.D.1.a and b and e–f, 5.D.2.b and d, 5.D.3.b and d with ills 5.1.2, 5.9.2, 5.11.1–2, 5.15.1 and fig. 5.22 (and ills of Roofs 5–8, 5–9 and 5–10); Winter, N. A. 2010; Crouwel 2010; Lubtchansky 2010; Lulof 2010a and 2010b (moulds 1, 3–4).

[18] Winter, N. A. 2006; 2009, 580f.; 2010.

[19] See especially Andrén 1939–40, 373f. nos I.1–2 and pl. 115: 406; 1974, 3 and figs 1–21; *La grande Roma* no. 7.4.1–5; Winter, N. A. 2009, 328, 336f. no. 5.A.3.b with ill. 5.3.2 and fig. 5.6 (Roof 5–15).

[20] Winter, N. A. 2009, 400, 447f. no. 6.D.1.a with ill. 6.13.1. and fig. 6.21 (and ills of Roof 6–2); Christiansen and Winter 2010, 26–31 and no. 2.

[21] Zevi 1975, 252, 284 and figs 13 and 17 (plan of tomb), also 252 and 284 no. 54 with figs 60–1 (iron wheel tyres), 280 and 282 nos 47–53 with figs 58–9 (bronze rings to fasten screening material), 252, 289 no. 56 with fig. 61 (two iron elements with one end sharply curving inwards), cf. 285 no. 55 with fig. 61 (iron element), 290 nos 66–7 with figs 63–5 (pair of iron horse bits); F. Cordano in *Civiltà del Lazio primitivo s.v.* cat. no. 82; Nebelsick 1992, 103f.; *Carri da guerra* 312, (Repertorio no. 19); Emiliozzi 1997, 96f. with fig. 1; *eadem* in *Memorie dal Sottosuolo*; Bietti Sestieri and De Santis 2000, fig. 16 (reconstruction drawing of chariot and other contents of the tomb).

[22] It has also been – implausibly – suggested by F. Müller (1995, 272–4) that the loop-shaped fittings provide the earliest evidence for a suspension system, as has been postulated for much later 'Celtic chariots' (see our p. 112 and note 26).

[23] See note 22 and p. 45, note 246. The tubular elements recall a find from Vaccareccia tomb VI at Veii; see Palm 1952, 63 no. 20 with pl. 13; *Carri da guerra* 326 (Repertorio no. 166).

from the Tomba del Carro in the Osteria cemetery of Vulci (dating to *c.* 680–670) and the Tumulo dei Carri in the San Cerbone cemetery at Populonia (dating to *c.* 675–650), have been restored with much more confidence in recent years (Pls 2–3).[24] This is thanks to their extensive metal parts and decoration, including bronze sheathing of the floor and siding frames and, in case of the vehicle from Vulci, to the survival of actual pieces of (elm) wood and leather belonging to different parts of the vehicle.

The construction and design of the two chariots are basically similar, the framework of their body comprising two main elements: a floor frame and a siding frame. The narrow floor frame (Vulci: length *c.* 0.65 m, width *c.* 0.40 m; Populonia: reconstructed length *c.* 1.10 m and width *c.* 0.65 m) resembles a capital U in plan. The curved part of the floor frame is formed from 1–3 pieces of wood, two of which are joined together at the front. The rear floor bar is broad and flat, and joins the curved part of the floor frame a short distance before its ends. On the Populonia chariot the rear floor bar curves outwards at the back, as is indicated by the bronze plaque that covered it, presumably to facilitate the occupant(s) mounting the vehicle. The remaining wooden parts indicate that, on the Vulci chariot, the junction of the rear floor bar to the curved part of the floor frame was by means of a mortise-and-tenon construction. On this chariot the projecting ends of the curved part of the floor frame were decoratively carved into knob-like finials. Both these finials and adjacent sections of the floor frame were subsequently covered by leather, which was held in place by bronze nails with large decorative rhomboid heads. On the Populonia chariot bronze caps with finials in the form of lion protomes facing backwards fitted over the ends of the side timbers. They also covered the junction with the rear floor bar.

The floor frame was held together by a mesh of rawhide or leather thongs, their ends passing through circular holes in the side timbers and rear floor bar, as indicated on the remaining wooden parts of the Vulci chariot. A mesh flooring, which at the same time provided a strong and resilient floor in an otherwise springless vehicle, was widely used on ancient chariots in different parts of the ancient world. The well preserved ones from the Egyptian New Kingdom are good examples.[25]

As restored, the bodies of the chariots from Vulci and Populonia are raised over the axle, which is itself rigidly fixed under the centre of the floor, as well as over the central draught pole. The pole has been restored as running in the same plane as the axle and ending where the two meet. If this restoration is correct, it would represent a weaker construction than that on the Egyptian and other ancient chariots. There, the pole ran all the way under the floor, between the floor frame and the axle, with the pole supporting the floor frame at the front and rear. Two further points of support for the body were provided by blocks, equal in thickness to the diameter of the pole, placed between axle and floor frame at either side. In Italy itself such an arrangement – with a pole running to the rear – is, in fact, postulated in the reconstruction of sixth century vehicles of Type I (see below).[26]

The siding frame of the Vulci and Populonia chariots extends across the front and sides in a series of probably heat-bent railings, leaving the rear open for quick access. In the case of the Populonia chariot, the surviving bronze sheathing shows that the siding frame is in three parts: a horizontal rail at the front (rising to *c.* 0.80 m), supported by vertical posts at the corners and dropping down some distance along the sides; further back are two lower, hoop-shaped rails similar to those in the same position on the Vulci

---

[24] For the Vulci chariot, see p. 8 and note 1. For the Populonia chariot, see Woytowitsch 1978, no. 67 and pl. 10; Emiliozzi 1992, 93–9 and figs 11–17; *Carri da guerra* 322 (Repertorio 123) (there is also a cart from the tomb, no. 124) 155–62 (A. Romualdi on the tomb and its finds), 163–8 (A. Emiliozzi on the chariot), 168–70 (A. Romualdi on the chariot decoration), 170–3 (F. Cecchi, F. Fiesoli and F. Gennai on the restoration of the chariot), 173–5 (R. Peccioli on radiographical analyses of metal decoration of the chariot) with figs 2–18 and pls 6–9; Emiliozzi, Romualdi and Cecchi 2000; Haynes 2000, 101–3 with fig. 185; *Principi etruschi* cat. no. 343 (F. Sciacca).

[25] Littauer and Crouwel 1985, 70; Crouwel 1992, 32 with n. 91.

[26] Cf. a fourth century Faliscan red-figure volute krater from Città Castellana by the Aurora Painter, clearly showing the (bound) axle as placed beneath the (similarly bound) draught pole and the U-shaped floor (our Pl. 49); see Sprenger and Bartoloni 1990, pls 228–9; Crouwel 1992, 34 and pl. 31: 1; Brendel 1995, 344f. and fig. 269; Steingräber 2006, ill. p. 243. The chariot depicted may be a slightly garbled version of our type I.

chariot. On the latter vehicle, the siding has been reconstructed in five parts: along the front, a hoop-shaped rail (rising to *c.* 0.70 m), supported by a central vertical post which forks near the top; along the sides, two lower, half-bent rails, followed by two still lower, hoop-shaped rails, their rear uprights anchored in holes in the side timbers of the floor frame where these join the rear floor bar.

On both chariots the lower parts of the siding frames were screened. At the centre front, the screening is thought to have extended upwards, narrowing towards the top rail. The presence of screening material and its width in this area is suggested by a length of bronze tube, with two knob-like finials, found with the Populonia chariot. The screening material – on the Vulci chariot restored as stretched leather – would have fitted over the centre of the top rail.

On the Vulci chariot, the leather screening material inside the lower part of the hoop-shaped rear side rails, as reconstructed, is fastened to the rear posts by triangular-headed nails. It is held in place by a series of leather thongs fastened to rings at the centre top of the rails – on analogy with the metal-wire thongs that are preserved in this place on the Populonia chariot. A similar arrangement is documented on surviving metal parts of some other chariots of the seventh century, and later it is often illustrated with chariots of the same and other types (see below). On the Populonia chariot, sets of leather thongs, fastened at the top to metal rings, held up the screening material within the half-bent rails that were placed further forward.

The chariot from Vulci was partly covered in bronze sheathing, made up of two decorated panels covering the lower part of the side rails and rising to a point at the centre front. The sheathing is folded around the vertical posts of the side rails where these meet, and also around the floor frame. The Populonia chariot carries even more elaborate bronze decoration, with additional inlays in iron. In fact, most of the floor and siding frames, and also the screening material, were covered in metal. A large ornamental bronze disc was fastened to the screening material inside the lower part of the rear hoop-like rails, and a similar but smaller disc has been placed near to the top of the front screening.

The smaller number of metal parts surviving from some other seventh century chariot burials suggests basically similar vehicles. One of these chariots, from the Tomba or Circolo del Tridente in the Costiaccia Bambagini-Lippi cemetery at Vetulonia in Toscana, has been reconstructed on paper. It carried elaborate metal decoration (Pl. 4).[27] From the Tomba Barberini in the Colombella cemetery at Palestrina in Lazio come parts of the bronze sheathing of hoop-shaped side rails (Pl. 5).[28] The hoops curve sharply inwards at what must be their rear side, resembling the rear curve of the siding of a Type I chariot of the sixth century from Roma Vecchia in Lazio (see below). Within the upper part of the hoop-shaped side rail are remains of bronze-wire thongs, recalling those of the Vulci and Populonia chariots. A hoop-shaped side rail with such thongs, this time not of bronze but iron, was found among the chariot remains from tomb 182 in the Crocifisso cemetery at Matelica in Marche (Pl. 6).[29] Metal-wire thongs are impractical and imitate the leather ones of less ornate and lighter chariots. Leather thongs helped to keep in place and under tension the leather or other screening material of the side rails' upper section. (Leather thongs have been reconstructed on the earlier, undecorated chariot from tomb 15 at Castel di Decima; Pl. 1a.) Curved side rails with thongs in their upper parts are illustrated on figured documents showing Type I chariots engaged in processions of some kind or in racing. As the latter activity required vehicles to be light and strong, leather thongs would have been used (see Chapter II.7).

From other seventh century tombs with vehicular remains – the Tomba Regolini Galassi in the Sorbo cemetery at Cerveteri (ancient Caere), tomb 8 (formerly LXI) in the Contrada Morgi cemetery at Narce

---

[27] *Carri da guerra* 327 (Repertorio no. 177); Cygielman and Pagnini 2006, 35–44 and figs 9–10 (reconstruction drawings).

[28] Curtis 1919, 40f. no. 77 and pl. 24: 1; Woytowitsch 1978, no. 8 and pl. 4; Emiliozzi 1997, 100 and fig. 2; *Carri da guerra* 313 (Repertorio no. 25).

[29] *Potere e splendore* 234f. (G. De Marinis), 235–41 and cat. no. 316 (L. Palermo).

and the Tomba Bernardini in the Colombella cemetery at Palestrina, all in Lazio – come pairs of terminals made of bronze or leather-covered wood.[30] These closely resemble the terminals at the rear of the floor frames of the type I chariots from Vulci and Populonia (Pls 2–3). In the case of the terminals from the Tomba Regolini Galassi at Cerveteri, other surviving metal elements from the tomb suggest that they belonged not to a Type I chariot but to one of Type III (Pl. 11; see below).[31]

According to a recent interpretation, the floor frame terminals helped to prevent the central-axled vehicles from overturning when the rigidly fixed draught pole was lifted up.[32] However, the bronze or leather-covered wooden terminals served no such practical purpose, but were simply decorative, like the calcite bosses on the projecting ends of the floor frames of extant Egyptian New Kingdom chariots.[33]

Highly decorated chariots from rich funerary contexts of the sixth century appear to have been basically similar to the earlier ones, with a U-shaped floor plan and a siding frame of hoop-shaped rails of unequal height. The chariot (mentioned above) from the Tomba della Biga in the Poggi di Castro cemetery at Ischia di Castro, which was buried together with its draught team of two horses, is particularly informative. Enough survived of this vehicle for a plaster cast to be made of its wooden parts. This heavily built, ornate vehicle with its elaborate, nailed-on bronze sheathing is on exhibit in the Villa Giulia Museum in Rome (Pl. 7). The other very informative chariot, which is closely related but even more splendid in that it is entirely covered in sheet bronze, comes from a tomb in the Collo del Capitano cemetery at Monteleone di Spoleto in Umbria. This vehicle, in the Metropolitan Museum in New York, has recently been newly reconstructed, allowing the correction of a number of points in the earlier restoration (Pl. 8).[34]

Both chariots have narrow U-shaped floors, only large enough for one standing person. The floor of the Ischia di Castro carriage is 0.46 m wide by 0.70 m deep. The Monteleone chariot is 0.50 m wide, but its floor may have been deeper than the current 0.54 m, to allow for the presence of low rectangular side panels (now missing) similar to those found on the other vehicle. New reconstruction drawings make the sides of the floor frames extend beyond the rear floor bar. The latter is given a curved rear edge, in line with the material evidence provided by the earlier chariots from Vulci and Populonia. The sides of the floor frame of the Monteleone chariot have knob-like finials at the rear – elements missing on the vehicle from Ischia di Castro. These finials recall the more elaborate ones in this position on the earlier chariots. Unlike their predecessors, the two sixth century chariots appear to have had a separate, smaller rectangular frame beneath the U-shaped floor frame, to accommodate the vehicles' axle and draught pole. The presence and shape of such a frame is indicated by details of the bronze sheathing of the lower part of the chariots. The frame consisted of deep side timbers, with central rectangular slots for the axle, joined fore and aft by thinner, round-sectioned ones. The sheathing includes a decorative disc at either side of the axle slot, indicating the shape and position of the round cross-timbers. A slot at the centre front of this frame took the pole, which probably ran all the way under the floor and through a similar

---

[30] *Carri da guerra* 320, 330, 313 (Repertorio nos 103, 203 and 24). See Emiliozzi 1988, 296–301 and figs 7b, 8A–C, 9, 10, above, 11C; 1992, 87–94 and figs 5–6, 9 and 10A–B, C, above; 1997, 100f. and figs 3 and 5, below.

[31] As A. Emiliozzi (1992, 104–6) has demonstrated, the pair of bronze terminals ending in horse protomes from the Tomba Regolini Galassi, together with bronze sheathing similar to that of the rear floor bar of the restored Populonia chariot, were erroneously incorporated in the reconstruction of an ornate bronze chair (usually called throne) and bed respectively from the same tomb. For the chair and bed, see Pareti 1947, no. 217 with pls 23–4, and no. 236 with pls 30–1; also Steingräber 1979, 202 no. 42 with pl. 2 (bed).

[32] See Emiliozzi 2001, 323f.

[33] Littauer and Crouwel 1985, especially 94f. with pls 8–9, 12, 16, 18–19, 27–8, 30–1, 54, 56–7 (all six chariots from the tomb of Tut'ankhamun), 68 and 70 (carriage of Yuia and Thuiu), 72–3 (Florence chariot).

[34] See especially Woytowitsch 1978, no. 85 with pls 14–15; Sprenger and Bartoloni 1990, pls 105–7; Bonfante and Emiliozzi 1991; *Antichità dall'Umbria a New York* 103–20 (A. Emiliozzi on chariot), 395f. (S. Leach on tomb), also 171 (F. Roncalli) and 398; Emiliozzi 1996; 2006, 135–7; *Carri da guerra* 319 (Repertorio no. 87), 179–81 (M. Bonamici on tomb), 181–3 (A. Emiliozzi on chariot), 183–90 (M. Bonamici on chariot decoration) with figs 1–6 and pls 12–17; *Art of the Classical World* no. 323; Eisenberg 2007 (arguing – unconvincingly – that the chariot is a pastiche); C Vogel, 'A more precise restoration of your chariot awaits', in The *New York Times* of March 29, 2007.

slot in the rear cross-timber. The axle was placed beneath the pole, fitting in the rectangular slots in the side timbers of the floor frame and, presumably, in a corresponding slot in the pole.

Nothing appears to have survived of the flooring of the chariots from Ischia di Castro and Montoleone di Spoleto, but it has been reconstructed as a series of lengthwise slats fitting into slots at either end. Such a flooring would not only have been much heavier but also much less resilient than the meshed thongs of the earlier chariots from Vulci and Populonia, and of those documented outside Italy. But then the Ischia di Castro and Monteleone chariots represent heavy, partly or entirely bronze-clad ceremonial carriages that would not have been driven hard at speed.

The siding of the two chariots is in five parts: one at front, and two at either side, leaving the rear open. At the front, there is a hoop which is closed by wooden panelling, partly or entirely bronze-sheathed. On the Ischia di Castro chariot the front hoop is approximately hip-high, but on the Monteleone carriage it rises to a height of 0.845 m. Behind the front hoop of both chariots is a lower one, again with a bronze-sheathed board filling (0.47 m in height on the Monteleone chariot). On the Ischia di Castro chariot, behind this hoop is a very low rectangular panel, also sheathed in bronze. The panels on either side are now missing on the Monteleone chariot (see above). The join between the front and side hoops is covered by a rectangular bronze plaque, terminating in a knob above the figure of a standing naked youth executed in repoussé technique; on the Monteleone chariot a lion's head is seen below the figure. As reconstructed, both front and side hoops have a board filling. On the Ischia di Castro chariot the lower part of the wooden front panelling is decorated by a palmette motif rising from the bronze sheathing of the floor and lower frames. In the case of the Monteleone chariot, the entire panelling served as a base for sheet-bronze decoration which includes elaborate figured scenes.

The same basic construction, design and proportions are repeated (except for details of the siding frame) in other, less well preserved actual chariots which similarly date to the sixth century. One of these, from the Tomba dei Bronzi at Castel San Mariano in Umbria, had highly elaborate sheet-bronze decoration that was originally affixed to the wooden panelling at the front and sides, exactly as on the Monteleone chariot (Pl. 9).[35] Remains of rectangular decorated bronze sheathing from the tomb may well have belonged to low side panels to the rear, like those still in place on the carriage from Ischia di Castro.

A chariot from Roma Vecchia, on display in the Vatican Museum, is heavily restored but includes part of a bronze plaque covering the join between the front and side hoops, like those seen on the Ischia di Castro and Monteleone carriages.[36] Unlike the latter two chariots, the rear post of the siding appears not to have been straight but drawn inwards as it approached the floor. This was a feature of the seventh century chariots from the Tumulo dei Carri at Populonia and the Tomba Barberini at Palestrina (Pls 3, 5), as well as of many of the vehicles of the same type illustrated in sixth–fifth century figured documents (see below). Surviving fragments from the bronze sheathing of the siding of the chariot from Roma Vecchia represent an incised animal skin, possibly reflecting the screening material of less ornate vehicles and seen in illustrations of Type II chariots (see below).

---

[35] The material is divided mainly between the Museo Archeologico Nazionale at Perugia and the Staatliche Antikensammlungen in Munich. See especially Petersen 1894, 274–96 no. 18; Woytowitsch 1978, nos 75–6 and pl. 13; Höckmann 1982, 42–4 no. 8, 43, 111–14, 116–18 and figs 70–1, pls 26–8 ('Streitwagen I'), cf. 7, 117f. and pls 29: 9 and 33: 2 (fragments of decorated sheet bronze); *Strade degli Etruschi* figs 45–6; Sprenger and Bartoloni 1990, pls 108–9; *Antichità dall'Umbria a New York* 131–40 and ills (A. E. Feruglio); Emiliozzi 1991, 119f.; *Carri da guerra* 320 (Repertorio nos 96–7), 206–7 and 213–25 (A. E. Feruglio), 210–13 (A. Emiliozzi) with figs 1–19 and pls 22–3; Bruni 2002, 26 and figs 3–4. For the two other vehicles – a chariot and a cart rather than a wagon – from this tomb, see p. 24 and note 95, and pp. 78–9 and note 60. Claims that fragments of decorated sheet bronze may have belonged to yet another chariot (Höckmann 1982, 7, 117f. with pls 29: 9 and 33: 2) have been rejected (*Carri da guerra* 320 s.v. Repertorio no. 987; Bruni 2002, 27).

[36] The vehicle was found in the Tenuta di Roma Vecchia cemetery on the Via Appia. See Pinza 1935, 175 with pls 85–6 (earlier reconstruction); Emiliozzi 1991, 116, 119f.; *Carri da guerra* 314 (Repertorio no. 36), 191–3 (F. Buranelli on the findplace), 194–200 (M. Sannibale on the conservation and – imperfect – restoration of the chariot), 201 (A. Emiliozzi on the chariot), 202 (F. Buranelli on the metal decoration of the chariot) with figs 2–9 and pls 18–19.

In the case of the chariot from the Tomba Dutuit in the Quattordici Ponti cemetery at Capua (present-day Santa Maria di Capua Vetere) in Campania, the elaborately decorated bronze sheathing, while extending over the floor frame and the front hoop, covered only the lower part of the side hoop (Pl. 10).[37] The latter's open upper part would have provided a convenient handhold in mounting.

Only parts of elaborate sheet-bronze decoration remain of yet other ornate sixth century chariots of our Type I. For example, the so-called Barsanti Bronzes and pieces from Todi include fragments of the sheathing of the lower floor frame similar to that of the Ischia di Castro and Monteleone chariots, and of low rectangular side panels.[38]

The Type I chariot frequently appears in figured documents. Its three-dimensional representation on the ivory pyxis lid from Marzabotto is of particular importance (Pl. 33). The model chariot has the U-shaped floor and a siding of three rails of unequal height, the front rail hoop-shaped and solid screened, the lower side rails screened only in their lower sections. As has been noted earlier, the vehicle is pulled not by horses but by a team consisting of two horses and two panthers.[39]

The numerous two-dimensional representations yield views of type I chariots in various settings, moving slowly and taking part in parades of some kind, or at speed and engaged in racing. Again, the floor appears to have been narrow, offering room for only the driver to stand at the front, but often deep enough to accommodate a passenger at the rear. This passenger is either shown inside the vehicle or in the act of mounting (Pl. 71a). The siding again consists basically of a light framework of bent wooden rails of unequal height, which are partly or entirely filled with screening material. In the case of one detailed profile representation, on the bronze sheathing of a side panel of the extant ornate chariot from Monteleone di Spoleto, the side screen carries a rosette. This recalls the discs in the same position on the restored earlier chariot from Populonia (Pl. 3). The siding of the chariot depicted on the Monteleone carriage has a knob at the join of the front and side rails. The side rails curve inwards at their lower rear and clearly do not extend to the very rear of the floor. Other representations may indicate, behind the side rails, the low rectangular panels such as were found on the extant chariot from Ischia di Castro (Pl. 7).

Detailed renderings on terracotta revetment plaques may show the knob at the junction between front and side rails, as well as a palmette motif on the solid front breastwork (Pl. 70a). The palmette, also seen in some vase paintings (Pls 43–44),[40] recalls the Ischia di Castro chariot and suggests a similar decorative bronze sheathing.

Other illustrated features include the thongs strung in the open upper part of the side rails, and appendages at the back of the floor. The latter presumably indicate decorative finials at the ends of the side beams of the floor frame (Pl. 70). A pair of scroll-like attachments may also be illustrated under the floor, one on either side of the central axle (Pl. 71a).[41] They are reminiscent of details of the decorative bronze sheathing on the floor frame of the chariot from Ischia di Castro.

The Type I chariots illustrated before or during a race were clearly light and small, designed for only

[37] In Paris, Petit Palais. See Woytowitsch 1978, no. 6 with figs 1–6 and pl. 4; Höckmann 1982, 42 and n. 252; *Strade degli Etruschi* 49 with fig. 47; Cerchiai, Colucci Pescatori and d'Henry 1997, 26–8 and fig. 1; *Carri da guerra* 312 (Repertorio no. 11) 301–3 (V. Bellelli); Emiliozzi 1997, 102 and fig. 6; 2006.

[38] For the so-called Barsanti Bronzes (in the Villa Giulia Museum, Rome), see Vighi and Minissi 1955, pl. 44; Brown, W.L. 1960, 86f. and pl. 31b; Emiliozzi 1997, 102 and fig. 7; *Carri da guerra* 334 (Repertorio no. 253; cf. no. 252: cart). For the finds from the Le Logge, Fondo Leli cemetery at Todi (kept in the Museo Archeologico, Florence), see Höckmann 1982, 109 n. 551; *Strade degli Etruschi* fig. 42; *Carri da guerra* 319 (Repertorio no. 92).

[39] See p. 7 and note 54.

[40] See also the incompletely preserved chariot in a wall painting of the fourth century from the Tomba Golini I at Orvieto (our Pl. 39; Woytowitsch 1978, no. 258 and pl. 44; Steingräber 1985, no. 33).

[41] See, in particular, the incompletely preserved chariot among the decoration of a bronze covering of an actual chariot from the Tomba dei Bronzi at Castel San Mariano (our p. 9, note 12).

the driver. The lower part of their front and side breastwork is usually shown solid, and sometimes again with straps strung criss-cross inside their open upper part to help tighten construction (Pls 34–6).

There are no local prototypes for chariot Type I in Italy, and a foreign origin may be assumed. Europe north of the Alps may be excluded: the actual vehicular remains of the Urnfield culture (thirteenth–eighth century) appear to have belonged to spoke-wheeled four-wheelers.[42] Illustrations of two-wheeled vehicles dating from the middle of the second millennium onwards are sketchy and do not appear to represent likely prototypes.[43]

Looking to the east, the particular combination of a narrow, U-shaped floor, accommodating one or two persons standing behind one another, and hoop-shaped front and side rails characteristic of the Type I chariots in Italy, finds no parallel among contemporary or earlier vehicles in the Near East, Egypt and Cyprus.[44] The chariots in those parts of the ancient world are of distinctly different types. This is particularly clear from such figured documents as the large-scale Assyrian and Neo-Hittite reliefs of the ninth–seventh centuries (Pls 125–127) and the Achaemenid ones of the late sixth century (Pl. 128). There is also ample documentation from Cyprus, which includes remains of actual chariots from eighth–seventh century tombs (Pl. 130), terracotta and stone models in the round, mainly of the sixth century, as well as detailed two-dimensional representations such as a sixth century sarcophagus from Amathus (Pl. 131). This does not mean that Italic chariots of Type I, and indeed others, are not indebted to the Near East, as will become apparent when discussing aspects of their wheels (see II.3).

As for Greece, the two chariot types attested on the mainland in the eighth century – the Rail and High-front chariots – could accommodate up to two people, standing side by side and not one behind the other as on Type I chariots from Italy.[45] Whereas the light Rail type with its D-shaped floor has an open siding consisting of only a single rail, supported at the centre front by a vertical post (Pls 132–134), the heavier High-front chariot combines a rectangular floor plan with a tripartite, fenestrated siding, the hoop-like front rail rising above the side rails (Pls 137–138). Of these two chariot types, the Rail chariot has clear Mycenaean antecedents and seems to go out of use after the eighth century. The High-front chariot, on the other hand, becomes the standard type in mainland Greece from the seventh century onwards, to judge from its many illustrations in various artistic media. High-front chariots are also frequently seen in figured documents made in the Greek colonies in southern Italy and Sicily, commonly referred to as Magna Graecia (Pl. 75).[46]

The Greek High-front and Rail chariots differ in several aspects from the Type I chariot of central Italy, but they do have in common an open or fenestrated railwork siding. Another feature shared by the Greek High-front chariot and the Italic type I chariot is that the rails are of unequal height. Mainland Greek types may then have provided inspiration for the Italic chariots of Type I (and more so for those of Type III, see below).

---

[42] See especially Piggott 1983, 109–14, 122–5; Pare 1987b, 33–63; 1992, ch. 3 and fig. 22 (distribution map); Clausing 1999; Winghart 1999.

[43] Crouwel 1981, 148 and pls 175–7; Piggott 1983, 92–4, 117–19 and figs 48, 50, 70; Pare 1987b, 28–30 and figs 5, 6 (distribution map) and 8; Larsson 2004, 383–97.

[44] See especially Littauer and Crouwel 1979a, chs 9 and 10; 1985; Crouwel 1987 and 1991.

[45] For what follows, see Crouwel 1992, ch. III; 2006. Add Heilmeier 1994 (the bronze models of Rail chariots from Olympia); Manakidou 1994 (numerous vase paintings with illustrations of High-front chariots).

[46] See a.o. Mertens-Horn 1992, 8–39, 105–10 and figs 1, 13–26, 45 and pl. 4 (terracotta revetment plaques of Frieze I from Metaponto, San Biago, in Puglia. Pl. 6: 1 shows a terracotta plaque with part a similar chariot from the Timone della Motta at Francavilla Marittima near Sybaris in Calabria); 2005–6 (terracotta plaques from Locri Epizephyrii, also in Calabria); Olbrich 1986, 137–45 (fig. 14 illustrates a terracotta perirrhanterion from Incoronata in Molise); Jantzen 1937, 26 no. 8 and pl. 10.41, and *I Greci in occidente* cat. no. 118 II (bronze belt from Noicattaro in Puglia); Franke and Hirmer 1964, a.o. pls 5–6 (silver coins from Syracuse); Von Mercklin 1916, and Woytowitsch 1978, no. 171 with pl. 40 (bronze model from Locri Epizephyrii). The rather summarily rendered chariots seen in fourth century painted tombs from cemeteries at Paestum in Campania cannot readily be attributed to any particular type, but they are clearly influenced by Greek artistic models showing High-front chariots; see Pontrandolfo and Rouveret 1992, 58–63 with many illustrations. Most unusually, the vehicles often have cross-bar and not spoked wheels (see our p. 72, note 26, pp. 81–2).

Inspiration may also have come from the Greek cities on the west coast of Anatolia, where chariots differ in various aspects from their mainland Greek counterparts. These so-called East Greek chariots, which are unfortunately documented only by profile representations and during a relatively brief period of time – the sixth to the earlier fifth centuries – fall into two types, on the basis of their floor plan and siding.[47] The first type probably has a more or less D-shaped floor and presents a variety of profiles, although the top edge is always curved and rises towards the front (Pl. 139). The siding is entirely screened, except for the usual handhold at the rear. The second, much less frequently illustrated type of East Greek chariot appears to have a rectangular floor plan (Pl. 140). The siding is formed by three separate rails, the one in front rising above the side rails. The screening material leaves a handgrip at the front, and there may be another handgrip at the upper rear corners. The chariots of East Greek types, their floor sometimes shown as wide enough for two occupants to stand side by side, differ from both the mainland Greek chariots and those of Type I in central Italy – in the details of their siding. At the same time, they share aspects of their traction system and harnessing with the Type I and other chariots from central Italy (see Chapter II.4 and 5). Another element in common is the palmette that decorates the front breastwork of some extant and illustrated chariots of Type I in central Italy. The palmette appears – in an upside-down position – on the chariots of East Greek type depicted on sheet bronzes found on Samos and at Olympia.[48] In fact, the palmette motif and much of the sheet-bronze decoration of the ornate chariots from sixth century central Italy derives from mainland and/or East Greece.[49]

Our Type I chariot is essentially the same as the Roman racing car, which in turn was still used in Byzantine times. An early representation can be seen on a stone relief of *c*. 50 BC, commemorating circus games.[50] Roman racing chariots are depicted in a variety of other two-dimensional representations (Pl. 143). There are also some bronze models, of which the one reportedly found in the Tiber river is the most detailed (Pl. 142).[51] This model represents a light racing car, with a narrow, U-shaped floor, the ends of the floor frame projecting at the rear. The flooring consists of interlaced thongs, probably of rawhide. The thongs held the floor frame together, as well as providing a resilient platform. The siding is formed of only one rail, supported by a vertical post at the centre front. The rail extends a short distance along the sides before running down in a curve, leaving an open platform at the rear. Screening material of leather or textile is attached to the rail by tabs.

Chariot Type II

In Italy before the Roman Imperial period, some two-dimensional representations show the front of the chariot body not vertical but dropping at a oblique angle towards the draught pole. The vehicle body thereby presents a distinctly triangular profile. The figured documents, restricted in date to the sixth and

---

[47] For what follows, see Crouwel 1992, ch. 3. Add sheet bronzes from Samos and Olympia, dated by P. Brize to the last quarter of the seventh century; see Brize 1995, 73–83 *s.v.* nos SA 3 (also Kopcke 1968, 286–9 no. 110 with fig. 32 and pls 119–20; Yalouri 1972, pl. 54), OL 3 (also Yalouri 1972, pls 52–3), OL 6 (also Yalouri 1972, pl. 51) and OL 10 (also Yalouri 1971; 1972, pls 55–6). Add also Braun 1998, no. 104 (fragment of an unprovenanced terracotta revetment plaque).

[48] See Brize 1985, nos SA 3 and OL 6.

[49] See recently, Höckmann 2006.

[50] Holliday 1994, 185 with fig. 103. See also Junkelmann 1990, fig. 135 (stone relief attributed to the tomb of the racing driver P. Aelius Gutta Culpurnianus on the Via Flaminia, showing a chariot with an – incompletely preserved – extension towards the rear).

[51] Walters 1893, no. 269; Woytowitsch 1978, no. 175 with pl. 41; Junkelmann 1990, fig 138. Two other bronze models, unprovenanced but probably also from the Roman Empire period, are related but have a solid front shield and open hoop side rails; Woytowitsch 1978, nos 173–4 with pl. 41; cf. also the unprovenanced bronze model in Von Mercklin 1933, 95f. with fig. 11. For Roman racing chariots, see Junkelmann 1992, 217–20 with fig. 197 (reconstruction drawing, largely based on the bronze model from the Tiber); 1990, 136–56 with many illustrations, especially figs 139–40 (terracotta so-called Campana placques, including our Pl. 143) and figs 122–4 (detailed illustrations on the Great Circus mosaic from Piazza Armerina in Sicily, for which see also Carandini, Ricci and de Vos 1982, figs 19–21, 202–5 and fol. LVI–LVII).

earlier fifth centuries, include Etruscan black-figure vase paintings which also illustrate chariots of Type I (Pls 40a–b, 44).[52] There is bronze sheathing with repoussé decoration, probably from the Isis Tomb in the Polledrara cemetery at Vulci (Pl. 54),[53] and a fragmentary terracotta stand with relief decoration from Poggio Civitate (Murlo), also in Toscana (Pl. 52)[54]. Type II chariots are also illustrated on terracotta revetment plaques from various sites: Tarquinia[55] and Roselle[56] in Toscana, and Cerveteri[57] and Satricum (present-day Borgo Le Ferriere)[58] in Lazio (Pl. 72). Other terracotta plaques, belonging to the Rome-Caprifico roof system, show a Type II chariot side by side with a chariot of Type III (Pl. 71b).

The siding of Type II chariots is in three parts: a rather low, solid triangular front shield, which extends some way along the sides, and two lower, hoop-shaped rails similar to those seen in the same position on Type I chariots, with the floor similarly extending at the rear. As on Type I chariots, the vehicles must have had a narrow U-shaped floor, offering room for a driver, and deep enough to accommodate a passenger standing to the rear. In fact, the Type II chariot is a variant of Type I, distinguished by its triangular front breastwork.

In some instances the lower front seems to take the form of the protome of a boar or other animal (Pl. 71b).[59] This feature may be interpreted as an exaggerated rendering of what is seen on highly decorated, extant chariots of Type I, such as those from Castel San Mariano and Monteleone di Spoleto (Pls 8–9). There, the central draught pole, upon emerging from under the vehicle body, passes under a bronze boar's protome or through the open mouth of a lion.[60]

In the case of the Type II chariots depicted on the bronze sheathing from Vulci and on an black-figure neck-krater by the Amphiaraus Painter from the same site, an animal skin is seen covering the triangular front part of the siding, the hairs being clearly indicated (Pl 40b).[61] This recalls the incised animal skin pattern on the remains of bronze screening of the actual chariot of Type I from Roma Vecchia.[62]

The hoop-like rear part of the siding is usually shown as a separate element, placed vertically, as on chariots of Type I. Similarly, the lower section is solid, the open upper section sometimes showing thongs to maintain tension. In addition, on the terracotta revetment plaques from Cerveteri a strap is indicated in paint, emerging from within the solid triangular part of the siding and running up at a slant. The strap ends in a loop held by the passenger, who is seen mounting the vehicle or maintaining his balance in it (Pl. 72).

---

[52] See p. 9, note 8: the neck-amphora by the Amphiaraus Painter (a Type II chariot is depicted on the neck – see Dorn 1966, ills 9–10; Hampe and Simon 1964, pl. 7: 1–2; 1967, pl. 30; Hannestad 1976, pl. 2 – whereas a race involving chariots of Type I appears in a body zone), the jug(?) by the Tityos Painter (showing Types I and II chariots as part of one scene), and the Polledrara hydria from Vulci (Smith 1894, pl. 7; the other side seems to show Type I chariots; see our p. 9, note 8.

[53] Walters 1899, no. 434; Haynes 1965, 13–25 with figs 7–10; Santoro 2006, 269 with fig. 3.

[54] Warden 1977, especially 203, 207f. with pls 101: 1, 106: 3, 107: 1–2; Camporeale 1993, no. 26.

[55] Andrén 1939–40, 66f. no. I: 1a–c with pl. 22:75; Cataldi 1993, especially 208 nos 7–8 with fig. 4 (see also nos 21–4); *Scavo con scavo* 83–87 nos I.e.21–36; Winter, N. A. 200, 375f. no. 5.D.5.d with figs 5.30 and 5.31.

[56] Winter, N. A. 2009, 360 no. 5.D.1.f and fig. 5.16.

[57] Andrén 1939–40, 14–17 nos I: 1a–d and pl. 4: 6–9; 1974, 4f. and figs 21–6; Melis 1986; Kästner 1988; *Die Welt der Etrusker. Archäologische Denkmäler* no. B 6.1.5; Cristofani 1990; *Italy of the Etruscans* no. 328; Winter, N. A. 2009, 236, 271f., 288–92 no. 4.D.8.g with ill. 4.12.1 and figs 4.30–4.31 (Roof 4–11); Christiansen and Winter 2010, no. 59.

[58] Maaskant 1991, 108 with fig. 33; Beyer 1993; Winter, N. A. 2009, 398–400, 445f. no. 6.D.1.a with ill. 6.12.1 and fig. 5.30 (Roof 6–1).

[59] For animal protomes in such a position, see also a decorated bronze sheathing from the Tomba dei Bronzi at Castel San Mariano (attributed by U. Höckmann to her 'Streitwagen II'; see our p. 24 and note 95), and a painting in the Tomba Golini I at Orvieto (Woytowitsch 1978, no. 258 with pl. 44; Steingräber 1985, no. 32).

[60] See p. 15 and note 37.

[61] See p. 9, note 8.

[62] See p. 14, note 36.

Chariot Type III

This type is only illustrated clearly on terracotta revetment plaques of the later sixth century, but it may also be represented among the actual vehicle remains. Considering the representations of chariots in procession on the Rome-Caprifico revetment plaques first, the chariot floor appears not to be U-shaped but rectangular. Four timbers meet at right-angles, to judge from the angular front corners (Pl. 71a–b). At the rear, the floor may have an upturned finial. The passenger shown in the act of mounting may well have stood beside rather than behind the driver, unlike the two occupants seen riding in chariots of Types I and II.

The siding consists of three separate rails, one extending across the front and the others at either side. The front rail, in vertical position and with a knob-like finial, rises well above the side rail to approximately hip height. The side rails have a horizontal upper edge and project backwards to form a large loop. Screening material of leather or textile is fastened to the side rails, leaving a large opening at the rear to serve as a handhold when mounting, and a smaller opening further forward.

A pair of thongs or, less likely, struts, is seen running down diagonally from the front to the side rail in order to reinforce construction. Under the floor, scroll-like attachments are visible, like those seen on the Ischia di Castro and other extant chariots of Type I. They may perhaps likewise indicate a decorative bronze sheathing of the floor frame.

The body profile recalls the High-front chariot of mainland Greece, which, as we have seen when discussing the Italic Type I chariot, is first attested in the eighth century and becomes the standard type there from the seventh century onwards. The High-front type, with its rectangular floor plan and tripartite siding of partly screened rails, also repeatedly appears on figured documents made in Magna Graecia (Pl. 75).[63]

Do the Rome-Caprifico terracotta revetment plaques represent chariots of a type that was actually used in Italy or do they simply copy Greek artistic models? First, it must be pointed out that the chariots on the plaques appear in processional scenes together with chariots of our Types I and II, neither of which has close parallels in (mainland) Greece. All three types of chariots are depicted in considerable detail. In addition, our Type III chariots display several features which are not found on Greek High-front vehicles, such as the finials of the front rail and floor frame, the thongs linking front and side rails, and the scroll-like attachments under the floor. At the same time, a characteristic element of the Greek High-front chariot – the thong pole-end support running from the top of the front rail to the upturned pole end – is notably absent. We may then conclude that the Type III chariots depicted on the revetment plaques, while ultimately deriving from the Greek High-front type, represent real vehicles of sixth century Italy.

The chariots depicted on somewhat later terracotta revetment plaques from Palestrina are less realistic (Pl. 73). These again are shown in processions, side by side with chariots of our Type I. The vehicles present the rectangular profile, the high front rail with its knob-like finial, and the lower side rail with its fenestrated screening of the Type III chariot. However, on the Palestrina plaques the front breastwork of a type I chariot can be recognised by its curved rear edge in the area where the oblique thongs or struts joining the front and side rails are shown on the Rome-Caprifico plaques. The chariot representations on the Palestrina plaques may therefore be interpreted as an artist's confused rendering of the bodies of our Types I and III.

Among the actual chariots from funerary contexts there may have been a few of Type III, to judge from surviving metal parts and decoration. One candidate is the chariot dating to *c.* 650 from the

---

[63] See p. 16, note 46.

Tomba Regolini Galassi at Cerveteri.[64] Though its published reconstruction (Pl. 11) may be questioned on many counts, the vehicle seems to have had a rectangular rather than a U-shaped floor, and a side rail rather like that of the Greek High-front chariot. Other features in common are found in the design and details of the wheels.[65] On the other hand, bronze elements like the sheathing of the rear floor bar and the sockets with their elaborate finials at the ends of the side timbers firmly link the Regolini Galassi carriage with the extant seventh century chariots with U-shaped floor frames of our Type I from Vulci and Populonia in central Italy (see above).

Some surviving metal elements from a tomb in the San Martino cemetery at Civitella San Paola (ancient Capena) in Lazio, dating to c. 700–650, have been tentatively attributed to a High-front type chariot and its draught pole.[66]

Another two-wheeler, from the Fossa della Biga in the San Cerbone cemetery at Populonia, dating to the early fifth century, has been reconstructed with a rectangular frame and a siding somewhat resembling that of the Greek High-front type.[67] However, the surviving metal parts and decoration do not appear to warrant such a detailed reconstruction.

It has been claimed that further evidence for chariots with rectangular floor plans is provided by bronze elements found in seventh century tombs with remains of two-wheeled vehicles in Toscana, Lazio and Emilia Romagna (Pls 12–13).[68] These objects come in pairs and consist of two sockets for round-sectioned pieces of wood, meeting at right-angles. They are either plain or decorated to varying degrees.

The metal elements have been classified as angle-sockets or 'Winkeltülle', on analogy with more or less similar finds from the Alpine region and beyond.[69] The angle-sockets from outside Italy, which come in pairs or fours, belong to the seventh and sixth centuries.

The *four* angle-sockets from some of the Hallstatt burials with four-wheeled vehicles have been convincingly reconstructed as fitting on the ends of the horizontal top rails of the siding (Pl. 15).[70] It has been argued that the *two* angle-sockets found in Italy and elsewhere were originally placed at the front corners of the floor frame or of the top railing of chariots with a rectangular floors.[71] This is difficult to imagine, at least in the case of the large, highly ornate pair of angle-sockets from the Tomba Barberini at

---

[64] Pinza 1907, 100–3 no. LIX; Pareti 1947, 120, 252–64 no. 227 and pl. 25; Hamblin 1975, ill. p. 48; Woytowitsch 1978, no. 30 and pl. 30; Emiliozzi 1992, 104–6; 1997, 100; also personal communication; *Carri da guerra* 320 (Repertorio no. 103).

[65] See p. 30 and note 136.

[66] *Carri da guerra* 329 (Repertorio no. 198), 286–9 nos B–D (E. Mangani), 289 (A. Emiliozzi) and figs 2–5, pl. 30: 1; Mura Sommella 2004–5, 257–9 and fig. 42. Some of the metal elements are decorated with inlaywork.

[67] De Agostino 1957, 14–21 (for reconstruction drawings, see figs 21, 34, 33–4); *Carri da guerra* 322 (Repertorio no. 122). Several of the decorative bronze elements recall unprovenanced ones of the fifth century which have also been attributed to chariots – in the Metropolitan Museum of Art in New York (see Richter 1939; De Agostino 1957, 21; *Carri da guerra* 334 s.v. Repertorio no. 256) and the Museo Archeologico Nazionale in Florence (Zaccagnino 2006, especially 225–7 with fig. 11b–g; *Carri da Guerra* 335 s.v. Repertorio no. 254).

[68] **Vetulonia, Tomba del Littore** (our Pl. 12): see Egg 1986a, 208, 210f. no. 15 with fig. 7; Woytowitsch 1978, no. 56h–i with pl. 8; Emiliozzi 1988, 296, 300 with fig. 8D; 1922, 87 with fig. 10D; *Carri da guerra* 1997, 268f., 272 with figs 5, 7 and pl. 29:1 (M. Cygielman: Veicolo B), 327 (s.v. Repertorio no. 174); *Signori di Maremma* cat. no. 3.84. **Castellina** in Chianti, tomb in the Monte Calvario cemetery: see Woytowitsch 1978, no. 68r and pl. 11; Egg 1986a, 207 no. 3; *Carri da guerra* 320 (s.v. Repertorio no. 98); Emiliozzi 2000, 19 and fig. 12. **Civiltà Castellana**, tomb: see Guidi 1983, 81 no. C1–2; Egg 1986a, 207 no. 4. Not mentioned in *Carri da guerra* 329f. (Repertorio s.v. Civita Castellana). **Palestrina**, Tomba Bernardini (our Pl. 13): see Curtius 1919, nos 90–1 and pls 65–6; Canciani and Von Hase 1979, 56f. no. 68 and pls 47–8; Emiliozzi 1988, 296–8 and figs 5–6, 7a, 11a; 1992, 87 and figs 3–4, 9, top; 1997, 101 and fig. 5; *Carri da guerra* 313 (s.v. Repertorio no. 24). **Verucchio**, Tomba del Trono: see *Carri da guerra* 332 (s.v. Repertorio no. 227); P. von Eles in *Guerriero e sacerdote* 88 nos 112a–b and fig. 29 and pl. 35; also Gentili 2003, pls 57 and CCLXXXI, no. 68.

[69] For the finds from Italy and elsewhere, see Woytowitsch 1978, 53; Guidi 1983, 29, 81f. with pl. 27: left (distribution map); Egg 1986a, 206–11 with fig. 8 (distribution map); 1987, 95–8 and fig. 21 (the same distribution map); Nebelsick 1992, 107–10 and fig. 10 (distribution map); Pare 1992, 100f., 170 and fig. 76 (distribution map); Camerin 1997, 35–7.

[70] Egg 1996a, 207–10 nos 2 and 17 (Ohnenheim in the Alsace and Birmenstorf in Switzerland); 1997, 92, 94 and figs 18, 23 and pl. 3 (Ohnenheim); 90 and fig. 20 (Birmensdorf); also Pare 1992, 100f. and cat. nos 12 (Ohnenheim) and 20 (Birmenstorf).

[71] See M. Cygielman in *Carri da guerra* 268 and fig. 5 (reconstruction drawing of part of the chariot from the Tomba del Littore at Vetulonia, see our note 68); Emiliozzi 1988, 296–301; 1992, 102–4; 1997, 101; Nebelsick 1992, 107–10.

Palestrina (length of sockets 0.220 m and 0.223 m respectively). With their human and animal figures, these objects would been most cumbersome in such a position on a chariot, but have fitted more easily on a piece of wooden furniture.[72] The widely distributed angle-sockets may in fact have served for different purposes. For instance, the pair of incompletely preserved objects identified as angle-sockets from the Tomba del Carrettino of the Ca'Morta cemetery at Como in the north, belonging to phase IB of the Golasecca culture and dating to *c.* 700, stand well apart from all the others.[73] Only where the similarities between the finds from Italy and Hallstatt Europe are sufficiently close, a common function and origin can be assumed.[74]

Chariot Type IV

Profile representations appear to illustrate chariots with a rectangular profile, suggesting that the floor was similarly rectangular in shape. The representations include an incompletely preserved ivory plaque from a tomb at Montefortini, Comeana di Carmignano, in Toscana (Pl. 56)[75] and three pyxides of the same material from tombs at Cerveteri and Chiusi in the same region (Pl. 57).[76] All date to the later seventh century. Similar chariots can be recognized on several of the funerary stelae of the fifth–fourth centuries at Bologna (ancient Felsina) (Pl. 61).[77] The same type of chariot is illustrated on bronzes belonging to the so-called Situla Art (Pls 164–166; see Appendix 1).

The lower part of the hoop-shaped rail siding on chariots of Type IV is mostly solidly-walled, leaving a convenient handhold above. Thongs may be seen running down from the top, as on chariots of Types I and II. In fact, the siding closely resembles the side hoops of those types of chariot, the difference being the absence of the higher breastwork at the front. By contrast, some of the representations of Type IV

---

[72] See p. 20, note 68. Steingräber (1979, 199f. no. 31 and pl. 6) includes these objects in his book on furniture from ancient Italy. A connection with furniture is perhaps also more likely in the case of the bronze figurines of couchant lions from this tomb, *pace* Emiliozzi 1988, 296 with fig. 11b; 1992, 87, 102f. with figs 7–8, 9, middle; see Canciani and Von Hase 1979, 56 no. 67 with pl. 46. The lion figurines are strongly reminiscent of those of dogs from the Tomba del Trono in Veruccchio (P. von Eles in *Guerriero e sacerdote* 88f. nos 109–11 with fig. 30 and pl. 34), which also contained angle-sockets (see our p. 20, note 68).

[73] Bertolone 1956–7, 38 with pl. C, fig. 1: 11–12; Woytowitsch 1978, no. 119 with pl. 20; Egg 1986b, 208–10 no. 5. For the vehicular remains from the tomb, see also Bertolone 1956–7; Woytowitsch 1978, no. 111 with pl. 18; De Marinis 1988a, 56; *Carri da guerra* 333 (Repertorio no. 238).

[74] Egg (1986a, 211) suggests that the angle-sockets originated in central Italy, from where they spread to the north.

[75] *Carri da guerra* 62f. no. s.4 with pl. I: 3 (F. Nicosia); *Principi etruschi* cat. no. 295 (M. Chiara Bettini).

[76] *Pyxis* from the Tomba Regolini Galassi in the Sorbo cemetery, Cerveteri: see Pareti 1947, 226 no. 168, pl. XVIII; Huls 1957, 31 no. 1 and pl. 2: 1, also 32 no. 2 and pl. 3: 1; Rebuffat 1962, 382–7 and ill. p. 384: above; Woytowitsch 1978, no. 211 and pl. 45; Pare 1987d, 211 and fig. 23: 3; 1992, 210 and fig. 151: 3. *Pyxis* from the same cemetery, and quite probably from the same tomb: see Rebuffat 1962 (ills pp. 371–4); Woytowitsch 1978, no. 213 and pl. 45. *Pyxis* from the Tomba della Pania, Chiusi: see a.o. Cristofani 1971, 63–89 and fig. 9; Woytowitsch 1978, no. 214 and pl. 45; *Etrusker in der Toskana* 269f. no. 2; Christiansen 1989, 48f. and figs 9–10; Pare 1987d, 221 and fig. 22: 2; 1992, 210 and fig. 151: 2; Camporeale 1993, no. 5; *Gli Etruschi* cat. no. 170.

[77] *Ducati 1910, no. 168* (Side A) and pl. 4 (our Pl. 61): see also Morigi Govi and Vitali 1982, 287 no. 168; Sassatelli 1989, 946f. and pl. 5b; Stary-Rimpau 1988, no. 168; Sprenger and Bartoloni 1990, pl. 206; Brendel 1995, 376f. and fig. 292; Lucassen 1995, no. 39); Bonaudo 2002–3, 104f. and fig. 2; E. Govi in Sassatelli and Govi 2007, 83, 86f., 89 and pl. 18a. *Ducati 1910, no. 11* and fig. 28: see also Stary-Rimpau 1988, no. 11; Lucassen 1995, no. 30. *Ducati 1910, no. 25* and fig. 4: see also Stary-Rimpau 1988, no. 25; Lucassen 1995, no. 18. *Ducati 1910, no. 42* (Side A) and fig. 79: see also Stary Rimpau 1985, no. 42; Macellari 2006, 245f. and pl. 160 (Arnoaldi, tomb 114, Stele A). *Ducati 1910, no. 47*: see also Stary-Rimpau 1988, no. 47; Lucassen 1995, no. 34; Macellari 2002, 252 and pl. 166 (Arnoldi, tombs 116 and 117, Stele D). *Ducati 1910, no. 77* and fig. 48: see also Stary-Rimpau 1988, no. 77; Lucassen 1995, no. 20; Macellari 2006, 212 and pl. 135 (Arnoaldi, tomb 100, Stele A). *Ducati 1943, no. 173* (Side A) and fig. 49: see also *Museo Civico Archeologico di Bologna* no. 173; also Stary-Rimpau 1988, no. 173; Lucassen 1995, no. 40. *Ducati 1910, no. 195* and fig. 24: see also *Museo Civico Archeologico di Bologna* no. 194; Stary-Rimpau 1988, no. 195; Brendel 1995, 375f. and 291; Lucassen 1995, no. 42. *Ducati 1943, no. A* and pl. 1: see also Stary-Rimpau 1988, no. 210; Morigi Govi and Sassatelli 1993, no. A and fig. 9; Lucassen 1995, no. 43. *Ducati 1943, no. C* and pl. 2, right: also Stary-Rimpau 1988, no. 212; Morigi Govi and Sassatelli 1993, no. C and fig. 12; Lucassen 1995, no. 44; E. Govi in Sassatelli and Govi 2007, 82, 84 n. 62 and pls 17d and 2o – extreme left. There are several other worn or fragmentary stelae where the type of chariot cannot be clearly established. See a.o. *Ducati 1910, no. 87* and fig. 78; also Stary-Rimpau 1985, no. 87; Lucassen 1995, no. 22.

chariots show a spiraliform element at the upper front of the siding (Pl. 56). The same element appears in the same position on several of the chariots depicted in Situla Art, including the two situlae found in northern Italy (Pl. 165–66; see Appendix 1).[78] The spiraliform element is also indicated on some of the chariots carved on funerary stelae from Padua in Veneto (Pl. 62).[79] These so-called Palaeovenetic stelae carry inscriptions in the Venetic language and have been attributed to the first century.

The spiraliform element at the top front of the chariots, which is illustrated in most detail on the ivory plaque from Montefortini, Comeana di Carmignano, has been linked with actual metal objects, always in pairs, from tombs containing remains of two-wheeled vehicles in Toscana and Lazio (Pl. 14).[80] These date to the seventh century. The vehicles were associated with warrior burials, and presumably were chariots rather than carts.

Similar finds occur in two warrior tombs with vehicular remains, again probably belonging to chariots, at Sesto Calende on the southern border of Lake Maggiore in northern Italy (Pls 15–16). Of these graves, the Tomba Guerriero A in the Castiona cemetery, has been dated to c. 600 (Golasecca culture, phase IC/IIA),[81] and the Tomba Guerriero B in the Carrera cemetery to the earlier sixth century (Golasecca, phase IIA).[82]

The bronze or iron objects are tubular, with one end spiraliform and the other open to fit into a piece of wood. There may also be a straight, tubular cross-piece fitting onto another piece of wood. These metal objects have been variously explained as handholds, holders for whips or goads, or simply as decoration. Another suggestion is that, like the two simpler iron tubular elements from the later eighth century tomb 15 found with remains of a Type I chariot at Castel di Decima (Pl. 1c),[83] they served for the attachment of traces (q.v.) that connected the outriggers of a three- or four-horse draught team to the chariot body.[84] As has been argued above, this is unlikely. Chariot teams in Italy before the Roman Imperial period appear to have consisted much more often of two rather than three or four horses. And when four-horse teams are illustrated, the traces are fastened differently, low down inside the vehicle, either to the axle or to the rear floor bar. Experiments with reconstructions of Greek chariots have

---

[78] See p. 109 and note 2: the so-called Arnoaldi Situla from Bologna and the Benvenuti Situla from Este.

[79] *Stele of Ostiala Gallenia* (our Pl. 62): see Zampieri 1994, 109 and fig. 153; also *Padova preromana* no. 75; Fogolari and Prosdocimi 1988, 105 and fig. 134; De Marinis 1988, fig. 103; (*Antichi genti d'Italia* cat. no. 786). *Stele Lapidario I:* see Zampieri 1994, 109f. and fig. 155; also *Padova preromana* no. 76. Possibly also Zampieri 1983 (fig. 5: reconstruction drawing). For other Padavian stelae, showing chariots without the spiraliform elements, see especially Zampieri 1994, 107–11 and ills; 1988 and 1999; Fogolari 1975, 132–6; Fogolari and Prosdocimi 1988, 99–105.

[80] *Circolo di Perazzeta at Marsiliana d'Albegna* in Toscana: see Woytowitsch 1978, no. 49a and pl. 11; Galeotti 1986–8, 100 and pl. 60: 1; *Carri da guerra* 322 (Repertorio no. 117). *Via Pontina cemetery, tomb 21* at Castel di Decima in Lazio: see Galeotti 1986–8, 100 and n. 43; *Carri da guerra* 313 (Repertorio no. 20). *Tumulo del Caiolo, tomb B,* at San Giuliano (Barbarano Romano) in Lazio: see Galeotti 1986–8, 100 and pl. 59: 1; *Carri da guerra* 280 (I. Caruso), 283 (A. Emiliozzi) with figs 5–6 and pl. 29: 2 (Veicolo A), 323 (Repertorio 323, no. 130). *Contrada Morgi cemetery, tomb 8 (LXI)* at Narce in Lazio (our Pl. 14): see Galeotti 1986–8, 100 and pl. 59: 3; Emiliozzi 1997, 101 and fig. 4; *Carri da guerra* 330 (Repertorio 330, no. 203). *Pizza Piede cemetery, tomb 20* at Narce: see Galeotti 1986–8, 100; *Carri da guerra* 331 (Repertorio no. 212). *Tomb below the 'Heroon of Aeneas'* at Pratica del Mare (ancient Lavinium) in Lazio: see Galeotti 1986–8, 100; Sommella 1971–2, 61 no. 3 and fig. 14, *Civiltà del Lazio primitivo* 311 no. 102 (P. Sommella); *Carri da guerra* 313 (Repertorio no. 28). *Tomba dei Flabelli* at Trevignano Romana in Lazio: see Galeotti 1986–8, 100 and pl. 60:2; *Carri da guerra* 324 (Repertorio no. 143). *Tomb in the Le Selve cemetery* at Vigna Batocchi: see *Carri da Guerra* 314 (Repertorio no. 39).

[81] Ghislanzoni 1944, 30 and pl. 10; Woytowitsch 1978, no. 109b–c and pl. 19; Galeotti 1986–8, 100 and pl. 59:4; Pare 1992, 210. For the vehicular remains from the tomb, see Frey 1969, 47–50; De Marinis 1975, 216; 1988b, 197; Woytowitsch 1978, no. 109 and pl. 19; Piggott 1983, 182f. (Sesto Calende A); Pare 1992, 57, 63; Camerin 1997, 39f.; *Carri da guerra* 333 (Repertorio no. 242). See also our p. 46 and note 249 (pair of horse bits).

[82] Ghislanzoni 1944, 30f. and figs 26–7; Woytowitsch 1978, no. 110a and pl. 19; Galeotti 1986–8, 100 and pl. 59:2; Pare 1992, 210 and pl. 135:2. For the vehicular remains from the tomb, see Ghislanzoni 1944; De Marinis 1975, 220f., 229 and pl. 7: 7–9; Woytowitsch 1978, no. 110 and pl. 19; Piggott 1983, 182f. (Sesto Calende B); Pare 1987d, 220 and fig. 24; 1992, 210, 356 no. XVII, 2; Camerin 1997, 39f., 42f. and fig. 8; *Carri da guerra* 333 (Repertorio no. 241); Koch, J. K. 2006, 161. See also our p. 46 and note 251 (pair of horse bits).

[83] Zevi 1975, 289 no. 56 and fig. 61; also Galeotti 1986–8, 100 and fig. 60: 3; Nebelsick 1992, 103 and fig. 11a.

[84] For discussion, see Galeotti 1986–8, 100; Nebelsick 1992, 103–7 and fig. 10 (distribution map); Emiliozzi 1997, 97, 283; Piggott 1983, 183; Pare 1992, 210, 212.

demonstrated the advantages of such a low attachment of the traces of outriggers (see II.5). All things considered, the paired metal elements with their spiraliform ending were probably part of a chariot's railwork siding, but their exact position and function remain uncertain.

The Type IV chariot has sometimes been thought to derive from the Rail type chariot of Greece.[85] However, the latter, with its D-shaped floor plan and entirely open-walled siding which lacks the spiraliform terminals, is quite different. In fact, the Type IV chariot in Italy has a better parallel in our Type I, except for the absence of the hoop-like front rail rising above the separate side rails. As mentioned above, the Type I chariots may have been inspired by Greek models. Influence of the Greek Rail type chariot, or its representations, may perhaps be detected in two vase representations, one of which is currently the first depiction of a chariot made in Italy. This unprovenanced neck-amphora by the Painter of the Heptachord, who probably worked at Cerveteri around 670, shows a horse-drawn chariot with only a low, semicircular rail siding (Pl. 46).[86] The second vase representation to be considered is on an incised Bucchero jug of the later seventh century. Although often referred to as coming from Ischia di Castro, the find place may rather have been Vulci, also in Toscana (Pl. 51).[87] The abrupt elevation at the front of the open side rail of the chariot depicted on this jug recalls representations of Rail chariots on late Mycenaean vases of *c.* 1100. However, as we shall see later, it is doubtful whether these two vase representations reflect the actual use of the Greek Rail type chariot on Italian soil, rather than (garbled) renderings of Greek artistic models.[88]

What look like chariots with an open railwork siding also appear on on a painted jug of the sixth century from Pomarico Vecchio in Basilicata in southern Italy (Pl. 47).[89] A series of light chariots is depicted here, possibly taking part in a race.

The so-called Stele or Pietra Zannoni should also be briefly considered here (Pl. 60).[90] This incompletely preserved tombstone with relief decoration from Bologna has been dated to the (later) seventh or early six century. What remains of the vehicle and its driver, who holds reins and what is probably a goad (*q.v.*) suggests a chariot with an open rail siding.

Chariot Type V

Under this heading may be loosely grouped a number of chariots depicted two-dimensionally, their siding presenting a variety of profiles but always rising towards the front. At the rear, the siding drops vertically or runs down in a curve, sometimes leaving an open handhold at the upper corner within the screening material. There may also be an open handhold at the top of the screened front. The screening material is sometimes shown as (elaborately) decorated. The chariots usually carry one, but sometimes two or even three occupants; in this last case the two passengers presumably stand abreast, and the driver at the front.

The figured documents include an Etruscan wall painting from the Tomba degli Hescanas at Orvieto

---

[85] Pare 1992, 210, 212.

[86] *Carri da guerra* pl. I: 1–2; Martelli 2001, 2–7 and figs 2–3; Crouwel 2006, 168f. and fig. 8. For the painter and his work, see also Martelli 1984 and 1988.

[87] Bloch 1950, 141–3 with fig. 1 and pl. 3: 1–2; Falconi Amorelli 1968, 171f. no. 10 and pl. 28; Bonamici 1974, 41 no. 48; Warden 1977, 205 and pl. 109: 2–3; Woytowitsch 1979, no. 236 and pl. 45; Stary 1981a, 95, 123, 129 and pl. 7: 1; Jannot 1985, 131 and fig. 4; 1986a, 111f. with fig. 1 and pl. 27:1; Torelli 1988, fig. 52; Camporeale 1993, no. 12; Crouwel 2006, 169 and fig. 9; Brouwers 2007, 312 and fig. 9. For the provenance of this and other Bucchero vessels in the Museo Nazionale di Villa Giulia, Rome, see Bartoloni 1979, 391 n. 33.

[88] See pp. 57–58.

[89] Tagliente 1994, no. 14; Colonna 1997, 18 and fig. 6.

[90] Ducati 1910, no. 202 and fig. 46; also De Ruyt 1934, no. 147; Woytowitsch 1978, no. 259 and pl. 46; Cerchiai 1987, 232f.; Stary-Rimpau 1988, no. 202 (the vehicle is incorrectly described on p. 253 as carrying a seated person and a parasol); Lucassen 1995, no. 2; Camerin 1997, fig. 7; *Principi etruschi* cat. no. 444 (M. Marchesi).

(Pl. 37)[91] and a series of Etruscan alabaster cinerary urns of the second-first century from Volterra (ancient Volaterrae)(Pl. 64).[92] Chariot Type V may perhaps also be identified on a few of the fifth–fourth century grave stelae from Bologna[93] and on one or two Etruscan stone sarcophagi of the fourth–third century from Vulci (Pls 65, 67).[94]

The chariots grouped under Type V may possibly have an ancestor in one of the ornate, bronze-sheathed vehicles that were buried in the sixth century Tomba dei Bronzi at Castel San Mariano in Umbria (Pl. 55).[95] In contrast to the Type I chariot with its siding in three or more parts from the same tomb (Pl. 9), the second chariot may have had a single-piece siding extending along the front and part of the sides. This is suggested by what remains of the shape and length of its highly decorated bronze sheathing. As reconstructed, the siding is *c.* 1.50 m long.

Looking forward in time, Type V chariots appear to be the direct prototypes of the ceremonial carriages with their rounded or angular sidings of the Roman Imperial period. This is clear from figured documents, such as large-scale state reliefs and life-size models in the round.[96] According to these sources as well as to textual information, Roman chariots were used in the *Triumphus* and at other ceremonial occasions by the emperors and their relatives, and by other high-status individuals.[97]

The Roman ceremonial chariots, sometimes large enough to accommodate up to three people, may have an open platform at the rear. Their siding, which rises to hip height or more, presents a variety of profiles: it sometimes drops down vertically at the rear, but more frequently in a curve. There often is an open handhold at the upper rear corner within the screening material. Such ceremonial carriages, with their often lavish decoration and four-horse teams, were used over a long period of time, lasting into the Byzantine era.

---

[91] Steingräber 1985, no. 34; 2006, 214f. and ills p. 214; Woytowitsch 1978, no. 257 and pl. 44.

[92] See a.o. *Corpus delle urne etruschi* 2, nos 216–17, 220–33; Lambrechts 1959, 150–69 and nos 21–31 and pls 17–34; Weber 1978, 102–6 and pl. 27: 1–3; Holliday 1990, 86–8 and figs 12–13. The decorated chariot depicted on one urn (Cateni and Fiaschi 1984, pl. 12; also Kähler 1958, pl. 40: above) is clearly different from the others in having a solidly-screened, hoop-shaped siding across the front and extending a short way along the sides, like the siding of our Type I chariots but without the lower elements further back.

[93] Ducati 1910, no. 169, side B and fig. 30; also Weber 1978, 86f. and pl. 25:2; Stary-Rimpau 1985, no. 169; Lucassen 1995, no. 26. The cross-hatched, probably wickerwork siding recurs on a stele fragment where the only partly preserved, spoked-wheeled vehicle may also have been a chariot rather than a cart (Ducati 1910, no. 54 and fig. 53; Stary-Rimpau 1985, no. 54; Lucassen 1995, no. 35; Macellari 2006, 246 and pl. 162: below (Arnoaldi, tomb 114, Stele C)). See also Ducati 1910, Side A of no. 61 (= Morigi Govi 1970, no. 61 with pl. 5c–d; Stary-Rimpau 1985, no. 61; Lucassen 1995, no. 7; Bonaudo 2002–3, 106 with fig. 4).

[94] Herbig 1952, no. 119 with pl. 28b (from the Monterozzi cemetery at Tarquinia; see also Van der Meer 2008, 44, 46 no. *H119* with figs 20–1), no. 5 with pl. 40c (our Pl. 65: sarcophagus of Ramtha Viśnai from Vulci, showing a chariot and a cart on the opposite short sides; see also Comstock and Vermeule 1976, no. 384; Höckmann 1982, 146f., 149, 153 no. E 14; Holliday 1990, 78f. and fig. 3; Brendel 1995, 381f.; Van der Meer 2008, 70–4 no. *H5*). The only partly visible chariot shown together with a cart on one long side of another sarcophagus, from the Ponte Rotto cemetery at Vulci, may possibly also be classified under our Type V (our Pl. 66); see Herbig 1952, no. 49 and pl. 42; Höckmann 1982, 144, 147 no. E 15; Brendel 1995, 382f. and fig. 295; Molteson and Nielsen 1996, no. 7; Van der Meer 2008, 81, 83 no. *H49* and fig. 45. For other sarcophagi, showing chariots of uncertain type, see our note 100.

[95] Höckmann 1982, 42–4 no. 8, 114–18 with figs 24–5 and pls 30–1 ('Streitwagen II'); *Strade degli Etruschi* figs 45–6; *Carri da guerra* 320 (Repertorio no. 97). According to Bruni (2002, 26 and figs 5–6), this chariot compares well to those seen on Clazomenian sarcophagi. However, this comparison seems unwarranted by the little that survives of the actual vehicle and by the lack of accuracy in the chariot depictions on these East Greek figured documents (see Crouwel 1992, 70).

[96] See a.o. Junkelmann 1990, figs 225–7, 230 (state reliefs), also 223–4 (marble chariot on display in the Sala della Biga in the Vatican; also Lippold 1956, no. 623; Helbig 1963, no. 507). This well-known restored carriage appears to have influenced the – unreliable – reconstructions of two much earlier chariots: the so-called Biga Sbrigoli from tomb 30 of the late seventh century in the San Martino cemetery at Civitella San Paolo (ancient Capena) in Lazio (Paribeni 1905, 324f.; 1906, 310f.; Woytowitsch 1978, no. 18; *Civiltà degli Etruschi* cat. no. 6.24 (F. Boitani); Boitani and Aureli 1988, 130 with pl. 62; *Carri da guerra* 329 *s.v.* Repertorio no. 200), the other reportedly from Orvieto in Umbria (London, British Museum 1911.4–18.1; see Loukomski 1930, pl. 57; also autopsy). For other representations of such chariots, see Junkelmann 1990, figs 220 (silver cup from Boscoreale), 221–2 (coins), 229 (terracotta bread mould).

[97] See especially Castritius 1971. For the *Triumphus*, see our p. 64 and note 370.

Chariots of uncertain type

There is also a large number of Italian-made figured documents of varying date showing chariots that cannot be grouped with any of the types discussed above. Classification is complicated by factors such as the poor state of preservation, summary rendering, artistic liberty, or a combination of these. In this category there are terracotta models[98] and two-dimensional representations on funerary stelae from Bologna,[99] on stone sarcophagi,[100] bronzework,[101] ivory plaques (Pl. 58),[102] ostrich eggs (Pl. 59)[103] and scarabs,[104] as well as wall paintings (Pls 38–39)[105] and painted vases (Pl. 48).[106] Other chariot representations, such as seen on Daunian stelae of the sixth–fifth centuries from Puglia[107] and on coins of the Roman Republic, may also be included here.[108]

---

[98] From a seventh century tomb at Fonte Cucchiaia near Chiusi; see Giglioli 1929, 473–5 and pl. 52:3; Breitenstein 1941, no. 783; Hencken 1968, 536, 582 and fig. 493b; Woytowitsch 1978, no. 162 and pls 36–7 (the metal 'yoke' does not belong with the vehicle); *Gli Etruschi* cat. no. 135. From Orvieto; see Giglioli 1929, 474 and pl. 52:4; Hencken 1968, 536, 582 and fig. 493d; Woytowitsch 1978, no. 161 and pl. 37. Possibly also a fragmentary model (of a chariot rather than a cart) from Tarquinia, Le Rose cemetery, tomb XLIII; see Hencken 1968, 424; Woytowitsch 1978, no. 155 and pls 31–2; Buranelli 1983, 48 no. 3 and fig. 49:3–4. Provenance unknown; see *Das Tier in der Antike* no. 298; Woytowitsch 1978, no. 160 and pl. 39. In other cases, the (incompletely preserved) models may be classified as carts rather than as chariots; see our p. 71 and note 9. There are also several terracotta horses and model wheels which once belonged to either chariots or carts; see a.o. Woytowitsch 1978, no. 153 and pl. 32 (Sopra Selciatello, tomb 44; also Hencken 1968, 292, 424, 535f. and pl. 280d; *Civiltà degli Etruschi* no. 2.4.8,5), no. 154 and pl. 31 (Tarquinia, Monterozzi cemetery; also Hencken 1968, 292, 336f., 340, 419f., 536f. and figs 280d, 441); Buranelli 1983, 38 nos 8–9 and fig. 38, 57 no. 3 and fig. 58, 86 no. 10 with fig. 89 (Tarquinia, Le Rose cemetery, tombs XXXIII, XLIX and Group C; also Iaia 1999, 24f., 45 and fig. 5:1). See also the chariot group represented by a fragmentary terracotta acroterion from Cerveteri: Andrén 1939–40, 47 no. III.3 and pl. 15:50; Briquet 1968, 66 and figs 24–6.

[99] See a.o. Ducati 1910, no. 2 (Side A) and fig. 83; also Sassatelli 1983, 50–60 and fig. 5; Stary Rimpau 1988, no. 2; Lucassen 1995, no. 9.

[100] Herbig 1952, no. 112 and pl. 70b (from Tarquinia; see also De Ruyt 1934, no. 153 and fig. 56; Lambrechts 1959, no. 5 and pl. 6), no. 113 and pl. 74b (from Tarquinia; see also Lambrechts 1959, no. 12 and pl. 11), no. 114 (from Tarquinia; see also Lambrechts 19659, no. 4 and pl. 5), no. 115 (from Tarquina; see also Lambrechts 1959, no. 16), no. 158 (from Tarquinia; see also Lambrechts 1959, no. 13 and pl. 12), no. 66 and pl. 80 (from Tuscania; see also Lambrechts 1959, no. 7 with pl. 7), no. 81 with pl. 43d (from Tuscania; see also Lambrechts 1959, no. 1 and pl. 2; Helbig 1963, no. 611; Holliday 1990, 84 and fig. 9; *Gli Etruschi* ill. p. 227; Van der Meer 2008, fig. 41), no. 12 and pl. 11, no. 66 and pl. 80a (from Vulci; see also Lambrechts 1959, no. 7 and pl. 7; Holliday 1990, 94f. and fig. 10), no. 71a+c (from Vulci; see also Lambrechts 1959, no. 6 and pl. 4), no. 71b and pl. 109 (from Vulci; see also Lambrechts 1959, no. 3 and pl. 4), no. 205 (from Musarna; see also Lambrechts 1959, no. 2 and pl. 3). See also Lambrechts 1959, nos 9, 10, 14–15 and pls 8–9, 13–14 (all from Tarquinia), no. 11 and pl. 10 (from Musarna). For lists, see Weber 1979, 96f; Van der Meer 2008, 74–8 and list on p. 76.

[101] **Legs of Etruscan cistae (caskets):** see Bordenache Battaglia and Emiliozzi 1979, nos II and 42; Jurgeit 1986, no. K 1, 1–3; *Italy of the Etruscans* no. 27. Engravings on cistae: see Bordenache Battaglia and Emiliozzi 1979, nos 7 (also Bonfante Warren 1964), 13, 20, 36, 42, 48 and 54; 1990, nos 69 (also Foerst 1978, no. 95; Woytowitsch 1978, no. 22 and pl. 44; Sprenger and Bartoloni 1990, pl. 235) and 89. Note that Bordenache Battaglia and Emiliozzi 1990, no. 73 (also Foerst 1978, no. 98) seems to illustrate a chariot of our Type I. **Etruscan bronze relief bands:** see Hanfmann 1937; Comstock and Vermeule 1971, no. 688; Colonna 1993, 149f. and figs 6–7.

[102] See p. 7 and note 51.

[103] Two ostrich eggs of the later seventh century, probably from the Isis Tomb at Vulci: see a.o. Torelli 1965, 336f. nos 9–10; Haynes 1977, 22 and figs 1–2; Jannot 1986, 112f. and fig. 25; Rathje 1986, 398f. and figs 4–5; Camporeale 1993, nos 2 and 10.

[104] See a.o. Zweierlei–Diehl 1969, no. 273; Boardman and Vollenweider 1978, nos 264–6.

[105] Steingräber 1985, no. 106 (Tarquinia, Tomba Querciola I = Tomba della Caccia al Cinghiale; also *Malerei der Etrusker* no. XI; Adam, A.-M. 1993; Jannot 1995; Steingräber 2006, 155 and ill. pp. 156f.), no. 32 (Orvieto, Tomba Golini I; also Woytowitsch 1978, no. 258 and pl. 44), no. 33 (Orvieto, Tomba Golini II).

[106] A selection: **Skyphoid krater** by the Swallow Painter of the later seventh century from the Osteria cemetery at Vulci: see Giuliano 1963, 186–90 and figs 2, 4, 11–12; 1975, 68 no. 7 and fig. 13; Martelli 1975, 6–8 no. 7; Cook 1981, 454 no. 7; Camporeale 1993, no. 4. **Etruscan black-figure jug** by the Tityos Painter, possibly from Vulci (our Pl. 48): see *CVA* Paris, Bibliothèque Nationale 1, IIIF, pls 28: 5, 31: 1–4 (no. 171); Ducati 1932, 17f. and pl. 19; Hannestad 1976, 59 no. 35. **Etrusco-Corinthian black-figure jug** from Cerveteri, belonging to the Group of the Painter of the Bearded Sphinx: see *CVA* Bibliothèque Nationale 1, IIIF, pls 11: 9–11 and 12 (no. 179); Krauskopf 1974, 41–6; Warden 1977, 205f. and pl. 110: 1–2; Jannot 1986, 112f. and pl. 25; 1989, 11f. and pl. 25; *La ceramica degli Etruschi* no. 62; Szilágyi 1992, 122, 124–6 no. 102 and pl. 41a–b (also no. 103 and pl. 41c–d: fragmentary olpe from Ischia di Castro; see also Camporeale 1993, nos 11 and 30); Menichetti 1994, 68f. and figs 40–1. **Etruscan red-figure amphora** fragment of the Alcsti Group: see Beazley 1947, 134f. and pl. 30:3. **Etruscan red-figure hydria** by the Painter of the Vatican Biga from Vulci: see Beazley 1947, 47, 2; *La ceramica degli Etruschi* no. 161; Haynes 2000, 320 and fig. 255.

[107] See a.o. Nava 1979, 35 and no. 518 and pl. 145, no. 527 and pl. 148, no. 748 and pl. 246, no. 986 and pl. 326; Simon 2006; Norman 2009, 42f. and pls 2 and 6.

[108] See Mattingly 1953; also a.o. Crawford 1974, pls 2–6 (so-called *quadrigatus* coins), 18, 23, 25–7, 31 (two-horse chariots); Holliday 2002,

Several of the above and other chariot representations, such as the painted so-called Amazon Sarcophagus of *c.* 350 from the Tomba François at Vulci and tomb paintings from the Paestum area in Campania, have distinct affinities with mainland or East Greek artistic models.[109]

The two chariots among the terracotta pedimental sculptures of temple B at Talamone (ancient Telamon) in Toscana, currently dated to *c.* 50, should also be mentioned here (Pl. 69a–b).[110] The vehicles appear in the mythological battle of the Seven against Thebes. The chariot of Amphiaraus has a simple rounded profile, while that of Adrastus has an angular, five-part siding that rises towards the front.

There are also figured documents illustrating chariots which are actual imports from the eastern Mediterranean, such as large numbers of Greek painted vases, ranging from the later seventh century onwards, and so-called Cypro-Phoenician gilded silver bowls of the seventh century.[111]

2. Axle

The wooden axle (*q.v*) was fixed rigidly to the vehicle body, with spoked wheels revolving on it. The fixed axle is obviously desirable for fast vehicles, in contrast to the alternative, revolving axle, which is suitable only for slow transport (see Chapter III.2). Round in section where the wheels revolve on it, the fixed axle permits them to rotate differentially, thereby facilitating turning. The projecting naves (*q.v.*) of the wheels may be greased internally, thus decreasing friction and noise. And individual wheels, secured to the axle by a linch pin (*q.v.*), which passed through a slot near its ends, may be easily removed for repair, replacement or storage. In antiquity, fixed axles were everywhere standard on horse-drawn chariots.

In Italy the presence of this type of axle and revolving wheels is confirmed by the round axle end that is often illustrated and by the finding of actual metal axle caps of circular shape along with linch pins.[112] Remains of the wooden axle itself, together with the nave and other parts of a spoked wheel, were found with the sixth century chariot burial in the Tomba della Biga at Ischia di Castro in Toscana. Here, as on the Monteleone and other contemporary chariots of our type I that were partly or entirely covered in sheet-bronze, the axle was rectangular in section, except for the area of the wheels (Pls 7–8). The axle's rectangular shape and position – halfway down the length of the body – are indicated by the

---

29 and fig. 4 (triumphal *quadriga*).

[109] See Pallottino 1952, 93–6 and ill. p. 94; Sprenger and Bartoloni 1990, pl. 215; Bottini 2007; *Il sarcofago delle Amazzoni*. The chariot shows affinities with the mainland Greek High-front type. The same can be said of chariots depicted in Paestan tombs (see our p. 16, note 46) and vase paintings, such as four Caeretan hydriae (Hemelrijk 1984, 149f., 176 nos 6, 28, 31 with fig. 35 and pls 41, 100a, 101d, 109; 2009, 30–2 *s.v* nos 6, 28 and 31, 28 with pls 27f, 10a and 27c, 17b and 27d, and no. 2 *bis* with fig. 16 and pls 24f and 27b), an Etruscan black-figure stamnos by the Micali Painter (Spivey 1987, 23 no. 138; *Un pittore etrusco* no. 29; Capelletti 1992, no. 21), and a Faliscan red-figure volute-krater by the Aurora Painter (see our Pl. 49 and p. 11, note 26). For vase representations of chariots showing affinities with East Greek types, see a.o. the so-called **Ricci Hydria** by the Ribbon Painter, belonging to the Campana Group and found at Cerveteri (Ricci 1946–8; Laurens 1986; Cerchiai 1995), another **Caeretan hydria** (Hemelrijk 1984, 149f., 176 no. 8 and pls 46a, 47a; 200g, 31f. and pls 28a and 30b), an **Etruscan red-figure hydria** of the Group of the Spouted Hydriae (Beazley 1947, 172 and pl. 34: 4), and twin neck-amphorae (see our p. 7 and note 56) and a **volute-krater** (Beazley 1957, 169, Volute-kraters no. 1; Capelletti 1992, no. 63; Bonami 2006, 526f. and fig. 3: top) of the Vanth Group from Orvieto.

[110] Andrén 1939–40, 223–7 no. 1 with pl. 82:295; Von Freytag gen. Loringhoff 1986, 85–113 and pls 4–5, 13, 27; Massa-Pairault 1996, 237, 241f. and ills.; *Gli Etruschi* cat. no. 307. See also our p. 111, note 19, and p. 112, note 24 (chariots with a Celtic-looking driver on a stone sarcophagus from Chiusi in Toscana and among the terracotta pedimental sculptures from Civitalbà in Umbria).

[111] Woytowitsch included some of these vases, like the Proto-Corinthian olpe known as the Chigi Vase and the Attic black-figure François Krater, in his catalogue (1978, nos 234 and 237 and pl. 46), as he also did with the metal bowls (1978, nos 220–5 and pls 47–8). For the latter, see especially Markoe 1985, nos E 2–3 (Palestrina, Tomba Bernardini; also Woytowitsch 1978, nos 224–5 and pl. 47; *Principi etruschi* ill. p. 126), no. E 5 (Palestrina, Tomba Barberini; also Woytowitsch 1978, no. 223 and pl. 47; Sprenger and Bartoloni 1990, pl. 17), nos E 6–9 (all from Cerveteri, Tomba Regolini Galassi; also Woytowitsch 1978, nos 220–2 and pls 47–8). See also the fragment of an ivory plaque found in the Tomba Bernardini at Palestrina but made in the Near East (Curtis 1919, 58f. and pl. 36:6 and 1; Woytowitsch 1978, no. 212 and pl. 45; Canciani and Von Hase 1979, 68 *s.v.* no. 120 and pl. 56:5; Stary 1981a, fig. 45:1).

[112] Actual linch pins, of bronze or iron, first appear, singly or in pairs, in tombs of the later eighth and earlier seventh century at Bologna and Verucchio; see Woytowitsch 1978, 4 and no. 104–5, 106a–b with pl. 18; Panichelli 1990, 203f.; Camerin 1997, 33f. and fig. 1, right. The so-called 'perni a spillone' of bronze, found in the same and other tombs, are unlikely to have served a similar function; see Camerin 1997, 33f. and figs 1, left and 2.

body's sheet-bronze covering. As mentioned above, the axle appears to have been attached not directly to the floor but to a separate rectangular frame. This also helped raise the floor over the axle, so that the draught pole could run between them (see Chapter II.1 *s.v.* Chariot Type I).

The remains of earlier, seventh century chariots of the same type do not yield evidence for such a frame. Instead, the axles of the Vulci and Populonia chariots have been reconstructed as fixed directly under the centre of the floor, the pole running up against them (Pls 2–3; see again II.1 *s.v.* Chariot Type I). As we have seen, such a construction would not have been very strong. The body may rather have been raised over axle blocks on either side, allowing the pole to run between the floor frame and the axle all the way to the back of the vehicle, as on surviving Egyptian chariots and others from elsewhere.

As for the lengths of chariot axles in ancient Italy, there is only one actual measurement: the excavators of the carriage from Ischia di Castro recorded the axle length as only 1.40 m, with a body width of 0.47 m and a nave length of 0.44 m. Other axles, from the contemporary Monteleone chariot as well as the earlier ones from Vulci and Populonia, have been reconstructed as being similarly short. These ornate vehicles, relatively heavy and slow-moving due to their metal decoration, would have been used only for ceremonial purposes. (The Ischia di Castro carriage was claimed – probably incorrectly – to have been made specially for burial.)[113] Other chariots that were put to more active use – and particularly racing – probably had a long axle, projecting well beyond the sides of the vehicle body. Such an axle permitted long naves, which helped to keep these from wobbling on the axle (these wooden elements not being able to fit together as tightly as corresponding ones of metal). A long axle also allowed for a wide wheel track (*q.v.*), which gave lateral stability to a light vehicle on fast turns.

As stated above, the axle of the actual chariots of our Type I from Ischia di Castro and Monteleone di Spoleto was located about halfway down the length of the floor. A similar axle location has been assumed for other chariots, including those from Vulci and Populonia. Profile representations of the same and other types of chariot usually show axles in a similar central position, or just rear-of-centre, judging from the location of the wheels under the floor and taking into account the part of the floor that might project beyond the siding at the rear. Since these axle locations appear so consistently, and in different artistic media, they presumably reflect reality. This is supported by the evidence of the Ischia di Castro and Monteleone chariots. The same axle positions for chariots, it may be noted, carry on into Roman Imperial times (Pl. 142).

For comparison, a central axle location is characteristic of the High-front chariot in mainland Greece in the first millennium (Pls 137–138). At that time chariots in the Near East are usually shown with their axle at or near the rear of the floor. The same is the case on East Greek chariots (Pls 139–40).[114]

As already mentioned, axles could be fitted with round caps at their ends and linch pins that prevented the wheels from slipping off. Metal axle-caps and linch pins have survived from several tombs containing vehicles in central and northern Italy (Pls 1–3, 16, 116–117). They are usually associated with chariots, but also occur with carts and four-wheelers.[115] The round axle caps of cast bronze belonging with chariot burials are usually 'hat-shaped', with a broad flange and a cylindrical or conical neck which is pierced for the linch pin and terminates in a flat disc.[116] Highly decorated bronze axle caps also occur, such as the pairs with a frontal lion's head, belonging in one case with an ornate chariot of our Type I of the sixth century from Roma Vecchia and in another case with one of the three vehicles buried in the contemporary Tomba dei Bronzi at Castel San Mariano (Pl. 9).[117] These axle caps are paralleled by

---

[113] Boitani 1985, 220; 1987, 89.

[114] Crouwel 1992, 34, 70.

[115] See pp. 79, 93.

[116] For illustrations, see Woytowitsch 1978, pl. 61:B.

[117] **Roma Vecchia:** see M. Sannibale in *Carri da guerra* 197, 199 and figs 6–7, pls XVIII, XIX:2. **Castel San Mariano:** see Woytowitsch 1978, no. 72 and pls 11 and 61:B 2; Höckmann 1982, 44f. no. 9 and pl. 29:1–3. The lion protomes at the ends of the bronze-sheathed axles presently

a pair from a rich vehicle burial of the later seventh-sixth century at Huelva on the southwest coast of Spain.[118] In all these cases the caps are pierced horizontally for linch pins, whereas other axle caps have linch pins in a vertical position.

The use of axle caps and linch pins made of metal is unknown in mainland Greece but is documented in the Near East from the earlier first millennium onwards. Simple bronze caps, extending back over part of the wheel, are known from Urartu, where they can be dated to the eighth century by the royal names sometimes inscribed on them.[119] More ornate axle caps, in the form of a frontal sphinx head and pierced by highly elaborate linch pins, have been found with the remains of a chariot buried at Salamis in Cyprus around 700.[120] On Assyrian palace reliefs, from the time of king Sennacherib (704–681) onwards, the axle ends of royal chariots are shown as decorated with a rosette, which suggests metal axle caps. Rosettes on axle ends can also be seen on representations of East Greek chariots (Pl. 140).[121] In Europe north of the Alps, flanged bronze axle caps are first documented in the early Urnfield period (thirteenth–twelfth centuries), to become more common in late Hallstatt times (sixth–early fifth centuries), when they are usually associated with ornate four-wheeled vehicles (see Chapter IV.2).[122] Among the various, fairly simple designs is the 'hat-shaped' axle cap which is also found in northern and central Italy (Pls 116–117).[123]

Instead, a few vehicle tombs in Italy have yielded simple ring-shaped axle endings, again together with linch pins.[124]

The bronze or iron linch pins, found with or without axle caps, usually have one or two holes for a thong to prevent them from being jolted out. The varying designs of the linch pin head may again have parallels among the iron ones belonging with late Hallstatt wagon burials.[125]

3. Wheels

We saw earlier (Chapter II.2) that the wheels of chariots in Italy before the Roman Empire revolved on a fixed axle. The wheels had long wooden naves (*q.v.*) in order to reduce their wobbling, and metal linch pins to prevent them from slipping off.

Figured documents illustrate chariot wheels with a varying number of spokes, from four to six to eight. A few of the illustrated wheels have as many as ten spokes. Actual remains of chariots confirm such numbers, ranging from four (Tomba Regolini Galassi at Cerveteri) and eight (Tomba del Carro at Vulci, Tumulo dei Carri at Populonia, Tomba di Guerriero B at Sesto Calende) to nine (Tomba della

seen on the Monteleone chariot, in fact, do not belong in this place; see Emiliozzi 1991, 115, and in *Carri da guerra* 183 and pls XII, XVII. Bronze axle caps of the Roman Imperial period may be decorated with frontal lion's heads or gorgoneia; see Von Mercklin 1933, 119 and figs 37–8, 165f and figs 92–4.

[118] Garrido Roiz and Orta García 1978, 167–71 with figs 35–6 and pls LIII:2–LVI ('La Joya' tomb 17, for which see also 66–87); Piggott 1983, 193f.; Stary 1989, especially 157f., 178 and fig. 1; Quesada Sanz 1997, 56 and pl. II:4.

[119] Özgen 1984, 114–16 and figs 43–5; Littauer and Crouwel 1979, 106.

[120] Karageorghis 1973, 70, 80f. and pls 101–5, 256–7; Crouwel 1987, 105. See also the pair of elaborate metal linch pins, without axle caps, found with other vehicular remains in Bintepeler tumulus 89 of the early fifth century at Sardes in Anatolia (Kökten Ersoy 1998, 117, 129–30 nos S/B.1–2 and fig. 6).

[121] Littauer and Crouwel 1979a, 105f.; Crouwel 1992, 70.

[122] Piggott 1983, 112–14 and fig. 66 (Early Urnfield example), 161, 164f., 184, 192; Pare 1992, 28, 30, 41f. (Urnfield period), 88–90 and fig. 72 (Late Hallstatt types).

[123] Pare 1992, 88, 90 and fig. 72: 13–15 (Wychen type). Cf. Woytowitsch 1978, pl. 61: B 1 (no. 112: Ca'Morta wagon), B 3 (no. 69: Siena) and B 4–5 (no. 31: Cerveteri wagon).

[124] Woytowitsch 1979, nos 91 and 95 and pl. 61: B6–7 (from Belmonte and Grottazolina).

[125] See especially linch pins with crescent-shaped heads, Woytowitsch 1978, nos 110, 112 and 72 and pl. 61: A1, B:1–2 and 11: 72a–b (vehicle burials from Sesto Calende and Ca'Morta; chariot burial from Castel San Mariano; see also Höckmann 1982, 44 and fig. 26 and pl. 29:1); Egg and France-Lanord 1987, 154f. and fig. 4: 1–2 and pl. 43: 1–4; 2003, 59 and pls 42: 1–2 and 43a–d (axle caps and linch pins from the late Hallstatt wagon burial at Vix in Burgundy); Pare 1992, 90f.

Biga at Ischia di Castro, Tomba del Carro at Monteleone di Spoleto).[126] For comparison, contemporary chariots in mainland Greece are usually, but not exclusively, shown with only four spokes, and those of East Greece with 4–10, but mostly six or eight spokes.[127] The chariots of the earlier first millennium in the Near East are depicted with six- to eight-spoked wheels; those of Achaemenid times have wheels with as many as ten or 12 spokes.[128] The actual chariots found in tombs of the eighth–seventh centuries at Salamis in Cyprus had wheels with eight or ten spokes (where the numbers could be calculated).[129]

The extant remains, and in particular the nailed-on iron tyres, also provide direct information on the diameter of chariot wheels, ranging from *c.* 0.60 m (Tomba del Carro at Vulci, Ischia di Castro, Monteleone di Spoleto) to *c.* 1.05 m (Populonia, Tumulo dei Carri).

The relatively well preserved, ornate chariot of the sixth century from the Tomba della Biga at Ischia di Castro furnishes valuable information on wheel design (Pl. 7). Its nine spokes, wrongly restored as rectangular in section, are inserted into mortises in cylindrical naves (length 0.44 m) which are made of oak wood. With the exception of their central part, which is thickened to receive the spokes, the naves are sheathed in bronze, in the same way as those of a sixth century chariot from Sirolo in Marche.[130]

The naves of other actual chariots, such as those from the Tumulo dei Carri at Populonia, the Tomba Regolini Galassi at Cerveteri and the Tomba di Guerriero B at Sesto Calende, may be entirely bronze-sheathed, with openings for short metal sockets through which the spoke ends passed before being inserted into the (lost) wooden core of the nave.[131] The bronze nave casings, of varying design and sometimes including decorative mouldings or metal inlays, are similar to those of several wagon wheels. The find places of the latter include the Tomba del Carro in the Ca'Morta cemetery at Como in northern Italy, dating to the earlier fifth century (Golasecca, phase IIIA1), and numerous sixth–early fifth century (late Hallstatt) graves in Europe north of the Alps (Pls 117, 159).[132]

The chariot from Monteleone di Spoleto is exceptional in that its nine-spoked wheels are completely sheathed in bronze – naves, spokes and felloes – as are its axle, body and draught pole (Pl. 8). Other chariot wheels in Italy, such as those from Castel di Decima tomb 15 and the Tomba del Carro at Vulci, have naves with only simple metal hoops at their ends, to prevent them from splitting (Pls 1–2).[133]

The wood of the nave and parts of the body of the chariot from the Tomba del Carro at Vulci has been identified as elm.[134] There is also material evidence from second and first millennium Egypt, the Near East and Greece to show that this timber was used on chariot wheels. Indeed, elm, a hard and tough timber, remained the wheelwright's preferred choice for naves over the centuries in different parts of the world.[135]

---

[126] See, conveniently, Woytowitsch 1978, 30–53 and plates. The choice of an uneven number of spokes is unexplained.

[127] See Crouwel 1992, 34f. An actual, fragmentary eight-spoked wheel was found at Olympia, its context dating to 450–425; see Hayen 1980–1, 185–9 and figs 26–8.

[128] Littauer and Crouwel 1979a, 106, 147.

[129] Crouwel 1987, 105f.

[130] E. Emiliozzi in *Carri da guerra* 253 and fig. 25 (Repertorio no. 85), also in *Eroi e Regine* 356 *s.v.* no. 124.

[131] See especially F. Cecchi, F. Fiesoli and F. Gennai in *Carri da guerra* 172 and fig. 10 and pls VI, IX: 3 (Repertorio 123: Populonia, Tumulo dei Carri; the bronze nave casings have iron inlays); Woytowitsch 1978, no. 30b and pls 6, 58: 5 and 60: C 5 (Cerveteri, Tomba Regolini Galassi), also no. 110 and pls 58: 1 and 60: C 8 (Sesto Calende, Tomba di Guerriero B).

[132] See Pare 1992, 167 and 169f. and fig. 113, citing parallels for the nave casings from the Tomba Regolini Galassi at Cerveteri and from the Santa Maria in Campo cemetery at Fabriano in Marche (probably the same as *Carri da guerra* 316 (Repertorio no. 59: cart from tomb 3). For the Como, Ca'Morta and Hallstatt wagons, see our pp. 90–96.

[133] See Woytowitsch 1978, no. 34g with pl. 7 (Vulci, Tomba del Carro; see also A. Emiliozzi in *Carri da guerra* 146 and pl. III), no. 88b, d with pl. 16 (Campovalano, tomb 2), no. 89c, f and pl. 18 (Campovalano, tomb 69), no. 95c, g and pl. 17 (Grottazzolina, tomb 20); M. Cygielman in *Carri da guerra* 266 and fig. 4c (Repertorio 174: Vetulonia, Tomba del Littore), and P. Santoro, *ibidem* 297 no. 26 and fig. 31 (Repertorio 319, no. 88: Sferracavallo, Colle del Forno tomb XI).

[134] G. F. Priori in *Carri da guerra* 153.

[135] Littauer and Crouwel 1985, 92f.; Littauer, Crouwel and Hauptmann 1991, 354f.; Crouwel 1992, 38.

It is questionable whether wheels with only four spokes, like those of the actual chariot from the Tomba Regolini Galassi at Cerveteri, and others depicted in figured documents, had their spokes mortised into a separate, cylindrical nave (Pl. 11). This construction might not have been strong enough for a four-spoked wheel. Instead, the wheels may well have been made according to a different nave-and-spoke construction which is best documented on surviving four-and six-spoked chariot wheels from fifteenth and fourteenth century Egypt (Pl. 144). There, spokes were formed from a single piece of wood bent halfway down its length at an angle of 90° (on four-spoked wheels) or an angle of 60° (on six-spoked wheels), then glued back to back along their length to form complementary halves of sister spokes. The apices of such bent pieces of wood also formed sections of the nave, which was extended by the addition of cylindrical flanges at either end. These parts were held together by glue and rawhide put on wet and allowed to shrink on, forming a tight, strong binding material. There is good reason to believe that this construction obtained not only in Egypt but also in parts of the Near East in the second half of the second millennium, as well as in contemporary Greece. In the later area, it continued in the case of four-spoked wheels well into the first millennium.[136] This sophisticated wheel construction, which also included a rawhide tyre (see below), was resilient, its tightness and tension permitting as few as four spokes. The wheel was, however, vulnerable to dampness and thus not suited to wet climates.

The four spokes of the chariot wheels from the Tomba Regolini Galassi seem to have widened where they joined the felloe, to judge by the 'trumpet-shaped' metal sheathing that covers them in this area (Pl. 11).[137] The sheathing is actually in two halves, made of bronze and iron respectively, which are nailed together horizontally. They recall the tubular bronze spoke casings of certain wheels from Europe north of the Alps dating no later than the Urnfield period (the thirteenth/twelfth–eighth centuries), and may conceal an actual thickening of the spoke ends.[138] The form of these spoke sheathings is also reminiscent of a construction attested on four-spoked chariot wheels in Greece, during the first millennium and quite probably already in the Late Bronze Age.[139] According to our most detailed representations – Greek vase paintings of the sixth and fifth centuries – the spokes tapered towards the felloe and were probably mortised into it. Triangular wooden wedges were placed on either side of the spokes, so as both to strengthen the vulnerable part of the wheel where spokes and felloe meet and to distribute the pressure more evenly over the felloe. Exactly how the spoke-and-felloe wedges were held in place is uncertain – possibly by glue and by rawhide lashings. In first millennium Greece, this aspect of four-spoked wheel construction is characteristic of the High-front type of chariot. This chariot type was presumably also used in southern Italy and – with some modifications – in central Italy, as our chariot type III (see Chapter III.1). Spoke-and-felloe wedges seem to be indicated with the Type III chariots illustrated on the Rome-Caprifico type of terracotta revetment plaques (Pl. 71a).[140] In the case of one of the chariots depicted, the eight spokes show a distinct thickening about halfway down their length. This may suggest a decorative carving or turning, a practice well attested on the wheels of sixth to earlier fifth century East Greek and Achaemenid chariots.[141]

Turning now to the wheel rims, the nine spokes of the ornate chariot from the Tomba della Biga at Ischia di Castro, as reconstructed, are mortised into a thick plank felloe (q.v.). The felloe has been reconstructed as composed of three thick butt-ended segments, encircled by (the remains of) an iron tyre with fastening nails driven in from the tread or running surface (Pl. 7). It is not clear how the felloe

---

[136] Littauer and Crouwel 1985, 76; Littauer, Crouwel and Hauptmann 1991; Crouwel 1981, 81f.; 1992, 35f.; Sandor 2004, 166–73.

[137] Woytowitsch 1978, no. 30 and pls 6 and 60: B 1 (no. 30).

[138] Pare 1987a, especially 45 and figs 4–5; 1992, 19f. and figs 23, 25: 3; Winghart 1993, especially 156f.

[139] For what follows, see Crouwel 1992, 36f.; 1981, 82f.; Sandor 2004, 171. Pare (1987a) interprets the Late Bronze Age chariot wheel representations in Greece as indicating a thickening of the spoke ends, a feature which was then adopted by the Urnfield wheelwrights.

[140] On the Etruscan so-called Amphiaraus Amphora (Pl. 40a) similar four-spoked wheels belong to chariots of our Italic type I (see p. 9, note 8).

[141] Crouwel 1992, 71 with n. 342, pls 15:2 and 16:1; Littauer and Crouwel 1979a, 147, fig. 80.

segments were held together – perhaps merely by being mortised together at their joints. There seems to be no evidence for metal felloe clamps, such as have been found together with similar nailed-on iron tyres in many other vehicle burials in central and northern Italy (Pl. 76c). The vehicles are mainly two-wheelers – chariots and carts – but also include wagons (see Chapter III.3 and Chapter IV.3).[142]

Similar bronze or iron felloe clamps and nailed-on iron tyres were used in Europe north of the Alps, where they first appear with the ornate wagons buried in tombs of late Hallstatt times (the sixth–early fifth centuries).[143] The Hallstatt wagon wheels, their spokes varying in number from six to 16, had diameters ranging from 0.70 m to 0.95 m (Pl. 159). The felloe clamps attested in Italy and further north present a variety of designs but divide into two basic types. One consists of a pair of iron plaques riveted together; the other type is basically U-shaped, made of a length of iron or bronze folded around the inner edge of the felloe, with the ends held together by nails.[144] Altogether, the similarities in both felloe clamps and nailed-on tyres are sufficiently close to suggest a similar wheel rim construction in Italy and further north.

Detailed study by C. F. A. Pare of the clamps and tyres of a large number of Hallstatt wagon wheels, taking into account the length of the fastening nails and the traces of wood grain left on them, has led to the identification of three types of felloe construction. The first, apparently most common, so-called Gottesberg type consisted of a single shallow felloe, requiring a single felloe clamp of the folded type to hold its ends together (Pl. 145a). The depth of the piece of wood used could not exceed 7.5 cm, if it were to be bent into a hoop of the size required for the wheel.[145]

The second and more complex, so-called Grosseibstadt type of construction involved a deep rim in two layers, the inner layer again of bent wood, the outer one made from a number of planks (Pl. 145b).[146] The reason for designing a wheel rim with two layers of wood rather than one has been pointed out by G. Kossack:[147] there are limits to the degree to which a length of timber of a given thickness can be bent – the thicker the piece, the less the degree to which it can be bent. Hence, if for any reason a heavier felloe is required (for instance, for carrying a heavier load, or because of the nature of the terrain), it must be in two parts. Moreover, these elements are often made in segments. In order to hold the two concentric layers together, the same author has plausibly suggested that a tongue-and-groove construction was used. In this a tongue on the inner surface of the outer layer lies in a groove in the perimeter of the inner one, or *vice versa*, with several riveted clamps securing the different parts, as well as joining the ends of the planks of the outer felloe layer. A folded clamp was used to hold the ends of the inner felloe layer together.[148]

The third, so-called Bruck type of wheel rim construction also involved a double felloe, but this time both layers were of bent wood (Pl. 145c).[149] The distinction between this and the Grosseibstadt type of felloe construction can usually only be made if enough wood is preserved still adhering to the shafts of the iron tyre nails to show the direction of the grain.[150]

In the case of the vehicles with two- or four-spoked wheels found in Italy it is often uncertain if the

---

[142] See especially Emiliozzi 2001, 316–20; also Woytowitsch 1978, 6f. and pls 58–9; various contributions to *Carri da guerra*.

[143] For what follows, see Kossack 1971; Piggott 1983, 165–70; Pare 1992, 43–63, 166–9; also 1987c.

[144] Pare 1992, 56f. and fig. 58 (Hallstatt clamps); Woytowitsch 1978, pl. 59: B (clamps from Italy).

[145] Pare 1992, 52f., 57, 61, 63 and fig. 53:1. According to Pare, the felloe depth should not exceed 0.075 m; Kossack (1971, 146) favours 0.065 m.

[146] Pare 1992, 52f., 56, 61, 63 and figs 53: 2 and 59 (distribution map).

[147] Kossack 1971, 144, 146, 156f.; see also Piggott 1983, 165f.

[148] Kossack 1971; see also Littauer and Crouwel 1979a, 107f. Such a construction has also been assumed by Kossack for the spoked wheels of the chariots illustrated on ninth–seventh century Assyrian palace reliefs and for those of actual chariots buried in eighth–seventh century tombs at Salamis in Cyprus; see also Littauer and Crouwel 1979a, 107f.; Crouwel 1987, 106; 1990; Spruytte 1994. It may be noted that the two-layered rim of an actual spoked wheel of the first millennium, acquired in Egypt and at present in the Brooklyn Museum, has no such construction and is held together merely by strips of rawhide; see Littauer and Crouwel 1979b; Wegener Sleeswyk 1987; Spruytte 1986, 41–74; Sandor 2004, 169f.

[149] Pare 1992, 52f., 57, 60f., 63 and fig. 53: 3.

[150] See Pare 1992, 52–63 and fig. 53.

felloes were of single- or double-layered construction. It is, for instance, usually impossible to ascertain whether the iron fastening nails of the tyres penetrated the whole depth of the felloe so as to determine the height of the felloe. When a two- rather than a single-layered felloe can be assumed, there is often doubt about the exact type of construction, due to the poor state of preservation and conservation of the metal elements and any remains of wood adhering to them. However, the first, Gottesberg type of wheel rim construction, with a single shallow felloe and one folded clamp, may be assumed for the wheels of the wagon from the Tomba del Carro at Como, Ca'Morta. The four-spoked chariot wheels from the seventh century Tomba Regolini Galassi at Cerveteri also appear to have been found with only a single felloe clamp (Pl. 11).[151] The felloes of the chariot wheels from Castel di Decima tomb 15 of the later eighth century were also probably in a single layer, as suggested by the fastening nails of the iron tyres which are only 0.07 m long. The same may be assumed for the small eight-spoked wheels, merely 0.60 m in diameter, of the ornate chariot from the seventh century Tomba del Carro at Vulci (Pl. 2). The eight-spoked wheels of the equally ornate seventh century chariot from the Tumulo dei Carri at Populonia, their iron tyres indicating a diameter of 1.04 m, have been reconstructed with a single-layered felloe made from four segments (Pl. 3).[152] The reconstruction includes four riveted rectangular felloe clamps of iron, placed at spoke ends so as to strengthen their junction with the felloe, and at the sime time holding together the four segments. These clamps alternate with four 'axe-shaped' iron plates which extend some way along the spokes and are nailed on. The latter recall the tongue- or T-shaped clamps of several sixth century chariot wheels from different parts of central Italy, the thicker part covering the felloe and the thinner part extending up the spokes.[153]

In several cases a two-layered felloe may be assumed, for instance where folded felloe clamps are present with a length of 0.20 m or more.[154] In a few cases – the two-wheelers from the Tomba del Carrettino at Como, Ca'Morta and from the Tomba del Guerriero A at the other northern site of Sesto Calende – study of the direction of the grain of the wood still adhering to the felloe clamps and tyre nails has led to the recognition of the Grosseibstadt and Bruck types of felloe construction respectively.[155]

Important information on wheel rim construction is also provided by the remains of a chariot and a cart from a sixth century burial at Sirolo in Marche. The wheels of these vehicles had diameters of 0.79 m and 0.90–0.91 m respectively (Pl. 76).[156] The wheel rims of both vehicles were of the Grosseibstadt type, the inner layers consisting of a single piece of heat-bent wood and the outer ones of three and four wooden boards respectively. The large number of folded clamps, preserved in situ on the nailed-on tyres of the chariot and cart wheels from Sirolo is unusual. The clamps are mostly simply U-shaped, but some have more decorative curved edges. At the same time, the long tyre nails of the Sirolo wheels are few in number and irregularly spaced. On the cart but not on the chariot wheels, a strong double-headed iron

---

[151] Como, Ca'Morta: see Pare 1992, 57, 61 and pl. 134:2 (clamp). Vulci: A. Emiliozzi in *Carri da guerra* 146 and figs 111, 113. Cerveteri: see Woytowitsch 1978, pl. 58: 5.

[152] For the wheels, see A. Emiliozzi in *Carri da guerra* 163.

[153] Woytowitsch 1978, no. 86a–b and pl. 5 (Monteleone di Spoleto; tyre segment preserved with U-shaped clamp *in situ*), no. 88a and pl. 16 (Campovalano, tomb 2), no. 89b, d and pl. 18 (Campovalano, tomb 69; see also D'Ercole and Martellone 2006, 80 and fig. 5), no. 93a–b and pl. 16 (Grottazzolina, tomb 5), and especially nos 95f and i and pl. 17 (Grottazzolina, tomb 20; see also Woytowitsch 1978, pls 58: 3 and 60: B 4; Annibaldi 1960, 376f. and figs 16–17).

[154] Long felloe clamps were used on chariot as well as cart wheels; see Emiliozzi 2001, 316–20. Among the vehicles with such long clamps are a chariot and a cart from San Giuliano (Barbarano Romana), Tumulo del Caiolo, tomb B (I. Caruso in *Carri da guerra* 280 nos 4, 11 and figs 3–4, 11, and Repertorio nos 130–1) and a chariot from the Tomba del Littore at Vetulonia (M. Cygielmann in *Carri da guerra* 266 and fig. 4b, and Repertorio 327, no. 174).

[155] Pare 1992, 56f., 60 and fig. 58: 1, pl. 132: B5–11 (Como, Ca'Morta, Tomba del Carrettino), 57, 60 and fig. 58: 10, pl. 136: 7–8 (Sesto Calende, Tomba del Guerriero B). The latter vehicle is not a wagon, as Pare assumed (1992, 60). In the case of the two-wheeler from Tomba del Guerriero A at Sesto Calende, it was impossible to reconstruct the type of felloe which was also fitted with a nailed-on iron tyre (Pare 1992, 63). For these two vehicles, see also our p. 22 and notes 81, 82.

[156] For the chariot wheels, see A. Emiliozzi in *Carri da guerra* 253 and figs 24 (tyre) and 25 (nave casings), and for the cart, 251, 253 with fig. 20 and pls 27, 28: 2–4 (see also 318f., Repertorio nos 85 and 86).

bolt passed horizontally through each of the ten spokes, where these were mortised into the felloe.[157] As for the iron tyres and their fastening nails, they were a common feature of the two- and four-wheeled vehicles that were buried in central and northern Italy from the later eighth century onwards. Among the earliest examples are tyres from tombs at Castel di Decima and Veii, apparently belonging to both chariots and carts (Pl. 1a and Fig. 6).[158] Nailed-on tyres provided a hard running surface and strengthened wheels, while at the same time increasing their weight and that of the vehicle as a whole. Similar tyres are materially documented in tombs in Europe north of the Alps from the Hallstatt period onwards, initially with four-wheelers, later also with two-wheelers.[159] Here, as in Italy, the tyres show considerable variation in width, cross-section and nailing. The nails vary in number and length, and may be close together or widely spaced. (In Italy, the nails appear to become more widely spaced as time progresses.) The heads of the nails, which may be countersunk, but often projected above the tyre surface, vary in size and design, including round, rhomboid, oval and rectangular ones. It is not exactly clear how these tyres were attached to the wheels. In the words of C. F. A. Pare:

> 'The tyres could be fitted to the felloe cold, their ends being held together by a nail or rivet. On the other hand, the ends of the tyre could be hammer-forged to form a hoop of exactly the right size, then heated over a fire to expand the metal. The red-hot tyre could then be fitted over the wheel: after cooling the tyre would shrink to give a tight fit, holding the tyre to the felloe and at the same time tightly holding together the nave, spokes and felloe.'[160]

In Europe north of the Alps, the fastening nails were often dispensed with in the later La Tène period. In Italy, such 'sweated on' tyres without nails are only known with certainty from the wagon of the earlier fifth century from Como, Ca'Morta (Pl. 117).[161]

In Greece, nailed-on iron tyres have been found, together with riveted rectangular and T-shaped felloe clamps, nave hoops and other iron fittings, in sixth century tumulus burials at Ayios Georgios in Thessaly.[162] Other such material comes from votive deposits in the sanctuary of Poseidon at Isthmia near Corinth, dating no later than c. 470–450, and from the sanctuary of Zeus at Olympia.[163] Similar finds have recently been reported from a temple at Kalapodi in Phocis, the find context pre-dating the destruction by the Persian army in 480.[164] It may be noted that riveted iron felloe clamps, but no nailed-on tyres, have also been found in a tomb of the later eighth century in Athens.[165]

---

[157] For this and other finds of such iron bolts from vehicle burials dating from the early seventh century onwards, see Emiliozzi 2001, 320–2 and fig. 14, 328–30. See also F. Healy in *Notizie degli scavi di antichità* (Serie 8) 26 (1972), 258 no. 9 and fig. 44 (example from Veii, Quattro Fontanili tomb AA *gammabeta*, without (other) vehicular remains.

[158] For Castel di Decima, see *Carri da guerra* 312f., Repertorio nos 18 (Tumulo Lanciani), 19 (tomb 15), 20 (tomb 21), 23 (tomb 101). For Veii, see *Carri da guerra* 325, Repertorio no. 158 (Quattro Fontanili tomb CC *alpha*), no. 159 (our Fig. 6. Same cemetery, tomb EE 10 B; also A. Cavalotti Batchvarova in *Notizie degli scavi di antichità* (Serie 8) 21 (146 no. 24 with fig. 35); *Carri da Guerra* 324 (Repertorio no. 146: Casal del Fosso tomb 821). For illustrations of other (later) tyres, see Woytowitsch 1978, pls 58 and 59: A.

[159] Piggott 1983, 167–70; Pare 1992, 166f., 169 and fig. 112 (showing similar tyres from Italy and Hallstatt Europe).

[160] Pare 1992, 128.

[161] Piggott 1983, 167, 215–17. Apart from the wagon from Como, Ca'Morta (Piggott 1983, 184; Pare 1992, 61, 128; also our pp. 90–96 with note 13), such tyres may have been present on the two-wheeled vehicle that was buried with its harness team in a third century tomb at Adria (see our p. 5 and notes 35–36).

[162] Tziafalias 1978, 175, 178 and figs 14–15, 21; 1994, especially 180f., 184f. and figs 1–3 (vehicles thought to have been wagons with small wheels at the front and larger ones at the rear – a combination not attested in ancient Greece or elsewhere); also Georganas 2004, 294.

[163] Raubitschek 1998, 100–2 and no. 336 (IM 776) and pl. 56 (part of tyre; its rather widely spaced fastening nails, with carbonized wood still adhering, are 0.109 m in length, thereby indicating a two-layered felloe (cf. nos 325 and IM 1077 with fig. 15 and pl. 57), nos 351–8 and figs 18–20 (riveted rectangular felloe clamps), nos 359–62 and fig. 18, 20–1 and pl. 58 (folded felloe clamps), also nos 337–9 (nave hoops), etc. (all from Isthmia). For a nailed-on iron tyre from Olympia, see Raubitschek 1998, 100 with n. 22.

[164] Whitley 2005, 55f. and fig. 98; 2006, 41 and fig. 49.

[165] Ceramicus, tomb 58 of Late Geometric IIa–b; see Kübler 1954, 252 nos M 125–7 and pl. 167; Müller-Karpe 1962, 125 and fig. 21: 13; Crouwel 1992, 87 and n. 441 (cf. n. 440, referring to doubtful iron nave hoops). The inscription listing 'iron' wheels among the temple inventories of the Acropolis at Athens may perhaps refer to wheels with tyres and other elements made of this metal; see Dunst 1972, 140 *s.v.* no. 6.

Further east, actual finds of similar iron tyres with fastening nails, together with felloe clamps of riveted as well as folded types and other vehicular remains, are known from funerary contexts of the later sixth to early fifth century in different parts of Anatolia. These finds, which may be accompanied by bridle bits and other horse gear, have invariably been attributed to two-wheeled vehicles (Pl. 146).[166] Here we should also draw attention to the royal chariots depicted in detail on Assyrian palace reliefs of the seventh century. The prominent domed nails closely studding the wheel rims may perhaps have been for traction rather than for securing an iron – or rawhide – tyre. A metal tyre may well be indicated beneath such nails on a contemporary Assyrian wall painting from Til Barsip in Syria. Tyres similarly studded with nails become commonly illustrated in the Near East with chariots of the Achaemenid period (Pls 128–129).[167]

The origin of the use of iron tyres has been sought in the Near East. From there the idea would have first spread to the Mediterranean, thence to be passed on to Europe north of the Alps.[168] The same may be assumed for the use of two concentric elements to form the wheel rim, which is first attested on one of the actual chariots buried in the tomb of Tut'ankhamun in New Kingdom Egypt, and then becomes widespread in the Near East in the earlier first millennium (Pl. 146).[169]

The concomitant use of metal felloe clamps of riveted and folded types may again derive from the Near East. All chariots illustrated on reliefs of Tiglath-Pileser III (745–727) and later Assyrian kings have eight-spoked wheels with two-layered felloes, held together with the help of two pairs of folded clamps placed opposite each other (Pl. 126).[170] The large size of these clamps recalls extant iron ones from Italy (see above). Folded as well as riveted iron clamps are materially documented from the Anatolian funerary contexts of the later sixth to earlier fifth century, which also yielded nailed-on iron tyres.[171] Among the riveted clamps are T-shaped ones with close parallels not only in Italy but also in a tomb of *c.* 400–350 at Toya in southern Spain, where the six-spoked wheels were similarly iron-tyred.[172] Finally, folded clamps were found with what remained of the eight-spoked wheels of an actual chariot from a eighth/seventh

[166] **Gordion, tumulus A:** see Kohler 1980, 69 and fig. 31: A–D (tyre segments), F–J (riveted felloe clamps, both rectangular and more or less T-shaped with curved edges), L (parts of two bridle bits), etc. **Balıkesir-Üçpınar, tumulus** (in Mysia, north-west Anatolia): see Kökten Ersoy 1995 and, in more detail, 1998, 110 nos UP/I.1–6 and fig. 2b–c (iron tyre segments, in one case with a folded felloe clamp remaining *in situ*; for another such clamp, see 114 no. UP/I.25 and fig. 4d. The rather widely spaced nails are 0.095–0.10 m in length, thereby pointing to two-layered felloes), 110 nos UP/I.14–17 and fig. 3c–d, 4a and pl. 6:4 (four riveted rectangular clamps), 110 nos UP/I.18–21 and fig. 4b–c (four riveted T-shaped clamps), 114–17 and fig. 5 (our Pl. 146; reconstruction drawing of spoked wheel, its diameter estimated as 1.10 m, incorrectly incorporating a single-layered felloe), see also 114 nos UP/I.23–23 and 24 and pl. 7: 1–4 (possible iron nave hoops, recalling Raubitschek 1998, nos 340–3 with fig. 17 and pl. 57 from Isthmia in Greece; see our p. 33, note 163). The finds from the tomb also included a pair of iron horse bits and of bronze frontlets, the latter recalling a pair from Cretone (Sabina Tibertina) in Lazio (see our p. 51 and note 282). In addition, there were bronze tubular strap crossings of a distinct type, also known from Greece, Italy and other parts of Europe (see our p. 49 and note 272). **Bintepeler tumulus 89** at Sardes: see Kökten Ersoy 1998, 122 no. S/I.16 (remains of tyres with closely spaced nails, 0.08–0.10 m long and indicating a two-layered felloe), 120f. nos S/I.10–13 and fig. 9b–e (six openwork, folded felloe clamps), cf. 120 no. S/I.5 with fig. 8b (iron bolt, reminiscent of those fixed horizontally through the outer spoke ends of wheels from Sirolo in Italy and Salamis in Cyprus (see our p. 33 and note 157, p. 35 and note 173), 122, 125f. and figs 11–12 (reconstruction drawing of wheel, its diameter probably too generously estimated as 1.60 m). The tomb also yielded a pair of decorated bronze linch pins, pointing to a two-wheeled vehicle (Kökten-Ersoy 1998, 117 nos S/B.1–2 and fig. 6).

[167] See Littauer and Crouwel 1979a, 108, 147. For illustrations, see a.o. Barnett and Lorenzini 1975, pls 65, 92, 103–5, 108, 117, 168; Parrot 1961, pl. 345 (Til Barsip).

[168] Kossack 1971, 159f.; Piggott 1983, 169f.; Pare 1992, 166f., 169; Egg and Pare 1993, 212; Emiliozzi 2001b, 315–19, 330.

[169] Littauer and Crouwel 1985, 27, 77 chariot A 4 and pls 5: below (Object nos 144–5) and 31. The composite double felloe of these six-spoked wheels was held together with the help of bronze thongs (instead of clamps) and presumably a rawhide tyre. For wheel construction involving a double wooden rim in the Near East in the earlier first millennium, see Kossack 1971 (comparing it with wheel construction in Europe north of the Alps); Littauer and Crouwel 1979a, 106–9; also Spruytte 1994.

[170] Kossack 1971, 157–9; Littauer and Crouwel 1979a, 108 and fig. 55; Spruytte 1994.

[171] See above note 166. The apparently very closely spaced tyre nails of the vehicle from Bintepeler tumulus 89 at Sardes strongly recall the hobnails of the chariot wheels seen on Assyrian and Achaemenid reliefs.

[172] Fernàndez-Miranda and Olmos 1986, especially 49–65 and figs 12–18 and ill. p. 64, see also 69–81 and fig. 19 and ills pp. 72 (Toya), 75 (El Mirador de Rolando) and 77 (Baza); Stary 1989, 172f., 181f. no. 7B and fig. 8:2, cf. 182 no. 7A and fig. 8:1; Quesada Sanz 1997, 57 and fig. 2.

century burial at Salamis in Cyprus. As reconstructed, the wheel rim here consists of two concentric elements, like that of another chariot from the same necropolis and of similar date. In the latter case, where metal clamps were absent, the outer ends of the ten spokes were held in place with the help of iron bolts fixed horizontally, exactly as documented on the sixth-century cart wheels from Sirolo in Italy.[173] In Cyprus, the wheels of these and other vehicles – both chariots and carts – were held together without iron tyres. Instead, there may well have been tyres made of rawhide, a material that was already used for this purpose on the extant Egyptian New Kingdom chariots from the tombs of Tut'ankhamun and others (see below).

The figured documents from Italy yield no firm information on the presence or absence of iron tyres on the wheels of chariots or other types of vehicle. The wheel rims are shown either as single or consisting of two concentric elements of varying thickness.[174] The depiction with a two-layered rim may indicate two wooden elements, or a single felloe and a tyre, the latter made of iron or rawhide. The use of rawhide tyres is best documented by the actual chariot wheels from the Egyptian New Kingdom, where the same material was used as a nave-and-spoke binding (see above). Shrunk-on wet, a rawhide tyre not only protected the running surface but also helped to strengthen the wheel as a whole. As was stated above, such tyres, unlike iron ones, were vulnerable to dampness. Nonetheless, rawhide tyres, in combination with low, single-layer felloes, are most likely for the wheels of racing chariots in Italy – as well as in Greece – which had to be light and fast.[175] (The same combination is materially documented on some of the New Kingdom chariots from Egypt.) In contrast, heavy iron tyres in combination with single- or double-layered felloes were used on the slow-moving, mainly ceremonial vehicles that were buried in tombs in Italy and north of the Alps.

Some representations from Italy reflect actual wheel construction by showing felloe clamps. Square, rectangular or T-shaped and with nails indicated, these fittings are usually placed where spokes and felloe meet. Other representations offer only misunderstood versions of such clamps.[176]

4. Traction System

Draught pole

Traction was provided by teams of two to four horses, two of which were under a yoke (*q.v.*). The yoke was connected to the vehicle by means of a single, central draught pole (*q.v.*). The pole of a two-wheeler is rigid and on ancient chariots usually ran all the way under the floor. This not only helped support the chariot body but made for a stronger pole, less apt to break during turns.

In Italy, the extant ornate chariots of Type I belonging to the sixth century, such as those from Ischia di Castro, Monteleone di Spoleto and Castel San Mariano, have been reconstructed with a pole running to the rear of the chariot body, passing in between the floor and the central axle (Pls 7–9). On the other hand, the reconstructions of the highly decorated Type I chariots of the seventh century from Vulci and

---

[173] Crouwel 1985, 106 *s.v.* chariots A 3 and A 7, from tombs 3 (chariot B) and 79 (chariot *Bèta*) respectively; Crouwel 1990; see also Kossack 1971, 155–7, 159 and fig. 34 (reconstruction drawing); Emiliozzi 2001, 321 and fig. 13. Cf. also the iron bolt among the vehicular from tumulus 89 at Sardes-Bintepeler (see our p. 34, note 166).

[174] A clear example is also the eight-spoked wheel in a scene of the death of charioteer Myrtilus on an alabaster cinerary urn from the Tomba delle Olimpiadi at Volterra; see Massa-Pairault 1992, 234 and fig. 218.

[175] For Greece, see Crouwel 1992, 37. In tomb paintings at Paestum, racing chariots are often shown with the heavier cross-bar type of wheel typical of carts (see our p. 16 and note 46, p. 82).

[176] See a.o. Woytowitsch 1978, no. 257 and pls 44 and 59: B 9 (our Pl. 37a; also Steingräber 1985, no. 34: painting from the Tomba degli Hescanas, Orvieto), no. 258 and pl. 44 (also Steingräber 1985, no. 32: painting from the Tomba Golini I, also at Orvieto), nos 74 and 232 and pls 8, 44 and 59: B 11 (also Höckmann 1982, fig. 25 and pl. 30: sheet bronze from the Tomba dei Bronzi at Castel San Mariano, which presumably contained remains of three actual vehicles; see our p. 14 and note 35).

Populonia show the pole ending at the central axle (Pls 2–3). Single T-shaped iron fittings, found among the surviving metal parts of other chariots, are thought to have helped fix the pole to the axle.[177] Such a construction, which is also seen with a later, Roman bronze model of a one-man racing chariot (Pl. 142) is probably unrealistic. It would have been much weaker than that involving pole running to the rear of the floor.[178]

On the Monteleone and other sixth-century actual chariots of Type I, from Ischia di Castro and Castel San Mariano, the pole passed through a bay cut in the wooden floor frame with its ornamental sheet-metal covering (Pls 7, 9).[179]. In the case of the Monteleone chariot, the pole is bronze-sheathed and emerges from under the mouth of a bronze boar's head at the front of the body Pl. 8).[180] On the so-called Dutuit chariot, also of Type I, from Capua, the pole actually passed through a socket in the form of a lion's head with open mouth.[181] Such an animal-headed socket can be seen with the Type I chariots depicted on a sheet-bronze panel belonging to one of the chariots from Castel San Mariano and on the walls of two fourth century tombs in Toscana (Pl. 55).[182] Terracotta revetment plaques and an Etruscan black-figure vase painting of the sixth century show an outsized boar's head in this position, the chariots here being of our type II (Pls 72, 44).

In the case of the Monteleone chariot, the bronze-clad pole describes a single curve upon emerging from under the floor and then continues to the yoke area at an oblique angle. In some profile representations the pole also rises in a single curve, while in others it seems to describe a double curve – upwards and then forwards – before disappearing behind the near horse.

The pole of several actual chariots – mostly of Type I but also including the Type IV carriage from the Tomba Regolini Galassi at Cerveteri – had a decorative bronze finial at its straight forward end (Pls 10–11). On the Monteleone chariot this fitting is still in place (Pl. 8a), as it is on the incompletely preserved pole which forms part of the remains of a life-size bronze chariot from Chianciano in Toscana. The remains were found in a third century sanctuary of the Moon Goddess Selene (Pl. 17).[183] The bronze pole finials of these and other actual chariots have a variety of shapes: heads of eagles, griffins, lions, rams or calves, facing forward and fitted by a socket to the straight, round-sectioned pole end.[184] A griffin's head is seen in this position on the chariots, possibly of Type V, depicted on two red-figure neck-amphorae of the fourth century from Orvieto in Umbria.[185] The chariot of Type V in a wall painting in the Tomba degli Hescanas at the same site, dating to c. 300, has a ram's head pole-end finial (Pl. 37).[186] A similarly shaped pole-end finial appears on a Roman bronze chariot model, said to be from the Tiber (Pl. 142);

---

[177] A. Emilozzi in *Carri da guerra,* 101.

[178] See p. 11 *s.v.* chariot Type I and p. 17 with note 51.

[179] See pp. 13–14.

[180] A. Emilozzi in *Carri da guerra* 181 and figs 4, 5, pl. XII. A similar arrangement, involving a boar's head, can be assumed for one the chariots from the Tomba dei Bronzi at Castel San Mariano; see Höckmann 1982, 44 and pl. 29:5; A. M. Feruglio in *Carri da guerra* 220 no. 4 and fig. 10; also Emiliozzi, *ibid.*, 213 and figs 4–5 (reconstruction drawings).

[181] Woytowitsch 1978, pl. 4, no. 6a; *Strade degli Etruschi* fig. 47; Cerchiai, Colucci Pescatori and d'Henry 1997, 27 with fig. 1; Emiliozzi 2006, 141f. no. 7 with pls 16–17, 24–6.

[182] See p. 9, note 12 (Castel San Mariano); Woytowitsch no. 258 with pl. 44, and Steingräber 1985, no. 32 (Orvieto, Tomba Golini I). See also our p. 7 and note 55 (chariot, possibly of Type I, depicted in the Tomba della Quadriga Infernale at Sarteano).

[183] Alberti-Parronchi and Piccardi 1950–1, 249–51 and fig. 1; Woytowitsch 1978, no. 169A and pl. 43; Stibbe-Twiest 1977, pl. 17: 1–2; *L'archeologia racconta* no. 52 (with bibl.); Littauer and Crouwel 1988a, 195 and pl. Va–b (= 2002, 548 and pl. 234a–b).

[184] Höckmann 1982, 43f. and pl. 29: 6–7, and A. Emiliozzi in *Carri da guerra* 220f. nos 5–6 and figs 11–12 (eagle- and lion-head pole-end finials attributed to two chariots from the Tomba dei Bronzi at Castel San Mariano); Pareti 1947, 258, fr. 28, and Woytowitsch 1978, no. 30c and pl. 6 (lion-head pole-end finial of the Type IV chariot from the Tomba Regolini Galassi); De Agostino 1957, 18f. and figs 17, 29 and 33 (ram's head pole-end finial of chariot from Populonia, San Cerbone tomb 2); F. Buranelli in *Carri da guerra* 202 and figs 7, 9, pl. XVIII (eagle-headed pole-end finial of the chariot from Roma Vecchia). A lion's head pole-end finial belongs with the unreliably reconstructed so-called Biga Sbrigoli from a late seventh century tomb at Civitella San Paolo (ancient Capena) in Lazio (see our p. 24, note 96).

[185] See p. 7 and note 56 and p. 26, note 109.

[186] Woytowitsch 1978, no. 257 and pl. 44; Steingräber 1985, no. 34.

in this case, the pole is turned up at its end. There are various other bronze fittings, Etruscan as well as Roman, not directly associated with vehicle burials, which have been regarded as pole finials. While this may sometimes be correct, they may also have been attached to pieces of furniture, firedogs or other objects, particularly when their sockets are not round but rectangular in section.[187] Among these fittings are griffin's heads, some of which come in pairs and so probably did not belong with the single-pole chariots of the time.

The actual pole-end finials help to explain the central Italian representations of harnessed chariots of Types I, II and III, in which a griffin's head – in one case a spiral curl – rises above the yoke area and faces backwards towards the driver (Pl. 71a–b). Griffin's heads, sometimes highly stylized, are depicted in the same position on East Greek chariots and sometimes also on those of mainland Greece and the Aegean islands (Pls 139–141). They also appear on chariots in Magna Graecia (Pl. 75).[188] In reality, these fittings will have faced forward, like the actual bird- and animal-head finials in this position. It may then be simply for clarity's sake that the artists depicted them as back to front.[189] The idea of such pole finials may well have been adopted in Italy from the east.

A pole with a sharply recurved forward end, and with what is either a yoke or a yoke peg lashed to it, seems to be indicated on a sixth-century ivory plaque from Tarquinia (Pl. 58).[190]

There is no evidence for a pole support or breastwork brace on any of the chariot types in use in central and northern Italy before or during the Roman Empire period, with the exception of the vehicles seen in Situla Art (see Appendix 1). These traction elements are also absent from East Greek chariots.[191] In marked contrast, chariots of the High-front type of the eighth century and later in mainland Greece are consistently shown with a thong running out horizontally from the top of the front rail to the forward end of the pole which in Greece was sharply upturned. This traction system, which is also illustrated in southern Italy and involved a pole maintained under tension by such a pole-end support, was an essential corollary of a dorsal yoke (Pls 135–137)[192] The straight-ended pole generally preferred in central and northern Italy – as in East Greece and the Near East at the time – was used in conjunction with a neck yoke and evidently did not need a form of pole support.[193]

Pole binding

While the pole of the ornate carriage from Monteleone is entirely sheathed in bronze, that of a chariot from Sirolo in Marche had a binding of bronze rings, set at regular intervals (Pl. 76a).[194]

Several figured documents indicate that the pole could be bound by thongs of organic material, to help prevent its splitting and to hold it together should this nonetheless occur (Pls 54–55, 59).[195] These

---

[187] See Woytowitsch 1978, nos 70–70A (pair of griffin's heads), 71–71A, 35, 9; Haynes 1985, nos 24–8 and pls 142–3; cf. Von Mercklin 1933, 95–101; Brown, W. L. 1960, 114f.; Hill 1974, 443f.; Crouwel 1992, 72.

[188] Crouwel 1992, 39, 71f. Add Braun 1998, no. 104 (unprovenanced East Greek terracotta revetment plaque). For chariots of the Greek High-front type with griffin's head pole ends from Magna Graecia, see p. 16 and note 46 (terracotta revetment plaques from Metaponto, San Biagio).

[189] Cf. the elaborate, gold-covered sun discs decorating the poles of royal chariots of the Egyptian New Kingdom. In order to render these forward-facing objects explicitly in the invariably profile views of harnessed chariots, the artists depicted them as if facing sideways; see Littauer and Crouwel 1985, 83.

[190] See p. 7 and note 51.

[191] Crouwel 1992, 71.

[192] Crouwel 1992, 40. For representations from southern Italy, see p. our 16 and note 46.

[193] See p. 39.

[194] A. Emiliozzi in *Carri da guerra* 53 with fig. 10. There is evidence for bronze sheathing of the pole in the area ahead of the body of the chariot from the Tomba della Biga at Ischia di Castro; see F. Boitani in *Carri da guerra* 206.

[195] See p. 18 and note 53, and p. 25 and note 103 (chariots, of Type II and unknown type respectively, depicted on sheet bronze and an ostrich egg probably from the Isis Tomb at Vulci) and a type I chariot illustrated on a sheet bronze from the Tomba dei Bronzi at Castel San Mariano (Woytowitsch 1978, pl. 8: 74; Höckmann 1982, 36f. and figs 19–20 and pl. 15: 7).

figured documents are of different dates and include profile representations, as well as the fourth century group of terracotta winged chariot horses from Tarquinia and the remains of the third century bronze chariot from Chianciano (Pls 68, 17).[196] The pole binding is sometimes shown as meshed. In the case of the Chianciano chariot, it covers most of the preserved pole length before the attachment of yoke braces (see Chapter II.5).

Pole binding appears with representations of the High-front chariots in mainland Greece from the seventh century onwards. It is not visible in illustrations of East Greek chariots.[197]

Note. There is no evidence for pole braces (*q.v.*) joining the pole to the lower front of the chariot body. One at either side, such braces restricted any sideways motion of the pole and reduced the stress at the point of connection between pole and floor frame. In Greece, short pole braces are seen in the many frontal views of High-front chariots.[198] In Italy, there is, in fact, only one such frontal view, of a racing chariot in a wall painting from the Tomba delle Bighe at Tarquinia of the early fifth century, where pole braces are notably absent (Pl. 34).[199]

5. Harnessing

In Italy before the Roman Empire, harness teams are depicted with one to four horses. In fact, when single draught is illustrated in profile views, it is merely a simplification devised by the artist; at the same time a draught pole, implying *paired* draught, is shown. Two-horse teams (*bigae*) are predominant among the representations of chariots of all types. Their use is also indicated by paired metal horse bits, found with and without chariot remains in tombs from the eighth century onwards, and by occasional paired horse burials, such as the one associated with the chariot of our Type I from Ischia di Castro (see II.2). Three-horse teams (*trigae*) also occur, sometimes together with two-horse ones harnessed to the same type of chariot, on terracotta revetment plaques of the later sixth century (Pls 70–71, 73). Four-horse teams (*quadrigae*) are attested too. They can be seen, for instance, on the series of terracotta revetment plaques from Cerveteri showing chariots of Type II (Pl. 72), and in two black-figure vase paintings illustrating Type I chariots (Pl. 45).[200]

There is also the plastically-rendered *quadriga* on the ivory lid of *c.* 600 from Marzabotto, where the team consists of two horses and two panthers (Pl. 33).[201] In addition, an actual four-horse team was found in a mid-sixth century tomb at Vulci, associated with the remains of a chariot.[202] And a terracotta *quadriga* stood over the front pediment of the temple of Jupiter Optimus Maximus on the Capitoline hill at Rome. According to tradition, the temple was inaugurated in 508.[203]

For comparison, chariots in mainland Greece had teams of 2–4 horses, with *quadrigae* predominating

---

[196] See p. 6 and note 41, and p. 36 and note 183.

[197] Crouwel 1992, 39. The actual chariots that have survived from much earlier, New Kingdom tombs in Egypt have the bearing surfaces of their poles bound with leather; see Littauer and Crouwel 1985, 79f.

[198] Crouwel 1992, 39f.

[199] Pole braces are also absent in later, Roman representations of *quadrigae* in frontal view; see a.o. Dunbabin 1982, 70–8 and pls 6–9.

[200] See p. 9, note 8 (the second neck-amphora by the Painter of Berlin Amphora 2154 and the Micali Painter's neck amphora). A team of four horses, implying a *quadriga*, is seen racing on an Etruscan black-figure neck-amphora from Vulci (London, British Museum GR 1865.1–3.2.5 = B 64) by the Micali Painter; see Beazley 1947, 2f. with pl. 2; Spivey 1987, 19 no. 102; Szilágyi 1991, 8–10 and figs 24–7; Moltesen 1982, 60–6; Van der Meer 1986; Brendel 1995, 195–8 and figs 129–30.

[201] Cf. the draught team of two lions and two griffins in the wall painting of the Tomba della Quadriga Infernale at Sarteano (p. 7 and note 55).

[202] See p. 4 and note 22.

[203] Winter, N. A. 2005, 247, 240. For this and other such *quadriga* groups of Roman Republican times mentioned in the literary sources and/or depicted on coins, see especially Schollmeyer 2001, 125–30, 200–3 nos B 11–24.

from the sixth century onwards, when *trigae* became obsolete.[204] In East Greece only bigae are in evidence,[205] while in Imperial Rome *quadrigae* far outnumber other teams which might range from two to ten animals.[206]

Yoke

In Italy, as in Greece, only two horses were under yoke (*q.v.*), this being the wooden element that connected them with the draught pole. Other horses, when present, were trace animals or outriggers (see below).

Our most explicit information on the type of yoke and its attachment to the pole is furnished by the remains of the life-size bronze chariot of the third century from Chianciano (Pl. 17).[207] Here we see a yoke which was meant to lie across the two animals' necks, just ahead of the withers. The yoke is of the so-called fitted type, i.e. shaped into bays for the neck of each horse. This type of yoke was used in the Near East from the eighth century onwards and also in contemporary Cyprus, replacing the neck yoke with yoke saddles (*q.v.*) that had previously been widely used in the eastern Mediterranean.[208] The fitted neck yoke also prevailed in East Greece, but not in mainland Greece. High-front chariots there, from the eighth century onwards, had a dorsal yoke (*q.v.*), i.e. one placed behind the withers on the horses' back, consisting of a slender straight rod with sharply upturned ends.[209] The quadrigae of Imperial Roman times again had a fitted two-horse neck yoke (Pls 142–143).[210]

The yoke of the Chianciano bronze chariot has decorative ridges in the centre and at either edge and roller-like fittings at the outer ends of the bays. The yoke is placed on top of the pole, just behind the latter's griffin-head finial, and is attached by lashings. The two protuberances on top of the yoke, one at either side of the pole, help secure the lashings.[211] The neck yoke of the pair of winged terracotta horses from the Ara del Regina at Tarquinia, of the fourth century, appears to be similarly shaped, again with raised edges and roller-like terminals (Pl. 68).[212]

As presently reconstructed, the highly decorated chariot of the sixth century from Monteleone di Spoleto includes the metal sheathing of a yoke that is too small and impractical (Pl. 8a). The yoke ends are in the form of lion heads, which recur on fragments of similar yoke sheathing belonging with one of the three ornate vehicles from the contemporary Tomba dei Bronzi at Castel San Mariano.[213]

Among the figured documents, the one representation of an unharnessed (racing) chariot, in the Tomba delle Bighe of the early fifth century at Tarquinia, shows only a shapeless yoke. This seems to have had attachments for harness straps at the ends (Pl. 34).

Sixth-century terracotta revetment plaques, depicting chariots of Types I, II and III, show a rectangular

---

[204] Crouwel 1992, 40f.

[205] Crouwel 1992, 71.

[206] See pp. 68–69 and note 404.

[207] See p. 36 and note 183.

[208] For the fitted neck yoke and its predecessor, see Littauer and Crouwel 1979a, 85, 113f.; Crouwel 1987, 108; 1992, 42.

[209] Spruytte 1983, 53, 57, 61; 1997, 71 (assuming that a neck rather than a dorsal yoke was used in Italy); Crouwel 1992, 42.

[210] Our Pl. 143 shows a terracotta, so-called Campana plaque of the first century AD; see Junkelmann 1990, fig. 140. For other representations, see Junkelmann 1990, fig. 122; Vigneron 1968, pl. 73c.

[211] A yoke with similar ridges can be seen on a Etruscan red-figure hydria by the Painter of the Vatican Biga from Vulci; see Beazley 1947, 47, 2; Haynes 2000, 320 and fig. 255.

[212] See also the yoke of the two-horse chariot belonging to the terracotta pedimental sculptures of the later second or first century at Civitalbà in Umbria (p. 112, note 24).

[213] The decoration of the fragments from the Tomba dei Bronzi at Castel San Mariano also included a panther; see Höckmann 1982, 44 with pl. 29: 4; A. E. Feruglio in *Carri da guerra* 221f. nos 7–8 and figs 13–14 and pl. XXIII: 4. Fragments remain of bronze sheathing of the yoke of the chariot from Ischia di Castro, see F. Boitani in *Carri da guerra* 206.

element lying over the horses' neck (Pls 70–72). This element, its lower edge sometimes cut out into a bay, is best explained as a pad of fabric or leather protecting the animal's neck from bruising or chafing by the yoke. It is notable that similarly shaped yoke pads, including the cut-out bay, occur in sixth-early fifth century chariot representations in East Greece (Pl. 139–141).[214]

In mainland Greece and southern Italy the dorsal yoke was standard on the High- front type of chariot which predominated from the seventh century onwards, always in conjunction with a relatively short draught pole. The sharply upturned forward end of the pole was obtained by bending under heat, and maintained by a thong running back to the top of the vehicle's front rail (Pls 135–137). In most Italic chariots, such a pole-end support – and the dorsal yoke – are not in evidence, even on Type III chariots which clearly derive from mainland Greek models (see Chapter II.1). A possible exception may be seen on an ivory plaque of c. 600 from Tarquinia. The incompletely preserved chariot here seems to have the mainland-Greek type of pole, a thong running back from its sharply recurved, hook-shaped forward end (Pl. 58).[215]

Yoke braces

The fragmentary bronze chariot from Chianciano shows two short metal straps coming from the pole, apparently as extensions of the pole binding and running to each yoke arm where they are bound (Pl. 17). Such straps are also seen with the unharnessed chariot shown in frontal view in the Tomba delle Bighe at Tarquinia (Pl. 34). They can be interpreted as yoke braces (q.v.) – harness elements which, lashed to the pole and yoke arms, helped to keep the yoke at right-angles to the pole and to distribute tractive stress.

Yoke braces appear to have been widely used in ancient harnessing.[216] They are seen, for instance, on Greek black-figure vases where High-front chariots are depicted in frontal view.

Harness straps

The two horses under yoke were harnessed by two elements – a neckstrap (q.v.), sometimes shown rather like a rigid collar, and a girth (q.v.).[217] When the animals advanced, they pressed against the neckstrap, which was fastened directly or indirectly to the yoke (see below) and transmitted the pressure to the draught pole by which the vehicle was pulled. The neckstrap, which also kept the yoke in place, is depicted as widening towards the front and thereby assuming a crescent shape. A neckstrap of the latter form stays lower down and better in place on the horse and helps to spread the pressure on the front of the neck.[218] Crescent-shaped straps are found with neck-yoke harnessing in East Greece and the Near East. The dorsal yoke of mainland Greek chariots has a breaststrap of similar shape, for the same reason.

The second harness strap, the girth, passed behind the horse's elbows. When combined with a neck yoke, the girth acted primarily as a backing element (q.v.). It prevented the continued forward movement of yoke, draught pole and vehicle when the animals slowed their pace or moved backwards. The girth was slack – necessary if the horse was not to be cut under the elbows – and ran at an oblique angle.[219]

---

[214] Åkerström 1954, 199; Crouwel 1992, 72 and pl. 16:1, 2a–b. Braun 1998, no. 104 (explicit illustration on unprovenanced East Greek terracotta revetment plaque).

[215] See p. 7, note 51. For mainland Greek High-front chariots in figured documents made in southern Italy, see p. 16, note 46.

[216] Spruytte 1983, 53; Crouwel 1992, 43.

[217] Coloured illustrations of chariots of different types on terracotta revetment plaques where the original paint is well preserved are particular informative as regards these straps and other harnessing elements; see Tomei 1997, no. 13g (plaques of the Rome-Caprifico type), *Die Welt der Etrusker. Archäologische Denkmäler* no. B.6.1.5, and *Italy of the Etruscans* no. 328 (Cerveteri), and Christiansen and Winter 2010, no. 2 (plaques of unknown provenance).

[218] Spruytte 1983, 53; Crouwel 1992, 43, 72.

[219] Crouwel 1992, 43, 72.

In contrast, the girth of High-front chariots in mainland Greece, which was used in conjunction with a dorsal yoke, was strapped more tightly and further back, enabling it to keep the yoke in place as well as to function as a backing element.[220]

In Italy, as in Greece, the girth is always shown as thin, and usually tied in a knot, sometimes with a loop hanging down (Pls 70–72). It should be noted that the girth is absent in a number of representations of two-horse teams. This is surely accidental, as this harness strap is essential for pole horses, though not for outriggers.

As regards the attachment of both neckstrap and girth, our most detailed document is the pair of winged terracotta horses of the fourth century from the Ara del Regina at Tarquinia (Pl. 68). These horses wear a wide neckstrap which is not fastened directly to the yoke, at least not on the outside where the strap ends in what looks like a metal pin, knobbed at either end. A short, narrow strap runs from there to the inside of the roller-like (metal) yoke end. The wide neck strap also has a rectangular slot near its pin-like end, through which the narrow girth passes before being tied in a knot further down.

A rather similar arrangement is indicated on the stone heads of a pair of yoke horses of the later fourth century from Vulci (Pl. 28).[221] Here the crescent-shaped neckstrap narrows towards the end and seems to be looped over the yoke end; the neckstrap has two triangular, possibly decorative slots. Of interest also is the yoke of the unharnessed chariot depicted in the Tomba delle Bighe at Tarquinia (Pl. 34). It has loops at the ends, quite probably to facilitate the attachment of the horses' neckstrap.

In profile representations of harnessed chariots a knotted narrow strap may be seen linking the neckstrap to the yoke end, similar to that on the Tarquinia team (Pl. 70). The terracotta revetment plaques of the Rome-Caprifico type seem to indicate a different way of attaching the crescent-shaped neckstrap to the yoke. Here the neckstrap divides into two or three short, narrow straps in the area of the yoke padding (Pl. 71a–b).

The neckstraps may sometimes have had an ornate bronze facing, such as is represented by the pairs of decorated bronze strips found in some rich tombs with vehicular remains of the seventh to early sixth centuries in central Italy. The strips, with straight or curving edges, have collared holes or loops at their ends for fastening.[222]

Figured documents offer glimpses of other harness elements. Thus a stone sarcophagus from Cerveteri illustrates a toggle fastening inside the neckstrap (Pl. 63).[223] The two-horse team here wears a necklace with disc-shaped pendents or *bullae* which must have been fastened in the same way as those worn around ladies' necks, by means of a horizontal tube at the top.[224] A similar narrow thong with *bullae* is worn around the upper neck of the pair of winged terracotta horses from Tarquinia (Pl. 68) and by the three-horse draught team depicted on terracotta revetment plaques of the late sixth century from Palestrina (Pl. 73).[225] In addition, actual bronze *bullae* have been found near the necks of buried horses at sites in Veneto.[226]

---

[220] Crouwel 1992, 43.

[221] Found at the entrance to a tomb in Camposcale necropolis. See Giglioni 1935, pl. 262:1; *La Tomba François di Vulci* no. 86; Helbig 1963, no. 610. Cf. also the incompletely preserved yoke and neckstrap attachment of the chariot team depicted on the terracotta frieze from Civitalbà (our p. 112, note 24).

[222] Curtis 1925, 46f. no. 83 and pl. 34 (Palestrina, Tomba Barberini. The pair of strips, 0.464 m long and hinged in two places, has been interpreted as belts. For the chariot remains, see our p. 12 and note 28). P. Santoro in *Carri da guerra* 296, no. 10 and figs 20–1 (Sferracavallo, Colle del Forno tomb XI. Length of complete strip 0.34 m. The strips, like two bronze headstalls from the tomb (see our pp. 49–50 and note 273), have been linked – for no apparent reason – to the cart rather than the chariot that was also buried in the tomb (*Carri da guerra* 313, Repertorio nos 88–9).

[223] See p. 9, note 14.

[224] For actual *bullae* and their representations, see especially Andrén 1948, 91–100.

[225] See p. 6 and note 41, p. 10 and note 19. They also appear with a chariot team depicted on Etruscan sheet bronzes; see p. 25, note 101.

[226] Gambacurta and Tirelli 1996, 71 and fig. 27; Gambacurta 2003, 94f. with fig. 6a (horse 13 from Le Brustolade at Altino – see our p. 5 and

The outriggers of *trigae* and *quadrigae* are shown with a neckstrap and girth similar to those of yoked horses, but they were otherwise not under yoke and harnessed very differently. This involved the use of traces (*q.v.*), one to each horse, running back to the chariot. Traces are explicitly shown only with the four-horse chariots of Type II depicted on terracotta revetment plaques from Cerveteri. The long thongs or straps are seen passing through a round hole in the lower siding of the triangular chariot body and running forward at an upward slant before disappearing between the horses (Pl. 72).[227]

Traces are a standard feature of High-front chariots with four-horse teams in mainland Greece. Experiments have shown that the straps or thongs, one to each outrigger, after passing through a loop suspended from the side rail, must have been attached to the central axle or, perhaps more likely, to the rear floor bar.[228] The use of traces with *quadrigae* is also attested – by figured and textual evidence – in chariot harnessing of the period of the Roman Empire (Pl. 143).[229]

As for the manner in which the traces were fastened to the outriggers, evidence of Greek chariot harnessing may again be helpful. Most explicit is a bronze statuette of a horse from Olympia, dating to 470–460 and originally belonging to a four-horse chariot group. Here, a trace was attached to a ring at the point over the horse's back where the breaststrap (which was used with the mainland Greek dorsal yoke) and the girth meet. When the team pulled, both breaststrap and trace would have been taut.[230]

We may note that in Greece the outriggers of *quadrigae* seem to have been prevented from swerving outwards by the reins being drawn inwards to pass through terrets (*q.v.*) on the yoke and by the charioteer's long goad (*q.v.*). In addition, the teams of two yoke horses and two outriggers may have had their mouths joined in front.[231]

It may be noted that in the case of the *trigae* illustrated in figured documents from Italy, there are no traces visible in the area between horses and chariot. This may suggest that the outrigger was connected directly to the yoke horse next to it, or to the end of the yoke, or both. Such an arrangement would recall the *trigae* and *quadrigae*, again with only two horses under yoke, which are depicted in great detail on ninth century Assyrian palace reliefs, where traces are also absent (Pl. 125).[232]

The outriggers cannot have contributed much to the pulling power of the harness team, as has been shown by experiments with two outriggers harnessed to a reconstruction of a Greek High-front type chariot. Depending on the use of the vehicle, these horses may have been for display or served as reserve animals.[233]

This section concludes with a brief consideration of a large group of cast bronze objects, often found – singly or in pairs – with remains of two-wheeled vehicles and horse bits in tombs of the late eighth and seventh centuries in central Italy. These objects mainly consist of simple rings and a variety of rectangular buckles, which will have been used for the attachment of harness straps or, in some cases, headstall straps. The buckles, sometimes with a flexible part on top, may be decorated with human figures, animals or birds, thereby recalling the decorated cheekpieces of bronze horse bits (Pl. 18a–b).[234]

---

note 29; Marchesetti 1993, 189, 269f. and pl. 30:1 and 8 (horse with bit, one *bulla* and other trappings from Santa Lucia di Tolmino). See also Peroni *et al.* 1975, 60 and fig. 10:15 (*bulla* from a tomb at Este); also our p. 4 and note 23 (finds from Populonia). A necklace with 14 bronze *bullae* comes from a looted tomb in the San Cerbone cemetery at Populonia (Milani 1908, 216f. and fig. 21; Minto 1943, 184–6 and pl. 49:5; see also our p. 4, note 21).

[227] A trace and a similar type of chariot can also be recognized on a fragmentary terracotta revetment plaque from Tarquinia; see Andrén 1939–40, 67 no. I: 1a and pl. 22: 75, right; Cataldi Dini 1993, 208 no. 7 and fig. 4, right.

[228] Spruytte 1978, 422f. and figs 12–15; Crouwel 1992, 44f.

[229] The Campana placque of Pl. 143 (see p. 39, note 210), illustrating an accident on the racetrack, shows a trace running back from where the neckstrap and girth meet. For traces, see also Junkelmann 1992, 223. For textual references, see Lewis and Short, *s.v. funalis*.

[230] See Crouwel 1992, 44 and pl. 4. A fragmentary terracotta relief of the mid-sixth century said to be from Metatarurus in southern Italy preserves part of a Greek-style frontal chariot group, with a trace running to the girth of an outrigger which is rearing up (Moore 1975, 41 and fig. 17).

[231] See p. 50 and note 277.

[232] Littauer and Crouwel 1979a, 115f. and fig. 53.

[233] Spruytte 1978.

[234] See especially Müller-Karpe 1974, 89 no. 14 (Veii, Grotta Gramiccia tomb 871); *Etrusker in der Toskana*, 138–42 nos 142–63 (Marsiliana

Related bronze harness elements consist of two plain or decorated articulating parts with ring-shaped or rectangular strap attachments at either ends.[235] These objects in turn are related to much more elaborate metal elements, some of which come from controlled excavations of tombs with vehicular remains in central Italy. Apparently single, these elements are made up of two or more articulating parts, linked by hinges and again with strap attachments at the ends (Pls 19–20). The articulating bronze objects, the highly decorated as well as the more simple ones, have sometimes been called 'distanziatori di cavalli', but their precise function remains uncertain.[236]

6. Control

The harness teams of horses were controlled by bitted bridles (*q.v.*). Reins (*q.v.*) ran from each animal's bit (*q.v.*) to the driver, providing him with directional as well as braking control.

Bits

The actual bridle bits that have survived completely or in fragmentary condition, whether for driven or ridden horses, are mostly of bronze or iron, or they combine an iron mouthpiece with bronze cheekpieces. In addition, there are remains of bits made from organic materials, which mostly antedate those made of metal.

The numerous metal bits come chiefly from tombs and are often found in pairs, indicating driving rather than riding. In several cases, remains of actual chariots and other vehicles have also been identified from the same tombs. The wear on a number of these bits, including highly decorated ones, indicates that they had actually been used.[237]

The metal bits may be broadly classified into three types, according to the specific action primarily of their mouthpieces (*q.v.*) but also of their mouthpieces in conjunction with the cheekpieces (*q.v.*).[238]

---

d'Albegna, Circolo di Perazzeta; see also Arietti and Martellotta 1998, pl. 10: 3; for the bronze horse gear from this tumulus, see also Dei 1996), 193f. nos 82–4 (Vetulonia, Circolo degli Acquastrini; see also Dei 1996); I. Caruso in *Carri da guerra* 280 nos 8–9 (San Giuliano, Caiolo, tomb B); P. von Eles in *Tomba del Trono* 2002, 117–19, 122–32 nos 136a–b, 137a–b, 138e–h, 141, 142a–b with figs 39–40 and pls 53, 56–8 (Verucchio, Tomba del Trono; also Gentili 2003, pls 157 (nos 71–2, 81–2), 158 (no. 83) and CCLXXXII (nos 72, 81–3). For finds from other tombs at Verucchio, see Gentili 2003, pls 66: 7 and 120: 10–11. See also Cygielman and Pagnini 2006, 45, 47 nos 27–31 (Vetulonia, Tomba del Littore). A large group of such bronze harness trappings, along with horse bits, was discovered by I. Balboni in 1894 in the Pozzuola cemetery at Veii; these finds remain unpublished, but are on display in the Museo Gregoriano Etrusco in the Vatican. The simpler, rigid rectangular buckles are somewhat reminiscent of the bronze so-called strap-unions, found in pairs with vehicle burials of La Tène date in Yorkshire in Britain. The position of these elements, near either end of the yoke, suggests they were to help fasten harness straps to the yoke; see Stead 1984, 32 nos 15a–b and fig. 2: 15 (Garton Slack); 1991, 47, 49f. nos 6–7 and figs 41–2 (Kirkburn). Differently shaped, paired metal elements serving a similar function are widely attested in the Roman Empire; see especially Radnóti 1961; also Von Mercklin 1933, 131f. *s.v.* no. 32; Garbsch 1986, 65 *s.v.* no. 46 and figs 48–50; Miniero 1987, 200 and fig. 29 (associated with wagon remains from a villa at Arianna near Stabiae in the Gulf of Naples; see our p. 91, note 23).

[235] See *Etrusker in der Toskana* 193f. no. 84 (Vetulonia, Circolo degli Acquastrini) and 140 nos 148–9 (Marsiliana d'Albegna, Circolo di Perazzeta); Cygielman and Pagnoni 2006, 47 no. 33 (Vetulonia, Tomba del Tridente).

[236] Most extensive discussion in Arietti and Martellotta 1998, 60 *s.v.* no. 21 with pls D and 7 ('tomba principescha' at Vivara, Rocca di Papa; see also Ghini 1987, 216 and fig. 13), 8:1 (Bisenzio, Buccini tomb 10; see also Galli 1912, 454 n. 15 and fig. 48); Bedini 1977, 300 and fig. 13), 8: 2 and 9: 1–2 (our Pl. 24; unprovenanced, London, British Museum 1851.8–13.139; see also Kemble 1855, 363 and pl. 27: 1, 8; Walters 1899, no. 356), 10: 1 (Castel di Decima, tomb 101; see also Bedini 1977, 297–303 and fig. 12, and in *Civiltà del Lazio primitivo*, no. 92, and in *Roma. Romolo, Remo* 192; Coarelli 1981, 24f.), 10: 2 (Civita Castellana, Valsariosa tomb 2; see also Cozza and Pasqui 1887, 310 no. h and pl. 6: 6; Woytowitsch 1978, no. 29 and pl. 43). See also Cuccini 1983, fig. 2 and pls 31–3: two closely related examples from Scarlino and Vetulonia (= Arietti and Martellotta 1998, pl. 11: 2), which in turn recall the elaborate, hinged handles with ring-shaped ends of incense burners of the seventh century Vetulonia type, for which see a.o. Pareti 1947, nos 444–9 and pl. 60; Vinattierri 1948–9, pl. 6: 2–3; Talocchini 1963, 447 and n. 23 and pl. 45b); Colonna 1997, 18f.; P. von Eles in *Tomba del Trono* 118 and n. 293.

[237] Von Hase 1969, 55, and Kilian 1977, 74 (Tarquinia, Tomba del Guerriero with chariot burial).

[238] The much used classification of horse bits from Italy by Von Hase (1969) is chiefly based on differences in the design of their cheekpieces (see his p. 6).

Type 1. Bits with bar canons, passing through the cheekpieces

This type is documented by a number of examples made of bronze, iron or a combination of both metals, from tombs in central and northern Italy, the find contexts dating to the eighth and seventh centuries (Pl. 21).[239]

The single canon mouthpiece (length, within cheekpieces, 0.09–0.127 m) is round in section, its ends passing through holes at the centres of the cheekpieces. The ends are rolled back on themselves to form loops that held rings or other attachments for the reins.

The accompanying cheekpieces are of varying design, including stylized horses (with their legs terminating in rings for the attachment of dangles), paired birds, solid plaques of squarish shape, and triple rings. In all cases, loops for attachment to bifurcated cheekstraps are present. Overall, this type of bit would have a rather mild action.

The horse-shaped cheekpieces, which also occur with bits of Type 2, are reminiscent of those from Luristan in south-west Iran and related ones found at Nimrud and among votive offerings at Greek sanctuaries on the islands of Samos and Rhodes. These all date to the eighth–seventh centuries.[240] The Luristan bits have single bar canons, like those of our Type 1, but with the loop ends bent in opposite directions; the other bits with horse-shaped cheekpieces from the east have jointed mouthpieces more like those of our Type 2.

Type 2. Bits with jointed canons, passing through the cheekpieces

Under this heading many more bits, with an even greater variety of cheekpiece designs, are grouped together (Figs 3, 6–7). The bits come from tombs in central and northern Italy, their find contexts ranging from the eighth to the sixth century.[241] The bits are made entirely of bronze or iron, or again they combine an iron mouthpiece with bronze cheekpieces. In addition, there are two complete mouthpieces and one fragment thereof from the so-called Contigliano Hoard in Umbria which dates to the first half of the ninth century.[242]

---

[239] See Von Hase 1969, a.o. nos 1, 16 and pls 1–2 (horse-shaped cheekpieces), 63–4 and pl. 6 (double-bird cheekpieces), 68–9, 71–2 and pl. 7 (solid-plaque cheekpieces). Add a.o. finds from the Quattro Fontanili cemetery at Veii: A. Cavalotti-Batchvarova in *Notizie degli scavi di antichità* (Serie 8) 19 (1965), 199 and fig. 100 (single bit from tomb HH II 9); M. C. Franco, P. Mallett and A. Wacher in *Notizie degli scavi di antichità* (Serie 8) 24 (1970), 302 nos 20–1 and fig. 78 (pair of bits from warrior tomb AA 1), and A. Batchvarova and M. Wheeler, *ibid.*, 238 nos 8–9 and fig. 34 (pair from tomb EEFF 6–7); M. Bedello in *Notizie degli scavi di antichità* (Serie 8) 29 (1975), 91 no. 4 and fig. 16 (our Pl. 21; single bit from warrior tomb DE 12–13).

[240] Moorey 1971, 114–18; Muscarella 1988, 155–61; Donder 1980, 28–32, 129f., type II nos 33–8 and pls 6 and 32:B (distribution map); also Littauer and Crouwel 1979a, 118f. Cheekpieces in the form of a galloping horse, identical in appearance to the actual metal ones from Nimrud, Samos and Rhodes, are shown on a few Assyrian reliefs of Sennacherib (704–681); see a.o. Von Hase 1969, 9f. and fig. 1; Littauer and Crouwel 1979a, 123 and fig. 72. Among the votive bronzes at Olympia are cheekpieces of Luristan types, as well as an Italic horse-shaped cheekpiece; see Herrmann, H. V. 1968; 1983, 283–5 and fig. 19; Kilian 1977, 121 and fig. 1.1. and pl. 24: 1; Kilian-Dirlmeier 1985, 247.

[241] See Von Hase 1969, a.o. nos 2, 5, 8, 13–15, 27–9, 36–7, 40–1, 43–4, 46–51, 53–5 and pls 1–5 (horse-shaped cheekpieces), 65–7, 73 and pl. 7 (squarish plaques), 80–3, 85, 87, 90, 94, 106, 108–11, 115 and pls 8–11 (decorated rod-like cheekpieces), 168–70, 172–81, 184, 187–91, 193, 195, 198–207 and pls 17–18 (triple-ring cheekpieces). Add a.o. several finds from the Quattro Fontanili cemetery at Veii: J. Close Brooks in *Notizie degli scavi di antichità* (Serie 8) 17 (1963), 213 no. e and fig. 88 (pair from warrior tomb JJ 14–15); A. Cavallotti-Batchvarova in *Notizie degli scavi di antichità* (Serie 8) 19 (1965), 178 no. 4 and fig. 87 (pair from warrior tomb Z 15 A); *eadem* in *Notizie degli scavi di antichità* (Serie 8) 21 (1967), 124 nos 10–11 and fig. 21 (pair from tomb DD 10–11'A), 146 no. 23 and fig. 35 (our Fig. 6; single bit from tomb EE 10 B), 169 no. 28 and fig. 51 (single bit from tomb FFGG 7–8); M. C. Franco, P. Mallett and A. Wacher in *Notizie degli scavi di antichità* (Serie 8) 24 (1970), 295f. no. 12 and figs 67 and 92 (pair from warrior tomb Z 1 *alpha*; L. Berni Brizio, M. Meagher and M. Pandolfini in *Notizie degli scavi di antichità* (Serie 8) 26 (1972), 212 no. 20 (single bit from warrior tomb Z *gamma*; M. Bedello in *Notizie degli scavi dia ntichità* (Serie 8) 29 (1975), 72 no. 3 and fig. 5 (pair from warrior tomb D 11–12), 146 no. 14 and fig. 52 (single bit from warrior tomb AB 12–13); E. Fabricotti *ibidem*, 170, 175 no. 7 and fig. 68 (single bit from tomb C 18–19). See also finds from the Casa del Fosso cemetery at the same site: Drago Trogoli 2005, 90 and fig. 5: 1–2 (pair from tomb 872), 105 and fig. 14: 29–30 (pair from warrior tomb 871). See further I. Caruso in *Carri da guerra* 280, no. 7 and fig. 8: pair from San Giuliano (Barbarano Romano), Caiolo Tomb B in Lazio.

[242] Von Hase 1969, 37 nos 211–13 and pl. 19; Ponzi Bonomi 1970, 123, 146 nos 77–9 and fig. 10: 10–12; Pare 92, 194.

The mouthpiece of this type of bit is jointed, consisting of two canons, either plain or made of twisted wire, interlocking in the middle. (The latter is also the case on the mouthpieces from the Contigliano Hoard.) The outer ends of the mouthpiece usually pass through holes in the cheekpieces, but sometimes through a ring fastened below the latters' centres, and have loops for ring-shaped or other rein attachments.

When made of bronze, the cheekpieces are often of designs also found on bits of Type 1: stylized horses (sometimes preserved with various dangles), squarish plaques and triple rings; the latter may be elaborated with human figures. Other bits of Type 2 have cheekpieces in the form of decorated rods bent at one end.

Other bronze cheekpieces are rod-like and/or crescent-shaped.[243] Of particular interest are crescent-shaped cheekpieces of openwork design, often with finials in the form of paired horse protomes or volutes. Pairs of bits with such cheekpieces and jointed mouthpieces are known from warrior tombs with vehicular remains in Marche (Pl. 22).[244] Similar bits belong with the ornate vehicle burials of the sixth century at Castel San Mariano in Umbria and Roma Vecchia.[245]

In marked contrast to most bronze bits, the all-iron ones of Type 2 usually have simple, crescent-shaped cheekpieces. Several such bits, single or again in pairs, have turned up in vehicle burials in different parts of central Italy, mostly dating to the seventh–sixth centuries. These include the tomb at Monteleone di Spoleto where the simple iron bits contrast starkly with the ornate, bronze-sheathed chariot (Pls 23, *cf.* Pl. 1d).[246]

---

[243] See a.o. Von Hase 1969, nos 122–6, 141–7 and pls 11–13. The variety of cheekpiece design of Type 2 bits is well illustrated by finds from the Tomba del Trono (tomb 89 in the Lippi cemetery) and various other tombs in cemeteries at Verucchio in Emilia Romagna; see P. von Eles in *Guerriero e sacerdote* 114–17, 119f. nos 134a–b, 135 and figs 36–7 and pls 51–2; Gentili 2003, pls 158 and CCLXXXIII, nos 92–3 (from the Tomba del Trono), also pls 46 (no. 31), 55 (no. 19), 62 (nos 12–13), 65 (nos 5–6), 78 (nos 22–3), 120 (no. 9), 127 (nos 19–21) and 130 (nos 14–15).

[244] Belmonte, tomb 17 (Dall'Orso 1915, 70–7 and ill. p. 37, see also ills pp. 37, 71, 73; Von Hase 1969, 25 no. 296a–b and pl. 21 (*Carri da Guerra 316*, Repertorio no. 54). Belmonte, Tomba del Duce (our Pl. 22. Von Hase 1969, pl. 21, nos 269–70 = *Eroi e regine* 251 cat. nos 436–7). Campovalano, tomb 69 (*Eroi e regine* 82 and fig. 54 and cat. no. 191; D'Ercole and Martellone 2006, 80 and figs 5–6). See also Von Hase 1969, 24f., pls 21–2; Stary 1981a, 265, 464 (W 58B); Buchholz and Wangenheim 1994, 252 and fig. 13a–b (also Von Hase 1969, no. 279 and pl. 22: complete example, with jointed iron mouthpiece, said to be from Chiusi in Toscana); Cahn, D. 1989, no. W 1d (incomplete bit, together with a bronze horse's muzzle belonging to a sixth century warrior burial – no. W 1a–d – reportedly from the Metaponto area in southern Italy); Naso 2003, no. 228.

[245] **Castel San Mariano**, the Tomba dei Bronzi: see Höckmann 1982, 45f. no. 11 and fig. 30: 1–4 and pl. 16: 4–6; A.E. Feruglia in *Carri da guerra* 225 no. 12 and figs 18–19 (cheekpieces and remains of bronze jointed mouthpiece with wire loops fastened at its ends). **Roma Vecchia:** see F. Buranelli in *Carri da guerra* 202 and fig. 10 and pl. 19: 3. See also Macintosh Turfa 2005, no. 111 (bit with differently decorated bronze cheekpieces and jointed iron mouthpiece, and four other such cheekpieces, reportedly from Cerneto near Tarquinia).

[246] Von Hase 1969, 25 n. 5; Crielaard 1996, 257f.; *Antiquità dall'Umbria* 409 no. 18 (our Pl. 23; from Monteleone di Spoleto); also a.o. Benedetti 1960, 450 and fig. 2 (also M. Cycielman in *Carri da guerra* 272 and fig. 6; *Signori di Maremma* cat. no. 3.93: pair from Vetulonia, Tomba del Littore); Camporeale 1967, 24f. and pl. A: 1 (pair from Vetulonia, Tomba del Duce); Falchi 1891, 165 and pl. 14: 10 (pair from Vetulonia, Primo Circolo delle Pelliccie); De Agostini 1957, 23 and fig. 32 (pair from Populonia, San Cerbone chariot tomb); Zevi 1975, 291 nos 66–7 and figs 64–5 (our Pl. 1d) (pair from Castel di Decima, warrior tomb 15); Minto 1921, 33 and pl. 46:5 (pair from Marsiliana d'Albegna, Banditella tomb 1); E. Mangani in *Carri da guerra* 286 no. F and fig. 6, and Mura Sommella 2004–5, 259 and fig. 40 (pair from Capena, San Martino tomb XVI); Annibaldi 1960, 378 no. 17 and fig. 15 (pair from Grottazzolina, tomb 20 in Marche); Percossi Serenelli 1992, 158 no. 35 and fig. 18b (pair from warrior tomb 1 in the Benaducci cemetery at San Egidio di Tolentino in Marche); Sgubini Moretti 1992, 184 and fig. 9c (pair from warrior tomb 31, Monte Penna cemetery at Pitino in Marche). There are also several such bits from the Quattro Fontanili necropolis at Veii; see J. Close-Brooks in *Notizie degli scavi di antichità* (Serie 8) 17 (1963), 213 no. e and fig. 88 (pair from warrior tomb JJ 14–15); A. Cavallotti-Batchvarova in *Notizie degli scavi di antichità* (Serie 8) 19 (1965), 199 no. k and fig. 100 (single bit from tomb HH II 9); A. Batchvarova and M. Wheeler in *Notizie degli scavi di antichità* (Serie 8) 24 (1970), 238 nos 8–9 and fig. 34 (pair from tomb EEFF 6–7). Similar bits are also known from southern Italy; see Pellegrini 1903, 260f. nos 48–9 and fig. 41 (pair from Cumae, Fondo Artiaco tomb 104; see also Crielaard 1996, 256f.; Guzzo 2000, 136 nos 48–9); Gàbrici 1913, 103 and fig. 46 (fragment from Cumae, Osta tomb 14) and 759 (iron bits – not illustrated – from early levels on the acropolis of Cumae); Mingazzini 1938, 914f. no. 1 and pl. 42:12 (single bit from Dea Marica sanctuary at the Garigliano). Note that a pair of simple iron bits has also been reported from the Tomba della Biga at Ischia di Castro (our p. 4 and note 20). Another pair was found in Monte Michele tomb 5 at Veii which contained the remains of a two- and a four-wheeler (Boitani 1983, 546 and pl. 98f.; 2001, 113, 118 no. I.G.8.22. Note that no bridle bits from this tomb are mentioned in *Carri da guerra* 325 (Repertorio nos 152–3). Of note is a single iron bit with plaque-like, V-shaped cheekpieces from Veii, Quattro Fontanili warrior tomb EE 10 B (our Fig. 6): A. Cavallotti-Batchvarova in *Notizie*

The action of this type of bit, with its variously shaped cheekpieces, would be more severe than that of type 1 with its single-bar canons, particularly when the jointed canons are of twisted wire.

Type 3. Bits with jointed canons, linked directly to the cheekpieces

A pair of bronze bits from Vetulonia in Toscana with a jointed mouthpiece and horse-shaped cheekpieces is exactly like those of our Type 2, except for the mouthpiece being fastened on top of the horses' bodies by means of a rivet rather than passing through a hole.[247] The same appears to have been true of two other pairs of bronze bits, which again have horse-shaped cheekpieces. One of these pairs, which are unprovenanced but clearly belong together, is incorporated in a reconstructed headstall of the seventh century in the British Museum, London (Pl. 24).[248]

Type 4. Bits with jointed canons linked to loops on the cheekpieces

In the case of the paired metal bits associated with vehicular remains in tombs of the Golasecca culture in northern Italy, the jointed canons are linked to loops on the rod-shaped cheekpieces. The latter also have loops for bifurcated cheekstraps, while large rings on the ends of the mouthpiece were for fastening the reins. The pair of such bits of iron from the Tomba di Guerriero A with its two-wheeled vehicle at Sesto Calende (Golasecca phase IC/IIA, *c.* 600) has cheekpieces with a knob at the slightly bent upper end.[249] These bits are closely paralleled by an iron pair from the Tomba del Carrettino at Como, Ca'Morta (Pl. 25; Golasecca phase IB, *c.* 700) and by metal bits from early Hallstatt burials north of the Alps.[250] The pair of iron and bronze bits associated with the two-wheeler buried in the Tomba di Guerriero B at Sesto Calende (Golasecca phase IIA, *c.* 600–550) has long narrow, U-shaped cheekpieces (Pl. 26), which can be matched by finds from late Hallstatt and early La Tène contexts, and which are illustrated in Situla Art (see Appendix 1).[251]

These bits would have a strong compressing action on the corners of the horse's mouth, because of the rigid connection between canon and cheekpieces. Such bits would also eliminate wear caused by friction between canon and cheekpieces.[252]

---

degli scavi di antichità (Serie 8), 31 (1967), 146 no. 23 and fig. 25.

[247] Von Hase 1969, 14 and no. 55 and pl. 5 = *Etrusker in der Toskana* no. 85 (from Vetulonia, Circolo degli Aquastrini). Rivets were also used for the mouthpiece-cheekpieces attachment of different types of iron bits of the fifth century in the lower and middle Danube region; see Werner 1988, pls 1–13.

[248] The unprovenanced bronze material in the British Museum (1873.8–20.246 and 247) appears to have belonged to two such headstallls. See Walters 1899, nos 357–8; Von Hase 1969, nos 56–7 and pl. 6; Macnamara 1990, 27 and fig. 26; Dei 1996, 201–3 and figs 4–6.

[249] De Marinis 1975, 216, 259f. nos 3–4 and pl. 3: 3; 1988b, 197; Piggott 1983, 182f.

[250] Bertolone 1956–7, 39 no. 19 (Sesto Calende, Tomba di Guerriero A). Kossack 1956–7, 48f. and pl. 24: 6–7; De Marinis 1988a, 56, 81 no. 138 and fig. 17; 1988b, 183, 197 and fig. 151, and 1997, ill. p. 20 (Como, Ca'Morta, Tomba del Carrettino); also Piggott 1983, 182; Dei 1996, 208; Dei 1996, 208. For related early Hallstatt bits, see Kossack 1954, 119f., 136, type Ib and especially fig. 23: A1 and distribution map 2; Pare 1992, 140 and fig. 101a (distribution map); Koch, J. K. 2006, 182f. Related too is a single bit possibly from the Arnoaldi necropolis, Bologna; see Hüttel 1981, 163 no. 247 and pl. 23, who attributed this bit to his Vadena type (pp. 163–7), named after a find (no. 246 and pl. 23; see also Ghislanzoni 1939, 325f. and fig. 8; Balkwill 1981, 431–3, group 3) from Pfatten/Vadena in the Alpine region. The Vadena type in turn has affinities with bits of the late Urnfield culture in central Europe and the Caucasus. Note also a fragmentary cheekpiece from the Francesco Depot at Bologna, again with parallels of late Urnfield date; see Von Hase 1969, no. 121 and pl. 11; Kossack 1956–7, 49 (for Urnfield parallels, see Kossack 1954, 118f., 136, bit type Ia, and fig. 11: s and distribution map 5); Hüttel 1981, 153f.

[251] Ghislanzoni 1944, 35 and figs 39, 40a–b, 43 and 40 *bis* (reconstruction drawing); Kossack 1956–7, 49 and pl. 24: 5; De Marinis 1975, 229, 233, 259f. and pls 7: 1–6 and 8: 2 (reconstruction drawing of bridled horse). Piggott 1983, 183f. For these bits and their parallels, see Egg 1986b (fig. 5: distribution map); Dei 1996, 208f.; Verger 1996, 650–6; Egg and Eibner 2005, 191, 193; Koch, J.K. 2006, 185–91, 258, also 336 (list 19 no. 43: Sesto Calende, Tomba di Guerriero B).

[252] See Littauer and Crouwel 1979a, 121, type 5 and fig. 69: bronze or iron bits acting on the same principle, from the earlier first millennium in central Anatolia and northwest Iran. Such bits were also used in Greece, their find contexts ranging from the seventh to the fourth century, and – under Greek influence – with ridden horses in southern Italy; see Donder 1980, nos 87–101, type IX; Crouwel 1992, 47, type 3; *Greci, Enotri*

Bits of organic materials

A number of antler-tine cheekpieces are known from sites of the Terremare culture of the Middle and Late Bronze Age (dated to *c.* 1700–1000) in northern Italy. They are rod-like, tapering towards one end and may have plastic or incised decoration (Pl. 171).[253]

These rod-like cheekpieces are singletons, without known find contexts. Whatever their precise dating, there is no overlap with the earliest metal bits found in Italy. Interestingly, the organic cheekpieces have counterparts in settlement and burial contexts in central and eastern Europe, some of which date back to the beginning of the second millennium or earlier.[254]

Antler-tine cheekpieces were used with a 'soft' mouthpiece, made of rope, gut or sinew. The ends of the mouthpiece passed through or were attached to holes in the cheekpieces in different planes from other holes for the bifurcated cheekstrap. Bits with such mouth- and cheekpieces may have been used on harness as well as riding horses.[255] In Bronze Age Italy, a use in driving is perhaps less likely. Other evidence for wheeled transport at that time – in the form of actual disk- and cross-bar wheels from the same and other sites in northern Italy – points to the use not of fast chariots but rather of carts or wagons which did not need bitted bridles for the control of their draught teams (see Chapter III.3). Representations of such vehicles, in one case quite possibly dating back to the third millennium, occur among rock art in the Alpine region of northern Italy, and another can be seen on a stele of similar date from the same area (see Chapter III.1 and Chapter IV.1).

Of note is a single bit from tomb 278 in the Benvenuti cemetery at Este (ancient Atestene) in Veneto, dating to *c.* 650–600. The bit combines a jointed bronze mouthpiece with boar's tusk cheekpieces strengthened by bronze wire. It was found together with other horse gear, and was probably used in riding.[256]

Bits in figured documents

It is often impossible to identify these actual bits on horses in figured documents from Italy. As is amply apparent from the above descriptions, similarly shaped cheekpieces might be used with different types of mouthpiece. The latter, being largely in the mouth, are hard to indicate in two-dimensional representations. Cheekpieces can be recognized in several pictures, from the sixth century onwards. In one instance, a wall painting of the earlier fifth century from the Tomba delle Bighe at Tarquinia, they look rather like straight rods (Pl. 34). Illustrated crescent-shaped cheekpieces are close in form to those of several surviving bronze or iron bits of our Type 2, which has jointed canons. The illustrated examples may represent actual openwork cheekpieces of bronze, such as have been discovered with sixth century vehicular burials at Castel San Mariano and Roma Vecchia. Alternatively, they may represent the much

---

e Lucani nella Basilicata meridionale 139 and 147 cat. nos 2.9.58 and 2.10.65 (warrior tombs 110 and 76, dating to *c.* 550, at Chiaromonte-Sillo la Croce near Taranto). For another such bit, reportedly from Italy, with rod-like crescent-shaped cheekpieces, see Dehn 1980, 327 and fig. 2.

[253] Woytowitsch 1978, 117–19 and pls 52–4; Hüttel 1981, 182–86 and pls 39–41; Werner 1988, 182–5 and pls 39–40; Provenzano 1997, 533, 542–4 and figs 294: H, 295: 21–26, 299: 3–4; Boroffka 1998, 100 and n. 22. For the Terramare culture and its chronology, see a.o. Cardarelli 1993, table XIV; Barfield 1994; and various contributions to *Le Terramare*.

[254] So-called 'Stangenknebel'. See especially Hüttel 1981; Boroffka 1998 (fig. 12: distribution map); Penner 1998, 123–36; also Pare 1992, 16f. (fig. 21: distribution map).

[255] In contrast, the so-called 'Scheibenknebel', combining a 'soft' mouthpiece with discoid cheekpieces made of bone or horn and often studded on their inner faces, were definitely driving bits. 'Scheibenknebel', like the 'Stangenknebel' going back to the beginning of the second millennium or even earlier, are mainly known from the southern Urals-Volga area, with outliers from the area east of the Carpathian mountains and as far south as the Peloponnese in Greece, but not from Italy. For these bits, see the literature cited in Littauer and Crouwel 2001, 233–6.

[256] See a.o. A. M. Chieco Bianchi in *Italia omnium terrarum alumna* 21, fig. 12; Capuis 1993, fig. 18. For this and other single (metal) bits from tombs at Este, see also Dei 196, 205–7. There are bits with cheekpieces entirely or partly made of organic material from Eberdingen-Hochdorf and other Hallstatt tombs; see Koch, J. K. 2006, 186, 188, etc.

simpler iron bits with rod-like cheekpieces that have been found in several other such burials. Among the latter bits are a pair from the chariot tomb at Monteleone di Spoleto, where the sheet-bronze decoration of the vehicle itself includes a representation of harnessed horses wearing such cheekpieces (Pl. 23).

The cheekpieces worn by the pair of fourth century terracotta winged horses from Tarquinia (Pl. 68), with their ends sharply drawn in and leaving only a small opening, recall the so-called omega-shaped cheekpieces of actual bronze or iron bits that are attested in different parts of Italy from the fourth century onwards. For example, such bits were found with buried horses at sites in Veneto (Pl. 27).[257] Similar bits were also widely used in other parts of Europe in the La Tène period and later.[258]

These metal bits are early variants of the so-called curb or leverage bit, which combines a single canon or jointed mouthpiece with a rod (the curb) or chain fastened below the horse's chin. When the reins were pulled, the curb was raised to press on the underside of the horse's lower jaw, which is thus compressed between the mouthpiece and the curb. Such bits were clearly designed for horses ridden in warfare rather than draught teams.[259] Their presence on the chariot horses of the Tarquinia pediment sculpture therefore seems unlikely (Pl. 68).

Two of the buried horses from Altino in Veneto were wearing the equivalent of modern so-called stallion or colt bits.[260] These are metal rings that fitted around the lower jaw. With a rope attached to it, the 'stallion bit' is used to lead refractory animals or ones with an inclination to rear up when led.[261] A led horse with what looks like such a bit is depicted on a polychrome ash urn of the late sixth century from Tarquinia.[262]

Other *in situ* finds of 'stallion' or 'colt' bits are known from ancient sites in Hungary and Spain.[263]

Headstall

The actual surviving metal bits, as well as those seen in representations, hung from divided cheekstraps (*q.v.*). This and the other straps belonging to the headstall (*q.v.*) are clearly illustrated on the team of terracotta winged horses from Tarquinia and a pair of life-size stone horse heads from Vulci (Pls 68, 28).[264] Here the two short straps, coming from the crescent-shaped cheekpieces, meet the cheekstrap proper low down on the horse's cheek; at this junction, a half noseband (*q.v.*), going over the front part of the nose only, is also fastened. A throatlash (*q.v.*) passes under the rear part of the jaw. In addition, the Vulci horses also wear a browband (*q.v.*), running across the forehead. Other representations, from the sixth century onwards, usually show similar headstalls, often including a browband (*q.v.*) (Pls 71–72).[265]

---

[257] Gambacurta 2003, 93, 96f. and figs 7a (horse 1) and 6c (horse 2) from Le Brustolade at Altino (see our p. 5 and note 29). At Adria, the remains of such a bit were found with the single horse, the yoked horses having different, simple bits (Frey 1968, 318 and pl. 40: 2; 1976, 172–4 and fig. 2; 1988, 123; Fogolari and Scarfì 1970, 73f. and pls 44–5. For the tomb, see also our p. 5, note 36). For other finds of single such bits from Italy, see Adamesteanu 1970, pl. 40, below, and Frey 1984, fig. 2 (our Pl. 27; from a sanctuary at Rossano di Vaglio in Basilicata); Jacobsthal 1944, 146 and pl. 258d, Oliver Jr. 1968, 13f. and fig. 2, and Frey 1984, fig. 3 (from tomb A at Canosa in Puglia); Krämer 1964 (figs 2 and 3 show one of five omega-shaped cheekpieces and two complete bits, all without provenance); Schönfelder 2002, 251, 253; Cambacurta 2003, 96f.

[258] Anderson 1961, 51–3; Frey 1964 and 1984; Werner 1988, 81–8, 101–6 with pls 37–60 (types XVI and VI); Schönfelder 2002, 251, 253–5.

[259] See a.o. Anderson 1961, 51–3.

[260] Gambacurta 2003, 94–6 (horses 14 and 1) with figs 6b and 7d (horse 1 also had a 'curb' bit). There is another *in situ* find of a ring-bit from tomb 24 at Montefortino di Arcevia in Marche; see Brizio 1899, 689; Cambacurta 2003, 95 and n. 29.

[261] Littauer and Crouwel 1988b. Also information G. Brownrigg.

[262] *Malerei der Etrusker* no. XX. See also a harnessing scene on a ninth century Assyrian relief of Ashurnasirpal II from Niniveh (Littauer and Crouwel 1979a, 326 with fig. 3).

[263] Jerem 1998 (Sopron in Hungary). For finds in Spain, see Mesada Oliver 2004, 179f. and fig. 2; Quesada Sanz 2003, 14 and fig. 1A–C; Lucas Pellicer 2004, 103–5 and figs 2–4.

[264] For the (nenfro) horse heads from Vulci (Camposcala necropolis), see especially Helbig 1963, no. 610; *La Tomba François* no. 86.

[265] Cf. also the headstalls, without indication of bridle bits, of two small ivory horse heads from the seventh century Tomba Barberini at Palestrina (Curtis 1925, 34 nos 56–7 and pls 15: 4–9).

Among the various bronze objects that may be identified as horse gear from tombs of the eighth century onwards, several seem to have belonged to headstall rather than to harness straps. The reconstruction of a bitted headstall in the British Museum, London, provides some idea of how and where such objects may have been fastened (Pl. 24).[266] This headstall includes, apart from a bit of our Type 2 with a jointed mouthpiece and horse-shaped cheekpieces, five discoid strap crossings, each with a raised central point, four pairs of volutes around the edge and a four-legged ring cage at the back. There are also a buckle and a large number of small appliqués, mostly bilobate but sometimes in the form of stylized bird protomes. The latter recur on other horse gear from central and northern Italy.[267]

The practice of decorating headstall straps – of draught and riding horses – was well-known in the Mediterranean and further east in the first millennium. The ornaments are mostly discoid and of bronze.[268] Discs are also often shown at the junction of headstall straps, indicating strap crossings. In Italy, groups of actual discoid strap crossings, with and without pairs of small loops around the edge, have been found, together with paired bits and other horse gear as well as vehicular remains (probably of chariots), in tombs at sites such as Bologna, Tarquinia, Vetulonia and Verucchio.[269] Similar discoid strap crossings are also known from the vehicle burial in the Tomba di Guerriero B at Sesto Calende.[270] These objects compare well to the bronze strap crossings, often referred to as 'Ringfussknöpfe' and 'tuduli', that have been found with bits and other horse gear in Hallstatt tombs.[271] Other bronze strap crossings in the form of crossed tubes, from tombs in different parts of central and northern Italy, also have counterparts in Hallstatt contexts, as well as in Thessaly in northern Greece and in northwestern Anatolia.[272]

Mention should be made here of the pair of elaborate bronze headstalls from Colle del Forno tomb XI at Sferracavallo (ancient Eretum) in Lazio (Pl. 29).[273] The rich tomb inventory contained remains of two vehicles (a chariot and a cart) and has been dated to *c.* 620–580. The headstalls have been attributed to the cart rather than to the chariot, without supporting evidence. They consist of two side pieces with their upper ends shaped as paired horse protomes, a browband and two nosebands, as well as a decorated

---

[266] See p. 46 and note 248. The reconstruction includes one unlikely strap, running from the pollpiece (*q.v.*) to the half-noseband. Cf. the more reliable reconstruction of the two bitted bridles found resting on the Hallstatt wagon from Eberdingen-Hochdorf (Koch, J. K. 2006, 83–7, 177–205, 231–7 and figs 201–2).

[267] See pp. 42–43 and notes 234–236.

[268] See a.o. Crouwel 1992, 49, 73 (mainland and East Greece); Littauer and Crouwel 1979a, 127, 151 (Near East). To mention one explicit representation from Italy, small discs outlining the headstall straps together with larger discs covering the strap crossings can be seen on fragments of sixth century terracotta roof decoration in the form of a pair of mounted horses from Cerveteri (*Italy of the Etruscans* no. 329).

[269] Frey 1969, 38 n. 191 and fig. 12: 15 (Bologna, Benacci Caprara tomb 39); Kilian 1977, 35, 73, 75 nos 56–63 and fig. 10:9–16 (Tarquinia, Monterozzi cemetery, Tomba del Guerriero), also 76f. *s.v.* nos 19–22 (fig. 10) for bronze buttons from this and other tombs in Italy, which belonged with bridle or harness straps; *Etrusker in der Toskana* 191–3 *s.v.* nos 80–1 (Vetulonia, Circolo degli Acquastrini), see also 193–6 *s.v.* nos 79–80, 82–6 (other bronze horse gear, including two pairs of horse bits, from the same tomb); Dei 1996, 200, 209–17; P. von Eles in *Guerriero e sacerdote* 123, 125 *s.v.* nos 140a–f and pl. 56 (Verucchio, Tomba del Trono; also Gentili 2003, pls 158 and CCLXXXI (no. 90), and – for discs from other tombs – pls 63 (nos 15–16), 66 (no. 9) and 79 (no. 25).

[270] Ghislanzoni 1944, 36–8 with figs 43–5; De Marinis 1975, pl. 7: 7–9.

[271] See a.o. Kilian 1977, 75 and nn. 253–7 (references); also Kossack 1954, 115–18 and figs 1 (reconstruction drawing of a headstall), 15: 7–8, 21: C 9, 23: A 6–7, 24: A 14, and distribution map 3; Frey 1969, 38 and n. 91; Guidi 1983, 26–8, 81 (catalogues B 2 and 3); Pare 1992, 140, 156, 346 (types 4–6), 356 (incorrectly called 'rein-knobs') with figs 100: 5–6, 102, 105 and figs 101b, 103 and 106 (distribution maps) and pls 94: B8, 12–13, 120: 2 (the button illustrated in fig. 105: 2 – from Woskowice Male/Lorzendorf in Poland – closely resembles those from Sesto Calende, Tomba di Guerriero B, seen in fig. 105: 4); Dei 1996, 209–13; Koch, J. K. 2006, 191–6.

[272] Kilian 1977, 34, 73, 76 *s.v.* no. 53 and fig. 16:6; Dei 1996, 213 and fig. 10; *Principi etruschi* 360 *s.v.* no. 508 (Bologna); P. von Eles in *Guerriero e sacerdote* 119, 132 *s.v.* no. 153 and fig. 41, left and pl. 61 (Verucchio, Tomba del Trono; also Gentili 2003, pls 157 and CCLXXXII, no. 78); Drago Troccoli 2005, 105 and fig. 14: 21 (Veii, Casale del Fosso tomb 871); Kossack 1954, 117, 120 with figs 11b, 18: C 8 and distribution map 3; see also Frey 1969, 38 n. 191; Kilian 1975, 179 and pls 75: 3 and 96: 3–12 (sanctuary of Enodia at Pherai and Valanida hoard in Thessaly); Kökten Ersoy 1998, 108, 127f. nos UP/B.7–12 and fig. 2a and pl. 6:1–2 (vehicle burial of *c.* 500 in the Balıkesir-Üçpınar tumulus; see our p. 34, note 166.

[273] Johansen 1979, 80 and fig. 19; P. Santoro in *Carri da guerra* 296f. no. 11 and fig. 22; Emiliozzi *ibid.* 300; 2001, 331f. and fig. 27. For the tomb, see recently Emiliozzi, Moscati and Santoro 2007 (fig. 4 and pl. 7b and 8a show the partially reconstructed cart as well as the headstalls); see also our p. 76 and note 51 and p. 85.

frontlet (see below). Originally nailed onto a leather backing, these metal headstalls must have had a purely ceremonial use.

Reins

Reins (*q.v.*) ran from the driver's hands to the head of each horse, where they were attached to the ends of the mouthpiece of the bit – either directly or indirectly by means of metal rings or hooks (see above).

Two methods of handling the reins are in evidence. One is illustrated with the *bigae, trigae* and *quadrigae* taking part in processions and with some of the racing *bigae* and *trigae* (a.o. Pls 70–74). The driver holds the reins in both hands, as was customary in Greece at the time. The other method, illustrated with the majority of racing *bigae* and *trigae*, involves the reins passing through one of the driver's hands before being tied in a knot behind his waist or back (Pls 35, 41–42, 45). The same practice is documented in Egypt and the Near East in much earlier times, and it continued into the Roman Imperial period.[274] In scenes of the Roman racetrack, with *quadrigae* viewed as if from above, the reins may be seen running back from the horses' mouths to be bundled above their backs and then to continue to the driver.[275] Such a bundling of reins is also illustrated with racing *quadrigae* in mainland Greece, the reins presumably sorted into left and right groups, but here they are not tied around the driver's waist.[276]

In some representations from Italy, the reins seem to run directly and in a straight line from the charioteer to the team's mouths. In others, they dip down towards the yoke area, suggesting the presence of metal rein rings known as terrets (*q.v.*). Terrets not only helped to keep slack reins from dangling but may have had a certain pulley effect, since they broke the straight line of action to the driver's hands and gave him greater control. On some of the terracotta revetment plaques showing *bigae, trigae* or *quadrigae*, terrets are explicitly indicated in the yoke area (Pl. 71). How many terrets there were and whether they were actually fastened to the yoke or to the yoke padding or both, remains uncertain. Terrets were a regular feature of ancient chariot harnessing. For example, we see them in mainland Greece with dorsal yokes and four-horse teams, and in East Greece with neck yokes and teams of two horses.[277] Terrets can also be seen in representations of *quadrigae* with a two-horse neck yoke of the Roman Imperial period.[278]

Frontlet

Representations of frontlets (*q.v.*) with driven (and ridden) horses appear to be confined to tomb paintings from the area of Paestum in Campania, dating to the fourth century.[279] Some actual bronze frontlets are known from Toscana and elsewhere. They include a pair of trapezoidal shape from a seventh century tomb at Marsiliana d'Albegna in Toscana (Pl. 30).[280] The frontlets are of trapezoidal shape and were suspended from a browband. They recall bronze frontlets from Samos and Miletus, which are also single-piece and without a hinge (Pl. 147).[281] The subject and style of the relief decoration of the pair

---

[274] See p. 67 and note 363.

[275] See a.o. Junkelmann 1990, fig. 124 (detail of the Great Circus mosaic from Piazza Armerina).

[276] Crouwel 1992, 49.

[277] Crouwel 1992, 50, 73 and pl. 16: 1, 2a–b. Add Braun 1998, no. 104 (explicit rendering on unprovenanced East Greek terracotta revetment plaque).

[278] Junkelmann 1990, fig. 122 (detail of the Great Circus mosaic from Piazza Armerina).

[279] See Pondrandolfo and Rouveret 1992, 102f. (ills 1, 3), 109f. (ills 1, 3), 142 and fig. 37 (= *I Greci in occidente* cat. no. 261 and ill. p. 469), 153 (ills 4–5).

[280] Minto 1921, 270, 272 and fig. 29 and pl. XXXV (Circolo di Perazzetta); Camporeale 1967; Cristofani and Michelucci 1981, 98 and fig. 220; *Etrusker in der Toskana* nos. 138–9.

[281] Donder 1980, 84f., 96f. no. 201 and pl. 20 (our Pl. 147; Samos), nos 202–3, 217 (Miletus) and pls 20–1; Kyrieleis and Röllig 1988 (Samos); see also Crouwel 1992, 51. For bronze and ivory frontlets from different parts of the Near East and from Cyprus, see a.o. Littauer and Crouwel

from Marsiliana d'Albegna point to manufacture in central Italy, whereas the frontlets from Samos and Miletus are probably imports from the Near East.

The design with curving outlines of a pair of probable frontlets found among tomb material of the eighth–seventh centuries at Cretone in Lazio (Pl. 31) recalls more elaborate frontlets from central and northwestern Anatolia (Pl. 148).[282] A decorated frontlet also forms part of the elaborate bronze headstall belonging to Colle de Forno tomb XI with remains of the vehicles at Sferracavallo (Pl. 29; see above). In addition, a pair of decorated bronze frontlets, this time with openings for the animal's eyes, was found – without vehicular remains – in tomb 4461 of the Corso Italia cemetery at Pontecagnano in Campania, which has been dated to the later eighth century (Pl. 32).[283]

Mention may be made here of bronze frontlets, mostly coming in pairs and together with paired breastplates, from recorded or unknown find contexts in southern Italy. They are of a type decorated with a frontal horse's head or, more rarely, a helmeted face or a gorgoneion. These frontlets have no parallels in the Near East but appear to derive from workshops in southern Italy and to date from c. 550 to the fourth century.[284]

A frontlet and breastplate have been identified among the incised decoration of a bronze statuette of a horse, dated to c. 700, from Banditella near Vulci in Toscana.[285] However, this identification is unlikely.

Later on, the Romans used elaborate bronze horse-head frontlets or chamfreins, with openings for the animal's eyes, on their mounts.[286]

There is no evidence, whether figured or material, for the use of blinkers (q.v.) in Italy, before or during the period of the Roman Empire. On the other hand, there are examples (mostly undated) from unknown contexts in Italy of an enigmatic class of metal objects but which has often been regarded as belonging to horse gear. These so-called *Stachelringe* consist of two rings and with sharp prongs in the middle. They were in use for a long time in different parts of Europe, before and during the period of the Roman Empire.[287]

1979a, 125f.

[282] Mari 1996, 307 and pl. 5 (said to be possibly from a round shield); Colonna 1997, 19 and fig. 7. For finds from Anatolia, see Kohler 1995, 74, 80f. nos TumKy 23–24 and fig. 32: E and pls 44: B, 46: C (frontlets found, together with bridle bits, *in situ* on two horses that were buried in the late seventh century in tumulus KY at Gordion); Kökten Ersoy 1998, 108, 127 nos. UP/B.5–6 and fig. 1: e–f and pl. 5: 3 (vehicle burial in the Balıkesir-Üçpınar tumulus).

[283] From the Corso Italia cemetery, tomb 4461 (*Carri da guerra* 311, *Repertorio* no. 8); see Cerchiae 1984; 1985, 31–42 nos 2–3 and figs 2–3 and pls 5–6; *Principi etruschi* no. 342 (L. Minarini).

[284] Where known, the decorative rather than protective frontlets and breastplates come from warrior tombs. See especially Lubtchansky 2005, 84–7, with discusssion of whether this equipment was used on chariot teams or on horses ridden by so-called mounted hoplites (see our p. 58 and note 330); also Jurgeit 1999, nos 189–95 and nos 185, 187–8 (breastplates); *Basileis* 34 with fig. 46 (graphic reconstruction of paired horses with elaborate frontlets and plain breastplates from Braida di Serra di Vaglio in Basilicata). See also Brize 1985, 64 (in a wide-ranging discussion of a highly decorated, sixth century bronze breastplate from the island of Samos). Note that a fragment of a horse-head frontlet of south Italian type was found in the sanctuary of Zeus at Olympia, while two others were acquired at Stemnitsa in Arcadia; see Kunze 1967; Berger 1982, nos B 4 and A 1 (see also 274, 279 and fig. 10: reconstruction of a frontlet on an alive horse); Donder 1980, nos 199–200. See also a pair of incompletely preserved, decorated bronze frontlets-cum-brownbands of unknown provenance and dating to the seventh century (Berger 1982, no. 118; Reussser *et al.* 1988, no. E/38A–B).

[285] D'Ercole and Trucco 1992, 81f. and figs 15–16; Bartoloni 2003, 191.

[286] See a.o. Garbsch 1978, especially 13f. An early representation of such a frontlet, on a stone relief of c. 80 from the Capitoline hill at Rome (Bertoldi 1968, 44 with fig. 5), strongly resembles those among the Gallic trophies depicted on the balustrade of the Athena temple of the early second century at Pergamun; see Droysen 1885, pl. 43; Jaeckel 1965, 115 and fig. 59; Gamber 1978, fig. 312; Donder 1980, 84. For other types of Roman frontlets, see a.o. Heres 1975; Pfrommer 1993, 14 and n. 88 and fig. 8 (horses' headstalls with rhomboid frontlets or 'protometopidia').

[287] See especially Jacopi 1974, 192–5; Adam, A.-M. 1984, *s.v.* no. 119; Sannibale 1988, 222–53; Schönfelder 2002, 273–5.

Whip and goad

Figured documents from the sixth century onwards frequently illustrate the use of whips (q.v.) or short sticks as instruments for urging on the teams of chariots of different types. Sometimes both whips and sticks are seen in the same scenes – with slow-moving as well as racing chariots (Pl. 41).

The whips may be shown with one or two lashes attached to the stock. The short sticks are almost certainly goads (*q.v.*), i.e. pointed for prodding. This usage is actually illustrated in scenes of chariot racing where the drivers are leaning forward and goading their teams. In the wall painting from the Tomba delle Olimpiadi at Tarquinia two of the racing drivers are seen using their goads, while the leading charioteer is holding up his instrument which is both pointed for prodding and carries two lashes for whipping (Pl. 35). Interesting details are also seen on terracotta revetment plaques of the Rome-Caprifico type: short whip stocks, with one or two knob-like finials at the lower end, and one or two lashes, in one case with knots or dangles at their ends (Pl. 71a–b).

The use of goads in Italy is also materially documented, at a time before their first representations. The evidence consists of a number of bronze tubes, with a spike at one end and a socket for the insertion of a wooden rod at the other. The tubes may be decorated and have a length of *c.* 0.12–0.15 m, including the spikes. They come from tombs of the eighth–seventh centuries, mainly at Bologna but there are also some examples from sites in Toscana. (Figure 7 shows the inventory, including a bronze goad and a pair of horse bits of our Type 2, of tomb 34 of the Benacci Caprara cemetery at Bologna.)[288] The use of these metal tubes as goad ends in driving is confirmed by their regular occurrence together with paired bits in tombs. Long goads are illustrated in Situla Art (see Appendix 1), and actual, iron goad-tubes have been found together with remains of wagons in late Hallstatt contexts north of the Alps.[289]

Long goads, for urging on the harness teams as well as directing them, were also used with the High-front type chariots of mainland Greece, whereas whips with one or more lashes are often shown with chariot drivers in East Greece (Pls 139, 141).[290] Finally, whips – but not goads – frequently appear on the Roman racetrack.[291]

7. Use

Until very recently, it was thought that the earliest firm evidence for the use of horse-drawn chariots in Italy dates to the eighth century. Apart from paired bronze bits and bronze goads to help enforce control on the harness teams,[292] the evidence of that date consists of the remains of actual vehicles from tombs at sites in central and northern Italy (see further Chapter V).[293] However, new finds from Lazio in central Italy suggest that chariots were already known in the eleventh–tenth centuries. The finds are two miniature bronze chariot models from tombs at S. Palomba sulla Via Ardeatina on the northwestern slopes of the Colli Albani, not far from Rome. The models were associated with male cremation burials of the end

---

[288] Woytowitsch 1978, 108–11 with pl. 49; Pincelli and Morigi Govi 1975, 460; Tovoli 1989, especially 282f. no. 158; Panichelli 1990, 203f., 203; Krausse 1992, 516, 522 with fig. 1: 3–4. See also Von Hase 1969, figs 2: A–D, 4A, 5A and 6A, showing tomb inventories, mainly from Bologna, which include both goads and horse bits; pl. 5A = our Fig. 7.

[289] Krausse 1992; Koch, J. K. 2006, 87f., 239f., 261f.; *eadem* in *La tombe princière de Vix* 251f.

[290] Crouwel 1992, 51, 73.

[291] See a.o. Junkelmann 1990, figs 122–4, 139, 152.

[292] Von Hase 1969, 53f.; also Stary 1979, 186; 1981a, 42f., 93f., 207; Pare 1992, 192–5. Earlier evidence for metal bits in Italy consists of three (complete or fragmentary) mouthpieces that formed part of the so-called Contigliano Hoard from Umbria and which has been dated to the first half of the ninth century. The mouthpieces are jointed and made of twisted bronze wire, thereby recalling bits of our Type 2 (see our pp. 44–46).

[293] See, conveniently, *Carri da guerra*, Repertorio nos 18–20, 23 (Castel di Decima), 35 (Rome), 38 (Velletri), 39 (Vigna Batocchi), 144–6, 148–50, 157–61, 166–70 (Veii), 207, 210–12 (Narce), 217, 219 and 221 (Bologna), 226 (Verucchio).

of the Bronze and the beginning of the Iron Age (Latial periods I and IIA1 respectively). The chariots, which have a railwork siding and four-spoked wheels, are being restored at the time of writing.[294]

Remains of actual vehicles, identifiable as chariots, become more numerous and widespread in tombs of the seventh and sixth centuries, mainly in different parts of central and northern Italy.[295] The chariot remains are mostly associated with male (warrior) burials, but sometimes with female burials. They may be accompanied by remains of other types of vehicle – two-wheeled carts and, if rarely, four-wheeled wagons (see Chapter V). It is in the seventh century that the first figured documents showing chariots become available, with many more dating from the next century. Evidence for chariots is also provided by some Impasto and Bucchero three-legged vessels of the seventh century. Their elaborate handle attachments are in the form of a standing driver and his two-horse team (Pl. 53).[296]

How would the chariots of eighth–sixth century Italy have been employed? Traces of wear on the horse bits and on some of the surviving metal elements of the vehicles indicate that they had been well used before being deposited in the graves. The frequent, but not exclusive association with military equipment, is suggestive of a role in warfare. Indeed it has been claimed that the first chariots in Italy are not only indebted to Near Eastern and/or Greek models for their their construction and the ways in which their draught teams were harnessed and controlled but also for their – military – use (see again Chapter V).[297]

A resumé of how horse-drawn chariots functioned in military and other contexts in the areas east of Italy is appropriate at this point. In the Near East, from sometime in the earlier second millennium down to the seventh century or later, chariots served primarily as an elevated, mobile firing platform for an archer standing beside his driver (Pls 125–127).[298] Bowcases and quivers of arrows were fixed outside the chariot body, providing reserve long-distance arms. A thrusting spear, axe and shield for man-to-man fighting could also be part of the equipment.

Recent experiments in southeastern Turkey with full-scale reconstructions of ninth century Assyrian chariots have demonstrated that these rear-axled vehicles were so stable that tight corners could be turned.[299] The archer standing beside the driver could quickly fire arrows in all directions, including to the rear, even when the two- or three-horse chariot was moving at considerable speed (up to 28 km per hour) in stony but reasonably flat terrain. The experiments, in which I participated, suggested that ninth century Assyrian chariots did not, as had previously been thought, run along the enemy front line to soften it up. Rather they attacked the enemy line frontally, and at different places simultaneously, firing, turning and getting away quickly enough so as not to offer easy targets to enemy archers. This manoeuvre would be repeated again and again.

There are, however, problems with such tactics. The often sizeable numbers of chariots of the armies in

---

[294] De Santis 2009, 362, 365 (tombs 1 and 2). I am most grateful to Dr A. J. Nijboer for alerting me to these as yet unpublished finds, and to the excavator, Dr A. De Santis, for information. A terracotta wheel model from tomb 1 in the area of the Arch of Augustus on the Forum Romanum in Rome is of similar date (De Santis 2009, 365). The first, fragmentary terracotta models of chariots or carts and/or their draught horses from other sites in central Italy date to the (late) ninth and eighth centuries (see especially Buranelli 1983, 106f.; Iaia 1999, 24, 45; also our p. 25 and note 98, p. 71 and note 9).

[295] See Carri da guerra, Repertorio (passim).

[296] See conveniently, Woytowitsch 1978, no. 157 (our Pl. 53; from Bisenzio, Palazetta cemetery), no. 158 (also from Bisenzio), no. 158A (the so-called Calabresi askos from Cerveteri; also Sciacca and Di Blasi 2003, 32–6 no. 1, cf. 36–8 no. 2); also Leprevost 1977, 7–9 with fig. 7; Reusser et al. 1988, no. E 5; Gran-Aymerich 1999, 385–8; Riva 2010, 167f. and figs 54–5.

[297] See especially Stary 1979, 186f., 190; 1980, 12–17; 1981a, 42–5, 93–5, 156f., 193f., 200, 207, 217, 245, 265, 272, 285f., 305f.; 2000, 215; Saulnier 1980, 65–70, 163. Pare (1992, 212, 218) writes of battle/war chariots, without further specification. A military use is also implied by the title of the great work Carri da guerra edited by A. Emiliozzi.

[298] For what follows, see Littauer and Crouwel 1979a, 90–4, 128–33; also 1983 (= 2002, 53–61) and 1996 (= 2002, 66–74); Crouwel 2004a, 78–84; Spruytte 1983.

[299] The experiments were conducted near Harran in the winter of 2002, as part of the preparations for a television documentary on Assyrian war chariots. The film, directed by Michael Barnes in his series 'Machines time forgot', has been widely shown on Discovery Channel.

the Near East mentioned in contemporary texts were not only limited in their field of operation to level and open ground but, despite the use of protective armour on the vehicle body and the harness team, they remained extremely vulnerable. The wounding of one horse or its laming from an obstacle-strewn field could bring the entire equipage to a standstill, thereby eliminating most of its effectiveness and making the elevated crew an easy target. At the same time, chariots remained too costly to manufacture and maintain, with a team and crew requiring extensive training, to be launched frontally against enemy chariotry. Were such a manoeuvre to take place, one's own chariots would be destroyed as well as those of the enemy. The charge would immediately result in a melée of broken legs and wheels since axles projected as much as 25 cm beyond the wheels (in order to provide stability on fast turns). The chariots of both sides would have to be very accurately spaced and able to maintain that spacing. This would be very difficult: as soon as any horse on either side went down, would the succeeding ranks be able to open up to avoid the fallen, and yet maintain their formation? Similarly, chariots were too vulnerable to be used as a *shock force* against a well-prepared, unbroken line of enemy foot troops. This is, in fact, true of all ancient military vehicles, with the exception of the scythed chariots of the later first millennium in the Near East. Even these were strictly limited to level and open terrain for their field of operation, unlike the modern tank with which chariots have so often, fallaciously, been compared.[300]

All the same, textual sources confirm that in the right circumstances Near Eastern chariots played an important role in warfare.[301] Combining speed with mobility and making use of the element of surprise, they were probably also used to harass an army on the march, and in pursuit of an enemy in defeat.

In the Near East, chariots were not only used in warfare, but also in ceremonies and prepared hunts (*battues*). In the course of the first millennium their military role became largely replaced by mounted troops who had the advantages of greater mobility, the ability to function in more rugged terrain, and of economy of man and animal power.

From the Near East the use of chariots spread in the course of the second millennium to Egypt, where this type of vehicle played a similar active role in warfare and hunting, and to Cyprus and Greece.[302] In Greece, during the period of the Minoan and Mycenaean palaces, the vehicles functioned in a markedly different military way – as a means of transport for warriors who fought not from the vehicle, but dismounted, mainly with thrusting spears and other short-range weapons.[303] There is no reliable evidence for the association between the chariot and the bow which is so well documented in the Near East and Egypt.[304] This limited military role must have been dictated to a large extent by the nature of Greek topography, with its often rough, stony ground, steep gradients and many natural obstacles. This was very different from the flat expanses in parts of the Near East and Egypt. So Greece was not really suited to bow-carrying chariots and even less to the deployment of sizeable numbers at speed. At the same time, the chariot still combined the advantages of relative speed, comfort and prestige, the warriors not having to march on foot.

In Greece, this form of military use of the chariot, as a conveyance for important warriors who actually fought on the ground, appears to have continued into the first millennium, and perhaps as late as the

---

[300] For the limitations of chariotry, see also Powell 1963, 165–7; Schulman 1979, 140–4.

[301] See a.o. Postgate 1980, 89–98.

[302] For Egypt, see Littauer and Crouwel 1985; Herold 2004; Hofmann 2004; cf. Fields 2006, 14–19, 45. For Cyprus, see Crouwel 1985.

[303] For what follows, see Crouwel 1981; 2006, 165–168; Littauer and Crouwel 1996; Dickinson 1999; cf. Fields 2006, 22–38, 46. For the weaponry used, see especially Fortenberry 1990.

[304] The few explicit representations of bows in chariots in Bronze Age and later Greece cannot be taken as reflecting actual practice since most are either strongly orientalizing or actual imports; see Crouwel 1981, 54 and n. 241; 1992, 60 and 33 n. 98. In the case of the hunting scene on a well-known gold ring from Shaft Grave IV at Mycenae, a prepared hunt may be depicted; alternatively, the ring may illustrate no more than an attractive motif borrowed from the Near East; see Crouwel 1981, 121f. no. G 2 and pl. 10; Littauer and Crouwel 1996, 300 n. 19 (= 2002, 71 n. 19).

eighth century.[305] The chariot's role in military transport, it may be noted, is very similar to that described in several passages in Homer's *Iliad*.[306] The fact that Homer makes no mention of bows in connection with chariots, but only of spears and swords, also corresponds with the archaeological evidence from Greece.

The eighth century evidence is ambiguous about whether chariots in Greece still had the same military function as in the Mycenaean period. Among the many scenes of fighting taking place on foot in Attic Late Geometric painting there is only one which involves a chariot (Pl. 135).[307] This is a well-known jug from a tomb in the Athenian Agora, where the role of one of the three vehicles depicted is the same as that proposed for the Mycenaean chariots, i.e. as a conveyance for a warrior who would dismount to fight on foot, while his driver looked after the vehicle and harness team. However, if it is assumed that this chariot crew, seemingly protected by a single checkered shield or corslet, does not consist of two mortals but, rather, of the much discussed Siamese twins known from Homer and Hesiod, the setting would be mythological. If so, this may suggest that the military use of chariots had in actual fact disappeared, as least in Attica, by the eighth century. Another rare example of chariots on a battlefield is provided by an eighth century amphora from a cemetery on the Cycladic island of Paros (Pl. 136).[308] Its painted decoration shows a battle, involving two chariots, riders on horseback and warriors on foot. The chariots only carry a driver, suggesting a similar use as a means of transport. But here again the vase representation may be mythological or generically heroic rather than a depiction of actual contemporary military practice.

According to a widely held view, at some time in the seventh century most of the high-ranking warriors had taken their place in a new military formation – the hoplite phalanx. (It has often been thought that an explicit, early illustration of the hoplite phalanx in action is provided by the Proto-Corinthian Chigi Vase (also called Chigi Olpe) of *c.* 640 which ended up in a tomb at Vulci in Toscana.)[309] Greek hoplites were heavily armed infantrymen, whose equipment included metal helmets, bell-shaped corslets and greaves, double-grip round shields and usually thrusting spears and swords. (The hoplites depicted on the Chigi Vase carry two spears, which are either two javelins or a javelin and a thrusting spear.) Individual combat or fighting in loose formation was replaced by fighting in tight formation – the hoplite phalanx – in which group discipline was a major factor.[310] However, this view was challenged in recent years. It was argued that fighting in tight formation was not essential for the effectiveness of the hoplite equipment, and that 'down to the early fifth century Greek hoplites continued to fight in a quite open formation, interspersed with light-armed troops.'[311] This view in turn has now come in for criticism. Indeed, it has been suggested that the hoplite phalanx already existed in the eighth century.[312]

The representations of chariots in a military setting in Greece, popular as they were in vase painting and other artistic media particularly during the sixth century, must refer to a phenomenon of the past which had assumed a heroic character. While most of the pictures illustrating warriors departing, fighting, waiting or wheeling around are generic, a number show identifiable deities or heroes in the chariots

---

[305] For what follows, see Crouwel 1992, 53–9, 105.

[306] See especially Latacz 1977, 215–23; Singor 1988, part II.1; Van Wees 1994, 9–13 and 137, 140f., 147; also Crouwel 1992, 106f.

[307] For this much discusssed scene, see a.o. Crouwel 1992, 57 with notes 265–6 (references); Papadopoulos 1999, 633–5 (more references); most recently, Dahm 2007; Hurwit 2011, 9.

[308] Zaphiropoulou 2006, 271, 275–7 with figs 1–4, 11.

[309] See a.o. Salmon 1977, 85–92 with figs 1–4; Amyx 1988, 32 no. A 3; Anderson 1991, 18–20; Schwartz 2009, 124–6 and figs 16–18 (including two aryballoi by the same painter, which illustrate hoplite fighting too; see Amyx 1988, 31f. nos A 1–2). But cf. Van Wees 2000, 134–42 with figs 9–11. For (various aspects of) the Chigi Vase or Olpe, see Hurwit 2002.

[310] For hoplite weaponry and phalanx tactics, see especially the contributions by J. K. Anderson, V. D. Hanson and others to *Hoplites* (1991); Schwartz 2009.

[311] See Van Wees 2000, ch. 5; 2004, chs 12–13; also Krentz 2002; 2007, 61–84. The quotation is from Rich 2007, 17.

[312] See Schwartz 2009, especially 143–6, 226–34.

– sometimes from familiar myths.[313] Similarly, the chariots depicted in wedding scenes in Attic and other vase paintings of the later seventh and sixth centuries cannot be taken as reflecting real-life practice. While the chariot-borne wedding party is usually anonymous, the deities seen riding in chariots at the wedding of Peleus and Thetis are identifiable. It is known from both figured and written sources that after a wedding the married couple and their guests drove to the bridegroom's house, not standing in horse-drawn chariots, as the gods did, but seated in mule-drawn, two-wheeled carts (see III.7).

In Archaic and Classical Greece, the chariot was reserved for other occasions, such as religious ceremonies and, in particular, racing with single, unarmed occupants. It may be assumed that similar use was made of chariots in the Greek colonies on the west coast of Anatolia and in Magna Graecia, i.e. southern Italy and Sicily.[314]

To return to central and northern Italy, the claim that chariots played a role in warfare there is largely based on the presence – in several tombs – of both chariot remains and weaponry. The weaponry occurs in different numbers and combinations, and is at first mainly of local forms of bronze or iron spearheads, axes, swords and daggers, helmets and shields. In the course of the seventh century, bronze helmets, corslets and greaves of Greek types were introduced.[315] Most of this equipment is for close-range fighting which would have taken place on the ground and not from moving chariots.

Direct material evidence for a connection of chariots and long-distance weapons is absent. There are a number of bronze arrowheads from the mid-seventh century Tomba Regolini Galassi at Cerveteri which contained two or three burials, accompanied by plentiful other grave goods, including a decorated chariot of our Type III and a four-wheeled vehicle.[316] The precise find circumstances of the arrowheads, their associations and use are unknown. Some of the spearheads found in other tombs with chariot remains may well have belonged to weapons meant for throwing rather than thrusting.[317] Apart from on the ground, these javelins could have been used from a moving or standing vehicle. It may be noted that there are some passages in the *Iliad* where the heroes are described as throwing spears from the vehicle before dismounting to fight on foot, and the same practice is textually documented for later, Celtic Britain.[318] We may also refer here to some late Mycenaean and Geometric vase paintings from mainland Greece where the shield-bearing passenger in the chariot is holding two spears rather than one – quite possibly javelins.[319] A couple of Roman coins of *c.* 50 from France show warriors brandishing single spears in 'Celtic' chariots (Pl. 169; see Appendix 2).

It has been claimed that the metal spearheads, thought to belong to thrusting spears of over four meters long and found together with vehicular remains in seventh–sixth century tombs in Marche (ancient Picenum), could only have been used from moving chariots.[320] Such a use, which has also been postulated for thrusting spears and chariots in Late Bronze Age Greece and further east, can probably be discounted on purely practical grounds. A thrusting spear, in contrast to a javelin, would have been difficult to use from a (fast-)moving chariot since, apart from it being a close-range weapon, there would have been the difficulty of taking aim. Besides, once the spear had struck home, the user would have

[313] See Moore 1971; Carpenter 1986, 104–17; Crouwel 1992, 59f.; Makanakidou 1994 (many illustrations); Sinos 1994, 101–12.

[314] See Crouwel 1992, 60–5, 74.

[315] For a comprehensive review of military equipment, and changes therein, in ninth–sixth century Italy, see Stary 1981a; also 1979; 1981c; 2000; D'Agostino 1990. Some elements, and particularly shields, were not for active use but for display.

[316] For the arrowheads, see Pareti 1947, 299f. nos 265–75 and pl. 39; Saulnier 1980, 52f. For the vehicles, see our pp. 19–20 and note 64, pp. 89–90 and note 8.

[317] For javelins, see Stary 1980, 12, 16; 1981a, 265, etc.

[318] See a.o. Wiesner 1968, 27f., 95f. For the Celtic practice, see a.o. Anderson 1965, 350f.; 1975, 177; Piggott 1983, 234f.

[319] Güntner 2000, nos. 24A and 24C and pls 7: 1a–d and 8: 1a–b (Tiryns); Crouwel 1992, 55 and pl. 7: 1–2 (Attica).

[320] Stary 1980, 12, 15f.; 1981a, 94f.

had to release his grip immediately and thus lose his weapon, or risk being dragged from the open rear of the vehicle.[321]

With regard to other possible sources of information on a military role for chariots in Italy, texts written by later Roman and Greek authors frequently refer to warfare in Italy at the time of the (Etruscan) kings and the Republic of Rome, but usually do not mention vehicles as being involved.[322] Clearly, not only the Romans of that time but also other Italic peoples relied on infantry and, to varying degrees, on mounted troops (for the latter, see Chapter V). When wheeled vehicles are mentioned – in the battles at Sentinum in Umbria (in 295), Telamon in Toscana (in 225) and Clastidium in Emilia Romagna (in 222) – they belong to invaders: Gauls, i.e. Celtic tribes.[323] Unfortunately, the texts yield no information on what these vehicles looked like or on their numbers. As to the way in which the vehicles were employed, Livy, in his account of the battle at Sentinum (10.28–30), refers to a sudden attack by Gauls with two types of vehicles (the terms used are *essedum* and *carrus*) on the mounted troops on the Roman left wing. Though Livy's account provides no details of their tactics, the headlong attack clearly took the Romans by surprise, quite probably because of their unfamiliarity with military vehicles. This would support the view that chariots were rarely put to active use in battle in Italy.

Yet another possible source of information on the use of chariots for military purposes in Italy is figured documents. The first such document to be considered here is in fact the earliest chariot representation currently known to have been made in Italy. It is an amphora by the Painter of the Heptachord, an artist who has been named after one of his other vase paintings (Pl. 46).[324]. This vase painter probably worked at Cerveteri around 675. The two-horse chariot depicted on the amphora has an open-rail siding and carries a driver holding reins and a goad. The vehicle is probably stationary, as a large impressive looking male figure is mounting the vehicle. The man is brandishing a sword in his raised right arm, surely to display his prowess and not with the intention to stab the unsuspecting driver in the back. No doubt the picture has narrative intent, drawing inspiration from Greek mythology and iconography, like other works by the same painter.[325] While the sword with its hilt ending in two curls is of the Italic, so-called antenna type,[326] the chariot is reminiscent of the Greek Rail type.

The vehicle on the amphora by the Painter of the Heptachord calls to mind another early chariot representation made in Italy. This is on an incised Etruscan Bucchero jug, probably dating *c.* 650–625 (Pl. 51).[327] Here, the two-horse vehicle is again of light, rail-type construction. It also carries an unarmed driver and is at a standstill or moving slowly. In front of the chariot, two men, armed with thrusting spears and protected by crested helmets of Greek type and by round shields, are locked in combat on the ground.[328] In between these heavily armed men and the vehicle, and partly beneath the hooves of the harness team, lies an archer on his back, still stretching his bow but clearly defeated. Behind the chariot there is an unarmed rider on a galloping horse, rendered at a smaller scale and suspended in the air. He is followed by two larger horses without riders and in a quiet pose. There is a conspicuous lack

---

[321] Littauer and Crouwel 1983 (= 2002, 53–61).

[322] See various contributions to *A Companion to the Roman Army* (especially Rich 2007 and Rawlings 2007) and to *The Cambridge History of Greek and Roman Warfare* vol. II; also Gage 2008; Roth 2009, chs 1–8.

[323] See a.o. Anderson 1965, 350; Piggott 1983, 230f., 234f. See also our p. 112 and note 24. According to Polybius (2.28–9), at Telamon (modern Talamone) two kinds of vehicle (called *hamaxa* and *synoris* in Greek) were used by the Gauls and stationed on the wings, but they seem to have played no part in the fighting. Note that Gauls had joined forces with Samnites in the battle at Sentinum.

[324] See p. 23 and note 86.

[325] See Martelli 1984; 1988; 2001, 2–7. The large-scale figures recall those appearing in mythological scenes in Proto-Attic vase painting; see a.o. Schefold 1993.

[326] See especially Bianco Peroni 1970, 112–25 and pls 45–51; Von Hase 1992, 240f.; Naso 2003, *s.v.* no. 181.

[327] See p. 23, note 87.

[328] A fragment of another, unprovenanced Bucchero jug shows a similar crested helmet and a shield(?) lying on what may well be a battlefield (Regter 2003, no. 134).

of coherence between the various motifs, defying any attempt to explain them as part of a single scene. However, the chariot seems to be associated with the two men fighting on foot, suggesting a military function for the vehicle. If so, the chariot's role would have been the same as that of the Rail chariots depicted on late Mycenaean vases of *c.* 1100. As previously mentioned, such a role is also described in the *Iliad*.

One of the warriors on the Etruscan Bucchero jug would have dismounted from his vehicle, the driver awaiting his return from the battlefield. It has recently been suggested that the other warrior is, in fact, a so-called mounted hoplite who, accompanied by an assistant known as a 'squire', used his mount only as a convenient means of transport to and from the field of battle where he left his horse in the care of the unarmed 'squire'.[329] In Greece, this military practice is frequently illustrated during the later seventh and sixth centuries, and it is quite possibly first hinted at in an Attic eighth century Late Geometric vase painting.[330] The practice appears to derive from the tradition of military chariot driving in Greece – the warrior and his driver having transferred to horseback.[331] In the case of the Etruscan Bucchero jug, it is doubtful whether the rider on the galloping horse seen directly behind the chariot can be identified as a 'squire'. On this vessel, no bowcases or quivers are shown attached to the body of the single chariot, and the relationship between the vehicle and the fallen archer remains unclear. The recent suggestion that the archer is actually being run down by the chariot is unlikely.[332] Rather, the position of the archer calls to mind the 'enemy beneath the team's hooves', a well-known theme in the Near East and Egypt. Its first, and probably only, appearance in Greece is on a stela from Shaft Grave V at Mycenae. Wherever the theme appears, it must be taken as merely symbolic of victory.[333] The position of the defeated enemies, including the archer on the Etruscan Bucchero jug, is not to be read literally, since horses and other equids avoid where possible stepping on bodies for fear of damaging their own limbs.

In any case, the Etruscan Bucchero jug provides no evidence for fighting *from* a chariot in Italy. The question is therefore whether this representation and the earlier one on the amphora by the Painter of the Heptachord reflect the adoption in Italy of Greek Rail-type chariots and their traditional military use. This is presumably not the case. More likely, the two vase representations reflect the influence of Greek artistic models and provide no more than a generally heroic ambiance rather than a literal reading. The same is probably true of two other figured documents, both made in Italy in the sixth century and showing chariots in a military setting. One is a decorated terracotta stand from Poggio Civitate (Murlo) in Toscana (Pl. 52).[334] In an incompletely preserved frieze, modelled in relief, we see a row of marching warriors with their single spears raised for attack, and a two-horse chariot, apparently of our Type II, coming towards them. The vehicle, which carries only an unarmed driver, is surely not going to join combat but may have brought a warrior (not shown) to the battlefield.

The other figured document, an Etrusco-Corinthian black-figure jug from Cerveteri, recalls the earlier Etruscan Bucchero jug in that four (not two) warriors are shown locked in combat with spears, in the presence of a chariot (of uncertain type) carrying an unarmed driver, and two men on horseback.[335]

---

[329] Brouwers 2007, 312 and fig. 9.

[330] See especially Crouwel 1992, 58f. and pl. 31: 2 (Late Geometric Attic neck-amphora, Buffalo Museum of Science C 12847); Moore 2006 40–5 and fig. 11 (the same vase, attributed to a painter from the Workshop of Athens 894); also Brouwers 2007, 309–17 (arguing – unconvincingly – that the double-grip hoplite shield was specifically developed for 'mounted hoplites').

[331] Note that in the Near East the first mounted warriors, shown on Assyrian palace reliefs of the ninth century, are also clearly derived from the two members off a chariot crew; see Crouwel 1992, 58–9 and pl. 32: 1–2.

[332] Brouwers 2007, 313. Even more unlikely is the view that the Bucchero jug bears a depiction of the stealing of a herd of cattle (Jannot 1995, 131).

[333] See Littauer and Crouwel 1979a, 32f. and fig. 3 (the so-called Standard of Ur), 62f.; Crouwel 1981, 119–21 with pl. 37 (Mycenae stele no. S 3).

[334] See p. 18 and note 54.

[335] See p. 23 and note 87.

Strong Greek artistic influences are apparent on an incompletely preserved and worn Italian-made ivory plaque of the later seventh century from Montefortini, Comeana di Carmignano, in Toscana (Pl. 56).[336] It shows Heracles wearing his lion skin and stretching his bow inside a chariot of our Type IV. Heracles is accompanied by his charioteer Iolaus who, like the impressive-looking man on the amphora by the Painter of the Heptachord, is mounting the vehicle while at the same time holding the reins and a long goad. (It has been suggested that Athena, Heracles' protector, was shown beside the two-horse harness team.)

A chariot-borne archer is depicted on a sixth century Etruscan black-figure jug by the Tityos Painter, possibly from Vulci (Pl. 48).[337] This time it is Apollo in a chariot, possibly an inaccurate rendering of our type I, which is drawn by winged horses. The god, accompanied by a dog and a griffin, is aiming at the fleeing Tityus and his wife. Here and in the case of the ivory plaque we have to do with Etruscan representations showing local types of chariot as part of strongly Greek-inspired mythological scenes. It may be noted that in Greece Heracles is also sometimes depicted drawing his bow from a chariot, while some fifth century silver coins minted at the Greek colony of Selinus in Sicily again depict Apollo in this role, accompanied by his sister Artemis.[338] None of these representations can be taken as depicting an actual practice, whether in Italy or Greece. In both countries, the bow-and-arrow was certainly used, but on the ground and, albeit much less frequently, on horseback (see Chapter V).[339] There are other seventh-century pictures of chariot-borne archers from central Italy but these are of less relevance here, as they appear on imports from the eastern Mediterranean.[340]

Altogether, there is no convincing evidence that chariots in Italy – or Greece – ever played an active role in battle, with warriors fighting *from* them, as they did in the Near East. This may to a large extent be due to differences in the terrain. Italy, like Greece, has much rough, stony ground and many natural obstacles. In both countries there is only limited ground for large-scale deployment of chariotry in the Near Eastern manner, with the exception of wide plains such as in the Po valley. As for the vehicles themselves, most chariots in Italy were not suited to carrying an archer standing beside the driver. According to both the material and figured evidence, the chariots of the most common Type I (as well as those of its variant, Type II) were only wide enough for the driver, who might be accompanied by a passenger standing behind him on the U-shaped floor. In addition, chariots in Italy, as in Greece, usually had their axle placed centrally under the floor, which would have offered a much less stable platform from which to shoot than the rear-axled chariots of the Near East. Moreover, there were no quivers of arrows or bowcases attached to the chariot's body.

If the chariot had a military function in Italy, it would have been the same as that in Greece – as a military transport for elite warriors, a use adapted to the nature of much the terrain. Such a use may be hinted at on the figured documents discussed above. In addition, it has often been assumed on the basis of the many other figured documents with chariot and warrior imagery of the later seventh to earlier fifth centuries. The representations begin with Etruscan carved ivory pyxides, ostrich eggs and fragments of another Bucchero jug, all dating from the later seventh century (Pls 57, 59, 50), and continue with Etruscan black-figure vase paintings and other two-dimensional representations, in particular on numerous terracotta revetment plaques (Pls 70–71, 73).[341]

---

[336] See p. 21 and note 75.

[337] *CVA* Bibliothèque Nationale 1, IIIF, pls 28: 5, 31: 1–4 (no. 171); Ducati 1932, 17f. and pl. 19: below; Hannestad 1976, 59 no. 35.

[338] Littauer 1968; Carpenter 1986, 73f. (Attic black-figure vase paintings); Franke and Hirmer 1964, pls 66–8 (coins from Selinus); see also Crouwel 1992, 60.

[339] For the use of bows in hunting in early Italy, see Camporeale, 88, 96, 99, 101.

[340] See p. 26, note 111. One of the chariots seen on a Cypro-Phoenician bowl from the Tomba Bernardini at Palestrina (Woytowitsch 1978, no. 225 and pl. 47; Markoe 1985, no. E2) and the incompletely preserved ivory plaque from the same tomb.

[341] For the terracotta plaques, see also Winter, N.A. 2009, index *s.v.* chariot procession.

These figured documents usually show slow-moving chariots, accompanied by varying numbers of men on foot and sometimes also on horseback, all taking part in what look like parades of some kind. There is considerable variety in the basic content of processional imagery. Military equipment is often included, but at the same time rarely is everybody armed. To illustrate this variety we may describe two processional friezes of the Rome-Caprifico type of terracotta revetment plaques and represented on the nearly complete roof of a temple at Caprifico near Cisterna di Latina in Lazio. These friezes are particularly interesting since they show no less than three different types of chariot as part of the same parades (Pl. 71a–b).[342]

One scene includes two chariots of Types I and III, drawn by three winged and two wingless stallions respectively, moving slowly to the right (Pl. 71a). The procession is led by a long-haired warrior on foot, wearing a crested helmet, a bell-shaped corslet over a short tunic, greaves, and carrying an upright spear and a curved trumpet. Behind him comes the *triga* – a chariot of Type III – which is driven by a probably female figure with long hair, wearing a cap and a long garment. The charioteer is holding the reins, a whip and a spear which is resting inside the chariot at an oblique angle. A long-haired warrior, again wearing a crested helmet, a bell-shaped corslet over a short tunic, and greaves, is stepping into the chariot. Next is the *biga* – a chariot of Type I – which is driven by a similarly equipped warrior, except that he is wearing a helmet with several attachments. This charioteer is holding the reins and a whip. Beside the harness team walks a long-haired, bare-headed man, wearing upward-pointing ankle-boots (known as 'calcei ripandi'); the man carries an upright spear and a staff with one curved end (like the Roman *lituus*) over his shoulder.

The companion frieze includes two chariots of Types II and III, drawn by two wingless and three winged horses respectively, moving slowly to the left (Pl. 71b). At the head of the procession walks a warrior wearing a crested helmet and greaves and carrying a round shield and an upright spear. Another warrior, wearing a crested helmet, a bell-shaped corslet over a short tunic, and greaves, is mounting the *triga* – a chariot of Type II; he is holding the reins, a whip and a spear, which is again resting inside the chariot at an oblique angle; a sword in a scabbard appears to be suspended at his waist. Beside the harness team walks a long-haired man, wearing an untied cap with a strap hanging down and 'calcei ripandi'; his left arm rests on the horses' backs, with the hand guiding reins, while with his raised right arm he holds a spear with the head pointing backwards. Next comes the *biga* – a chariot of Type III – with its unarmed, probably female driver with long hair, wearing a long garment and holding the reins and a whip. Beside the harness team walks another long-haired man, bare-headed and wearing 'calcei ripandi'; he is looking back while guiding the reins with his left hand; with his raised right arm he is again holding a spear pointing backwards.

These and other processional scenes present a complex mixture of Italic and Greek elements. With regard to the chariots, they are of the local, if Greek-inspired Types I, II and III. Quite often an armed man is seen mounting the vehicles, as is also the case on the much earlier amphora by the Painter of the Heptachord and the ivory plaque from Montefortini, Comeana di Carmignano (Pls 46, 56). In the processional scenes, the heavily armed man is strongly reminiscent of the 'departing hero' (sometimes identified as Amphiaraus), or 'mounting hoplite', seen in various Greek artistic media of the later seventh–sixth centuries.[343] It seems certain that this is another theme adopted from Greek iconography.

Indeed some of the armed men seen mounting chariots, going on foot, or on horseback, look like Greek hoplites, with their bronze helmets of Corinthian type, bell-shaped corslets and greaves of the same

[342] See p. 10, note 17. See especially Winter, N.A. 2009, 323f., 358–60, 368f. nos 5.D.1.e–f, 5.D.3.b with ills 5.11.1–2, 5.15.1 and fig. 5.22 (Roof 5–8); Crouwel 2010, 123, 128; Lulof 2010a, 34–40; 2010b, 84–90 (moulds 3 and 4); also Lubtchansky 2010, 140–67.

[343] See especially Wrede 1916; Krauskopf 1984; Serneels-Hofstetter 1992; Winter, N. A. 2009, index *s.v.* departing hero. For an early representation, on a Middle Proto-Attic lid (*c.* 675–600) from the Ceramicus at Athens, see Kübler 1970, 437–40 and pls 17, below and 18, above.

material, and a single (thrusting) spear. Other warriors are shown with Italic (horned) helmets, axes, or large knives with a curved blade, or with a combination of these. Among the non-military equipment, some is also clearly not Greek but local, such as the curved staff (in Rome known as *lituus*) and curved trumpet. The garments and caps worn by unarmed men and women are also of local types. The heavily armed men seen mounting chariots have sometimes been described as *apobates*, a term known from Greek literary texts and inscriptions.[344] According to these sources, races were held in Athens and elsewhere, in which heavily armed men jumped on and off moving four-horse chariots large enough to accommodate them and and their drivers standing side by side.[345] The *apobates*-race, which is most graphically illustrated on the Panathenaic frieze of the Parthenon at Athens, must ultimately derive from the military use of chariots that was typical of Greece, i.e. as conveyances for warriors who fought dismounted. However, there is no evidence that this practice was ever adopted in Italy. Running warriors and a slow-moving chariot can be seen on the fragments of a Bucchero jug (Pl. 50), but here the men are not running alone but in single file.[346]

Much has been written about the Italian-made processional scenes and their meaning.[347] They represent not only a mixture of indigenous and Greek elements, but also of the real and unreal. This is well illustrated by the presence of chariots with wingless and winged draught horses in the same parade. And what are we to think of presence of Heracles with the Cretan bull and the Nemean lion, in processions depicted on terracotta revetment plaques of *c*. 560–550 from Acquarossa and Tuscania in Toscana (Pl. 74)?[348] Another parade, on plaques of the Veii-Rome-Velletri roof system, involves a *triga* and a *biga* and is led by a figure on foot, who with his brimmed hat and particular type of staff resembles the god Hermes-Turms.[349]

Equally difficult to interpret is the presence of female figures as chariot drivers or passengers on revetment plaques of the Veii-Rome-Velletri, Rome-Caprifico and Palestrina roof systems (Pls 70–71, 73). There is nothing obviously divine about these figures and their identity must remain uncertain.[350] There is clearly not one simple, correct 'reading' of the processional scenes. At any rate, it is clear that Greek myths and images offered a resource to Italic peoples which could be adapted in various ways to local needs.[351]

As already mentioned, in Greece the use of chariots as military conveyances had probably ceased by *c*. 700, if not earlier. In different parts of Italy, in the course of the seventh century, the Etruscan and other polities adopted weaponry characteristic of Greek hoplites, such as the bronze bell-shaped corslet and greaves. It is not altogether clear how this Greek weaponry was integrated into the existing warrior

---

[344] See a.o. Torelli 2001, 315f. An *apobates* has also been identified on grave stele no. 61 from Bologna (see Bonaudo 2000–3, 106f. and fig. 4; for this stele, see also our p. 24, note 93.

[345] See Crouwel 1992, 56 (and bibliography in nn. 253–4); more recently, a.o. Müller, S. 1996; Reber 1999.

[346] See Camporeale 1993, especially 13–19.

[347] See especially Chateigner 1989; Jannot 1989, 120–6; D'Agostino 1991; Bartoloni 1992a; 1993, 271–4; Torelli 1992 (= 2007, 87–121); 2001, 312–19; Menichetti 1994, 92–102; Von Mehren 1997, 226f. (suggesting – on no good grounds – that the processional scenes on the terracotta revetment plaques are of Near Eastern origin); Lubtchansky 2010, 140–67.

[348] See, recently, Strandberg Olofsson 2006, and figs 12.1–2; Winter, N. A. 2009, 231, 233, 235, 250, 266f., 269f., 275, 277, 580 and ills. 4.8.2, 4.8.4, 4.10.1–2 and figs 4.15, 4.19 (Acquarossa Roofs 4–5 and 4–9, Tuscania Roof 4–6); also Von Mehren 1997, 225f.; Torelli 1992, 263f. (= 1997, 104, 106); 2001, 315f.

[349] Winter, N. A. 2009, 362f., 367 nos 5.D.2.a and 5.D.3.a and ills. 5.13.1, 5.14.1 and fig. 5.20 (Roof 5–7).

[350] See especially Torelli 1992, 252–60 (= 1997, 91–101); 2001, 313; Winter, N. A. 2009, 364 and 369 (Veii-Rome-Velletri: female passengers; see our p. 10, note 16), 360 (Rome-Caprifico: probably female charioteer; see our p. 10, note 17), 336 (Palestrina: female charioteer; see our p. 10, note 19; Lubtchansky 2010, 144, 146, 163). The presence of a female chariot passenger on a revetment plaque from Acquarossa (our Pl. 74) is not universally accepted (see a.o. Torelli 1992, 264 = 1997, 104; Strandberg Olofsson 2006, 126f.; Winter, N. A. 2009, 267, description of plaque 4.D.4.b, ill. 4.8.2 and fig. 4.15).

[351] Osborne 2001, especially 290. For the reception of Greek myths and images in central Italy, see also a.o. Hampe and Simon 1964; Krauskopf 1974; Martelli 1984a and 1988; Camporeale 1989; Menichetti 1994, especially 4–90; *Le myth grec dans l'Italie antique*.

equipment, which included non-Greek weapons such as axes and large knives with a curved blade. Apart from Greek imports such as the Proto-Corinthian Chigi Vase, local illustrations of what looks like a hoplite phalanx begin to appear before 600, with more dating to the sixth century. Here again it is difficult to say to what extent the Italian-made representations can be read literally or in fact reflect Greek artistic influence. Indeed, it has been much debated whether the hoplite phalanx was ever adopted in central Italy (as it probably was in the Greek colonies in the south) as the standard tactical formation. However this may be, the adoption of Greek weaponry in central Italy may not have involved radical changes in fighting methods, let alone in the existing clan-type organisation under aristocratic leaders.[352]

The question remains whether such leaders used chariots to go to and from the battlefield, as has often been suggested.[353] We have noted earlier (see Chapter II.1) that some of the chariots of Types I and II illustrated in processional scenes on sixth century terracotta revetment plaques, and on painted vases bear decoration resembling the sheet bronze decoration of actual chariots of type I that were buried in central Italian tombs dating to the same century (Pls 43–44, 71a). The decoration which they have in common includes a palmette on the front breastworks and a boar-headed socket for the draught pole where it emerges from under the vehicle body. The actual bronze-decorated chariots were certainly prestige vehicles, offering room for only one person, and were too heavy to move at anything but a slow pace. One of these ornate type I chariots, from Ischia di Castro in Toscana (Pl. 7), was buried along with its harness team of two horses, one of which was found with a bridle bit still in place. It has been suggested that this chariot had been especially made for burial.[354] This is unlikely in view of the repairs that have been noticed on the even more ornate, entirely bronze-clad chariot of the same type from a contemporary tomb at Monteleone di Spoleto in Umbria (Pl. 8). The evidence indicates that even this cumbersome conveyance was repeatedly used in its lifetime.[355] It must be the case that such magnificent one-man chariots were prestige possessions of important individuals, like the supposed aristocratic clan leaders mentioned above. The vehicles did not travel far or over rough ground – and certainly not all the way to and from a battlefield – but must have been used on special occasions. (The important individuals riding in them were mostly men, but sometimes also women, to judge from the character of the burial goods.)

A ceremonial function may already be assumed for the decorated chariots buried in rich tombs of the seventh century at Vulci, Populonia and other sites in central Italy.[356] This use continued into the sixth century, and later when vehicle burials became rare.

There is hardly anything military about the chariots in figured documents of the fifth century and after. Apart from chariot racing, which is depicted from the sixth century onwards (see below), the often single male figures standing in chariots and their entourage on foot or on horseback appear to be engaged in purely peaceful activities. An unusual, helmeted figure in a chariot of uncertain type is painted on the wall of the Tomba Querciola I at Tarquinia (Pl. 38).[357]

To a large extent the iconography now appears to be local and not Greek-inspired. The chariot images occur mainly on funerary monuments from central and northern Italy and include stone sarcophagi, funerary

---

[352] See especially Stary 1979, 191–7; 1981a, 130–7, 307–9 D'Agostino 1990; Spivey and Stoddart 1990, 127–39; Jannot 1989, 1991, 1995 and 2007; Cornell 1995, 183–90; Rawlings 2007; Rich 2007.

[353] So a.o. d'Agostino 1990, 73f., 81; Colonna 1997, 15–17. Stary (1980, 9f., 15f.; 1981a, 45, 95, 125, 156) assumed that active 'Near Eastern' military use was replaced by the 'Greek' way with the introduction of the hoplite phalanx, c. 650. Pare (1992, 195, 212, 218) speaks of battle/war chariots, without further specification. A military use is also implied by the title of the great work *Carri da guerra* edited by A. Emiliozzi.

[354] Boitani 1985, 220; 1987, 89.

[355] Emiliozzi 1991, 110; 1997, 183; Bonante and Emiliozzi 1991, 53.

[356] So also Colonna 1997, 17–22.

[357] See p. 25, note 105.

stelae, cinerary urns, as well as tomb paintings (Pls 61–67).[358] Both these and other figured documents also illustrate female figures in carts, seated alone or with their drivers (see below and Chapter III.7).

All of these representations have frequently been interpreted as showing the journey of important individuals to the Underworld, while at the same time reflecting contemporary life.[359] Indeed a painting in the Tomba Golini I at Orvieto in Toscana, which according to its inscription belongs to a high official, shows the dead man in his chariot, accompanied by a death demon (Pl. 39).[360] On the grave stelae of the fifth and fourth centuries from Bologna, chariots as well as carts may also be accompanied by winged or other death demons, emphasizing the funerary and supernatural character of the drive. In addition, the draught horses may have wings (Pl. 61), as in some earlier, non-funerary representations where they appear together with chariot teams of wingless horses (see above).[361] A death demon also appears in a scene on an Etruscan sarcophagus of the later fourth century from Vulci (Pl. 66).[362] The scene shown here is of a bearded man, standing alone in a chariot and accompanied by two others on horseback, meeting three women who are seated side by side and behind their driver in a cart. Behind the cart are two figures on foot: a woman holding a jug and a bearded man with a mallet; he is clearly Charun, the guardian of the Underworld. Behind the horseman is a leafless tree and under the forelegs of the chariot horses a rock. This scene has been interpreted as the reunion of an important man, accompanied by his sons, with his wife and her servants on his journey to the Underworld. According to another interpretation, the three (motionless) female cart passengers are divine figures from the Underworld awaiting the arrival of the dead man.[363]

There is also the somewhat earlier sarcophagus of Ramtha Viśnai, wife of Arnth Tetnie(s), again from Vulci.[364] The couple is named in the accompanying inscription and shown lying down together on the lid of the sarcophagus. One of the short sides shows a bearded man, presumably Arnth Tetnie(s), mounting his chariot, while another male figure holding a curved staff stands beside the harness team (Pl. 65). On the opposite short side of the sarcophagus, a cart carrying two seated women (one of them probably Ramtha Viśnai) and their driver are depicted, along with a female death demon (Vanth) holding a snake in either hand (Pl. 109). The elaborate scene on the front side, involving a married couple on foot (presumably Ramtha Viśnai and Arnth Tetnie(s)) and various attendants, has been interpreted in different ways. Elements explicitly referring to the Underworld are absent here.[365]

Several other third century sarcophagi, from different sites in central Italy, show on one of the long sides a procession of men in their chariots, accompanied by people on foot. These may include attendants carrying a bundle of rods (in Rome known as *lictores* and *fasces*) and one or more death demons (Pl. 67).[366]

Explicit references to the Underworld are conspicuously absent on a sarcophagus from Cerveteri (Pl. 63) of which the lid has a relief sculpture of a bearded man lying down.[367] The front side depicts a procession in great detail, with paint still preserved on the relief decoration. The procession is led by

---

[358] *Vacat.*

[359] See a.o. Blásques Martínez 1957; Weber 1978, 71–116; Holliday 1990; Torelli 2002. Cf. Höckmann 1982, 152–7.

[360] See p. 25, note 105.

[361] See p. 21, note 77. For the interpretation of the scenes involving chariots and carts on the Bologna stelae, see especially Ducati 1910, 590–8; Weber 1978, 74–93; Stary-Rimpau 1985, 80, 113f.; Holliday 1990, 85; Morigi Govi and Sassatelli 1993, 106–8, 119; Bonaudo 2002–3; Maggiani 2003; Govi 2009.

[362] See p. 24, note 94.

[363] The most recent discussion is by Van der Meer 2008, 81–3.

[364] See p. 24, note 94.

[365] The most recent discussion is again in Van der Meer 2008, 81–3.

[366] See pp. 24–25 and notes 94, 100. For discussion, see especially Lambrechts 1959; Weber 1978, 94–101; Schäfer 1989, 36–43; Holliday 1990; Tassi Scandone 2001; Van der Meer 2009, 74–8, 88f. with lists (pp. 76, 88).

[367] See p. 9, note 14. The most recent discussion is again by Van der Meer 2008, 68–71.

a trumpet player, who is making dancing steps. He is followed by four men, including one carrying a curved rod, a citharist and a piper. Then comes what is clearly a married couple – most probably the deceased man, who is bearded and holding a staff, and his wife who is making dancing steps. They are followed by a young attendant carrying a stool on his shoulder (often identified with the *sella curulis* of Roman magistrates), and by a beardless charioteer driving a two-horse chariot of our Type I, probably that of the deceased. On this and the other funerary monuments, the deceased men, shown in or outside their chariot and accompanied by their retinue, appear as if they are alive. In real life they must have been important dignitaries, who used chariots for civic purposes, the vehicles being symbols of their special status and authority.

The many late Etruscan cinerary urns of the second–first centuries from Volterra often depict such dignitaries riding no longer in two-horse chariots but in *quadrigae* (Pl. 64). They are shown accompanied by what look like Roman lictors holding *fasces*, and other officials on foot or on horseback, but no death demons. Four-horse chariots appear in a distinct mythological setting on other Volterran urns. (Yet other urns illustrate processions involving carts with passengers reclining under an arched tilt (Pl. 112)).[368] The processional scenes are thought to reflect the realities of Etruscan life under Roman rule, as well as to anticipate the imagery of the Roman Imperial Triumph.[369] According to the written sources, the Triumph was a solemn procession in which the victorious emperor rode in a lavishly decorated *quadriga* into the city of Rome, accompanied by magistrates and senators as well as prisoners and spoils of war. It ended at the temple of Jupiter Optimus Maximus on the Capitoline hill.[370] The written sources clearly indicate that the Triumph goes back to Republican times and even to the (Etruscan) kings of Rome. For instance, Livy (5.23) tells the story of Camillus who as triumphator at some time in the fourth century caused uproar among the people of Rome by using a team of white horses – thereby identifying himself with Jupiter.[371] Literary tradition also indicates that wall paintings showing triumphal processions already existed in Rome by the third century. Remains of one such painting, including traces of a quadriga, have survived from the Tomba Artiei on the Esquiline hill at Rome, and date to the second half of the second century.[372]

It is commonly accepted that Etruscan processions lie at the root of the Roman Triumph.[373] As we have seen, there is a long history of processional scenes involving chariots in central Italy, beginning in the later seventh century. At first, such scenes appear on non-funerary, private and small-scale documents, such as Bucchero vases, ivory pyxides and ostrich eggs, to be followed in the sixth century by terracotta revetment plaques on temples and other public buildings. The images have military as well as peaceful and supernatural connotations. From the fifth century onwards, processions increasingly appear on funerary monuments, where the imagery of the chariot-borne high official was adapted by the addition of death demons leading the way to the Underworld, and occasionally also of mourners. Chariots, it should be noted, were to play no part in Roman funerals or their imagery.[374]

We may conclude our review of the use of chariots in Italy before the Roman Empire by considering their prominent role in racing. Explicit illustrations of chariot racing become available from the second half of the sixth century onwards, and include wall and vase paintings, terracotta revetment plaques, stone

---

[368] See p. 71 and note 12.

[369] See especially Weber 1978, 102–9; Massa-Pairault 1985, 222–38; Holliday 1990, 86–93; 2002, 43–6; Moscati, P. 1997.

[370] See especially Alföldi 1970, 93; Versnel 1970; Coarelli 1988, 364–437; Künzl 1988, especially chs 5–6; Holliday 2002, ch. 1; Junkelmann 1990, ch. 8; Bastien 2007, especially 258–65.

[371] See a.o. Versnel 1970, 61, 70ff. (testimonia X and I: Livy 5.23.5 and Plutarch, *Camillus* 7); Hague Sinos 1994, 112.

[372] Holliday 1990, 89f. and fig. 10; 2002, 36–43 and fig. 12.

[373] See above note 369. See also Bonfante 1970; Holliday 1990, 86–90; Zevi 1995, 311–13 and n. 38 (recent bibliography); Bartoloni 2003, 176–8.

[374] For these, see Holliday 2002, ch. 4.

cippi, bronzework and 'impressed red ware' pottery (Pls 34–36, 40–43, 45, 71c). These documents come from different parts of central Italy.[375] There are also fourth century painted sarcophagi from Paestum in Campania showing racing,[376] as well as other sources – pictorial and textual – more specifically relating to chariot racing among the Greek colonies in southern Italy and Sicily.[377] (For representations of chariot racing in Situla Art, see Appendix 1.)

The various representations from central Italy show light chariots of Type I, drawn by two or, less often, three horses; in some cases, *bigae* and *trigae* are seen competing in the same race (Pl. 71c). Racing with four-horse teams is rarely illustrated (Pl. 45).[378] The racing cars are depicted one behind the other or overlapping, their single unarmed drivers shown leaning forward to indicate speed. The drivers are sometimes looking back at their competitors and are often depicted as whipping or goading their harness teams, which are shown at a gallop (Pls 35–36, 41–43, 71c).

On terracotta revetment plaques of the Veii-Rome-Velletri and Rome-Caprifico roof systems the impression of speed is accentuated by the depiction of a running hare, or of a dog in pursuit of a hare and a backwards-looking deer in the free space beneath the chariot teams, or the animals may be alone (Pl. 71c). The (improbable) combination of a chariot race and a hare hunt recurs in East Greek representations of the sixth century, whence this theme probably derives.[379] Another feature in common of central Italian and East Greek iconography is the bird that is sometimes seen flying above racing (or parade) chariots.[380]

There are other iconographic links between chariot racing as depicted on terracotta revetment plaques and figured documents in central Italy and East Greece.[381] Like their East Greek counterparts, the racing drivers in central Italy wear short, thigh-length tunics with short sleeves. This type of dress may help identify racing chariot representations, where the context is otherwise not clear. In contrast, racing drivers in mainland Greece, from the eighth century onwards, wear long girdled robes, as is most explicitly illustrated by the famous bronze charioteer from Delphi.[382]

The drivers of racing chariots in central Italy may be bare-headed or wear a close-fitting, conical cap with earflaps (Pls 35, 71c).

Of the four racing charioteers depicted in the Tomba delle Olimpiadi of the late sixth century at

[375] See especially Bronson 1965 (with list of illustrations); also Åkerström 1954, 192–200; Humphrey 1981, 12–17; Rawson 1981 (information yielded by Greek and Roman texts); Thuillier 1976; 1985, 626–9; 1997a and 1997b; Steingräber 1985, 52 (discussion of tomb paintings); Decker 1991; Von Mehren 1997, 223–5; Letzner 2009; Winter, N. A. 2009, especially 328, 351, 353–5, 292f., 392f., 400, 445, 447 (Roofs 5–2, 5–3, 5–6 and 5–7 of the Veii-Rome-Velletri system, Roof 5–8 of the Rome-Caprifico system, and Roof 6–2 from an unknown site), also index *s.v.* chariot race; Crouwel 2010, 123, 128f.; Lulof 2010a, 27–30; 2010b, 82 (mould 1).

[376] See Pondrandolfo and Rouveret 1992, 58–61 (*bigae*), 61f. (*quadrigae*) with many illustrations. Some vehicles are shown not with spoked but cross-bar wheels typical of carts (see Chapter III.3). For these and other ideosyncracies, see Bronson 1965, 104f. with n. 58. From Pomarico Vecchio in Basilicata comes a sixth century vase painting (see our Pl. 47 and p. 23, note 89) showing a row of light chariots with single, unarmed riders; this may suggest a race, although the vehicles are moving slowly.

[377] For a vivid representation, see the bronze belt from Noicattaro (p. 16, note 46); also coins minted by various cities in Sicily (Franke and Hirmer 1964, pls 5–6, 14–15, 22–6, 28–30, 32–4, 37–40, 44–5, 48, 52–4, 56, 61, 69). Rulers and other inhabitants of Sicilian cities were among the winners in chariot racing at Olympia and the other Crown Games in Greece (see Moretti 1953 and 1957).

[378] On an Etruscan black-figure neck-amphora by the Micali Painter (see p. 9, note 8). On another neck-amphora by the same painter, from Vulci, the chariot is left out but a team of four horses is seen passing the winning past (see p. 38, note 200).

[379] Cook 1952; 1981, 115; Hemelrijk 1984, 176; Crouwel 1992, 74; Von Mehren 1997, 223–5 (the motif of a dog hunting a hare first appears in Proto-Corinthian vase painting). For East Greek representations of chariot racing, mainly on terracotta revetment plaques and stone reliefs, see especially Åkerström 1951, especially figs 4, 33, pls 1–7 and I–IV; 1966, fig. 33: 2–6 and many plates; Crouwel 1992, 74 with pl. 15: 2; Von Mehren 1997, 223–5.

[380] Von Mehren 1997, 224.

[381] As stressed by N. A. Winter (2009, 392f.).

[382] For a long time the Delphi Charioteer was thought to belong to a chariot group that was dedicated by Polyzalus, tyrant of Gela in Sicily, after a victory in 478 or 474 (see especially Hampe 1941; Chamoux 1955; Rolley 1990; Stewart 1990, 149 and pls 301–2), but see now Adornato 2008. For the costumes of mainland Greek and East Greek racing drivers, see Bronson 1965, 96f.; Crouwel 1992, 61, 74. Note that the charioteers on the Etruscan Amphiaraus Amphora wear the mainland Greek long robe (pl. 40a).

Tarquinia, three are bare-headed, while one wears a different, round cap, looking rather like a crash helmet (Pl. 35). Such headgear is unknown in Greece, but later recurs in Roman racing, along with leather strapping to protect the drivers' ribs.[383] Charioteers depicted in the wall paintings from the Tomba delle Bighe of the earlier fifth century at Tarquinia, and in a contemporary Etruscan black-figure vase painting are shown with criss-cross straps around their knees (Pl. 34). These presumably are to absorb the shocks of locomotion and protect the knees from being injured against the front of the chariot.

The paintings from the Tomba delle Bighe do not show the actual chariot race but its preliminaries, with two horses being brought up by grooms to be harnessed to a waiting chariot. An attendant holds the light chariot by the pole. Other *bigae* are ready and moving slowly (Pl. 34).[384] The drivers here have the reins tied around their waists – a characteristic feature of chariot racing in Italy, as we will see below.

The same tomb also shows various athletic contests, and a wooden stand with an awning for spectators.[385] On one of the sculpted cippi we see a scribe and officials seated on a stand, the row of amphorae below presumably representing prizes.[386]

The contexts in which these chariot races and other contests are depicted – tomb paintings and funerary monuments in the form of cippi – suggest a funerary connection, and we may have here glimpses of games in honour of the dead. We known from Homer and textual sources that in Greece chariot races and other games were held as part of the elaborate funeral ceremonies of epic heroes like Patroclus and – at least for a time – of important real-life individuals.[387]

No funerary associations are apparent in other representations of chariot racing from central Italy, such as vase paintings and terracotta architectural friezes. These may refer to racing as part of religious festivals, as was common in ancient Greece.[388] In Rome too, chariot racing seems to have had cultic origins, before becoming a primarily secular affair with strong political overtones.

We know a good deal about chariot racing in ancient Greece, and in Rome of the later Republic and the Empire, thanks primarily to textual sources.[389] To these may be added the numerous illustrations of racing, and the remains of ancient hippodromes, such as the famous Circus Maximus and others in Rome itself and elsewhere.[390]

In both Greece and Rome, chariot racing consisted of a series of laps, involving 180° turns. At the Olympic and other Crown Games in Greece, there were 12 laps and 23 turns, the estimated total length of the race varying from 9 km to over 18 km. In Rome, each race consisted of seven laps, making up a length of over 5 km. This would suggest that what was required was not only speed but also endurance and tactical driving skills.

What may have started as no more than a reasonably level field, a marked starting and finishing line and a turning post, was to develop into hippodromes proper with permanent installations. In Greece,

---

[383] See Junkelmann 1990, figs 114, 122–4 (details from the Great Circus mosaic from Piazza Armerina, Sicily; see our p. 17, note 51), 129, 139, 141.

[384] Preparations for a chariot race can also be made out in wall painting from the Tomba del Letto Funebre at Tarquinia (Steingräber, 1985, no. 82).

[385] For the athletic and other contests depicted in this and other Etruscan tombs, see especially Thuillier 1985.

[386] Jannot 1984, no. C,I,8b and pl. 171; Humphrey 1981, 13f. and fig. 4; Thuillier 1985, 629–31 (for this and other stands).

[387] Decker 1991, 9. For the Homeric and other Greek textual references, see especially Roller 1991a and 1991b.

[388] See Colonna 1993b, 322 (discussing the 'pan-Etruscan' games which, according to Livy v.1, 4–5, were held at the sanctuary at *Fanum Voltumnae*, near modern Orvieto); also Thuillier 1985, 222; Massa Pairault 1993, 276f.

[389] Of the vast literature, see a.o. Vigneron 1968, 191–206; Harris 1972, chs VII–X; Rawson 1981; Scanlon 1984 (bibliography); Junkelmann 1990, ch. IV (273f.: bibliography for the Roman circus and chariot racing); Decker 1992; Messerschmidt 1993.

[390] For Roman hippodromes, see especially Humphrey 1981, *passim*; Junkelmann 1990, 102–30. For Roman figured sources, see a.o. Dunbabin 1982, 78–82; Junkelmann 1990, ch. IV. Particularly informative is the Great Circus mosaic from Piazza Armerina in Sicily; see Gentili 1957, 2–27; 1959, fig. 3 and pl.7; Carandini, Ricci and de Vos 1982, figs 202–5 and fol. LVI–LVII; Dunbabin 1999, 133 with fig. 136; Junkelmann 1990, figs 121–4.

none of these has so far been excavated, but we know from texts that the hippodrome at Olympia had elaborate starting gates to ensure an equal chance for the many teams that might compete in the races. In Rome, the history of the Circus Maximus and other hippodromes, which accommodated large crowds, is said by Latin and Greek authors to go back to the times of the Etruscan kings (*c.* 600). These authors also report that starting boxes with gates were in existence by 329, and the *spina* – a stone wall dividing the racetrack and linking both turning posts (*metae*) – by 174. At some time during the Roman Republic, the number of participating chariot teams became established at 12, under the colours of four factions. These factions were to stay throughout the Roman Empire period and, in Byzantium, even later.[391]

The figured documents illustrating chariot racing in early Italy reveal little about the setting in which it took place, apart from the occasional stand and turning or finishing post. Tomb paintings and cippi may show a row of trees, to mark the line between the turning posts or simply to indicate an open country setting.[392] At most, six or seven chariots are shown competing together, but this number should not be taken at face value.

The drivers of racing *bigae* and *trigae* in Italic representations may be shown holding the reins with both hands, as in Greece (Pl. 40a). More often, the reins are seen to pass through their hands and then to be tied in a knot at the driver's waist or at the small of his back (Pls 34–36, 41–42, 45). This practice recalls much earlier, second millennium representations from the Near East and Egypt.[393] These illustrate a royal or high-ranking personnage alone in his chariot attacking the enemy or wild animals, usually with a bow, the reins tied around his hips. Egyptian reliefs of the earlier twelfth century also show two-men war chariots, with one man holding up a shield and guiding the reins which are tied around the waist of an archer. Thus both crew members were able to use the reins to prevent themselves from falling out of the rear of the backless chariots, and at the same time to handle their weaponry.

Having the reins tied around the waist in a racing context and using them with one (left) hand, the charioteer would be able to hold a whip or short goad with his free (right) hand. This is quite often illustrated in Italic representations. By leaning against the reins, the driver could also slow down or brake his team, as well as reduce the risk of falling out of the back.

While this driving technique had practical advantages, it was surely also intended as an exhibition of skill and daring. Thus it is frequently seen in representations of racing – with *quadrigae* – in the Roman circuses (Pl. 143). This practice rendered the racing drivers liable to be dragged if thrown off the chariot in accidents. For this reason they carried a curved knife to cut themselves loose from the reins, as is seen most explicitly in a statue of a victorious Roman charioteer.[394]

Chariot racing, in Imperial Rome as well as earlier in Italy and in Greece, was a hazardous affair, particularly at the repeated 180° turns, which must have provided frequent 'spills and frills' for the spectators. It must have been the case that highly trained drivers took part in it. At the major games in classical Greece and in Rome it was not the owners of the vehicles and harness teams themselves who drove; professionals were employed.

Accidents on the race track will have been frequent, as is indeed recorded in Greek and Latin texts and seen in representations, particularly of the Roman Imperial period (Pl. 143).[395] Among the earlier figured documents from Italy illustrating chariot racing are some depicting chariots crashing. The wall painting

---

[391] See Cameron 1976; also 1973; Gabelmann 1980; Junkelmann 1990, 130–6.

[392] See Steingräber 1985, no. 15 (wall painting from the Tomba del Colle Casuccini in Chiusi); Jannot 1984, nos C,I,8, C,II,22 and C,II,33 with figs 172, 265 and 286 (cippi, presently in Palermo). The Lebes Barone from Capua (see our p. 9 and note 11) illustrates two free-standing Doric columns to mark the turning posts, recalling representations in Archaic art of mainland Greece (McGowan 1995, 622–8).

[393] Littauer 1972, 146f.; Littauer and Crouwel 1979, 63, 91f., 94f.; 1985, 103.

[394] Junkelmann 1990, 148 and fig. 141 (statue), see also a.o. figs 110, 124, 139 (reins tied in knot at back of driver).

[395] Crouwel 1992, 63–5 (Greece). For pictures of accidents on the Roman racetrack, see a.o. Vigneron 1968, pl. 73c; Junkelmann 1990, figs 123 (detail of the Great Circus mosaic at Piazza Armerina), 140 (a terracotta, so-called Campana placque, our Pl. 143).

from the Tomba delle Olimpiadi at Tarquinia, mentioned above, depicts a dramatic scene involving four *bigae* racing towards a post at the far left (Pl. 35). The driver of the leading team is glancing back, the next two are vigorously goading their teams, and the last chariot is collapsing, with one horse lying on its back, its legs entangled in the reins, while the other horse rears up and the driver himself is tossed into the air. In another wall painting, from the Tomba di Poggio al Moro of the second quarter of the fifth century at Chiusi, a biga driver is again seen hurtling through the air while still holding on to the reins (Pl. 36).[396]

Similar and other details of racing are furnished by an Etruscan black-figure vase painting of the early fifth century (Pl. 41).[397] Here we see six *trigae*, again racing to the left. At the far right stand two trumpeters, who may have just sounded the last turn. Ahead of them a chariot has overturned, the driver tumbling down and an assistant coming up to grapple with the entangled horses. The other chariots race past another assistant who looks back at the accident. At the far left stand two gesticulating officials, quite probably at the finish line. Another such vase painting illustrates the first of four *quadrigae* passing the turning or finishing post, with one of its horses falling to the ground, its head shown frontally.[398]

With regard to the origin of chariot racing in Italy, this is presumably to be sought in Greece, where the practice can be traced back to late Mycenaean times (the later twelfth century).[399] Chariot racing may have been introduced in central Italy from Greece, either directly or through the various Greek colonies in southern Italy and Sicily. Some features of racing in central Italy, such as the type of dress worn by the charioteers and the use of whips, point rather to a connection with East Greece. (In mainland Greece and southern Italy long robes and long goads were standard.)[400] Chariot racing, it may be noted, is not documented among the non-Greek populations of the Near East at this time.

It is in central Italy, however, that we first see head and knee protection for the drivers as well as the practice of tying the reins around the drivers' waist or back. These two features of chariot racing are unknown in either mainland or East Greece. The driving technique involving reins tied around the charioteers may well have been independently invented in central Italy in the sixth century, to be passed on to the Romans. Other features, such as the short driver's dress and the use of a whip, were probably also passed on – as indeed was the idea of chariot racing itself.[401] As we have seen, the type of chariot used in Roman racing also derives from Etruscan models (see Chapter II.1 *s.v.* chariot Type I).

According to our figured documents, chariot racing in pre-Imperial Italy usually involved two or three horses (of small size, see Chapter II.2). Racing teams of four horses were, however, not entirely unknown. There is the story of Ratumenna who, as related by ancient authors, gained victory at Veii with a *quadriga*.[402] For comparison, chariot racing in mainland Greece involved two or, more often, four horses, again of small size, whereas in East Greece *bigae* were standard. Figured documents and textual sources make clear that three-horse teams were also raced.[403] In Rome, as in mainland Greece, *quadrigae* were the most popular, though teams of two, three or even eight or ten animals are occasionally mentioned

---

[396]   Steingräber 1985, no. 22 and pls 191–2; Jannot 1986b, 194 and pl. I: 1–2; Decker 1991, 4f.

[397]   A neck-amphora, the name piece by the Painter of the Berlin Amphora 2154, from Vulci see p. 9, note 8). For discussion, see Bronson 1966, 24–8; Humphrey 1981, 17.

[398]   Neck-amphora by the Micali Painter (see p. 38, note 200). For discussion, see Moltesen 1982 (fig. 2 shows this detail).

[399]   Crouwel 1981, 142; 1992, 57. A passage in Herodotus (I, 167) may be relevant here: the Pythia at Delphi ordered the Agyllans (the inhabitants of Caere/Cerveteri) to set up funerary games, including equestrian events, in honour of the Phocaeans who had perished in the sea battle off the coast at Alalia *c.* 550 (see a.o. Von Mehren 1997, 223; Thuillier 1997b, 262).

[400]   For discussion of the East Greek connections, as regards racing practices and their iconography, see especially Bronson 1965, 94, 104; Von Mehren 1997, 223–5.

[401]   Bronson 1965, 98f.; Rawson 1981; Humphrey 1981, 12, 16f.; Thuillier 1990; Decker 1991, 9f.

[402]   As told by Festus 340 L. See a.o. Rawson 1981, 2f.; Thuillier 1985, 495–9, 515f., 520; 1992; Decker 1991, 10.

[403]   For the size of racing teams in Greece and in the Homeric poems, see Crouwel 1992, 61.

in textual sources.[404] It may be therefore that the Romans in their preference for racing with four-horse teams were influenced by Greek practices. Such influences may have come directly from Greece or via the various colonies in southern Italy, which regularly competed in *quadriga* racing at Olympia and the other Crown Games on the Greek mainland.

Whatever the exact number of horses, only two animals were under yoke – in Italy, as in Greece. When present, the one or more outriggers, being attached to the chariot by only a trace, did not notably contribute to the pulling power of the team, whether on the straight or on the turns. The extra animals must have been mainly for display, creating a more spectacular effect.[405]

---

[404] See a.o. Junkelmann 1990, figs 140, 142; Bronson 1965, 103f.; Humphrey 1981, 16f. (*trigae*).

[405] Spruytte 1978 (experiments with a team of two yoke horses and two outriggers harnessed to a mainland Greek type of chariot); Crouwel 1992, 65. For different views, see Bronson 1965, 101–3; Muzzolini 1991.

CHAPTER III

Carts

Our knowledge of the existence, construction and functions of two-wheeled carts (*q.v.*) – and also of four-wheeled wagons (*q.v.*) – in Italy in pre-Imperial Roman times depends chiefly on actual remains of such vehicles in tombs of the eighth-sixth century and on a variety of figured documents dating from the seventh century onwards. In addition, isolated disk and cross-bar wheels (q.v.) found at northern Italian settlements, and dating back to the second millennium, belonged to carts or wagons rather than to chariots.

Vehicles other than chariots are mentioned in Latin or Greek texts relating to pre-Roman Imperial times in Italy. It is difficult to establish whether carts or wagons are referred to, since the number of wheels is rarely stated explicitly. Information on the construction and appearance of these vehicles – called *carpentum, carrus, pilentum, plaustrum/plostrum* or *tensa* – is in any case extremely limited.[1] Interestingly, Latin terms such as *carpentum* are clearly of Celtic origin, thereby suggesting a case of 'borrowed names for borrowed things'.[2]

In the sections to follow textual information will be used with caution, and mainly when it complements the archaeological record.

Among the remains of actual vehicles encountered in tombs dating from the eighth century onwards in different parts of Italy, carts may be distinguished from both chariots and wagons by their surviving metal parts – the wood usually having decayed.[3] Only in one case – a rich female burial of the late sixth century from Sirolo (ancient Numana) in Marche – could the cart be reconstructed more or less in its entirety, thanks to the large number of metal elements found *in situ* (Pl. 76). The rectangular tomb 4, known as La Tomba della Principessa, measures 5.10 by 2.20 m and was dug within large tumulus 1 of the I Pini cemetery. The tomb in fact contained the remains of two vehicles: the cart, which was in an upright position so as to save space, behind a much less well preserved chariot (Pl. 76a).[4]

The carefully recorded and recently published Sirolo cart helps to identify other carts in tombs elsewhere in Italy by the presence of similar distinctive metal elements.[5] In particular, it is now firmly established that the frequently found but previously unexplained type of metal fittings commonly known as 'poggiaredini' formed part of the composite draught pole of carts (see below, *s.v.* Type 1).

---

[1] See *DarSag s.v.*; *RE s.v.*; also Abaecherli 1935–6; Lucchi 1968; Pagnotta 1977–8; Höckmann 1982, 133f. (with extensive references to earlier studies).

[2] Piggott 19983, 229–231. For Celtic loan-words for vehicles in the Latin language, see also a.o. De Simone 1978.

[3] For cart remains, see *Carri da guerra* 337–9 (table); also Bartoloni and Grottanelli 1984 (= 1989); Galeotti 1986–8. Important recent publications of cart remains include P. von Eles in *Guerriero e sacerdote* 87–90 and nos 105, 108, 117–22 (the Tomba del Trono of *c.* 700 from Verucchio in Emilia Romagna; *Carri da guerra* 332, Repertorio no. 228), Cygielman and Pagnini 2006, 31–4 (the seventh century Tomba del Tridente at Vetulona in Toscana; *Carri da guerra* 327, Repertorio no. 177), L. Palermo in *Potere e splendore* 241–3 nos 320–6 (seventh century tomb 182 in the Crocifisso cemetery at Matelica in Marche); see also Drago Troccoli 1995, 89–94 and fig. 5 (Casal del Fosso tomb 872 of the later eighth century at Veii; *Carri da guerra* 325, Repetorio no. 149).

[4] For the necropolis, the tumulus and the tomb, its contents, and the recovery and conservation of the two vehicles, see *Carri da guerra* 229–41 (M. Landolfi), 242–7 (G. de Palma), 247–9 (C. Usai), 318f. (Repertorio nos 85 and 86); Landolfi 2001.

[5] For the study and reconstruction of the Sirolo cart, see Emiliozzi in *Carri da guerra* 249–53 and figs 19–23, pls 25–8 (Repertorio 319, no. 86); *eadem* 2001, 319–25, and in *Eroi e regine* 355f. cat. nos 121–3.

Figured documents illustrating carts are extensive. They may begin with a few representations among the large corpus of rock carvings from Val Camonica in the Italian Alps (Pl. 100). Difficult to date as they are, most of these petroglyphs seem to belong to the first millennium, and to the eighth–seventh centuries in particular. The two-wheelers, depicted schematically and in plan view, may be identified as carts rather than chariots on account of what look likes a forked Y-pole (see below *s.v.* Types and body).[6]

Other representations of carts include some small bronze models from sites in Toscana. One of these, from Vetulonia, may belong to the early seventh century (Pl. 87).[7] Three others – from Bolsena, Sarteano and Civiltà Castellana respectively, have been given dates ranging from the fifth to the third century (Pls 88–90).[8] There are also some cart models of terracotta from Toscana which may date to the seventh century.[9] Among the profile representations of carts from Toscana are terracotta revetment plaques of *c.* 580–575 from Poggio Civitate (Murlo) (Pl. 113),[10] stone sarcophagi of the later fourth and third centuries (Pls 109, 66),[11] and also numerous second-first century alabaster cinerary urns from Volterra (Pl. 112).[12] Carts are also depicted on a gem (Pl. 101)[13] and on some gold finger rings of the sixth century (Pl. 102),[14] as well as on some fifth and fourth century red-figure vases (Pls 96–97)[15] and on the wall of a tomb probably of the second century.[16] From Bologna come several sculpted funerary

---

[6] See Van Berg–Osterrieth 1972, 73–80 and figs 30–4; Piggott 1983, 108, 119; Züchner 2004, 405, 407 and figs 8: 9–10 (also for dating).

[7] From the Poggio alla Guardia necropolis; see M. Cygielman in *Carri da guerra* 65 no. s.9; Amann 2000, 74. The material of this very small model, which may have been used as a pendant, was previously thought to be terracotta (so Falchi 1895, 311 and fig. 165; Montelius 1904, 834 and pl. 178: 14; Hencken 1968, 582; Woytowitsch 1978, no. 165 and pl. 31; Höckmann 1982, 142, 146 no. E 2).

[8] For the models from Bolsena and Civiltà Castellana, see p. 6, notes 48 and 45. For the model from Sarteano near Chiusi (formerly thought to come from Amelia), see Walters 1899, no. 602 and pl. 12 Lorimer 1903, 135f.; Richardson 1953, 90f. and fig. 5 (the rosette-shaped 'wheels' illustrated with the cart almost certainly do not belong); Woytowitsch 1978, no. 169 and pl. 43; Höckmann 1982, 144, 147 no. E 12; Haynes 1985, 282 and pl. 100 (seated female figure only).

[9] From Bisenzio, Porto Madonna tomb 2; see Milani 1894, 126f. and fig. 3; Woytowitsch 1978, no. 159 and pl. 36. From Pitigliano, tomb; see Hencken 1968, 582 and fig. 493; Woytowitsch 1978, nos 163 and 164 and pl. 31. No provenance; see Woytowitsch 1978, no. 166 and pl. 35, and no. 167 and pl. 34; Höckmann 1982, 144 no. E 13. In the case of other (incomplete) models it is not certain whether carts or chariots were intended, see our p. 25, note 98.

[10] From the so-called Upper Building; see a.o. Andrén 1974, 5f., 11 and figs 46–9; Gantz 1974; Mackintosh 1974, 30–2 and fig. 3; Woytowitsch 1978, no. 251 and pl. 46; Höckmann 1982, 142, 146f. no. E 3; Rathje 1989, 79–81; 1993, 137f.; Holliday 1990, 76 n. 21; Von Mehren 1993 (distribution and number of plaques); Torelli 1992, 253–5 (= 1997, 93f.); Phillips Jr. 1993, 42f.; Hague Sinos 1994; S. Coggioli and N. Camerin in *Carri da guerra* 65 no. s.10; *Principi etruschi* cat. no. 117; Winter, N. A. 2009, 157, 185f. no. 3.D.5b with ill. 3.7.2 and fig. 3.17 (Roof 3–8; for the building, see 153–9).

[11] *Sarcophagus of Ramtha Viśnai* from Vulci, its short sides showing a cart and a chariot respectively (Pls 65 and 109; see p. 24, note 94); for the scene with the cart, see Herbig 1952, pl. 40d; Comstock and Vermeule 1976, no. 384; Littauer and Crouwel 1977b, 102 and pl. XI; Höckmann 1982, 144, 146f. no. E 14; Holliday 1990, 78f. and figs 3–4; Van der Meer 2008, 74 (incorrectly called chariot). *Another sarcophagus from Vulci*, one of its long sides showing both a cart and a chariot (Pl. 66; see our p. 24, note 94); for the cart, see also Höckmann 1982, 144, 147 no. E 15; Van der Meer 2008, 81, 83 (also called chariot). *Two sarcophagi from Camna I-tomb* in the Poggio del Cavalluccio cemetery at Tarquinia: see Van der Meer 2008, 86–90 no. *G19* and fig. 49 (our Pl. 111: tilt cart; also Weber 1978, 101f. group b, no. G 19; De Ruyt 1934, no. 153 and fig. 56) and 88–90 no. *G29* and fig. 51 (also Weber 1978, 101f. group b, no. G 29).

[12] See *Corpus delle urne etrusche di età ellenistica* 2, nos 188–213; also Weber 1978, especially 102–16 and pls 28–9 (Groups 1a–c and 2); Höckmann 1982, 145–9 *s.v.* no. E 18; Cateni and Fiaschi 1984, pls 14–15, 37; Moscati, P. 1997; Van der Meer 2008, 87–9 and fig. 50.

[13] Richardson 1964, pl. 33; Woytowitsch 1978, no. 214A with pl. 46; Höckmann 1982, 142, 146 no. E 5; Hague Sinos 1994, 101 and fig. 11.5–6.

[14] *Paris, Louvre Bj 1070:* see Boardman 1967, no. B II 10 and pl. 2; Richter 1968, no. 718; Woytowitsch 1978, no. 218 and pl. 46; Höckmann 1982, 142f., 144 no. E 6. *Paris, Louvre Bj 1071:* see Boardman 1967, no. B II 11 and pl. 2; Richter 1968, no. 717; Woytowitsch 1978, no. 219 and pl. 46; Höckmann 1982, 142, 146 no. E 4.

[15] *Neck-amphora of the Praxias Group*, from Vulci (our Pl. 96 : see Lorimer 1903, 142 and fig. 8; Dragendorf 1928, 344 and fig. 14; Beazley 1947, 195, Amphora no. 3; Höckmann 1982, 143, 147 no. E 9. *Twin stamnoi*, one from Bomarzo near Vulci (our Pl. 97) and the other unprovenanced: see Ambrosch 1837, pls 2–3; Albizzati 1918–19, 55, 61f. and figs 3–4; Beazley 1947, 61–3; Höckmann 1982, 143, 148 *s.v.* no. E 10; *Die Welt der Etrusker. Archäologische Denkmäler* no. D. 1.17. *Volute krater* from Orvieto: see Giglioli 1921, 85, 94f. and fig. 6, above; De Ruyt 1934, 76f. no. 83; Beazley 1947, 62, 169, 1 (Vanth Group); Höckmann 1982, 144, 148 no. E 11; Capelletti 1992, no. 63; Bonami 2006, 526f. and fig. 3: top.

[16] From Tarquinia, Tomba del Cardinale; see Höckmann 1982, 144f., 149 no. E 16; Steingräber 1985, no. 54 (badly effaced).

stelae, or fragments thereof, illustrating carts. Like those with chariot depictions, most of these stelae have usually been dated to the fifth–fourth centuries (Pls 106–108).[17] In the case of the Stela di Via Tofane, the cart scene apparently belongs to a re-carving of the original surface and has been dated to the seventh or early sixth century (Pl. 105).[18] Carts are also depicted on a stone funerary relief from Sulmona in Abruzzo which has been attributed to the first century (Pl. 111)[19] and on a stone relief from the Basilica Aemilia (dated 55–34) on the Forum Romanum in Rome.[20]

Important comparative material derives from southern Italy. It includes a bronze cart model from Rossano di Vaglio in Basilicata (Pl. 91)[21] and two others from Crotone (Pl. 92).[22] The latter vehicles are cast onto the superstructure of a ship model which is thought to be an import from Sardinia and to date as early as the ninth century (Nuraghic culture). There is also a terracotta cart model from Pithecusae on the island of Ischia, its find context dating to c. 650–580 (Pl. 93).[23] Profile representations of carts from southern Italy include a fifth century terracotta plaque from Locri Epizephyrii in Calabria (Pl. 114)[24] and terracotta revetment plaques from Metaponto in Puglia dating to c. 600 (Pl. 115).[25] In addition, carts appear in fourth century tomb paintings from Paestum (ancient Posidonia) in Campania (Pl. 94),[26] and in a few contemporary Paestan and Apulian red-figure vase paintings (Pls 98–99).[27] Finally, racing

---

[17] *Our Pl. 106:* see Ducati 1910, 437f. no. 164 and pl. 2b; also De Ruyt 1934, no. 149 and fig. 55; Stary-Rimpau 1988, no. 164; *Museo Civico Archeologico di Bologna* no. 164; Sassatelli 1989, 940 no. 28 and pl. 5a; Lucassen 1995, no. 38; Sassatelli and Govi, E. in Govi and Sassatelli 2007, 89 and pl. 19d. *Our Pl. 107:* see Ducati 1910, no. 169 (Side A), and pl. 5; also De Ruyt 1934, no. 148 and fig. 54; Woytowitsch 1978, no. 260A and pl. 46; *Museo Civico Archeologico di Bologna* no. 169; Stary-Rimpau 1988, no. 169; Sassatelli 1993, 64–6 and fig. 7; Lucassen 1995, no. 26; Govi, E. in Govi and Sassatelli 2007, 82 f. and pls 17b and 20: above, right. *Our Pl. 108:* see Ducati 1910, no. 63 and fig. 50; also Woytowitsch 1978, no. 260B and pl. 46; Star-Rimpau 1988, no. 63; Lucassen 1995, no. 36; Camerin 1997, 43 and fig. 12; Macellari 2002, 353f. with pl. 218 (Arnoaldi, tomb 146, Stele A); Govi 2009, 457 and fig. 2. *Ducati 1910, no. 12* (Side A) and fig. 52; see also Stary-Rimpau 1988, no. 12; Lucassen 1995, no. 31; E. Govi in Sassatelli and Govi 2007, 82f. and pls 17d and 20: second from left. *Ducati 1910, 456f. no. 194* (Side A) and fig. 5: 1; see also Stary-Rimpau 1985, no. 194; Lucassen 1995, no. 41. *Ducati 1943, no. E* (Side A) and pl. III, left (fragment): see also Stary-Rimpau 1988, no. 214; Lucassen 1995, no. 28; Morigi Govi and Sassatelli 1993, 119 and fig. 14. *Morigi Govi and Sassatelli 1993, no. G* and fig. 5. On some fragmentary stelae, carts rather than chariots are suggested by the presence of wheels of cross-bar type: *Ducati 1910, no. 45*; also Stary-Rimpau 1988, no. 47; Lucassen 1995, no. 33; Macellari 2002, 261 and pl. 171: top, left (Arnoaldi, tomb 19, Stele D). *Ducati 1910, no. 158* and fig. 18; also Stary-Rimpau 1988, no. 158.

[18] Bermond-Montanari 1962, 50f. with fig. 4 and pl. 8; Woytowitsch 1978, no. 260 and pl. 46; Cerchiai 1987, 228f., 232f. and fig. 54: 1; Stary-Rimpau 1988, 51–3, 57–9, 254f. no. 205; Lucassen 1995, no. 1; *Principi etruschi* cat. no. 445.

[19] Rostovtzeff 1957, *s.v.* pl. III: 5; *Antiche gente d'Italia* cat. no. 733 (with bibliography).

[20] Junkelmann 1990, fig. 96.

[21] From a sanctuary of Mefitis. See Adamesteanu 1970, pl. XL; 1974, ill. p. 191; Adamesteanu and Dilthey 1992, 69 and fig. 74; Höckmann 1982, 30, 138 no. G 34.

[22] From a sanctuary of Hera at Capo Colonna. See Spadea 1994, 22–4 no. 33; 1997, 250 and fig. 15, and in *Tesoro di Hera* 56, 109 no. 4.

[23] Fully published in d'Agostino 1996, 17–18 nos 7–8, 67f. and pls 4, 7: 1, 4–5, 20; see also 18f. nos 9–12 and pls 7: 2, 20–1 (remains of other such models and draught animals); also Woytowitsch 1978, no. 281 and pl. 40; Crouwel 1992, 79 and pl. 33: 3.

[24] Zancani Montuoro 1955; 1996, 203–26 and especially 204–8 and pls 73, 75; Prückner 1968, 19–22, type 3 and fig. 2; Höckmann 1982, 136f., 140 no. G 20; Crouwel 1992, 81 and pl. 34: 2; Schenal Pileggi 2003, 764–86 (type 7/3) and fig. 51 and pl. 133.

[25] Fully published in Mertens-Horn 1992, 46–73, 110–17 and figs 27–35, 46 and pls 8–15 (Frieze II, dating to c. 600, from San Biagio Temple C I; for fragments of the same series from the 'Timpone della Motta' at Francavilla Marittima near Sybaris and from Siris-Polieion in Calabria, see Mertens-Horn 1992, 47, 51f., 118–20 with pls 16: 1–2 and 17; also Maaskant-Kleibrink 1993, 33–6), 73–5, 118–20 with figs 36–44 and pls 18–19 (Frieze III of the sixth century). For the cart depictions, see also Woytowitsch 1978, no. 252 and pl. 46; Fabbricotti 1977–9, 162–70; Höckmann 1982, 136f., 140 no. G 20; Olbrich 1986, 145–9; Crouwel 1992, 79 and pl. 34: 1; Sinos 1994, 101f.; *I Greci in occidente* cat. no. 49.

[26] These mule-drawn vehicles, carrying one or, more rarely, two seated male or female figures, are sometimes shown with two wheels side by side or overlapping, and are surely meant to be carts rather than wagons; see Pontrandolfo and Rouveret 1992, especially 46f., also 325 with ills. pp. 118: 3 (Andriuolo, tomb 61), 339 and ills pp. 162: 1 and 163: 5 (Andriuolo, tomb 86), 343 and ills pp. 171: 5, 172: 1 and 181: 3 (Andriuolo, tomb 89), 345 (Andriuolo, tomb 80), 380 and ill. p. 259: 5 (Gaudo, tomb 2; see also Sestieri 1958, 51–3 and fig. 12; 1959, ill. p. 39 = our Pl. 94), 358 (Laghetto, tomb XVIIII; no ill.)); also Rouveret and Pontrandolfo 1983, 125–7 and figs 39–40 (Spinazzo, tomb 113); Weege 1909, 113–16 no. 29 and figs 6–7, and Nicolet 1962, 478 and fig. 7 (from Paestum, but lost); Sestieri 1958, 51f. and fig. 13 (Frarita). See further Weber 1978, 83, 93 n. 255; Höckmann 1982, 32, 138 nos G 30–1; Holliday 1990, 75, 85.

[27] *Paestan red-figure bell-krater* by Python from Ruvo: see *Antiquities and Islamic Art. Sotheby's Sales Catalogue* (New York, 23 June 1989) lot 196 (now New York, Metropolitan Museum of Art 1989.144). *Apulian fragment* from Ruvo (now lost): see Diehl 173, 185 and pl. 48: 2; Prückner 1968, 21 n. 137 (attributed to the Circle of the Darius Painter by A. D. Trendall); Höckmann 1982, 137–40 no. G 29; Crouwel 1992, 90 and pl. 34: 3.

carts can be seen on silver coins that were minted at Messana (ancient Zancle) in Sicily and at Reggio di Calabria (ancient Rhegium), not far away on the Italian mainland, in the earlier fifth century (Pl. 104).[28]

1. Types and body

Two types of carts can be identified – on the basis of differences in the form of the draught pole and its connection with the vehicle body.[29]

Cart Type I: the Y-poled cart

This type is best documented by the actual cart from the Tomba della Principessa at Sirolo (Pl. 76; see above). The vehicle had a basic framework formed by two parallel timbers, made of elm wood and joined together by cross-pieces. The two lengthwise timbers projected a short distance at the rear. At the front they bent somewhat inward, in order to run contiguously out to the yoke, thereby forming a composite, so-called Y-pole (*q.v.*). The floor area, being 1.04 m long by only *c.* 0.67 m wide, probably offered room for only one person.[30] Iron elements, found *in situ*, allowed for the reconstruction of a seat with low side supports, placed over the axle which ran under the centre of the floor area and was somehow fastened to the side timbers of the floor. (A fragment of decorated sheet bronze from Perugia in Umbria is thought to have covered the side support of a similar cart seat.)[31] At Sirolo, the evidence for a seat suggests a cart with a plank flooring rather than one of woven thongs, such as would have been convenient for the (standing) occupants of chariots.[32] Two metal rings have been convincingly interpreted as belonging to a board that was suspended from the side timbers for the seated occupant to put his or her feet on. The use of such a suspended foot support on carts is documented for mainland Greece, a sixth century Attic black-figure lekythos by the Amasis Painter being its most detailed representation (Pl. 149).[33] The carts depicted there carry four seated passengers, two abreast, protected by a rail siding. Like the Sirolo cart, the vehicles must have been open at the front.

Whereas the Greek carts probably had a single, central draught pole, that of the Sirolo cart was a composite, so-called Y-pole (*q.v.*). This Y-pole rose in a concave curve, as is indicated by details of the three closely spaced bronze tubes, joined together by cross-pieces, that fitted over the ends of the pole's arms and held them together. Unfortunately, the find circumstances in the Sirolo tomb yielded no information on the yoke and its attachment to the composite pole.[34] On the other hand, it is clear that the timbers which formed the sides of the floor frame and the composite pole were bound by a series of broad iron rings, set at regular intervals. These helped prevent the wood splitting.

The complex metal pole ending occurs with vehicular remains in several tombs in different parts of central Italy. When known, the find contexts date mostly to the seventh century, but in the case of the

---

[28] See a.o. Crouwel 1992, 81 (references in note 405), 96 and pl. 33: 2.

[29] P. von Eles (in *Guerrriero e sacerdote* 84–6 with n. 231) also distinguishes two types of cart, one called *carpentum* and the other 'calesse'. In her view, the first type is pulled by two animals, one on either side of a draught pole, whereas the 'calesse' has a single draught animal between shafts. In fact, there is no evidence for shaft harness in Italy before the Roman Imperial period.

[30] In a reconstruction drawing two persons are shown seated side by side; see Emiliozzi in *Carri da guerra* 253, fig. 22.

[31] Bartoloni 2006, 427 and figs 1–2, 4–5.

[32] Emiliozzi (in *Carri da guerra* 251) assumes a thong flooring.

[33] Crouwel 1992, 79, 81 and pls 38–40; Oakley and Hague Sinos 1993, 29f. and figs 68–70; *Carri da guerra* pl. 24 (see also N. Eschbach *ibidem*, 61f. no. s.3 for another such vase painting). Note that a terracotta cart model from a tomb of *c.* 525–500 at Thespiae in Boeotia features two (divine ?) female figures, seated side by side and with their legs seemingly hanging down in front; see A. K. Andreiomenou in *EAA Secondo Supplemento* 1971–94, vol. V, 741 and fig. 951.

[34] Cf. the reconstruction drawings *Carri da guerra* 250, 253, figs 19, 22.

Sirolo tomb to the late sixth. Commonly called 'poggiaredini', the multiple pole ending is made up of three to five tubes of bronze or iron, 0.10–0.15 m long and linked by two or more crosspieces. The tubes often have bird or other decorative finials at their forward end (Pls 76, 80a).[35] In the light of the evidence from the Sirolo tomb, where the 'poggiaredini' were found *in situ*, their function is now firmly established as the ending of the composite pole of an Y-poled cart.

Among the other graves that have yielded 'poggiaredini' is tomb B of tumulus I in the Caiolo cemetery at San Giuliano (Barbarano Romana) in Lazio. Here the dromos yielded two rich burials of *c.* 675, one male and the other female, and each with the remains of a two-wheeled vehicle. The male burial was accompanied by a pair of metal handholds of a type known from several other tombs and often considered to belong to chariots of our Type IV.[36] The female burial had 'poggiaredini' as well as metal rings which probably belonged to the cart's suspended footboard.[37]

In other cases, such as tomb 8 of *c.* 700 in the Fornace cemetery at Verucchio in Emilia Romagna, the 'poggiaderini' occurred together with a metal fitting consisting of three parallel rings through which the pole arms may have passed on the way to the yoke area (Pl. 80b).[38]

In the Tomba del Littore of *c.* 630 at Vetulonia in Toscana, there is again evidence for two vehicles. 'Poggiaderini' are absent, but a series of metal bands has been interpreted – in the light of the Sirolo evidence – as the bindings of a cart's composite Y-pole (Pl. 77).[39]

Y-poled carts were used in ancient and recent times in different parts of the world.[40] Among them, the carts represented by bronze votive models of the later first millennium from Collado de los Jardines, Despeñaperros in southern Spain recall the Sirolo carriage in being small, equid-drawn conveyances with only q seat (Pl. 150).[41] Closely related but of simpler construction is the so-called A-frame cart (*q.v.*), a type of vehicle also known from the ancient world (but not from Italy) and widely used until recently (Pl. 151).[42] Here, the composite draught pole is similarly formed from a continuation of the side timbers of the floor frame, but these do not converge in front and meet only at the yoke, thereby giving the whole equipage the shape of a capital A.

The Y-poled and A-frame carts of antiquity and of more recent times often feature one or more timbers in between the poles to the vehicle body, sometimes extending all the way to the rear and beyond – to reinforce the construction and, where there is one, to support an extension of the vehicle floor at the

---

[35] A. Emiliozzi in *Carri da guerra* 102f., 249, 251; 2004–5, 140f.; P. von Eles in *Guerriero e sacerdote* 85 n. 231, 87f.; G. Baldelli in *Eroi e regine* 251f. *s.v.* cat. no. 439. For earlier discussions of these objects, see Galeotti 1986–8, 101–4 and pls 61–2 (interpreted as belonging to the front breastwork of carts); Nebelsick 1992, 101.

[36] See p. 22, note 80.

[37] Emiliozzi 1997, 103; I. Caruso in *Carri da guerra* 131, 280, 282 nos 12–15 and figs 12–15 and pl. 29: 3–4, also Emiliozzi *ibidem*, 283 (Repertorio 323, no. 131). For other possible suspension rings, see also a.o. P. von Eles in *Guerriero e sacerdote* 90, 107 nos 121–2, pl. 45 (from the Tomba del Trono at Verucchio; *Carri da guerra* 332, Repertorio no. 228); Cygielman and Pagnini 2006, 34 no. 8 and fig. 3e (from the Tomba del Tridente, Vetulonia; *Carri da guerra* 327, Repertorio no. 177); Emiliozzi 2004–5, 140–3 nos 4–4ter and fig. 2 (from Piazza Risorgimento cemetery tomb 928 at Pontecagnano in Campania; *Carri da guerra* Repertorio 312, no. 10).

[38] See Camerin 1997, 37 and notes 52–4; *Carri da guerra* 332 (Repertorio no. 230). Tomb 13 of the Lippi cemetery also at Verucchio yielded no 'poggiaredini' but only the triple rings; see Camerin 1997, 37 and fig. 5; *Carri da guerra* 333 (Repertorio no. 235).

[39] M. Cygielman in *Carri da guerra* 265f. and fig. 2 (veicolo A), 327 (Repertorio no. 173).

[40] Littauer and Crouwel 1977b, and 1979a, 109, 147 (a Y-pole construction may also be suggested for ninth century Assyrian chariots and some later chariots in the Levant and Cyprus; see also Crouwel 1987, 107. For more recent Y-poled carts, see Deloche 1983, pl. 26: b (India); Galhano 1973, figs 70–1, 87–88 (Portugal); White 1984, fig. 133 (France). A recently used A-frame cart was on public display at the site of the Hippodrome in central Istanbul (November 2002).

[41] Férnandez-Miranda and Olmos 1986, 117f. and pl. 24; Hayen 1986, 128f. and ills p. 129; Quesada 1997, 59 and pl. II: 3; Gail 1986, 158f. and ills pp. 158–159.

[42] Littauer and Crouwel 1977b; Piggott 1983, 75–7 and figs 32 and 37 (actual carts from second millennium burials at Lchashen in Armenia); Koşay 1951, pls 15–16 (central Turkey); Gegeschidse 1956, a.o. pls 1, 9, 24–5, 30–4, 55–6, 60 (Georgia); Deloche 1983, pl. 26: a (India). See also Schlichterle 2004, 302–4.

front. This may explain why the Italian 'poggiaredini' consist of three or more tubes.[43] However, in the reconstruction drawings of the Sirolo cart no timber is inserted in the central one of the three tubes of its 'poggiaredini' (Pl. 76b).

In Italy, Y-poled carts may be identified on figured documents with varying degrees of certainty. First, there is the equid-drawn cart seen in profile view on a sarcophagus of the second half of the fourth century from Vulci (Pl. 109). Here the driver is seated on a cushion ahead of the two passengers who are seated side by side on a high-backed chair. The cushion is placed on what look like extensions of the side beams of the cart. Then there is the bronze cart model from Rossano di Vaglio in Basilicata in southern Italy, showing a rounded, dropped extension at the front of the body. This extension has a solid siding and appears to have rested over the Y-pole (Pl. 91). The vehicle also shows three lengthwise beams projecting beyond the solid flooring at the rear. A similar rounded extension can be made out on one of the funerary stelae from Bologna, where the driver is placed at a much lower level than the seated passengers in the equid-drawn cart (Pl. 107). The extension has a solid hip-high siding which is decorated with a bird. Other Bologna stelae show drivers perched in front of the cart body (Pls 106, 108). Something similar is seen on a fifth century red-figure neck-amphora from Vulci (Pl. 96).[44]

The vehicles with an extension at the front are strongly reminiscent of the Y-poled cart that is depicted in plan view on a stone relief of the second century from Bharput in India (Pl. 152).[45] Here, the bullock cart, its three lengthwise floor beams projecting beyond the solid rectangular floor at the rear as on the bronze model from Rossano di Vaglio, is extended by a curved, thong-floored platform for a driver at the front. This platform, which has no breastwork, is supported on the two arms of the Y-pole and on the central timber.

A bronze model, probably of a Y-poled cart with arched tilt, found near Kolhapur in the Maharashtra in India and dating to the second century AD, provides valuable information too (Pl. 153).[46] Here the small platform at the front is also supported on the two poles and a central timber, the poles rising in a concave curve (as on the Sirolo cart) to the yoke which itself is attached near their ends. Moghul miniatures of the sixteenth–seventeenth centuries AD from India show drivers in a kneeling position ahead of the main vehicle body, between the two poles, which here describe a more pronounced convex curve.[47]

In Italy, a Y-poled cart may also be recognized in the bronze cart model possibly dating to the early seventh century from Vetulonia in Toscana, where the pole is shown as forking just ahead of the vehicle body (Pl. 87). The equid-drawn vehicle with its two occupants seated side by side is closed at the sides and rear but open at the front. In addition, it is possible that the schematic petroglyphs from Val Camonica in the Italian Alps include representations of Y-poled carts (Pl. 100).[48]

Cart Type II: the central-poled cart

The second type of cart is best documented by the three detailed Etruscan bronze models of the fifth century or later (Pls 88–90). These attest to a basic framework formed by three parallel pieces of wood, joined together by cross-pieces. The three lengthwise timbers project at the front and rear, the central one continuing forward as the draught pole (see below, Chapter III.4). This construction, involving a central rather than a Y-pole, is found on many carts, ancient and recent, from different parts of the

---

[43] See pp. 73–74.

[44] See p. 71, note 15.

[45] Gail 1986, ill. p. 157.

[46] Gail 1986, ill. p. 159.

[47] See a.o. Paturik 1985, no. 5; Gail 1986, ill. p. 165; *Oriental Manuscripts and Miniatures. Sotheby's Sales Catalogue* (London, 22 May 1986), frontispiece and p. 46.

[48] Van Berg-Osterrieth 1972, 73–80 and figs 30–1, 33–4; Piggott 1983, 119.

world (Pls 149, 154, 156).[49] In Italy, the construction with a central pole is indicated not only on the Etruscan bronze models but also on the terracotta model of *c.* 650–580 from Pithecusae (Pl. 93). Other terracotta models from different sites confirm the rectangular floor, but give no details. Among the profile representations of carts, the terracotta plaques from Metaponto of *c.* 600 are particularly informative (Pl. 115). They show the ends of the cross-pieces of the floor frame as mortised into the side-pieces which project at the front and rear, and the central floor timber continuing forward as the draught pole. It may be noted that in the case of the Etruscan bronze model from Bolsena the central pole is joined by two pole braces (*q.v.*), round-sectioned timbers running back all the way to the rear of the vehicle body and thereby reinforcing the overall construction (Pl. 88).[50]

By no means all carts attested by surviving metal parts or illustrated in the figured documented can be grouped under the Y-poled or central-poled type. This is particularly difficult in the case of carts in profile representations. With regard to the carts of which there are material remains, the vehicle from the Tomba dei Bronzi at Castel San Mariano has been reconstructed as a Y-poled cart, even though no 'poggiaredini' or other conclusive evidence have been found (Pl. 79; see below). On the other hand, the cart from Colle del Forno tomb XI at Sferracavallo, where such evidence is lacking too, is assumed to have had a central pole (Pl. 78).[51]

Notwithstanding the paucity of evidence, some conclusions can be drawn about the size and construction of the vehicles. The width and depth of the cart floor varied considerably. Some carts must have been small, like the Etruscan bronze model from Sarteano and that on a black-figure Pseudo-Chalcidian neck-amphora which was quite probably made in Italy (Pls 90, 95);[52] these carts carry single passengers, their feet resting on the pole or dangling in front. Other carts in Italy were more capacious and accommodated up to three people: two seated side by side, and a driver seated separately at the front (Pl. 109). An Etruscan sarcophagus from Vulci appears to show as many as three female figures side-by-side, as well as a driver at the front (Pl. 66).[53] A fairly large floor is also implied by two Etruscan red-figure vase paintings, and by the series of cinerary urns from Volterra. All these depict one or, more rarely, two figures reclining or lying down lengthwise (Pls 97, 112).[54] As we have seen, other figured documents illustrate Y-poled carts with an extension at the front, designed to accommodate a driver.

Carts are essentially convertible and multi-purpose vehicles. Those in ancient Italy are no exception. Their framework may be left open, as on the Etruscan bronze models and the terracotta example from Pithecusae (Pl. 93), or floored over, as on the bronze model from Rossano di Vaglio (Pl. 91), depending on the use for which the vehicle was intended. A solid, plank flooring would obviously have been useful when the cart was carrying people seated on benches or chairs, as is illustrated on the terracotta revetment plaques from Metaponto and in several other figured documents (Pl. 115).

The cart's platform could, by the addition of a suitable superstructure, be adapted to different kinds of transport. Thus, the Etruscan bronze model from Sarteano is shown carrying a female figure seated on a folded cushion, without the protection of any siding (Pl. 90). At the same time, this and the bronze

---

[49] See a.o. Crouwel 1985, 203f. (Iron Age Cyprus), and 1992, 79 (Greece); Galhano 1973 (carts with central poles, A–poles and combinations of these were used side by side until quite recently in Portugal).

[50] Cf. Galhano 1973, fig. 110: a Portugese cart, apparently combining a Y-pole and a central pole. In Portugal such vehicles existed side by side with various Y-poled and central-poled carts until recently, as illustrated in Galhano's book. See also Crouwel 1985, 216 no. LM and fig. 1 (ancient lead model from Salamis in Cyprus).

[51] *Carri da guerra* 291–8 with figs 1–17 and pl. 30: 2–3 (P. Santoro), 299f. and reconstruction drawing fig. 33 (A. Emiliozzi), 319 (Repertorio no. 89); Emiliozzi 2001b 329–32; Martelli 2005; Emiliozzi, Moscati and Santoro 2007 and figs 3–9, pls 7b and 8a–b (fig. 4 and pl. 7b show the partial reconstruction of the cart, on display in the Ny Carlsberg Glyptotek in Copenhagen); website www.principisabini.it ('La tomba del principi sabino – Il calesse'); see also Johansen 1979, 86–9 (bronze sheathing of siding); our pp. 49–50 and note 273.

[52] Rumpf 1927, 156 and pl. 199, left (Group of Memnon Amphora); Canciani 1980, 145f. n. 14, no. d, 150, 154 and fig. 17; Steinhart 1990; Crouwel 1992, 80 and pl. 28: 1.

[53] See p. 71, note 11.

[54] See p. 71, notes (twin stamnoi, one from Bomarzo) and note 12.

model from Civiltà Castellana (Pl. 89) have removable front and tail boards, which are grooved in three places at the bottom to fit over the pole and the side beams. The head and tail boards are also grooved on top, presumably to support some removable superstructure. The latter may have been basket-like[55] or – more likely – similar to that of the bronze model from Bolsena, where the front and tail boards are rendered in less detail and cast in one piece with the floor frame (Pl. 88). Its superstructure is formed of two rods, round in section and running parallel to the side beams of the framework, the rear ends of which pass through the tail board; the two rods are lashed to the tailboard and converge in front to be fastened to the pole at some distance ahead of the vehicle body. Six other, transverse rods are lashed on top of the rods and form a cradle for the central floor beam. Such a superstructure is clearly designed not for a human load but for hay or other farm produce.[56]

The carts represented in two- and three-dimensional figured documents are shown with and without a siding. In addition to the bronze model from Sarteano with a female figure seated on a folded cushion (Pl. 90), a siding is absent from the cart seen on the Pseudo-Chalcidian neck-amphora, where the male driver is seated on what looks like cargo rather than a cushion (Pl. 95). Some of the carts depicted in representations from southern Italy have no siding, while carrying a single female figure seated on a chair with a backrest (Pls 98, 114).

Other figured documents illustrate carts with (removable) seats or benches, placed between a siding to help keep them in place. The siding of these carts is usually low and the seats – with or without back, armrests, or cushions – are seen rising above it. The siding often consists of a horizontal rail supported by a number of vertical posts, as is most explicitly illustrated on the terracotta revetment plaques from Poggio Civitate (Murlo), and others from Metaponto (Pls 113, 115). Such a siding is seen with contemporary carts in mainland Greece (Pl. 149).[57] Indeed a railwork siding, often removable and extending around the rear and sides but open at the front, is a feature of many carts, through the centuries in different parts of the world.

In Italy and elsewhere, the siding of carts may also be solid, as seen for instance on an Etruscan sarcophagus from Vulci and on the Rossano di Vaglio bronze model (Pls 66, 91). The carts depicted on funerary stelae from Bologna have a low siding, its latticing or cross-hatching suggesting wickerwork, with a row of loops on top (Pls 106–107). The loops recur on other figured documents, including the Etruscan engraved gem and one of the red-figure vase paintings, as well as some of the Volterra cinerary urns (Pls 101, 112). The latter also show arched tilts, open at the front. The loops here may have helped to secure the (removable) hood to the low siding, with straps running both up straight and obliquely across the hood. A cart with an arched tilt is also illustrated on a sarcophagus from Tarquinia (Pl. 110).[58] Furthermore, tilt carts, associated with female members of the Imperial family, are depicted on coins of the early Roman Empire period.[59]

An open cart with a rather fancy siding, its curved top ending in scrolls at either side, is seen on one of the Etruscan gold rings, the vehicle carrying a driver and a figure apparently seated on an elaborate chair (Pl. 102). This kind of siding recurs with the wagon depicted on a (lost) Etruscan stone relief (Pl. 121). It is also materially documented by the highly decorated bronze sheathing of one of the vehicles buried in the sixth century Tomba dei Bronzi at Castel San Mariano. This particular vehicle has been reconstructed – on paper – as a wagon, but there is now a much more convincing full-scale reconstruction

---

[55] As first suggested by Lorimer 1903, 135.

[56] So also Piggott 1983, 192. The superstructure calls to mind carts that were quite recently used in Turkey; see *Asia Minor* (with introduction by M. Osward; Munich and London 1957) pl. 142.

[57] Crouwel 1992, 81 and pls 17: 3, 18: 6, 23: 1a–b, 2, 25: 1, 3, 38–39, see also pls 20: 3 and 26: 4.

[58] See p. 71, note 11.

[59] See a.o. Lucchi 1968; Pagnotta 1977–8, 169f.; Weber 1978, 118–21 and pl. 30: 3.

as a cart (Pl. 79).[60] One argument against a four-wheeler is the length of the body, which in the earlier reconstruction was estimated as 1.42 m. (The bronze side sheathing is preserved to a length of 1.10 m.) This would leave little room for two pairs of wheels to revolve without touching each other, even when they were small and placed near the ends of the floor.

It may be helpful to adduce here the evidence provided by the remains of two other actual vehicles. The first is the cart, associated with a rich warrior burial of *c.* 620–580, from tomb XI of the Collo del Forno cemetery at Sferracavallo in Lazio (see above). The body of this vehicle is estimated to have been 1.28 m long, based on its decorated bronze sheathing which is of more angular appearance than that from Castel San Mariano (Pl. 78). The second actual vehicle is a wagon from San Michele tomb 5 at Veii, dating to *c.* 675–650. Here the vehicle body is estimated to have been *c.* 2.00 m long, the wheels having a diameter of 1.00 m (for this vehicle, see also IV.1).

In both the earlier and new reconstruction, the vehicle from the Tomba dei Bronzi at Castel San Mariano has highly decorated bronze-sheathed panels along the sides (0.44 m high) and at the rear (0.60 m wide and 0.43 m high), but is open at the front (Pl. 79). The new reconstruction as a Y-poled cart, with a suspended foot support for a single seated occupant, is largely inspired by the cart from Sirolo. However, as reconstructed, the wheels of the Castel San Mariano vehicle are not spoked, but of the cross-bar type (*q.v.*), based on those of the cart with a similarly-shaped siding depicted on the gold ring mentioned above. They are fixed on a revolving axle.

2. Axle

The extant cart from Sirolo appears to have its axle centrally located under the floor (Pl. 76b). The figured documents of carts usually show the axle in a similar position. A central axle is, in fact, characteristic of most carts, both ancient and more recent, and is suitable for stable loads or passive, i.e. seated or reclining, passengers.

The material and figured evidence attests to the existence of two types of cart axle in ancient Italy – one fixed, with the wheels revolving on it, the other revolving and with the wheels fixed on it. The first type of axle, rigidly fixed to the vehicle body and only round where the wheels revolved on it, is shared with chariots (see Chapter II.2). Its presence on the Sirolo cart is indicated by the iron hoops that encircled the projecting naves of the spoked wheels, exactly as those of chariots. The wheels of this cart were similarly kept in place by iron linch pins, their simple design also occurring with chariot burials elsewhere in Italy. The spoked wheels seen on carts in some figured documents must have similarly revolved on fixed axles (Pls 66, 97, 110, 112–113).

Other figured documents yield explicit evidence for the second type of axle, which revolved with the wheels and was held in place by axle brackets (*q.v.*) beneath the sides of the floor frame. This type of axle, round in section where it revolves within the brackets and rectangular where the wheels are fixed on it, is suitable for relatively slow transport. The revolving axle requires only a simple naveless wheel, in contrast to the fixed axle with revolving wheels which is essential for fast vehicles.

The detailed bronze cart models from Bolsena, Sarteano and Civiltà Castellana show straight-sided axle brackets, whereas the model of the same material from Rossano di Vaglio in southern Italy indicates

---

[60] **Pro wagon:** Petersen 1894, 256–74 no. I and fig. 1 (reconstruction drawing); Woytowitsch 1978, nos 77–8, 84 and pl. 13; Höckmann 1982, 10–32 (especially 31f.), bronzes sheathings nos 1–3 ('Sitzwagen'), 158 and figs 4–11 and 12 (reconstruction drawing, reproduced in Camerin 1997b, fig. 10), pls 1–13 and Beil 1. **Pro cart:** Emiliozzi 1997, 95 n. 3; *Carri da guerra* 319, (Repertorio no. 95); E. Feruglio in *Gli Etruschi* 580–2 cat. no. 127 (full-scale reconstruction, incorporating bronze sheathing and statuettes dispersed over several museum collections, first displayed in Venice in 2000 and since then in the Museo Archeologico Nazionale dell'Umbria in Perugia; see *I carri etruschi di Castel San Mariano* (Perugia 2002); Bruni 2002, 27–35 and figs 8–9, 11–14.

brackets with curved sides (Pls 88–91). The bronze models from Bolsena and Civiltà Castellana still preserve the revolving axles. Their rectangular-sectioned ends are pierced for wedge-like linch pins, which helped keep the wheels in place; the latter are naveless and of disk type (see below, Chapter III.3). Just inside the wheels, the axles thicken to prevent the wheels from running into the vehicle body.

A rectangular axle end, a wedge-like linch pin and a disk wheel are clearly indicated on the equid-drawn cart on the Stele di Via Tovana from Bologna (Pl. 105), and on a hand-drawn cart in a fourth century Paestan red-figure vase painting by Python (Pl. 99).[61] Other figured documents, dating to the sixth century and later, also attest to revolving axles by showing rectangular axle ends – sometimes together with linch pins and axle brackets – but in combination with wheels of the different, cross-bar type (see below, Chapter III.3).

There are remains of actual wooden wheels from northern Italy, presumably going back to before the period of our first figured documents of carts (see below, Chapter III.3). Three of these wheels are naveless solid disks, thus implying a revolving axle (Pl. 81–83). Another – a cross-bar wheel with a tubular, inserted nave – must have revolved on a fixed axle (Pl. 84). Among the vehicular remains from later funerary contexts there is the bronze and iron sheathing of a pair of exceptionally large wheels (diameter 1.14 m) and their accompanying axle from the Tumulo dei Carri of c. 675–650 at Populonia (Pl. 86).[62] The elaborate sheathing of the naves leaves a square opening for the axle. This points to wheels that were fixed on a revolving axle, indicative of a cart, not a chariot.

The metal axle caps with square rather than round openings from the Tomba del Littore at Vetulonia and from Colle del Forno, tomb XI at Sferracavallo indicate that the carts buried there similarly had revolving axles with wheels fixed on them.[63]

Other material evidence for revolving axles, it has been claimed, is yielded by a distinct type of metal objects. It is found, mostly in pairs, among vehicular remains in several tombs, including Colle del Forno tomb XI at Sferracavallo (see above) and Case Nocera tomb A at Casale Marittimo in Toscana (Pl. 80c).[64] These objects, in Italian referred to as 'staffe' (stirrups), consist of a flat piece of bronze or iron bent into a U-shape and with stirrup-like fastenings (width across on average c. 0.06–0.07 m; height c. 0.09–0.10 m). The 'staffe' would have hung from the cart floor with the axle revolving within them.[65] However, such an arrangement has no parallels among other carts, ancient or recent. Apart from the problem of attachment to the vehicle, these objects would have suffered from wear by the revolving axle.

Axle brackets, on the other hand, not only served to keep the axle in position but also to raise the vehicle floor. On carts in ancient Italy and elsewhere, the Y- or central pole often formed an integral part of the vehicle floor, being a continuation of the central floor board and running out horizontally or at a slight angle to the yoke area. Axle brackets helped to keep the floor in a horizontal position rather than tilting, their height depending on the size of the wheels and that of the draught animals.

---

[61] See p. 72, note 27.

[62] Woytowitsch 1978, no. 66 and pl. 9; *Etrusker in der Toskana* 217–19 (A. Romualdi); *Carri da guerra* 176f. and pl. X (A. Emiliozzi), 322 (Repertorio no. 124); *Signori di Maremma* cat. no. 1.121.

[63] Tomba del Littore: see *Carri da guerra* 266 and fig. 1d (M. Cygielman), 327 (Repertorio no. 173); also *Signori di Maremma* cat. no. 376. Sferracavallo tomb XI: see *Carri da guerra* 297 no. 19 and fig. 25 (P. Santoro), 319 (Repertorio no. 89).

[64] Emiliozzi in *Carri da guerra* 297 no. 27 and fig. 26 (Colle de Forno tomb XI); Emiliozzi 2001a 44f. and figs 34–5, 38 (Casale Marittimo, tomb A; *Carri da guerra* 319, Repertorio no. 94). See also Emiliozzi 1997, 103; Cygielman and Pagnini 2006, 31f., 34 *s.v.* nos 4–7 with fig. 3a–d and pl. IIe–f (four 'staffe', attributed to two carts, from the Tomba del Tridente at Vetulonia; *Carri da guerra* 327, Repertorio no. 177). Earlier discussion in Nebelsick 1992, 101 and n. 94 (called *Klemmschnallen*). For the pair from Colle del Forno tomb XI at Sferracavallo, see P. Santoro in *Carri da guerra* 297 no. 20 and fig. 26. Four such objects, along with 'poggiaredini', are known from tombs III and V of c. 700 in the Varreccia cemetery at Veii; see Palm 1952, 61 nos 10–11 and 62 nos 7–10 with pls 12–13; Emiliozzi 1997, 103 and fig. 8; *Carri da guerra* 326 (Repertorio no. 165). A pair of 'staffe', along with 'poggiaredini', are also among the cart remains from tomb 182 at Crocifisso, Matelica in Marche (*Potere e splendore* 242f. cat. nos 322 and 326; see our p. 12, note 29).

[65] For a reconstruction drawing, see Emiliozzi 2001a, fig. 35.

This arrangement contrasts sharply with that of ancient chariots where the pole was made of a separate timber, lying between the axle and the floor and curving upwards rather more sharply in front of the vehicle to reach the necessary yoke height (see Chapter II.4).

Axle brackets, open and concave as they are at the bottom, permit the cart body and pole to be lifted off the axle at any time for convenience – e.g. for storage or in the event of the vehicle becoming stuck in mud. Metal bearing shoes on the concave bottom of the wooden brackets were used to protect the latter from wear by the revolving axle (Pl. 154, cf. Pl. 155).[66] It may be noted that there is as yet no material evidence for axles with metal bearing shoes in ancient Italy.

3. Wheels

The figured documents illustrate cart wheels of three different types – disk, cross-bar and spoked (*q.v.*).

Disk wheels are seen with the Etruscan bronze cart models from Bolsena and Civiltà Castellana (Pls 88–89).[67] The wheels are naveless, with a rectangular hole in the centre for the revolving axle on which they were fixed (see Chapter III.2). The two outward-curving elements flanking the axle hole on the outer side of the wheels indicate that these were composite and probably tripartite, held by battens.

On most tripartite disk wheels – a type well-known through the ages in different parts of the world – a central plank, as long as the diameter of the finished wheel and half as wide, is flanked by planks half its width. The three planks have flush surfaces and are held together by internal dowels or by battens let into one or both of the outer faces of the wheels, or by a combination of these.[68]

Two lake sites of the Terramare culture of the Middle or Late Bronze Age (*c.* 1700–1000) in northern Italy provide early material evidence for disk wheels with bonding elements. The wheels were excavated in the 1860s and their find contexts and precise dating are unknown.[69]

One of these sites, Castione dei Marchesi in Emilia Romagna, has yielded fragments of what was probably a tripartite disk wheel made of walnut wood (Pl. 81).[70] The diameter of the wheel has been variously reported as 0.69–0.70 or 0.85 m. Its component parts were held together by two pairs of battens kept in channels, and by two pairs of transverse slats driven into dovetail mortises. The slats were on one side of the wheel, each pair flanking the central axle hole which is now oval in shape and measures *c.* 0.11×0.07 m. There are lunate openings cut into the side planks on either side of the axle hole. Such openings are a feature of many tripartite disk wheels, ancient and more recent (Pl. 154). They may be a means of getting a handhold on an object otherwise awkward to grasp, e.g. when the vehicle was stuck in mud; they may also have permitted the passage of a pole through opposite wheels, in order to lock them.[71]

---

[66] Metal bearing shoes, attested in Iron Age Cyprus and possibly in the Near East, were recently still in use on carts in Portugal; see Crouwel 1985, 208 and fig. 1: A1(b); 1992, 84; Galhano 1973, especially figs 138 and 16, 18, 21–2.

[67] The wheels of the third model, from Sarteano (see p. 71, note 8), are rosette-shaped and therefore an anomaly; for illustrations see Walters 1899, pl. XII; Richardson 1953, fig. 5.

[68] See a.o. Lucas 1972; Littauer and Crouwel 1977a, 95–9; Hayen 1987, 173–5; Piggott 1993, especially 24–6; Schlichtherle 2004, 297–301.

[69] See a.o. Piggott 1983, 86, 97f.; Rottoli 1997.

[70] Woytowitsch 1978, no. 1 and pl. 2: 1a–b; Cornaggia Castiglioni and Calegari 1978, 42f. no. 5 and pl. IVA–C; Piggott 1983, 86; Mutti, Provenzano, Ross and Rottoli 1988, nn. 5, 214 and fig. 131: 2; Rottoli 1997, 485 with fig. 275: 17; Schlichtherle 2004, 301 and fig. 7: below. From the same site comes a wooden disk, only 0.14–0.155 m in diameter, with a square central opening (0.015 m²), which might be a model wheel; see Woytowitsch 1978, no. 206 and pl. 40; Cornaggia, Castiglioni and Calegari 1978, 39f. no. 2 and pl. IIA; Piggott 1983, 86; Rottoli 1997, fig. 275: 9. For other small pierced wooden disks from sites in Lombardia, see Cornaggia, Castiglioni and Calegari 1978, 37f. no. 1 (from Lagozetta), 40f. no. 3 (diameter 0.38 m, from Isolon delle Moradelle), cf. 41f. no. 4 (?imitation of spoked wheel, only 0.16 m in diameter, from Barche di Solferino).

[71] For tripartite disk wheels with lunate openings, see Lucas 1972; Littauer and Crouwel 1979a, 103f.; Hayen 1980–1, 44; Piggott 1983, 25, 86;

What was also probably a tripartite disk wheel, now only preserved in a plaster cast (Pl. 82), comes from Mercurago at the south end of Lake Maggiore in Piemonte.[72] Its diameter has been calculated as 0.78–0.80 m. As on the disk wheel from Castione dei Marchesi, the planks of the Mercurago wheel were held together by a pair of internal battens in channels. In addition, mortises were was cut in the surface of the wheel, symmetrically located on either side of the axle hole; into the mortises a flexible batten was inserted and held in lateral tension. The wheel shows traces of repairs on one side. A separately made, tubular nave (0.25–0.28 m long and 0.08–0.10 m in diameter) was inserted into the round axle hole. The nave must have helped prevent the wheel from wobbling on the fixed axle on which it revolved.

Two planks (now lost), also from Mercurago, have been interpreted as the outer members of a much larger tripartite disk wheel, c. 1.32 m in diameter (Pl. 83).[73]

The crescent shape of the bonding elements of the disk wheels of two Etruscan bronze cart models suggests battens let into channels and held in lateral tension, as on the first Mercurago wheel. Something similar is seen on the Stele di Via Tofana from Bologna and on an Etruscan cippus of the earlier fifth century, the vehicles here being a cart and a four-wheeled platform respectively (Pls 105, 120).

Other evidence for the use of disk wheels in Italy before the Roman Empire is yielded by the fourth century Paestan red-figure vase painting by Python, which illustrates a hand-drawn cart in a mythological setting (Pl. 99).[74] Here the wheels are clearly tripartite, the straight-sided central plank carrying no nave but only a square hole for a revolving axle. Bonding elements are not indicated.

Some terracotta models show what appear to be disk wheels with raised centres, but it is not certain whether these simple documents should be read literally.[75]

Neither the figured documents illustrating carts with disk wheels, nor the actual wheels of this type, provide evidence for a tyre (q.v.). This would have helped consolidate the wheels and protect the tread or running surface. Only much later, during the Roman Imperial period, can tyres sometimes be made out on depictions of disk-wheeled carts which were used in heavy transport.[76]

Figured documents ranging from the sixth century onwards more often illustrate carts with wheels of cross-bar type (Pls 94–96, 98, 101–102, 107–109, 114–115) . Individual wheels of this type appear as a motif on Etruscan silver and bronze coins (Pl. 103).[77]

Although varying in details of construction, the cross-bar wheel is characterized by a diametric bar through which the axle passes, with lighter cross-bars at right angles to the diametric bar, between it and the felloe. This type of wheel has a long history, going back to the later third millennium in the Near East, and it still existed in recent times in different parts of the world.[78] In antiquity it was normally

---

Boehmer 1983, 37–40; Burmeister 2004b, 332; Schlichtherle 2004, 308f. Such wheels openings are common on recent Portugese carts, see our Pl. 154 (adapted from Galhano 1973, figs 22 and 138b; see also his figs 70–1, 110, 136).

[72] Woytowitsch 1978, no. 2 and pl. 1: 2a–c; Cornaggia Castiglioni and Calegari 1978, 44f. no. 6 and pls VA–C, VIIIB–C (Mercurago no. I); Piggott 1983, 86 and fig. 43; Schlichtherle 2004, 309 and fig. 15: top.

[73] Cornaggia Castiglioni and Calegari 1978, 46 no. 7 and pl. VIB–C (Mercurago no. II); Piggott 1983, 86.

[74] See p. 72 and note 27. Cf. also a Paestan tomb painting of similar date showing a boy seated in a toy cart (Andriuolo tomb 8; see Pontrandolfo and Rouveret 1992, 340 and ills p. 166: 1, 3). The latter scene recalls the toy carts depicted on many Attic red–figure miniature choes; see Van Hoorn 1951, especially figs 258–61.

[75] See Woytowitsch 1978, pls 32–3, 36 and 39.

[76] See a.o. Pisani Sartorio 1988, figs 67–8, 70; Adam and Varène 1980, and Raepsaet 2002, 219 and fig. 116 (wall painting from Stabiae). See also Carandini, Ricci and de Vos 1982, pl. I and foglios XXVIII and XXX; Dunbabin 1999, figs 135, 142 (the Great Hunting mosaic from Piazza Armerina, Sicily). Nailed-on iron tyres belonged with the disk wheels of a cart of which remains were found in a villa near Boscoreale; see De Caro 1994, 206–8 no. 228 with fig. 54; Raepsaet 2002, 229 and fig. 128.

[77] Minted at Vulci; see Franke and Hirmer 1964, pl. 3: middle, left (our Pl. 103); Woytowitsch 1978, no. 226 and pl. 46; Crouwel 1992, 86 n. 437 and pl. 36: 2. Minted at Populonia; see Cahn, Mildenberg, Russo and Voegtli 1988, 18 no. 1. Bronze coins minted at an unknown place; see *Welt der Etrusker. Archäologische Denkmäler* no. H 26; Catalli 1990, 102f. nos 80–1.

[78] For the cross-bar type of wheel, its properties, origin and distribution, see Lorimer 1903; Atkinson and Ward 1965; Littauer and Crouwel 1977a (= 2002, 272–88); Hayen 1980–1; Piggott 1983, 97f.; Boehmer 1983, 36f.; Wegener Sleeswyk 1992, 490–2 (called H-spoked wheel);

associated with carts – in Italy as well as in Greece and the Near East – but not with wagons or chariots. A notable exception from Italy are the racing chariots with cross-bar wheels in tomb paintings of the fourth century from Paestum.[79]

As in the case of the disk wheels, there is also material evidence for the use of cross-bar wheels in Italy before the Roman Empire. Remains of two such wheels have been found at Mercurago, the same Terremare site that yielded evidence for disk wheels. The cross-bar wheels again date to some time in the second millennium, i.e. long before the first figured documents of this type of wheel in Italy.

One of the Mercurago wheels, now preserved only in a plaster cast, had a diameter of 0.88–0.90 m (Pl. 84).[80] Over the years different woods – walnut and chestnut – have been mentioned for different parts of this wheel. The diametric bar was thickened in the centre to accommodate a separately made tubular nave. The latter (originally *c.* 0.30–0.36 m long and 0.06 m in diameter) must have revolved on a fixed axle. The ends of the diametric bar were spade-shaped and formed part of the felloe. The felloe was made in two segments, one on either side of the diametric bar and mortised into the latter's ends. There are two thin cross-bars, passing through the diametric bar close to its centre and curving slightly outward before being mortised into the felloe segments. The curve of the cross-bars, applied under tension, may well be intentional, to help hold the wheel together rather than to transfer weight, as spokes would.

Very little was found of the second cross-bar wheel from Mercurago: one felloe segment with the ends of two straight cross-bars mortised into it (Pl. 85).[81] The felloe was reportedly made of oak wood and suggests a wheel of more massive construction than the first one, with an estimated diameter of *c.* 0.89 m.

These material remains may be compared with two other cross-bar wheels that have survived, albeit incompletely, from antiquity. One comes from Olympia in Greece, its find context dating to the earlier fifth century (Pl. 157).[82] The other was found at Gordion in Anatolia, in a context of the sixth century (Pl. 158).[83] The Olympia wheel, its diameter estimated as 0.78 m, had an inserted tubular nave, made of oak wood, and must have revolved on a fixed axle, like the best preserved cross-bar wheel from Mercurago. In contrast, the larger wheel from Gordion (diameter reconstructed as 1.15 m), with its subrectanglar axle end, appears to have been naveless and fixed on a revolving axle. The diametric bar of the Olympia wheel is mortised at each end into the felloe, at a place where two of the latter's four segments are joined together by mortise-and-tenon. The two rather thick, straight cross-bars of this wheel pass through the diametric bar and felloe. Unlike the best preserved Mercurago wheel, the cross-bars are straight and end in the tread (*q.v.*), where they are secured by wedges. Beech wood was used for the felloe of this wheel, as well as for its diametric and cross-bars. The more clumsy-looking wheel from Gordion has been reconstructed with six felloe segments, held together where the diametric and rather thick cross-bars join them.

None of these surviving cross-bar wheels, whether from Italy, Greece or Anatolia, shows evidence of a tyre of any sort. Instead, on the Olympia wheel the wedges at the ends of the cross-bars, driven in from the tread, helped to hold the wheel together when in use. This was also the purpose of the spade-shaped ends of the diametric bar on the best preserved Mercurago wheel (Pl. 84).

However, a nailed-on iron tyre is a feature of a cross-bar wheel that has recently been identified at a sanctuary site at Monteleone Sabino (ancient Trebula Mutuesca) in Lazio. The wheel remains belong to

---

Crouwel 1992, 85–7.

[79] See p. 16, note 46.

[80] Littauer and Crouwel 1977a, 101f.; Woytowitsch 1978, no. 3 and pls 2–3; Cornaggia Castiglioni and Calegary 1978, 46f. no. 8 and pls VII, VIIIA (Mercurago no. III); Hayen 1980–1, 162–74 no. D 4–1 and figs 14–19; Piggott 1983, 28, 97f. and fig. 53; Crouwel 1992, 85f. and pl. 36: 4; Schlichtherle 2004, 309 and fig. 15, middle.

[81] Cornaggia Castigioni and Calegari 1978, 47f. no. 9 and pl. VIA (Mercurago no. IV); Piggott 1983, 98; Schlichtherle 2004, 309f. and fig. 15: bottom.

[82] Hayen 1980–1, especially 153–62, 183–5 no. D 3–1 and figs 10–13, 20; Crouwel 1992, 85–7 and pl. 17: 1.

[83] Kohler 1980, 69 and fig. 32; Crouwel 1992, 85f. and pl. 36: 2.

a foundation deposit of the third century. Iron was used to cover the transverse bar and two crescent-shaped(?) cross-bars of the wheel, which had a diameter of 0.93 m and revolved on a fixed axle.[84]

Some of the figured documents from Italy showing cross-bar wheels indicate rectangular axle ends. A good example is a sixth century Etruscan silver coin minted at Vulci, where a linch pin is also indicated (Pl. 103). This would imply a wheel fixed on a revolving axle, thus requiring no nave, as on the actual cross-bar wheel from Gordion. Another Etruscan coin, unprovenanced and made of bronze, shows a cross-bar wheel combined with a round axle end, thereby implying a naved wheel revolving on a fixed axle, as on the Olympia wheel and on the best preserved one from Mercurago (Pls 157, 84).

The lines running across the diametric bar seen on the silver coin from Vulci and in some other figured documents, suggest a binding to protect it from splitting under pressure from the axle (Pls 103, 108).[85] The two cross-bars are straight or, more often, curving outwards. As noted above, one of the two much earlier actual cross-bar wheels from Mercurago also has outward curving cross-bars. They also recall the similarly curving battens of the tripartite disk wheels of two of the Etruscan bronze cart models (Pls 88–89) and of the wagon depicted on an Etruscan funerary relief (Pl. 120).

It is commonly accepted that the cross-bar type of wheel represents an attempt to lighten the tripartite disk wheel.[86] The particular variant with cross-bars curving away from the diametric bar is documented not only in ancient Italy, but also in Greece. However, in Greece the cross-bars are more often shown as straight.[87]

Other figured documents from Italy, of the sixth century and later, illustrate carts with spoked wheels (Pls 97, 106, 110, 112–113). This type of wheel seems to be standard on the actual carts of which remains have been found in tombs of the seventh and sixth centuries (Pl. 76c).[88]

The spokes of these wheels vary from four to eight and appear to have been of similar construction to those of contemporary chariots, which have projecting naves that revolved on fixed axles (see Chapter II.3). The cart wheels represented by actual surviving metal parts had felloes with folded U-shaped or riveted clamps, and nailed-on iron tyres, exactly like those of chariot wheels. As in the case of some chariot wheels, the folded clamps may be so large that they indicate a double-layered felloe.[89]

The iron tyres usually yield diameters of the same size as those of chariot wheels. On the other hand, the pair of wheels represented by their elaborate bronze sheathing from the Tumulo dei Carri at Populonia belonged to a cart rather than a chariot, in view of details of the naves and accompanying axle (Pl. 86).[90] These wheels are exceptional in having a diameter as large as 1.14 m. They are also exceptional in presenting the appearance of two four-spoked wheels, one within the other; the respective spokes are staggered.

To conclude, in Italy carts (and wagons) could be fitted with three different types of wheels. Of these the disk type was suitable only for slow, heavy transport. The cross-bar type is lighter than the tripartite

---

[84] Vallarino 2006, especially 86 and figs 3–4 (from Area I). Remains of another wheel of smilar date were found in Area III at the same site; the wheel also had a nailed-on iron tyre (indicating a diameter of 0.84 m), but was apparently spoked and originally fixed on a revolving axle (Vallarino 2006, 86 and figs 6–7).

[85] Such a binding may also be illustrated with cross-bar wheels in Greece; see Crouwel 1992, 86 and pls 18: 2, 20:2 and 5, 23: 1a–b, 24: 2, 28: 2, 38–39.

[86] See p. 81, note 78.

[87] Littauer and Crouwel 1977a, 102; Höckmann 1977, pl. 51: 2; 1982, 135 no. G 7; Crouwel 1992, 86 and pl. 18: 4 (pl. 28: 2 is taken from a so-called Tyrrhenian black-figure amphora by the Guglielmi Painter; see Beazley 1956, 96, no. 9; Carpenter 1989, 25). This and other 'Tyrrhenian' black-figure vases were probably made in Attica and not in central Italy (Etruria); see Carpenter 1984; Kluiver 1992.

[88] It may be noted that remains of a pair of eight-spoked wheels have been identified at the Terramare site of Barche di Solferino in northern Italy. With a diameter of 0.12–0.13 m, the objects may have been models of some kind; see Ornella Acanfore 1970, 216–22 and figs 34/1, 41/1; Woytowitsch 1978, no. 4 with pl. 3; Piggott 1983, 94.

[89] See Emiliozzi 2001, 318 and fig. 6 (Veii, Vaccareccia cemetery, tombs V, VIII and XVIII of the later eighth century; also *Carri da guerra* 326, Repertorio nos 165, 168, 170). For long felloe clamps of chariot wheels, see our pp. 33–34 and note 156.

[90] See p. 79 and note 62.

disk wheel. In comparison with the spoked wheel, the cross-bar type is simpler to make and repair, but heavier and not as strong. This makes it suitable for the relatively slow cart (and wagon), but not for the fast chariot, which in Italy and elsewhere usually had spoked wheels.

4. Traction system

As in the case of chariots, traction was provided by teams of animals under a yoke. This was connected to the vehicle by means of a draught pole. As already noted, there were two types of draught pole – the central pole, formed simply of a continuation of the central lengthwise timber of the vehicle floor, and the composite so-called Y-pole. A different type of Y-pole is attested on four-wheelers. It is not rigidly fixed, as on two-wheelers, but often articulates vertically.[91]

In profile representations, the draught pole may be shown as rising at a slight slant to the yoke area or at a steep angle, reminiscent of chariot poles (see Chapter II.4). In other profile representations, the pole is seen running out horizontally from the vehicle body. The latter is also the case on the Etruscan bronze models with their central draught pole.

A pole-end finial, apparently in the form of a bird's head, is seen on one of the carts depicted on the cinerary urns from Volterra.[92] Also of note is the stationary mule-cart on the Apulian red-figure vase fragment from Ruvo, where a prop is seen supporting the pole at its junction with the yoke (Pl. 98).[93]

5. Harnessing

Carts were drawn by two animals – equids or bovids – under a neck yoke (*q.v.*). This lay just in front of their withers, as in contemporary chariot harness in Italy (see Chapter II.5).

Information on the shape of the yoke is furnished chiefly by the Etruscan bronze cart models from Bolsena, Civittà Castellana and Sarteano (Pls 88–90). On the last model, the yoke is explicitly associated with bovid traction. Representations on later cinerary urns from Volterra confirm that similarly-shaped yokes were used on equids (Pl. 112). The bronzes show the yoke with bays shaped for the neck of each individual animal, like the yoke of chariot horses.[94] In the case of equids, a padding would have been present to protect the animals' necks from being bruised and rubbed by the wooden yoke.

The bronze cart models yield evidence for two different ways of attaching the yoke to the pole, near the latter's forward end. On the models from Bolsena and Sarteano the yoke lies on top of the pole, which may have notches above and below to help secure the lashings by which the yoke was held in place (Pls 88, 90).[95] The model from Civittà Castellana instead shows the pole as lying on top of the yoke, but this would seem to be an anomaly (Pl. 89). The same model, more realistically, has corresponding holes in yoke and pole – quite possibly for a (missing) yoke peg (*q.v.*). This would have helped to consolidate the position of the yoke at right angles to the pole.

The two animals were each harnessed under the yoke by means of a neckstrap (*q.v.*). This arrangement is seen in profile representations, and two of the bronze models have holes on either side of each bay for fastening neckstraps (Pls 89–90). In some representations of mule-carts, the neckstrap may be shown as attached not directly to the yoke, but by means of a separate, narrow strap (Pls 113–115).

In contrast to contemporary chariot harness, there is no girth (*q.v.*) running under the animals' chest

---

[91] See pp. 91, 94–95.

[92] Volterra Museum 183 (autopsy).

[93] Such a prop is also shown with the mule-cart depicted on an Attic black-figure plaque by Exekias; see Crouwel 1992, 90 and pl. 21: 1.

[94] (Parts of) actual wooden yokes with wider bays for the team's necks have survived from Europe north of the Alps; see Piggott 1983, 219 and figs 137–8 (La Tène period), cf. 170–2 and figs 106–8 (late Hallstatt period); Crouwel 1992, 89 and pl. 36: 5.

[95] A similar attachment is shown with the yoked oxen of the bronze plough group from Arezzo, see p. 6, note 49.

just behind the forelegs. This strap acted as a backing element (see Chapter II.5). A girth is also absent from mule-cart harness in ancient Greece, and was obviously not considered essential.[96] Neither is there evidence for a 'drag' (a weight to reduce speed on downwards slopes) or other braking device.[97]

6. Control

Figured documents indicate different ways in which the equine animals pulling carts were controlled. On the one hand, there are representations where the people in the vehicles are not concerned with controlling their harness teams (Pl. 113). The vehicles must have been slow-moving and led by attendants on foot. Several documents indeed show such figures, sometimes holding lead ropes that were attached to the noseband of the team's halters (*q.v.*). For instance, the slow-moving mule-cart depicted on terracotta revetment plaques from Metaponto is led by a man on foot, while at the same time one of its seated female passengers is holding a two-lashed whip (Pl. 115). For comparison, in ancient Greece mule-cart teams were usually controlled by a long stick or goad (*q.v.*) or by a whip, and the animals also often wore a halter (Pl. 149).[98]

Bridles were invariably used on horse-drawn chariots in Italy (see II.6), and are to be assumed in some of the cart representations (Pls 94, 107). There, reins are seen running from the driver's hands to the team's heads, while the driver may also hold a short stick or goad, or a whip. The pair of elaborate sheet-bronze headstalls of the seventh century from Colle del Forno tomb XI at Sferracavallo in Lazio should also be mentioned here (Pl. 29).[99] For no obvious reason they have been attributed to the cart rather than the chariot that were both buried in the tomb.

7. Use

Most of our evidence concerns the use of carts as conveyances for human beings who in the figured documents are shown seated, reclining or lying down but never standing, as chariot occupants do. The vehicles, drawn by teams of mules or horses, are usually shown moving slowly and their passengers unarmed. Unfortunately, the nature of the journey and the identification of the passengers often remain uncertain. They may be mortals, depicted during their lifetime or on their way to the Hereafter, deities or mythological figures.

What is probably a wedding procession is depicted on the Etruscan gem of the sixth century (Pl. 101). We see two people seated side by side and a driver at the front holding a whip, in a vehicle drawn by four horses(?) and led by a man on foot. A team of four draught animals is most unusual for carts in Italy, which are normally pulled by two equids or bovids. The large size of the team here may have been influenced by chariot draught which does make use of three or four horses, though more often of two (see Chapter II.5). The cortège includes other people on foot: a double-flute player in front and a woman carrying a basket or bucket on her head at the rear. The opposite side of the gem shows a house as well as various people on foot. The two scenes, when taken together, can be interpreted as analogous to contemporary practices in Greece, where after the wedding feast the bride was taken to the groom's house in a mule-cart. Written sources confirm this practice, while the fullest representation of such a wedding procession can be found in the Attic black-figure vase painting of *c.* 550–530 by the Amasis Painter (Pl. 149).[100]

Wedding processions, mostly mythological in nature, have been recognized in several other

---

[96] Crouwel 1992, 90.
[97] Wildhaber 1979; Molin 1984, 107f.; Crouwel 1992, 90.
[98] For the long goad in Greece, see Crouwel 1992, 92.
[99] See pp. 49–50 and note 273.
[100] See p. 73 and note 33. For discussion, see also Oakley and Hague Sinos 1993, 26–34; Hague Sinos 1994, 107f.

representations involving carts from Italy.[101] These, however, are not so straightforward and allow for different interpretations. It may be noted that there is no textual evidence for the use of carts or other vehicles at weddings in Italy, before or during the Roman Empire period.

A good example of the problems of interpretation is presented by the terracotta revetment plaques from a large building of the early sixth century at Poggio Civitate (Murlo) in Toscana (Pl. 113).[102] These illustrate a processional scene involving two figures, at least one of them female with her head covered, seated in a mule-cart. The draught team is led by two men on foot, who are followed by two others with fans and baskets or buckets in their hands. The men also carry a lidded container and an up-turned stool on their heads. The female cart passengers are seated side by side on a chair with a backrest. One of them holds a parasol, its shaft resting on the cart floor. This scene has been variously interpreted as a (mythological) wedding party, a journey to the underworld, a procession to a sanctuary to pay respect to the deities depicted on other revetment plaques from the same building, or as a procession at an unspecified occasion involving a ruler and his consort.[103]

The scene from Poggio Civitate (Murlo) recalls another procession, involving two female figures seated on chairs with high back- and armrests in a mule-cart, depicted on the terracotta revetment plaques dating to c. 600 from Metaponto in Puglia (Pl. 115). The vehicle is led by a man on foot and followed by three women, each holding a flower, as does one of the cart passengers. It has been persuasively argued that the figures in the cart are a priestess and her companion being driven to a local sanctuary.[104]

Mule-carts carrying single female figures seated on chairs appear in two other figured documents from southern Italy – a fourth century Apulian red-figure vase painting where the woman is holding a hydria (Pl. 98), and a terracotta votive plaque of the fifth century from Locri Epizephyrii in Calabria (Pl. 114). In the latter case a supernatural setting is suggested by the presence of a winged female figure above the vehicle. However, according to a more recent interpretation, the seated person is a priestess being taken to a sanctuary of Aphrodite.[105] A single seated female figure in a mule-cart is depicted on a fifth century red-figure neck-amphora from Vulci, her driver being seated at the front (Pl. 96).

Carts with seated female figures are also shown on a variety of funerary monuments from north and central Italy. (These and others also illustrate men standing in chariots; see Chapter II.7.) Among these monuments are stelae of the fifth–fourth centuries from Bologna, depicting one or two seated passengers, one of them holding up a parasol, along with a driver (Pls 106–108).[106] The presence of death demons emphasizes the funerary and supernatural nature of the journey.

A winged death demon with snakes in either hand appears in the cart scene on one of the short sides of the Etruscan sarcophagus of Ramtha Viśnai, wife of Anth Tetnie(s), from Vulci in Tuscany, dating to the second half of the fourth century (Pl. 109). The horse-drawn vehicle carries two seated women, one of them presumably Ramtha Viśnai herself and both holding the shaft of the same parasol, with their driver perched at the front. The same document shows, on the opposite short side, a man mounting a chariot – presumably Anth Tetnie(s) (Pl. 65).[107] The parasol, seen here and on the Poggio Civitate

---

[101] Thus particularly Höckmann 1982, 134–41; Fabbricotti 1977–9, 161–70.

[102] For this so-called Upper Building and its functions, see a.o. Phillips Jr. 1993, 7–12 (also 105–40: annotated bibliography for the site by him and I. Edlund-Berry).

[103] See p. 71 and note 10.

[104] See p. 72 and note 24. Mertens-Horn 1992 (a similar procession was depicted on the second, somewhat later series of revetment plaques from Metaponto, San Biagio). Some bronze statuettes of standing female figures from Francavilla Marittima, dating to c. 600, have been interpreted as representing cult statues that were carried in carts during processions; see Stoop 1970–1, 39f. no. 2, 45–8 no. 5 and pls 16a–d, 18a–c; Maaskant 1993, 35f. and nos 81–2, 145.

[105] See p. 72 and note 245. Mertens-Horn 1992, 55, 57. For earlier interpretations, see Zancani Montuoro 1955; Prückner 1968, 19–22; Höckmann 1982, 140 s.v. no G 20.

[106] For discussion of the scenes with carts, see especially Weber 1978, 77f., 81–4, 86–92 (Group b); Höckmann 1982, 145–8 s.v. no. E 19; Stary-Rimpau 1988, 80–8, 113f.

[107] See p. 63 and p. 24, note 94.

(Murlo) revetment plaques and the Bologna stelae, provided shade but also points to the high status of the cart passengers. Its usage in wheeled vehicles can be paralleled at different times and places.[108]

Another sarcophagus from Vulci, dating to the later fourth century, depicts on one of its long sides the meeting of a man, riding in a chariot and with an escort on horseback, and three female figures women with their driver in a horse-drawn cart (Pl. 66).[109] The cart is accompanied by a female figure on foot holding a jug and by a bearded man with a mallet identifiable as Charun. A sarcophagus of the second half of the third century from Tarquinia depicts a mule-drawn cart with an arched tilt in procession, accompanied by various male and female figures on foot, including death demons (Pl. 110).[110] Inside the cart is a veiled woman.

Processions, involving carts with arched tilts, drawn by horses and accompanied by death demons and mortals on foot or on horseback, are seen on a series of late Etruscan cinerary urns from Volterra (Pl. 112).[111] Inside the vehicles are one or two figures, apparently in a reclining position and, when a pair, presumably representing a married couple.

Single reclining men in open mule-carts can be seen in twin Etruscan red-figure vase paintings of the fourth century (Pl. 97). Another such vase painting, from Orvieto, shows a man lying on his back and holding a long knobbly stick, again in an open mule-cart.[112]

The people depicted seated, reclining or lying down in carts on these and other funerary monuments have often been interpreted in the same way as those seen standing in chariots – as the deceased on their journey to the Underworld or on arriving at their destination (see also Chapter II.7). Even where this is explicitly so, the pictures presumably reflect real-life activities, the chariots and carts providing comfortable and prestigious means of transport.[113] The cart scenes recall sixth-century terracotta models from Cyprus showing people similarly reclining or, more rarely, stretched out, in carts – with and without arched tilts (Pl. 156).[114] On these terracottas the passengers are sometimes seen resting with their elbow on a cushion. Cushions are seen on models of empty carts. The reclining position is the same as that portrayed in contemporary banquet scenes, in Cyprus and elsewhere, involving privileged and wealthy people.[115] One of the Cypriot cart models shows a man holding up what looks like a drinking cup, while another presents two adults reclining side by side, a boy playing a double flute perched on their laps.[116]

The arched tilts, when present, gave protection against the elements, while at the same time providing privacy. Greek texts tell us that in the Near East, at the time of the Achaemenid empire, women and grandees travelled in covered vehicles.[117] As for Italy, carts with arched tilts are illustrated in Roman Imperial times.[118] According to Livy, King Numa Pompilius of Rome (traditionally dated to 716–674) ordained that the priests of the god Fides use covered carriages.[119] Other Latin texts refer to the use of carts – or wagons, but not chariots – in Italy before the time of the Roman Empire, mainly by women,

---

[108] Crouwel 1973; Höckmann 1982, 32 n. 210; cf. Miller 1992.

[109] See p. 24 and note 94, p. 71, note 11.

[110] See p. 77 and p. 71, note 12 (Van der Meer 2008, no. *G19*). Another sarcophagus, from the same tomb at Tarquinia, shows a woman seated in an open cart and accompanied by mortal attendants and death demons; see p. 71, note 12 (Van der Meer 2008, no. *G29*).

[111] See p. 71, note 12.

[112] See p. 71, note 15. The mule-cart is shown together with a chariot (of uncertain type), drawn by four horses and driven by Hades–Aita, who is escorted by Charun and a a death demon (Vanth).

[113] As was stressed by Höckmann 1982, 149f., 154, 156f.; see also Walde-Psenner 1992.

[114] Crouwel 1985, 204, 212 nos SM 1, 3–4, TM 1–4, 12, 21, 23–6, 34 with fig. 1 and pls 31–3; Karageorghis 1995, 121–3 nos II(iv) 1–9 and pls 73–4.

[115] For this theme, see especially Fehr 1971; Dentzer 1982.

[116] Höckmann 1982, 148 and pl. 68: 5; Crouwel 1985, 212 nos TM 34 and pl. 33: 7 and TM 1 and pl. 31: 4 (from a tomb at Alambra); Karageorghis 1995, 122 nos 4 and 5 and pl. 72; Karageorghis, Mertens and Rose 2001, 151 no. 239.

[117] Lorimer 1903, 141; Vigneron 1968, 166f.; Fehr 1971, 22f.; Höckmann 1982, 133 and n. 705, 148f.; Crouwel 1985, 206, 211f.

[118] See p. 77 and note 59 (coins showing a covered cart, named *carpentum*, associated with female members of the Imperial family). Pisani Sartorio 1988, figs 58–9 (wagons; cf. reconstruction, fig. 60).

[119] Livy 1.21.4 (*bigis curru arcuato*).

for journeys in and around Rome and to attend religious ceremonies and games.[120] Interestingly, at various times laws were promulgated, or rescinded, to restrict the use of such carriages in Rome. For instance, in the *Lex Oppia* (dating from 215–195) women are forbidden to drive to Rome, except for public religious services. This prohibition was rescinded after 195.[121] The *Lex Julia Municipalis*, variously dated to 65, 60 or 45, stipulates that only the Vestal Maids, the *Rex Sacrorum* and the *Flamen Dialis* – two important priests – may go into the city by vehicle (called *plostrum*) by daylight, other wheeled traffic being confined to night time and early morning.[122] This points to a concern over traffic congestion.[123]

Many of the figured documents considered above associate mule- or horse-drawn carts with seated or reclining women, surely of high status, the vehicles being driven by men or led by men on foot. In marked contrast, horse-drawn chariots in Italy, both before and during the Roman Empire, were used primarily by men who remained standing and often drove themselves. This distinction is particularly well illustrated by sarcophagi and grave stelae showing men and women riding in their respective vehicles.

It has been suggested that the distinction – chariots for men and carts for women – can also be observed in funerary contexts.[124] This does not apply, however, to cases such as the tombs at Sirolo and Sferracavallo, repeatedly referred to above, where chariots and carts are associated with single male and female burials respectively.

Carts were also used for other purposes, in particular the transport of goods. Multi-purpose carts are well illustrated by the Etruscan bronze models. One of these, from Sarteano, shows a female figure, often identified as the goddess Demeter but quite probably mortal, seated on a cushion placed on the floor frame (Pl. 90). This recalls the Pseudo-Chalcidian amphora illustrating a bearded man seated on cargo (Pl. 95). The model cart from Sarteano has head and tail boards for the attachment of a (removable) superstructure possibly of the kind seen on the bronze model from Bolsena (Pl. 88). As already mentioned, this superstructure was probably intended for hay or other bulky agricultural produce. A use of such carts in slow, heavy transport is implied by the bronze model from Civiltà Castellana, where the draught team of two bovids is preserved (Pl. 89). The two, bovid-drawn carts forming part of the bronze ship model from Crotone in southern Italy apparently each carry a tree trunk on their open platform (Pl. 92).[125] In addition, the stone funerary monument from Sulmona apparently illustrates farmers with their flock, along with goods strapped to an equid-drawn cart (Pl. 111).[126]

Textual sources refer to agricultural use of heavy-duty vehicles, whether carts or wagons, during the later Roman Republic.[127] It is during the period of the Roman Empire that textual – and figured – evidence for the important role of such vehicles as carriers of bulky and/or heavy goods, for instance in the military baggage train, becomes extensive.[128]

---

[120] For the textual evidence for the use of vehicles other than chariots in carrying privileged women and men, before and during the Roman Empire, see especially Abaercherli 1935–6; Gagé 1963a, 155–66; Alföldi 1970, 106–10; Weber 1979, 1983 and 1991; Pagnotta 1977–8; Höckmann 1982, 133f.; Grottanelli 1987; Bartoloni and Grottanelli 1984, 389–93 (= 1989, 63–7); Johner 1992; Van Tilburg 2007, 41–4. See also our p. 106. For the story, related in several ancient texts, of king Servius Tullius being run over in Rome by the *carpentum* of his daughter Tullia, see a.o. Gagé 1963b, 25–42; Grottanelli 1987.

[121] Livy 24.1.

[122] *Corpus Inscriptionum Latinarum* I² no. 593, ll. 56–67 (term *plostrum* used); Höckmann 1982, 134; Humphrey, Oleson and Sherwood 1996, no. 10.45; Van Tilburg 2007, 128–30.

[123] See Van Tilburg 2007, 85–170.

[124] Galeotti 1986–1989; Bartoloni and Grottanelli 1984 (= 1989, 383–410).

[125] See p. 72, note 22.

[126] See p. 72, note 19.

[127] For example, Cato (*De Agricultura*, chs 10–11) consistently uses the term *plostrum* in lists of equipment and animals needed for work in the olive and vine yards. For these and other references to wheeled vehicles and/or their draught animals in Cato's work and in Varro's *Rerum rusticarum*, see *DarSag s.v. plaustrum*; *RE s.v. plaustrum*.

[128] See p. 3 and note 17; also a.o. De Azevedo 1938, 15–18; Vigneron 1968, pls 57a–b, 59b, 60–1, 62b–d, 63; Mitchell 1976; Pisani Sartorio 1988, 61–9 with figs 67–70, 79 (carts), figs 71–5, 78 (wagons). See also Bassi and Forno 1988 (similar use of carts – and wagons – in Italy during the Roman and more recent periods). For evidence for such transport in Iron Age Greece, see Crouwel 1992, 97f.

CHAPTER IV

Wagons

Representations of four-wheeled vehicles from Italy before the the time of the Roman Empire are rare, with the exception of the rock carvings from Val Camonica in the Alps where wagons are much more numerous than two-wheelers.[1] One group of petroglyphs (Rock II at Cemmo near Capo di Monte), which includes pictures of a bovid-drawn wagon and a plough, may date back to the middle of the third millennium (Pl. 118). A similar date has been proposed for a stone stele showing a four-wheeler from Lagundo in the Alto Adige in northern Italy (Pl. 119).[2]

Two other representations of wagons are Etruscan – an incompletely preserved cippus relief of the beginning of the fifth century, quite probably from Chiusi (Pl. 120),[3] and a relief on a stone house-shaped urn of similar or slightly earlier date from Vulci; the latter document is now lost and only known through old drawings (Pl. 121).[4] To these funerary monuments may be added the two equid-drawn four-wheelers that form part of the elaborate carved decoration on the backrest of a wooden chair from tomb 89 in the Lippi cemetery at Verucchio in Emilia Romagna (Pl. 122).[5] In the literature this rich warrior tomb, dating to c. 700, is usually referred to as the Tomba del Trono, and the chair as the Verucchio Throne. The tomb also contained the remains of three actual vehicles – a chariot and two carts – and much metal horse gear.[6]

Etruscan stone urns of the second-first century from Volterra include one showing an equid-drawn four-wheeler, amongst the many illustrating carts and chariots (Pl. 123).[7]

Only very few wagons have been identified among the vehicular remains from tombs in central and northern Italy, chiefly on the basis of surviving metal parts. First, there is a four-wheeler from the Tomba Regolini Galassi in the Sorbo necropolis of Cerveteri dating to c. 650 (Pl. 116).[8] The different sections of

---

[1] Most of the petroglyphs from Val Camonica showing wagons have been dated to the first millennium; see Van Berg Osterrieth 1972, 13–23, 29–72, 99–194 (eighth–sixth century); Piggott 1983, 106–8, 119, 151, 153f.; Züchner 2004, 405, 407 (ninth–first century); also Bevan 2006, 15–18. For two-wheelers, see our and p. 71 and note 6.

[2] Stele Lagundo I; see Van Berg Osterrieth 1973, 105f.; Piggott 1983, 53f. and fig. 22: A; Züchner 2004, 404 and fig. 8: 2. The four-wheelers thought to have been depicted on two other stelae from Caven in Valtellina, a valley neighbouring Val Camonica (Van Berg Osterrieth 1972, 105–7 and figs 40–1; Piggott 1983, 53 and fig. 22: B–C), are regarded as daggers in sheaths by Züchner (2004, 404).

[3] Rumpf 1928, no. E 30 with pl. 20; Woytowitsch 1978, no. 255 and pl. 46; Höckmann 1982, 29, 143 no. E 8; Jannot 1984, no. C, II (Berlin 1227) and fig. 225 (for this cippus, see also figs 226–7).

[4] Martha 1889, 360 and fig. 249; Woytowitsch 1978, no. 254 and pl. 46; Höckmann 1982, 28–30, 142 no. E 7 and fig. 13: 1–5; Pare 1987, 217 and fig. 20: 1; 1992, 210 and fig. 147; Colonna 1997, 15.

[5] See especially Gentili 1987, 243–6 no. 93a–b and fig. 162; 2003, 296–301; Pare 1989, 94 and fig. 14; 1992, 210 and fig. 148; Kossack 1992 and figs 2 and 6: 5–6; 1999, 64–7; Colonna 1997, 15 and fig. 1; *Principi etruschi* cat. no. 253; Torelli 1997, 52–86; Sassatelli 1996, 261–5; *Guerriero e sacerdote* 235–7 (P. von Eles), 237–68 (A. Boiardi and P. von Eles), 269–72 (P. von Eles) with figs 120–1, 123–4, 129 and pls V: 1–2, VII: 2; Bonfante 2005, 30–42 and fig. 29a–b; Eibner 2007, 444f. and fig. 12; Gleba 2008, 28, 173f.

[6] For the vehicular remains and horse gear, see *Carri da guerra* 332 (Repertorio nos 227–228), *s.v.* Sotto la Rocca, Fondo Lippi cemetery, tomb 89); P. von Eles in *Guerriero e sacerdote* 83–132.

[7] Brunn and Körte 1916, pl. 83: 10; Maggiani 1976, 119 and pl. 32a; Höckmann 1982, 29, 145, 147 no. E 17; Nielsen 1990, 56 and figs 9 and 9a.

[8] Reconstruction on display in Rome, Vatican Museum. See Pinza 1907, 85–100 no. LVIII; Pareti 1947, 119f., 286–9 no. 237 and pl. 31 (as restored); Helbig 1963, no. 671; Woytowitsch 1978, no. 31 and pls 12, 61: B4–5 (axle caps); Höckmann 1982, 29 and notes 191–2; Camerin 1997, 90, 92 and fig. 9; *Carri di guerra* 320 (Repertorio no. 102).

the tomb probably contained two burials, thought to have been a male warrior cremation and a female inhumation, and masses of often precious goods. Among these were two vehicles – the four-wheeler, placed in the so-called 'anticamara', and a chariot.[9]

Second, there are remains of a four-wheeled vehicle from tomb 5 of the Monte Michele cemetery at Veii dating to c. 675–650.[10] It carried the bronze urn with the remains of an adult person. The tomb chamber also contained another cremation burial, of an 18 year old male, as well as remains of a two-wheeled vehicle, probably a cart.[11]

A third wagon has been identified among the highly decorated bronze panels and other vehicular remains from the sixth century Tomba dei Bronzi at Castel San Mariano in Umbria. However, the vehicle is more likely to have been a cart.[12]

Finally, more extensive remains of a wagon come from the rich Tomba del Carro in the Ca'Morta cemetery at Como in northern Italy (Pl. 117). They were associated with a female cremation burial of the Golasecca culture (phase IIIA1), dating to the earlier fifth century.[13] This vehicle has good parallels among the wagons buried in graves of important individuals during the Hallstatt period (later eighth–early fifth centuries) in central and western Europe. As in Italy, the wooden parts had usually completely decayed, but various metal elements of the vehicles had survived, though mostly not in their original position.[14]

Mention may be made here of the various bronze models of four-wheelers bearing vessels, known from rich tombs in central and northern Italy and mostly dating to the seventh century. These often elaborately decorated models have close parallels among the so-called *Kessel-*, *Vogel-* and *Beckenwagen* from Urnfield and Halstatt funerary contexts in other parts of Europe. Intended for cultic purposes, they do not reflect actual vehicles, except for details of their four-spoked wheels.[15]

There is also a terracotta model of the eleventh–tenth centuries from Frattesina di Fratta Polesine in the Po delta in northeast Italy, representing an equid which originally rolled on four wheels (now lost). The rectangular container placed on the animal's back may perhaps suggest a vehicle rather than a pack animal (Pl. 124).[16]

---

[9] See pp. 12–3, 19–20 and note 64. For the burials and the find places of the vehicles and other finds in the tomb, see especially Colonna and Di Paolo 1997; also Strøm 1971, 160–8; Höckmann 1982, 29 n. 191; *Carri da guerra* 320 (*s.v.* Repertorio nos 102–3); Rathje 2000, 296f.; Riva 2010, 98, 151f.

[10] In Rome, Museo Nazionale di Villa Giulia. See Boitani 1983, 545–9 and fig. 4 (plan of tomb) and pl. 96c–e (for the tomb, see 538–49); Boitani and Aureli 1988, 128–30 with pls 58–9; Camerin 1997, 90; *Carri da guerra* 325 (Repertorio no. 152); Barker and Rassmussen 1998, 121 with fig. 40 (plan of tomb); Boitani 2001, 113–18; *Etruschi. Le antici metropoli del Lazio* cat. no. 251.

[11] *Carri da guerra* 325 (Repertorio no. 153). The identification as a cart is based on remains of iron tyres belonging to six wheels, not all of the same diameter, and on two metal axle caps with rectangular and not circular openings (personal information A. Emiliozzi).

[12] The remains of four iron tyres or other metal fittings found in some other tombs may be attributed to two two-wheelers rather than to a single wagon; see Woytowitsch 1978, 41 *s.v.* no. 49 (Marsiliana d'Albegna, Circolo di Perazzetta) and 43 *s.v.* no. 61 (Vetulonia, Pietrera tumulus); Emiliozzi 1997, 95, 103, and M. Cygielman in *Carri da guerra* 263, 265 (Vetulonia, Acquastrini, Tomba del Littore; Repertorio nos 173–4); cf. Schauer 1987, 23.

[13] For the tomb (excavated in 1928) and its vehicle, see Baserga 1929; Ghislanzoni 1930; De Marinis 1988b, 198f.; 1991, 97f. and ill.; De Marinis and Premoli Silva 1968–9, 137–42; Saronio 1968–1969, 63–9 and figs 3–7; *Popoli e civiltà dell'Italia antica* 4 (1975), pl. 167; Woytowitsch 1978, no. 112 and pl. 20; Piggott 1983, 183f. and fig. 113; Egg 1987, 89; Egg and France-Lanord 1987, 155 and n. 33 (dating), 158, 163, 173; 2003, 62, 64, 66f., 69, 72 (see also P.-Y. Milcent, p. 313 and n. 90); Pare 1987c, 131–3 and figs 13, 21; 1987d, 194, 210; 1992, 2, 82, 86, 100, 105, 128–32 with fig. 95 and pls 133–4; Camerin 1997, 90 and fig. 8; *Carri da guerra* 333 (Repertorio no. 239); Koch, J. K. 2006, 217f. and 323 (list 9, no. 6), 247 and 317 (list 1, no. 278). Vehicular remains from another tomb of the Golasecca culture in northern Italy – the Tomba del Guerriero A at Sesto Calende – have been attributed by Pare (1992, 63) to a wagon. For this vehicle, which was surely two-wheeled and presumably a chariot, see our p. 22 and note 82 (Pare himself refers on p. 210 of the same publication to this tomb and the the Tomba del Guerriero B at the same site as 'the Sesto Calende chariot graves).

[14] See especially Piggott 1983, 152–4; Pare 1992; Egg and France-Lanord 2003, 58–75; Koch, J. K. 2006; also various contributions to *Vierrädrige Wagen*, *Zeremonialwagen* and *Prunkwagen*; Egg and Lehnert 2006b.

[15] See especially Woytowitsch 1978, 54–66; Piggott 1983, 114f., 120–2; Egg 1991, 191–207; Pare 1989; 1992, 179–86 (fig. 123: distribution map); Riva 2010, 104–6.

[16] F. Rittarore Vonmiller in *Popoli e civiltà dell'Italia antica* 4 (1975), 410 and pl. 8: 1; Woytowitsch 1978, no. 143 and pl. 29. Cf. Crouwel 1992,

1. Body

The single wagon in early rock art from Val Camonica and the other on a decorated stele from the Italian Alps, similarly shown in plan view, have rectangular bodies, sometimes with cross-timbers indicated, what look like disk wheels, a central draught pole and a yoke for paired bovids. The pole forks just before joining the front of the vehicle body (Pls 118–119). This is a feature also of the four-wheeler shown according to the same pictorial convention on a pottery vessel of the Funnel Beaker Culture (later fourth millennium) from Bronocice in Poland.[17] The forking of the pole anticipates a common practice in wagon-building – ancient and recent. Its purpose is to strengthen the attachment of the pole to the vehicle body or, more often, to permit the pole articulate vertically, thereby reducing the strain on wagon and draught team.[18] In these early four-wheelers the prongs of the fork may have hooked over the transverse timber at the front of the vehicle body or this timber may have passed through the ends of the prongs, in order for the pole to move up and down.

The many four-wheelers shown in plan view in the later rock art of Val Camonica are similar, but are often depicted with spoked wheels and equid draught.[19] Apart from the forking pole, they may also show the front and rear axles as joined by a central bar which bifurcates at the rear junction. This bifurcating bar recurs, together with the forked pole, on the wagons depicted in plan view on some figured documents of the late Urnfield and Hallstatt periods (eighth–early fifth centuries) in central and western Europe (Pl. 161).[20] The same elements can be recognized on the best preserved of the two four-wheeled vehicles depicted on the Verucchio Throne of c. 700 (Pl. 122). We have here the earliest illustrations of what is technically known as a perch (q.v.; also called wagon pole): the central bar, bifurcating towards the rear (whence the often used name Y-perch), in order to help keep the rear axle at right-angles (see Fig. 5).[21] The presence of a Y-perch and the undercarriage (q.v.) of which it forms part have been assumed also for actual wagons that were buried in Hallstatt tombs and were themselves the prototypes of the representations (Pl. 159).[22] But the Y-perch and the undercarriage are first attested materially at a later time, on a wagon from Dejbjerg in Denmark probably dating to the first century (Pl. 160). From then on they were to remain salient elements of wagon construction in Europe.[23]

The Dejbjerg wagon and later ones had a front axle that was not rigidly fixed to the vehicle frame but could pivot on a so-called kingpin (q.v.), a metal bolt passing vertically through the centre of the front axle as well as the forward end of the perch, to facilitate the turning of the vehicles in motion. In the case of a pivoting front axle, the draught pole must be connected to the axle, not to the frame of the wagon – so that the axle turns *with* the draught animals and not differentially. For a draught pole to be

83 and nn. 417–19 (terracotta models of equids on four wheels from Greece and Cyprus).

[17] Piggott 1983, 41f. and figs 10–11; Schauer 1987, 5f. and fig. 5; Bakker, Kruk, Lanting and Milisauskas 1999, 784–6 and fig. 7; Bakker 2004, 288f. and fig. 6; Drenth and Bakker 2005/6, 15–19 and fig. 6.

[18] Littauer and Crouwel 1973, 116f.

[19] Four- as well as two-wheeled vehicles are commonly shown in plan view in the rock art of different parts of Europe and central Asia; see Littauer 1977, especially 257; Piggott 1983, 78–82, 116–19; Schumacher 1983, 70f.

[20] Pare 1992, 204, 207, 210 and figs 142 (the bronze couch from Eberdingen-Hochdorf; also Piggott 1983, fig. 94, and *Principi etruschi* cat. no. 593), 143, 144:A 1 (also Piggott 1983, fig. 91), 144: B, 145: 1–6, 149 (also Piggott 1983, fig. 69).

[21] See Piggott 1983, 119, 152 and fig. 98 (diagram); Pare 1992, fig. 1.

[22] See discussions and reconstructions of Hallstatt wagons in the literature mentioned in p. 90, note 14.

[23] In fact, two wagons were discovered in a peat bog near Dejbjerg in western Jutland, one of which was subsequently reconstructed and displayed in the National Museum, Copenhagen. For this and later wagons in Europe, their undercarriage and pivoting front axle, see especially Hayen 1983 (457–9 and fig. 16 – undercarriage of Dejbjerg wagon); Piggott 1983, 225–8 and fig. 141; Wegener Sleeswyk 1987; Pare 1987c, 132 and fig. 3; 1992, 129f., 132 and fig. 94; F. Kaul in *The Celts* 536f.; Schönfelder 2002, especially 97–107 and figs 61–6. It may be noted that a Y-perch, together with a swivelling front axle, is included in the reconstruction (on paper) of a four-wheeler from the Villa Arianna at Stabiae near Pompeii which was destroyed by the eruption of Mt Vesuvius in AD 79; see Miniero 1987, especially fig. 7a–b (reconstruction drawings); 1991–2, 223–7; Rega 1991–2; Raepsaet 2002, 228f.

attached to the axle and still to clear the front edge of the floor as it swings, the axle would have to be placed lower than than the wagon foor. In other words, an undercarriage would be needed. A factor to be considered with a pivoting axle is the danger of the rim of the front wheels running into the edges of the floor during turns. This may be obviated in one of three ways: there may be a mechanism to limit the degree of turning, as on modern four-wheeled vehicles; the floor may be raised so high over the front wheels that it completely clears them; or the diameter of the wheels may be so small and the axles so long that there is little likelyhood of the wheel rims running into the floor.[24] In the reconstruction of the wagon from Dejbjerg the vehicle body is raised over the front and rear axles on wooden boards (Pl. 160a).

It has been convincingly argued that an undercarriage – and a vertically articulating draught pole – were already present on the ornate actual wagons from Como, Ca'Morta in northern Italy and a number of Hallstatt burials, such as those from Vix in Burgundy and Eberdingen-Hochdorf in Baden-Württenberg (Pls 117c, 159).[25] The evidence, in fact, consists of bronze cylinders and sheathing of the wooden draught-bar and traction arms (see also below, Chapter IV.4).

The Hallstatt four-wheelers all had a small rectangular body (1.48–1.85 m in length, and 0.585–0.84 m in width). A very low siding, apparently not exceeding 0.15 m in height, extended all around and was variously decorated in bronze.[26] In most cases the vehicle body has been reconstructed as resting directly on the undercarriage. The reconstruction of the wagon from Vix, however, shows the body as raised on tall metal posts over the axles. The decoration of the low siding here consists of a series of bronze balusters alternating with plaques.[27] Balusters were also found with the remains of the equally ornate wagon from Como, Ca'Morta. In the present reconstruction of this vehicle two rows of such objects, placed one above the other and in all 0.22 m high, held in place by a bronze pin, support the body well above the axle beds. Similar balusters, placed between bronze-sheathed borders, form the low siding (Pl. 117a–b).[28]

The four-wheeled carriage from the Tomba Regolini Galassi at Cerveteri, as reconstructed and displayed in the Vatican Museum, is also raised high over an entirely hypothetical undercarriage (Pl. 116a). Its rectangular body has been reconstructed as measuring 1.92 by 0.83 m, in order to accommodate the bronze bed (itself 1.87 by 0.73 m) that was also found in the 'anticamara', though not inside the vehicle (Pl. 116a shows the bed placed inside the vehicle).[29] A frieze of cut-out bronze palmettes is thought to have covered the low wooden siding of the vehicle body.[30]

There is at present little detailed information on the construction of the wagon from Monte Michele tomb 5 at Veii.[31] Its body dimensions have been estimated as 2.00 by 0.80–0.90 m, on the basis of the surviving sections of a decorated bronze frieze that once ran along its siding to a height of only 0.14 m.

As for the figured documents showing four-wheelers, the (lost) relief from Vulci depicts a long vehicle, carrying two or more occupants, seated behind each other (Pl. 121). The siding is clearly open at the

[24] Littauer and Crouwel 1973, 111f. (= 2002, 252f.).

[25] See Piggott 1983, 153, 156–8; Pare 1987c, 132f. and figs 1–2 (Como, Ca'Morta); 1987d, 210f.; 1992, 129–32 and fig. 95 (Como, Ca'Morta); Egg and France-Lanord 1987, 158, 160; 2003, 62–4, 74; Koch, J. K. 2006, 215–19 and 121–7.

[26] Piggott 1983, 154f.; Pare 1987d, 209; 1992, 133–5.

[27] Egg and France-Lanord 1987, 160–79 and especially figs 25–6, pls 62–4 and X–XI (reconstructions); 2003, 69–72, 75; Pare 1987d, 211; 1992, 132f.

[28] See p. 90 and note 13; also Egg and France-Lanord 1987, 163 and fig. 13; 2003, 72; Pare 1992, 105 and pl. 134.

[29] For recent discussion, see Colonna and Di Paolo 1997, especially 155–61. For the bed, see also Pareti 1947, 119f., 285f. no. 236, pls 30–1 (the latter shows it placed inside the four-wheeler); Steingräber 1979, 202f. no. 45 and pl. I; *Principi etruschi* 167 (reconstruction drawing, showing the four-wheeler and the bed next to each other in the 'anticamara').

[30] Pareti 1947, 288 (fr. 25–8).

[31] See p. 90 and note 10.

front, since the driver has his feet resting on the draught pole. The side screen has a double-curved upper edge which seems to end in a bird protome at the rear. The screen's profile recalls that of the cart carrying a seated driver with a passenger behind, illustrated on an Etruscan gold ring (Pl. 104). It is also strongly reminiscent of the decorated bronze side panels of what was probably a cart rather than a wagon from Castel San Mariano (see above).

The seated wagon passengers depicted on two other figured documents – the Verucchio Throne and the late Volterra urn – are not protected by any siding (Pls 122–123). The fragmentary cippus quite probably from Chiusi also appears to illustrate an open four-wheeled platform. What was originally carried on it is uncertain (Pl. 122).

2. Axle

The four-wheeler buried in the Tomba Regolini Galassi at Cerveteri had revolving axles, to judge from its surviving bronze axle caps. The caps have openings that are square and not round, recalling those of some actual carts and similarly indicating that the (spoked) wheels were fixed on them (Pl. 116a–b; see Chapter III.2).[32] The axle caps are pierced vertically by plain linch pins, recalling the linch pins of one of the Etruscan bronze cart models which has a revolving axle and disk wheels (Pl. 89). Revolving axles are also indicated by the iron stirrup-shaped objects ('staffe' in Italian), similar to those found with cart burials in other tombs.[33] The four-wheeler from Monte Michele tomb 5 at Veii also appears to have had revolving axles, in view of the square openings in the iron nave hoops, resembling those of the two-wheeled vehicle that was buried in the same tomb.[34]

In contrast, the bronze axle caps of the four-wheeler from Como, Ca'Morta are round in section, indicating fixed axles for the revolving spoked wheels that belonged with these vehicles (Pl. 117a). The axle caps are hat-shaped, a type that can be paralleled both among the chariot burials in Italy and the wagons from late Hallstatt tombs north of the Alps.[35] The same is true of the lunate linch pins. These were inserted vertically and had a small loop below the head for a thong, to help prevent the pin from jumping out of the axle.[36]

Enough remains to assume that the front axle of the Como, Ca'Morta wagon pivoted on a kingpin (*q.v.*) in order to facilitate the turning of the vehicle. A similar horizontally articulating front axle has been reconstructed on some of the wagons buried in Hallstatt tombs (Pl. 159; see above, Chapter IV.1). Whether the other wagons documented in Italy before the Roman Empire also had a pivoting front axle, is unknown.

3. Wheels

In early Italian rock art, wagon wheels are rendered as solid disks, but in later petroglyphs as spoked. The wheels of the wagon depicted on the Verucchio Throne also look like simple solid disks (Pl. 122). More detail of construction is yielded by the cippus relief quite probably from Chiusi, where the wagon wheels are solid disks with crescentic battens on either side of the naveless axle hole (Pl. 120, exactly as seen on Etruscan bronze cart models (see Chapter III.3; Pls 88–89). The wheels may likewise have been

---

[32] Pareti 1947, 121, 287 (Fr. 20); Woytowitsch 1978, no. 31a–d with pls 12, 31a–d and 61: B4–5; *Carri da guerra* 325 (Repertorio no. 152).

[33] Pareti 1947, 288 (Fr. 24); *Carri da guerra* 320 (Repertorio no. 102). For 'staffe' associated with cart burials, see our p. 79 and notes 64–65.

[34] Boitani 1983, 545, 549 and pl. 96c; 2001, 117 no. I.G.8.21. See also our p. 90 and note 10.

[35] Woytowitsch 1978, no. 112c with pls 20 and 61: B1 (length 0.037–0.04 m; diameter 0.055 m). Cf. Pare 1992, 88, 90 and fig. 72: 13–15 (Wijchen type); Woytowitsch 1978, no. 69 with pls 11 and 61: B 3 (Siena, Roman period).

[36] For the Como, Ca'Morta linch pins (length 0.11 m), see p. 90, note 13. For parallels, see Pare 1992, 90f. and pl. 21: 1 (Vix; see also Egg and France-Lanord 1987, 155 and fig. 4: 2).

tripartite and fixed on revolving axles. Four-spoked wheels may be indicated on the wagon on the (lost) stone urn relief from Vulci (Pl. 121).

As for the wheels belonging to the buried wagons, the reconstruction of the vehicle from the Tomba Regolini Galassi includes six-spoked, revolving wheels (Pl. 116a). However, the four bronze axle caps with their square openings indicate revolving axles, with the wheels fixed on them (Pl. 116b).[37] The Regolini Galassi wagon wheels had a diameter of 0.65–0.67 m, to judge from fragments of iron tyres.[38] These were held on by closely spaced nails, like those of the two-wheeled vehicles found in the same and other tombs.[39] Rectangular felloe clamps and nailed-on iron tyres were found with the wagon in the Monte Michele tomb at Veii. The spoked wheels of this vehicle, with a diameter reported as 0.70 m or 1.00 m, were again fixed on revolving axles. This is indicated by the square openings of the surviving metal axle caps.[40]

The Como, Ca'Morta wagon had wheels with ten-spokes, set in sockets projecting from elaborately bronze-cased naves which revolved on fixed axles (Pl. 117).[41] In the current reconstruction the wheels have very short spokes, entirely sheathed in bronze, and enormously deep plank felloes. As S. Piggott has pointed out, the latter are "quite unjustifiable" and a much shallower felloe and longer spokes sheathed for only part of their length are to be preferred.[42] It has, in fact, been plausibly suggested that the felloe was made of a thin, single piece of bent wood, its ends joined by a clamp – a type of construction well documented by several late Hallstatt wagon wheels from north of the Alps (see Chapter II.3).[43] The unusually thick (c. 0.024 m) iron hoop tyres of the Como, Ca'Morta wagon are 0.90–0.95 m in diameter. They have no fastening nails and must have been secured merely by 'sweating on'. Such metal tyres are materially documented in Europe north of the Alps but only from the later La Tène period onwards.[44]

4. Traction system

The reconstruction of the four-wheeler from the Tomba Regolini Galassi at Cerveteri includes a pair of incompletely preserved iron objects at the front of the low body, suggesting handholds (Pl. 116a).[45] This four-wheeler may, therefore, have been hand-pulled. In contrast, the Como, Ca'Morta wagon was provided with a central draught pole and must have been drawn by paired animals – one on either side of the pole, exactly like the Hallstatt carriages. The same traction system and animal draught is indicated on two of the figured documents of wagons: the (lost) funerary relief from Vulci and the Verucchio Throne (Pls 121–122).

The draught pole of four-wheelers must normally have been able to articulate vertically, permitting the vehicle and team to adapt differentially to uneven terrain (see also above, Chapter IV.1). In this way they are quite unlike two-wheelers, which require a rigidly fixed draught pole. The Como, Ca'Morta wagon provides material evidence for such an articulating pole. According to the surviving bronze sheathing, the pole ended in a transverse cylinder which hinged up and down the draught bar or pole axle of the vehicle's fore carriage (Fig. 5; Pl. 117c). A similar arrangement, but with a forked rear end of the pole, has been reconstructed on some of the wagons from Hallstatt burials north the Alps (Pl. 159). It is

---

[37] For the fragments of nave hoops, see Pareti 1947, 287f. (fr. 21).

[38] Pareti 1947, 286f. (fr. 1–19).

[39] See pp. 32–3 and p. 83.

[40] Boitani 2001, 113 (wheel diameter given as 1.00 m); cf. *Carri da guerra* 325 (Repertorio no. 152; wheel diameter given as 0.70 m).

[41] See p. 90, note 13. Woytowitsch 1978, no. 112e and pl. 20, cf. pl. 60: B 3 (spoke sheathing); Egg and France-Lanord 1987, 155 and fig. 7: 1; Pare 1992, 82, 86 with fig. 62 and pl. 134: 1.

[42] Piggott 1983, 184.

[43] Baserga 1928, figs 48–9; Egg and France-Lanord 1997, 155 and fig. 7:3 ; Pare 1992, 61 and pl. 34: 2.

[44] See p. 33.

[45] See Pareti 1947, 289 (fr. 29–31).

also definitely attested on the reconstructed wagon from Dejbjerg, where the pole is again forked at its rear end (Pl. 160).

5. Harnessing

Figured information on the harnessing of wagon teams is very limited, but since we know that draught in antiquity was mostly with a pole-and-yoke, the same harness system may be assumed here.

The yoke of the wagon buried at Como, Ca'Morta had a bronze sheathing and knob-like terminals of the same material. Its present reconstruction has, however, no validity.

6. Control

As in the case of harnessing, evidence for the way animals pulling four-wheelers were controlled is extremely limited. On the (lost) relief from Vulci and the Verucchio Throne the seated drivers hold reins, implying a bridle (*q.v.*), and what look like a long goad; the Vulci relief also features a whip or goad (Pls 121–122).

Control by bitted bridle may be indicated by the pair of iron bits found in Monte Michele tomb 5 at Veii, assuming that they belonged with the wagon and not with the two-wheeler that was also buried in this grave.[46] It may be noted that no bits were recorded from the Regolini Galassi tomb at Cerveteri, nor from the Como, Ca'Morta wagon tomb. For comparison, actual bits and various metal parts of headstalls are known from several Halstatt wagon burials, as are the bronze parts of goads.[47]

7. Use

The few figured documents of four-wheelers show them taking part in processions, as carts often do too. Once again, the setting is not really clear. Of the three Etruscan funerary monuments, the (lost) urn relief from Vulci (Pl. 121) depicts the equid-drawn wagon as carrying a female figure on a seat, recalling the seats placed on carts. A driver is seated at the front, whereas the two female figures seen further back may be seated too or walking beside the wagon. A bird is shown above the reins, and an animal (dog?) walks between the wheels. The setting has been variously interpreted as a funeral or a wedding.[48] On the cippus relief quite probably from Chiusi the wagon is also accompanied by people on foot, including both men and women, some of whom are preserved with their arms raised (Pl. 120). Not enough remains to confirm the suggestion that the vehicle is being used as a hearse. There are no traces of draught animals, and the vehicle may well have been hand-pulled, like the actual four-wheeler that was buried in the Tomba Regolini Galassi at Cerveteri. It is often assumed that the latter vehicle had served as a hearse for a human body lying on the heavy, six-legged bronze bed that also ended up in the tomb (as shown in Pl. 116a).[49]

Such a function is more firmly documented for the four-wheeler from Monte Michele tomb 5 at Veii, which was actually discovered carrying a bronze cremation urn together with a dagger, three spearheads and a sceptre.

The use of wheeled vehicles as hearses is well paralleled in antiquity, for instance by figured documents

---

[46] Boitani 1983, 546 and pl. 98f.; 2001, 117 no. I.G.8.22. Note that the bridle bits, which are of our type 2 (our p. 45, note 246), are not mentioned in *Carri da guerra* 325, Repertorio nos 152 (four-wheeler) and 153 (two-wheeler).

[47] See especially Koch, J. K. 2006, 81–3, 177–91, 204f., 231–7 (bits and headstalls), 87f., 207f., 239f., 260f (goads); *eadem* in *La tombe princière de Vix* 251f.

[48] Martha 1889, 360 (funeral); Höckmann 1982, 143, 146 *s.v.* no. E 7 (wedding); Colonna 1997, 15 (wedding).

[49] See p. 92 and n. 29. Recently, Rathje (2000, 156f.) assigned the wagon, bed as well as the chariot to the (?female) inhumation burial.

from Greece dating from the eighth to the sixth century.[50] The vehicles (wagons and carts) are seen carrying a bier and being drawn by paired equids and not hand-pulled. The conveyances from the rich tombs at Cerveteri and Veii, which may best be described as floats with low decorated sides, are most unusual among four-wheelers, ancient or more recent, in having revolving rather than fixed axles. Thus the vehicle bodies could be quickly lifted off when needed.[51]

The equally ornate, animal-drawn four-wheeler from the rich burial at Como, Ca'Morta would have been used for ceremonial purposes too, as would its counterparts from richly fitted Hallstatt tombs north of the Alps (Pls 117, 159).[52] Interestingly, the metal parts of the Como, Ca'Morta wagon, in common with some of the Hallstatt vehicles, show considerable wear, therefore pointing to repeated use before being buried.

In a much illustrated but unsubstantiated reconstruction drawing (Pl. 117a), the Como, Ca'Morta wagon is shown with a metal-decorated seat placed on it, thereby resembling the materially documented seat that belonged with the later vehicle from Dejbjerg (Pl. 160a).[53]

Wagons, drawn by teams of equids or oxen, were widely used in the transport of people and heavy and/or bulky goods in the Roman Empire period, when an arched tilt might be added.[54] One particular type of Roman four-wheeler, its use extending into Byzantine times, is the so-called *Sesselwagen*, named after the elaborate chair that was placed on it (Pl. 162).[55] This horse-drawn conveyance, mounted on four, spoked wheels, consisted of no more than an open platform, with a driver seated on it at the front and with the emperor or one or two high-ranking functionaries seated on the chair. The *Sesselwagen* is anticipated by the horse-drawn, wheeled platform carrying a seated female figure (identified as Thana Velui by the accompanying inscription) depicted on the late Etruscan urn from Volterra (Pl. 123).[56] The earlier urn from Vulci and the still earlier Verucchio Throne also come to mind (Pls 121–122).

On the Verucchio Throne, the two wagons each appear in a very similar scene, on either side of a central panel. Apart from a person seated on a chair with a high backrest (in one case clearly shown as decorated) and a driver on a stool at the front, the long platform of the vehicles carries a pair of figures at the back, standing opposite each other and busying themselves with some object placed between them. Directly behind the vehicles but on the ground, is another figure (Pl. 122). Much has been written about the carved decoration of the Verucchio Throne, and about the identity and gender of the people seated on the two wagons. Interpretations vary greatly, but the various scenes may well represent real-life ritual activities.[57]

---

[50] Crouwel 1992, 94 with pls 1: 4 and 22: 1–2.

[51] Independent evidence for funerary use of wheeled conveyances is yielded by the wheelruts (Höckmann 1982, 31, n. 204: wheel track 1.42 m) in the Banditacchia necropolis at Cerveteri; see our p. 2 and note 11, and *Strade degli Etruschi* fig. 23; Macnamara 1990, fig. 12; Quilici 1997, 80.

[52] The ceremonial use of the horse-drawn Hallstatt wagons did not include that as hearses; see Pare 1992, 135, 204, 217f. In a much illustrated reconstruction drawing, the Como, Ca'Morta four-wheeler is shown with a seat placed on it; see a.o. Ghislanzoni 1930, pl. II; Camerin 1997, 90 and fig. 8.

[53] Ghislanzioni 1930, pl. 2; also Pare 1992, fig. 3; De Marinis and Premoli Silva 1968–9, 137–42; Camerin 1997b, 90 and fig. 8. Piggott 1983, 227 and fig. 141 (Dejbjerg wagon). The seats assumed for Hallstatt period wagons from Ohnenheim in the Alsace (Egg 1987, fig. 3) and Mitterkirchen in Austria (Pertlwieser 1988, 63 and ills pp. 95f.) have been rejected by Pare 1992, 134 and cat. nos 178b and 12; see also Egg 1987, 98.

[54] See a.o. Pisani Sartorio 1988, 54–61 with figs 54–64, and 65, 67f. with figs 71–5; De Azevedo 1938. See also our p. 91, note 23 (two actual wagons from the Villa Arianna at Stabiae).

[55] See a.o. Weber 1978, especially 45–51 and pl. 11 (our Pl. 162) and many other illustrations; 1979; 1983; 1986, 99 and ills pp. 97–8; 1991, 16–20 and figs 2, 4–6; Ghedini 2009, 18–26 (in a study of the so-called Tensa Capitolina, an actual vehicle of Roman Imperial times that was restored with four wheels and carried highly elaborate sheet-bronze decoration; see also E. Simon in Helbig 1966, no. 1546). Note that the Arch of Galerius at Thessaloniki shows the emperor as seated in a similar vehicle but with two wheels (Laubtscher 1974, 61–4: Fries B II 19 and pls 45: 1, 46, 48); Weber 1979, 140–2 and figs 4–5.

[56] See p. 89, note 7. The wheeled platform also carries a standing person at the rear.

[57] See the literature cited in p. 89, note 5, and especially the contributions by P. von Eles.

CHAPTER V

Concluding Remarks

Since the focus of this study has been mainly on chariots and other wheeled vehicles, it would be easy to make the mistake of under-estimating the role of other forms of land transport in Italy before the Roman Empire. In fact, it should be emphasized that even at the time of the large-scale building of paved and graded, carrigeable roads by the Romans, land transport in Italy was, to a considerably extent, conducted on foot or animal back. A comparison with transport by boat is beyond the scope of this study, but it is clear that transport over naviageable rivers and by sea was also of great importance.[1]

Pack animals – asses as well as mules – will have been widely used in Italy, as in Greece and other Mediterranean countries.[2] The advantages they provide for transport, particularly in more hilly and mountainous country, are obvious. They can carry larger loads over longer distances than human porters,[3] and can function over terrain which would only be accessible to vehicles after considerable efforts had been made to build roads. Moreover, pack asses and mules are more economical both to use and to maintain than vehicles. In countries such as Italy where asses and mules were available, these animals were usually preferred to horses for such work. In temperament, asses and mules are better suited to the pack train, as they are stronger, more disease-resistant animals than horses. They are also much cheaper to feed and have a much higher thirst threshold. In addition, asses and mules are surer-footed in mountainous going and have harder hooves – a distinct asset particularly before the horseshoe had been invented.[4]

If we find only very limited figured evidence for pack animals in Italy before the Roman Empire, it is surely because the subject was of no real interest to the patrons of art. An Etruscan funeral cippus of the early fifth century from Perugia is exceptional in showing mules with loads strapped to what appear to be rigid-framed pack saddles.[5] Roman textual sources attest to the wide use of asses and mules in packing in later Republican and Imperial times – in a variety of civilian roles and as part of the military baggage train.[6]

Conditions for the horse varied in Italy. Some regions, such as the Po valley, offered wide stretches of open land suitable to the large-scale keeping and employment of this animal. Other regions with broken or mountainous terrain had less favourable conditions.[7] Osteological remains of the horse first appear among assemblages of bone refuse from sites of the Early Bronze Age (c. 2300–1700 BC). The first – indirect – evidence for the use of the domesticated horse is yielded by the antler-tine or bone

---

[1] For such a comparison, see Laurence 1998, who argued that the role of land transport – by pack animal as well as wheeled vehicle – has often been underestimated; see also Laurence 1999, chs 7 and 8 (on transport by inland waterways); Erdkamp 1998, 21, 62–70; Adams, C. 2007, 4.

[2] For what follows, see Crouwel 1981, 43f., 147; 1992, 101; Landels 1978, 170–3; Ohler 1986, 35–42. For important observations on the advantages of pack animals in the Mediterranean area, see Sion 1955; Mitchell 1976, 123.

[3] For porters, see Vigneron 1968, 141–3; White 1984, 127–9; For important general observations, see Landels 1978, 170–3; Cotterell and Kamminga 1990, 196f. and table 8.1 (carrying capacity of human porters and pack animals).

[4] The nailed-on horseshoe was first used in Imperial Roman times, see a.o. Clark 1995.

[5] Jannot 1984, 43f. no. C,I,1 and figs 158–9 (the pack mules belong to a frieze possibly illustrating the return from a military expedition); Sprenger and Bartoloni 1990, pl. 167; *Gli Etruschi* cat. no. 171. Mules carrying loads appear in a Paestan tomb painting of the fourth century; see Pontrandolfo and Rouveret 1992, 345f. and ills pp. 179: 3, 180: 1 and 181: 5 (Andriuolo, tomb 80).

[6] For pack animals – and wheeled vehicles – in the Roman army train, see a.o. Vigneron 1968, 130–7, 147–50; Toynbee 1973, 191–5; White 1984, 128f., 131f.; Adams, J. N. 1993, 42, etc.; Laurence 1999, 123–35; Roth 1999, 202–7, etc.; Adams, C. 2007, 56–8, 60–2; Erdkamp 1998, 21–3, 68–83; 2007, 102–4.

[7] Later Roman sources mention Apulia (Puglia) and Sicily but mostly areas outside Italy as suppliers of horses; see a.o. Anderson 1961, 19–39; Toynbee 1973, 168. See also our p. 5 and note 37 (Venetic horses from north-eastern Italy).

cheekpieces of bridle bits of organic materials that have turned up at sites in the north (Pl. 171).[8] These sites belong to the Terramare culture of the Middle and Late Bronze Age (*c.* 1700–1000). The isolated, rod-like cheekpieces have good parallels in central and eastern Europe, whence they were presumably introduced. The original bits must have been used on horses rather than other equids, but whether in riding or driving or both remains uncertain.[9]

Horseback riding is first explicitly documented in the eighth-seventh centuries, by figured documents. Among the earliest representations is a terracotta vessel of *c.* 700 from Bologna; attached to it is the figure of a horse bearing a helmeted rider with a shield slung on his back.[10] More representations, in different media, become available by the later seventh and the sixth century. Horseback riding may also be inferred from the single instead of paired metal bits that have been found in tombs of varying dates in northern and southern Italy, where they are associated with warrior equipment.[11] The design of the so-called curb bits which came into use in the fourth century also suggests horse-riding.[12]

We have already discussed the incised decoration on an Etruscan Bucchero vessel of the later seventh century, which includes two warriors engaged in battle on foot, a vanquished archer, a chariot, and an unarmed rider on horseback (Pl. 51).[13] We have also discussed the numerous figured documents of the later seventh and sixth centuries from central Italy showing slow-moving chariots accompanied by varying numbers of warriors or unarmed men on foot, and also by riders on horseback (Pl. 163). The latter, riding singly or in pairs, may be unarmed or equipped like the warriors in the chariots or on foot – with a helmet, round shield and single spear. We have pointed out the strong Greek artistic influences apparent in these scenes (e.g. the often repeated detail of the warrior mounting a chariot), and have interpreted them as depicting parades, with strong heroic and mythological overtones, rather than real-life armies going to, or returning from war.

Some terracotta revetment plaques from sites in Toscana and Lazio do not illustrate men on horseback together with others in chariots or on foot, but on their own.[14] Armed or unarmed, they are again riding singly or in pairs, either slowly or, more often, at a gallop. When paired riders are shown, one is armed, usually but not exclusively with hoplite equipment, including a round shield and a single spear, while the other rider is unarmed. This combination recalls the theme of the so-called mounted hoplite and his attendant or 'squire', which is frequently illustrated in Greek art of the later seventh and sixth centuries.[15] Terracotta plaques of the Rome-Caprifico decorative roof system show a hare, a backward-looking deer and a pursuing dog beneath the galloping horses, as is also the case on the plaques of the same roof system depicting chariot racing (Pls 163, 71c).[16] The presence of these animals accentuates speed, as do the birds shown above the galloping mounts (Pl. 163).

---

[8] See p. 47 and note 253.

[9] See p. 47 and note 255.

[10] From tomb 525 in the Benacci Caprara cemetery; see a.o. Stary 1981a, 95 and pl. 68: 1; Sprenger and Bartoloni 1990, pl. 11; Brendel 1995, 90 and fig. 59; Lubtchansky 2005, 38–41. Cf. Hencken 1957 (helmeted riders as decoration of bronze tripod cauldrons of the seventh century from sites in Toscana). See also Stary 1981a, 57, 95; Menichetti 1994, 30f.; Lubtchansky 2005, 38–41.

[11] See Von Hase 1969, 3f.4 and 39f. nos 252–7 with fig. 7 and pl. 20 (tombs at Este in northern Italy); Carter 1998, and Lubtchansky 2005, 90f. (tombs in southern Italy)

[12] See p. 48 and notes 257–258.

[13] See pp. 57–58.

[14] See lists and discussion of the mould-made plaques in Von Mehren (1997, 219, 219) and Lubtchansky (2005, 227–65 and 285–9); also Winter, N. A. 2009, index *s.v.* horse rider.

[15] See p. 58 and note 330.

[16] Winter, N. A. 2009, 331f., 337f. nos 5.A.1.d, 5.D.1.d with ills 5.2.5, 5.10.1 and fig. 5.3 (Roofs 5–8 and 5–10). For the plaques showing chariot racing, see pp. 64–65 and note 375. The combination of a horseback rider, a flying bird and a 'dog-after-hare' recurs on a terracotta plaque from the Greek island of Thasos (Picard 1941; Winter, N. A. 1993, 254, 256 and pl. 102; Von Mehren 1997, 222 and n. 7; Lubtchansky 2005, 238 and fig. 171). Birds and speeding chariots are seen together on East Greek terracotta revetment plaques (Åkerström 1951, fig. 33: 2–6; 1966, pls 21: 1 and 25: 1–4). Note that on a plaque from Tarquinia a bird is associated with a slow-moving chariot and a pair of riders on horseback (Winter, N. A. 2009, 260f. no. 4.D.3.d and ill. 4.7.4).

In Greece, the theme of the 'mounted hoplite' almost certainly reflects actual practice, involving a heavily armed nobleman who used his mount only as a convenient – and prestigious – means of transport and who fought dismounted, while his 'squire' looked after the horses. The weaponry shown is typical of the hoplite but not suitable for fighting from horseback: a helmet, bell-shaped corslet and (often) greaves, all of metal, together with a round shield and a heavy thrusting spear. In Greece, this military practice derives from a tradition of chariot driving – the warrior and his driver having transferred to horseback. A parallel may be drawn with the chariot warrior and driver in Assyria, who began to be transferred to two horses during the ninth century.[17]

As for the sixth century representations from central Italy, the question again arises as to whether we are dealing with the adoption of an actual practice from Greece or merely of Greek artistic models, like those of the dog pursuing a hare, and the hoplite mounting a chariot. Here it is important to note that the shield-carrying warrior of the galloping pairs on the revetment plaques is sometimes not shown holding a spear, but wielding a sword or an axe (Pl. 163).[18] The latter offensive arms are not associated with (mounted) hoplites in Greece, but are commonly found in Italy among actual weaponry that was buried in tombs and seen in representations. Swords and axes – like the single spears intended for close-range fighting – will primarily have been used by warriors on foot, particularly when they are shown held together with shields. But they may also have been used on horseback.

On other sixth century terracotta revetment plaques, from Acquarossa and Tuscania in Toscana, and from Cerveteri and Satricum in Lazio, bows and arrows are associated with men galloping or moving slowly on horseback. The bow, a long-range weapon, may be carried in a case slung over the riders' backs or may be shown in use.[19] On the plaques from Cerveteri and Satricum, which were made in the same workshop at Cerveteri,[20] the riders are in pairs, one shooting and the other presumably controlling both mounts. Such representations suggest the existence of actual, lightly-armed mounted troops in central Italy at the time. However, some of these and other archers on horseback are seen employing the so-called Parthian shot, i.e. shooting back over the horse's croup.[21] In addition, the archers may wear oriental- or Scythian-type pointed caps and clothing. They have sometimes – erroneously – been taken for Amazons.[22] It should be noted that the 'Parthian shot' is also seen in Greek iconography and is probably again an artistic borrowing, ultimately deriving from the Near East.[23]

All in all, it is difficult to sort fact from fiction, though the figured documents leave little doubt that riding on horseback played a role in military affairs in central Italy at the time, and became a popular subject for artistic representation.[24]

---

[17] Littauer and Crouwel 1979a, 134f.; Crouwel 1992, 59.

[18] On terracotta revetment plaques of the Veii-Rome-Velletri and Rome-Caprifico types. See Lubtchansky 2005, 286 nos R 48, R 44; Winter, N. A. 2009, 331f., 357f. nos 5.A.1.c–d, 5.D.1.c–d with ills 5.2.5, 5.10.1–2 and fig. 5.3 (Roofs 5–2, 5–3, 5–6, 5–7, 5–8 and 5–10).

[19] **Acquarossa and Tuscania** (files of slow-moving single riders, some of them carrying a bow in a case, others unarmed or equipped like hoplites): see Lubtchansky 2005, 234, 288 nos R 59–60 and fig. 160; Winter, N. A. 2009, 241, 244 nos 4.A.2.a, 4.A.2.d and ills 4.2.1, 4.2.1.3, figs 4.1 and 4.3 (Roofs 4–3, 4–4). **Cerveteri** (pairs of galloping riders, one of them shooting backwards or simply holding the bow): see Knoop 1987, 56f., 60 and pl. 76a; Kästner 2006, 78–82 nos 2–5 and figs 7.2–6; Winter, N. A. 2009, 449–51. **Satricum** (pairs of galloping riders, one of them shooting backwards or simply holding the bow): see Knoop 1987, 51–66 with fig. 30, 237–9 nos 173–4 and figs 6–7, 10 and pls 72–6; Lulof 1997, fig. 1 (reconstruction of frieze); Lubtchansky 2005, 234f., 287f. no. R 56 and fig. 155; Winter, N. A. 2009, 448–50 no. 6.D.1.b and ill. 6.12.2 (reconstruction of frieze belonging to Roof 6–1).

[20] Winter, N. A. 2009, 450.

[21] Among the other representations are the so-called Lebes Barone from Capua and other bronze vessel attachments (see Haynes 1965, pls 3–4; Adam, A.-M. 1980, 642–7; Jannot 1987; Lubtchansky 2005, 95–9), and a black-figure neck-amphora by the Paris Painter from Vulci (see Ducati 1932, pls 8a, 9a; Beazley 1947, 1 and pl. I: 1; Hannestad 1974, 44 no. 3).

[22] See Jannot 1987; Adam, A.-M. 1980, 646; Lubtchansky 2005, 96f.; Kästner 2006, 79, 81f.

[23] See Greenhalgh 1973, 139–41 and fig. 76 ('Chalcidian' neck-amphora); Littauer and Crouwel 1979a, 135 (also Jettmar 1967, pl. 44: ninth century Assyrian palace relief), 157 and fig. 85 (Achaemenid gem).

[24] One intriguing representation, on a terracotta revetment plaque of c. 520 from Tarquinia should be mentioned here (Winter, N. A. 2009, 334 no. 5.A.2.a with ill. 5.3.1 and fig. 5.5). It shows two pairs of galloping riders, wearing a crested helmet, carrying a round shields and brandishing a spear; beneath the first pair lies a vanquished enemy in a short tunic and wearing a 'Phrygian' cap; behind the horsemen runs a large figure,

When it comes to textual sources for horseback riding and its military role in Italy before the Roman Empire, these are so extensive that they would require a separate study. One notoriously controversial subject is the socio-political position of the *equites* ('horsemen') and the role of mounted troops in early Roman history. Suffice it to say that the textual sources leave no doubt that between the sixth century and the Second Punic War (218–201) mounted troops, with warriors who actually fought *from* horseback, became a regular and important part of the armies of Rome and other polities in Italy.[25]

The appearance of mounted troops in Italy seems then to be rather late – as it is in Greece – when compared to the Near East, where they are firmly attested from the ninth century onwards.[26] It should be noted that cavalry (*q.v.*), a term that may be properly applied only to mounted troops when these are trained to such a degree that they can function with precision as a unit, seems first to have developed into a truly formidable force only during the fourth century in the plains of Macedonia in northern Greece. Even this force, which still lacked saddles and stirrups, would not have been used in a frontal assault with couched lances on a well-prepared infantry line.[27] In Greece – and in Italy as well – mounted troops were presumably employed as a fast flanking and pursuing arm, in surprise attacks, as well as in scouting, patrolling and guarding an army on the march. Roman cavalry by the first century AD came to be exclusively made up of auxiliary units from other parts of the Empire where there were large grassy plains suitable for horse raising and training.[28]

Horses were also ridden in Italy in parades, for sport and probably also in hunting.[29] Racing on horseback is vividly illustrated on terracotta revetment plaques of *c.* 580–575 from Poggio Civitate (Murlo) in Toscana. The jockeys, with their pointed caps, short tunics and capes, are seen racing past a stand carrying a bronze prize-vessel.[30] Roman texts refer to horseback racing and acrobatics in Republican and Imperial times, involving single or pairs of horses.[31]

In Italy, the earliest evidence for wheeled vehicles (with disk wheels and employing the pole-yoke harness system) appears to date to the third millennium. It consists of the first of a long series of rock carvings of two- and four-wheeled vehicles from Val Camonica in the north, and of a wagon representation on a stone stele, also from the Alpine region (Pls 100, 118–119).[32] The use of vehicles with disk wheels, at this time and earlier, is also documented by finds of actual wheels, and by a few representations in Switzerland and other parts of Europe, although not in Greece.[33] Carts and wagons with similar wheels

carrying a spear.

[25] For discussion, based on textual as well as archaeological sources, see Stary 1981a, 95–9, 124., 149f., 157–71, 194f., 200, 218, 264f.; Saulnier 1980, 109–14; Adam and Rouveret 1995 (with bibliography); Junkelmann 1991, 27–54; Adam, A.-M. 1995a; Jannot 1986a; 1989; 1995; Lubtchansky 2005, *passim*.

[26] For the Near East, see Littauer and Crouwel 1979a, 134–9; Spruytte 1983; also Mayer 1978, 181–6. For Greece, see Bugh 1988; Junkelmann 1991, 15–27; Spence 1993; also Anderson 1961 and 1970 (index *s.v.* cavalry); Greenhalgh 1973; Crouwel 1991, 102f.; Van Wees 2004, 65–8; Lubtchansky 2005, 13–31. Cf. Drews (2004, 71): 'shock cavalry may have been employed as early as the eighth century in the ancient world'.

[27] For the riding saddles of the Roman Empire period, see Connolly 1987; Connolly and Van Driel-Murray 1991; Junkelmann 1992, 34–74; also Herrmann, G. 1989 (saddles of the Parthians and Sasanians in the Near East). For the early history of stirrups, see especially Littauer 1981.

[28] For Roman cavalry and its equipment, see a.o. Vigneron 1968, 235–54, 261–77, 309–14; Bishop 1988; Junkelmann 1991, 1992 and 1996; Dixon and Southern 1992; Goldsworthy 1996, ch. 5; Feugère 2002, 83f. and ch. 7; MacCall 2002.

[29] For hunting, see Camporeale 1984.

[30] Root 1973; Thuillier 1985, 82–7; Lubtchansky 2005, 231–3, 238 (no. R 29), 285 with fig. 156; Winter, N. A. 2009, 157, 183, 185 no. 3.D.5.a with ill. 3.7.1 and fig. 3.16 (Roof 3–8 of the so-called Upper Building, which was also decorated with a frieze showing carts; see our Pl. 113 and p. 71 with note 10). The capes have been – erroneously – taken for quivers by Jannot (1986, 128; 1987, 699–702; 1995, 21). For this frieze, see also D'Agostino 1991, 225f.; Massa-Pairault 1990. Revetment plaques from Poggio Buco similarly show unarmed riders at a gallop, but no prices; see Lubtchansky 2005, 231–3, 238 (no. R 33), 286 and fig. 157; Winter, N. A. 2009, 157, 183, 185 no. 3.D.5.a and ill. 3.7.1 and fig. 3.16.

[31] See a.o. Vigneron 1968, 209f.; Humphrey 1985, 16; Thuillier 1987 (the so-called *desultores* and their Etruscan predecessors, for which see also Thuillier 1985, 97–109); Lubtchansky 2005, 99–127.

[32] See p. 71 and note 6, and p. 89 and notes 1–2.

[33] See especially Piggott 1983, ch. 2; Bakker, Kruk, Lanting and Milisauskas 1999; various contributions to *Rad und Wagen* (especially Bakker 2004; Maran 2004a and 2004b; Schlichtherle 2004); Drenth and Bakker 2005/6.

were also used in parts of the Near East at the same time and earlier.[34] Taking this into account, the first vehicles in northern Italy may owe much to external stimuli, from beyond the Alps rather than the eastern Mediterranean.

The first *material* remains of carts or wagons in Italy consist of single wheels of the disk and cross-bar types which have survived from lake sites of the Terramare culture.[35] They date from the Middle and Late Bronze Age (*c.* 1700–1000), again in the north (Pls 81–85). The disk wheels are tripartite and held by slats – a construction shared by actual wheels found in Switzerland and elsewhere in Europe, as well as in parts of the Near East.[36] One of the tripartite disk wheels from northern Italy has lunate openings in the outer planks – a feature that can again be seen in other parts of Europe.[37] The other, cross-bar type of wheel is not documented elsewhere in Europe at this time, but may ultimately derive from the Near East, where it has a history going back to the later third millennium.[38] Apart from the wheels, there is no information on the construction of the Terramare vehicles. In view of the types of wheel, the vehicles must have been slow-moving and therefore carts or wagons, rather than chariots with two spoked wheels.

Isolated finds of cheekpieces of horse bits at Terramare sites in northern Italy may perhaps be evidence for horse-drawn chariots (Pl. 171). The cheekpieces are made of antler-tine and have excellent contemporary and earlier parallels in central and eastern Europe. Bits with such cheekpieces and a 'soft' mouthpiece made of rope, gut or sinew may have been used on driven as well as ridden horses (see above).

The antler-tine cheekpieces and the bits to which they belonged bear no relationship to the bronze ones that are first found in the Contigliano Hoard of *c.* 900–850 in Umbria and then in funerary contexts of the eighth century (the later part of the Early Iron Age) at Bologna and other sites in northern and central Italy.[39] The new bronze bits are of two basic types and their cheekpieces may carry (elaborate) decoration. Some of the cheekpiece designs, as well as the use of a metal bit, are probably inspired by models from the Near East, where all-metal bits have a long history.[40]

The bronze bits from eighth century tombs in northern and central Italy are found mostly in pairs, and at Bologna sometimes together with bronze terminals of wooden goads and, albeit rarely, with metal linch pins (Figure 7 shows the inventory of Benacci Caprara tomb 34).[41] The presence of pairs of bits in the tombs presumably implies driven and not ridden animals, the accompanying goads helping to enforce directional control of the teams of horses pulling faster chariots and not slower carts or wagons where bits are not essential. These horse bits, which often show signs of wear, may be regarded as *pars pro toto,* pointing to the existence of horse-drawn chariots.

On present evidence, the deposition of metal horse bits and other gear in tombs seems to precede that of vehicles, if only by a short time span. Remains of chariots and carts (but not wagons) are first found in eighth century tombs at Veii and other sites in central and northern Italy. The vehicles or horse bits and other gear are mainly associated with (rich) male burials. Men have usually been identified on the basis of accompanying burial goods such as bronze razors and weaponry. For instance, the cremation

---

[34] See especially Littauer and Crouwel 1979a, chs 4–6; Crouwel 2004a, 69–78.

[35] See pp. 80–82 and notes 70–73.

[36] For the recent debate on the 'monocentric' or 'polycentric' origin of the (disk) wheel in fourth millennium Mesopotamia and/or Europe, see especially Burmeister 2004; Maran 2004a and 2004b; Sherratt 2004 and 2006; Jacobs 2005, 430–4.

[37] See especially Schlichterlee 2004, 305, fig. 13 (distribution map).

[38] See p. 81 and note 78.

[39] See pp. 44–47.

[40] Von Hase 1989, 1045–9; 1995, 275, 277 with figs 33 and 34 (distribution map); Stary 1981a, 59. But cf. Hencken 1968, 564f. (preferring an independent origin in Italy). For the bits, see Chapter II.6.

[41] Pincelli and Tovoli 175, 458–60; Panichelli 1990, 203–8, 322f.; Pare 1992, 192; also Von Hase 1969, figs 2A, 4, 5A and 6A (inventories of tombs at Bologna and Volterra). For linch pins, see also our pp. 27–28.

burial of a *c.* 40-year-old male warrior in Quattro Fontanili tomb EE 10B at Veii is accompanied by weaponry, fragments of nailed-on tyres, one horse bit and 'dente equini' (Figure 6: tomb plan).[42] There are also tombs where the evidence points to female or children's burials.[43]

Thus begins the practice of vehicle burial which is to become more frequent and widespread, particularly in central Italy in the seventh and sixth centuries (Figure 8: distribution map). There are also some chariot burials from the fifth century, and one dating as late as the third century (at Adria on the north-western Adriatic coast).[44] Vehicle burials are not often attested in southern Italy where Greek colonies exerted strong cultural influences. Nor do they appear to have extended into Imperial Roman times anywhere in Italy.

The vehicles accompanying human burials in tombs of the seventh century and later were mainly chariots. Carts and, if only in a few cases, wagons are also attested. The wooden parts had usually decayed but metal parts were preserved, albeit rarely *in situ.* Identification of two- and four-wheelers is facilitated by the number of iron wheel tyres, and in some cases also by that of metal axle caps or other elements. Chariots and carts can often be distinguished by the presence or absence of metal parts known to be characteristic of either type. In some seventh and sixth century tombs identification, and at least partial reconstruction – is greatly helped by the survival of wooden elements and/or the extensive use of metal sheathing of the wooden parts. The vehicles were quite often accompanied by paired metal bridle bits and other horse gear.

In most cases the available material evidence suggests the presence of a single vehicle in a tomb. When identifiable, the vehicle is usually a chariot, sometimes a cart, and in one case (the Tomba del Carro at Como, Ca'Morta of the earlier fifth century) a wagon.[45] There are also instances where a chariot and a cart were deposited in the same tomb, and two cases (the Tomba Regolini Galassi at Cerveteri and Monte Michele tomb 5 at Veii, both in Lazio and dating to the seventh century) of the deposition of a chariot or cart and a wagon.[46]

The maximum number of vehicles buried in the same tomb appears to have been three: two chariots and a cart (the sixth century Tomba dei Bronzi at Castel San Mariano in Umbria)[47] or one chariot and two carts (the seventh century Tomba del Tridente at Vetulonia in Toscana and the Tomba del Trono of *c.* 700 at Verucchio in Emilia Romagna).[48]

Where the find circumstances are sufficiently clear, the chariots are mostly associated with male, and carts with female burials. Gender distinctions are, however, not clear-cut. For instance, a chariot and a cart were associated with the single warrior burials in Tomba A at Casale Marittimo in Toscana and Colle del Forno tomb XI at Sferracavallo in Lazio, dating to the earlier seventh century and *c.* 520–480 respectively.[49] The chariot and two carts in the Tomba del Trono at Verucchio belonged to a warrior burial.

---

[42] See A. Cavalotti-Batchvarova in *Notizie degli scavi di antichità* (Serie 8) 21 (1967), 138–46; Nebelsick 1992, fig. 27; *Carri da guerra* 325 (Repertorio no. 159); Pacciarelli 2000, fig. 140A; Seubers 2008, 7. See also our p. 4 and note 24. For another eighth century cremation burial from the same cemetery – Quattro Fontanili tomb AA 1 – with weaponry, fragments of nailed-on tyres and a pair of horse bits, see M. C. Franco, P. Mallett and A. Wacher in *Notizie degli scavi di antichità* (Serie 8) 24 (1970), 296–308; *Carri da guerra* 325, (Repertorio no. 157); Pacciarelli 2000, 264; Torelli 2006, 414f., 418 and fig. 12; Seubers 2009, 7; *Etruschi. Le antiche necropoli del Lazio* no. 241.

[43] See, for instance, A. Cavalotti-Batchvarova in *Notizie degli scavi di antichità* (Serie 8) 21 (1967), 252–8; *Carri da guerra* 326, (Repertorio no. 160); Piaccarelli 2000, fig. 140B; Torelli 2006, 415, 421 and fig. 14; Seubers 2008, 7 (Veii, Quattro Fontanili tomb HH 6–7: cremation burial of two children, *c.* 9–11 years old and accompanied by weaponry, a pair of bits and fragments of nailed-on tyres).

[44] For a catalogue of – in all 280 – vehicular burials in Italy, see *Carri da guerra* 305–34 (Repertorio), 335f. (Supplemento), 337–9 (tombs with vehicular remains and weaponry); see also Riva 2001–3, 75–85. For the tomb at Adria, see our p. 5 and note 36, and p. 33 and note 161.

[45] See p. 90 and note 13.

[46] See p. 90 and note 10.

[47] Höckmann 1982; *Carri da guerra* 319f. (Repertorio nos 95–7). See also p. 14 and note 35.

[48] Cygielman and Pagnini 2006, especially 35, 43; P. von Eles in *Guerriero e sacerdote* especially 85; also *Carri da guerra* 327, 332 (Repertorio nos 172 and 227–8).

[49] See p. 76, note 51, and p. 79, note 64.

On the other hand, a cart and a chariot were found with the single female burial in the sixth century Tomba della Principessa at Sirolo in Marche (Pl. 76).[50] It may be noted that horse bits also occur with both male and female burials.[51]

As in the case of the eighth century burials with vehicles or horse gear, the gender identifications usually rest on the character of the other grave goods. However, the presence of burial goods such as chariots, carts or horse bits is clearly not (always) gender specific and may simply indicate high social status.[52]

The vehicles were rarely buried together with their harness team, an exception being the third century tomb at Adria mentioned above. Its single, warrior(?) burial was accompanied by a two-wheeled vehicle, together with the harness team of two horses, apparently still under yoke, and a third horse, which was presumably a mount rather than a spare draught animal. All three animals were bitted. The sixth century Tomba della Biga at Ischia di Castro in Toscana yielded an ornate chariot and a pair of horses (one of them with a bit in its mouth), but in different parts of the tomb.[53] In the case of the above mentioned tomb at Sirolo and another at Populonia in Toscana,[54] paired animals – surely draught teams – were buried without gear near the tombs containing one or more vehicles.

In central and northern Italy, the tombs with vehicles, like the early ones with only bridle bits and goads, represent only a small percentage of the total number of tombs in the cemeteries in which they occurred. The tombs were clearly special, as is confirmed by the richness of the rest of the funerary assemblage and sometimes by their architecture as well. Some of the tombs, from different regions, have often been regarded as representing a special category, the so-called Tombe Principesche which date to the Orientalizing period (*c.* 750/700–600).[55] Apart from the often monumental aspects of their architecture, the 'Tombe Principesche' are characterized by the exceptionally rich funeral gifts that are associated with male and sometimes female burials. The grave goods include many of Near Eastern or Greek origin or inspiration. This points to a shared funerary ideology of an elite group, which participated in a wide network of gift-exchange. The vehicles, which were often decorated in metal, would have been appropriate to the life-style of their owners and designed to enhance their status.

One of the 'Tombe Principesche' belongs to the Fondo Artiaco cemetery at Cumae in the Gulf of Naples. This warrior tomb 104, which dates to *c.* 700 or slightly earlier, contained among its rich grave goods a pair of simple iron horse bits and, it was claimed, a few metal remains of a vehicle. According to Greek textual sources, Cumae was an Euboean colony, and the Fondo Artiaco tomb is often thought to belong to a colonist from that Greek island.[56] There are indeed striking similarities in the funerary arrangements with those attested in the West Cemetery at Eretria on Euboea dating to the later eighth century.[57] The Eretria tombs, however, did not produce evidence for the presence of chariots or other vehicles. In Greece as a whole, the practice of vehicular burial is attested only rarely. All we have are metal elements of spoked wheels from two ninth–eighth century tombs in the Ceramicus at Athens and from sixth century tumulus burials at Ayios Giorgos in Thessaly.[58]

---

[50] See p. 70 and note 4.

[51] See P. von Eles in *Guerriero and sacerdote* 116f. (Verucchio); Bartoloni and Grottanelli 1984, 284 (= 1989, 56) (Veii).

[52] For discussion, see Bartoloni, Cataldi and Zevi 1982; Bartoloni and Grottanelli 1984 (= 1989); Bartoloni 1993, 274–87; 2003, 170–93; P. von Eles in *Guerriero e sacerdote* 83–87. For distinguishing male and female burials on the basis of the tomb finds, see also Robb 1996; Toms 1998; Riva 1999, 89f.; 2001–3, 81f., 85f.; 2010, especially 95–107; Amann 2000, 66–75; Rathje 2000; Thiermann 2009, 185–9.

[53] See p. 4 and note 20.

[54] See p. 4 and note 21.

[55] See especially Waarsenburg 1995, 182–5, 321–4; Winther 1997; Fulminante 2003; also Barker and Rasmussen 1998, 118–25.

[56] See p. 45, note 246. For Cumae as an Euboean colony, see Crielaard 1996, 252–73; Coldstream 2003, 231, 395.

[57] Crielaard 1996, 75–93; also 2004; Coldstream 2003, 196–201.

[58] See p. 33, note 162. In addition, *paired* metal bits, but no vehicle remains, were found in tomb XXVII of *c.* 900 in the Athenian Agora (Blegen 1952, 287, 290 nos 8–9 with fig. 3 and pl. 75c.; Donder 1980, nos 111–12; Crouwel 1992, 48) and in eleventh century tomb 219 of the North

On the other hand, vehicle burials are well attested in eighth–seventh century Cyprus. At Salamis on the east coast, chariots and carts were associated with the same burials. The vehicles were left in the wide entrance corridor of chamber tombs, together with their harness teams of horses or asses, the animals still under yoke and fitted out with their bridle bits and other elaborate gear (Pl. 130).[59] In the Near East, first millennium burials of vehicles are only known from different parts of Anatolia. The find contexts are tumulus graves dating to the later sixth and early fifth centuries.[60]

Vehicle burials of the first millennium are also known from parts of Europe other than Italy and Greece. They include two-wheelers, presumably chariots, from coastal regions of Spain dating from the seventh century and later,[61] and many two- and four-wheelers from areas north of the Alps. Here, vehicle burials first appeared in the Urnfield period and continued in the Hallstatt and La Tène periods.[62]

As in Italy, the tombs with chariots and/or other types of vehicle always formed only a small percentage of the total number of graves in the cemeteries in which they were deposited. Clearly, vehicle burial represents a practice common to ruling groups at different times and places in the ancient world, extending from Britain to China and from the Netherlands to Egypt. The burial of vehicles was intended to enhance the status of their owners in an act of conspicuous consumption.

The practice of vehicular burial in Italy from the eighth century onwards has been thought to derive from the Near East, with the Phoenicians acting as middlemen.[63] However, as we have seen, evidence for vehicle burial in the Near East at that time is limited to a few examples from Anatolia. In Italy, the practice appears to have a local origin and be connected to the rise of indigenous élites. Features of this process are the energy invested in the construction of larger tombs and the placing in them of the trappings of wealth, including complete chariots or other wheeled vehicles.

In Chapters II–IV the various components of chariots, carts and wagons of the eighth to the first centuries in Italy were discussed. We also discussed the ways in which the draught teams were harnessed and controlled, and the use to which the equipages were put. It became clear that there were similarities as well as differences as compared to contemporary and earlier vehicles elsewhere. What should we now conclude about the different vehicles attested in Italy, their origins, development and foreign connections?

Beginning with *carts*, two types are attested in the material record and among the figured documents – the Y-poled cart and the cart with a central draught pole (Chapter III). Both types have much in common with carts known from different parts of the world in ancient and recent times.[64] The same is true of the two types of axle – one revolving, and with the wheels fixed on it, the other fixed rigidly to the cart frame but with revolving wheels. As to the wheels, the figured documents of the seventh century and later often show the disk and cross-bar types, which are already attested earlier in northern Italy. In contrast, the actual carts buried in tombs of the eighth century and later appear to have had spoked wheels of a construction very similar to that of contemporary chariots, with single- or double-layered felloes held by bronze or iron clamps and secured by nailed-on iron tyres.

Cemetery at Knossos, which also contained two horses (Catling 1996, 569–71 nos f 92, f 102, f. 103a with fig. 168 and pls 282–3). At Lefkandi on Euboea, two of the four horses associated with the tenth century burial under the so-called Heroon were found with iron mouthpieces of bits in their mouths (Popham 1993, 21f., 76 no. SF.1 and pls 22, 32, 34; Crouwel 1992, 47f.), like the two horses from tomb 68 in the Toumba cemetery (Popham 1993, 22; Popham, Calligas and Sackett 1989, 118; Popham and Lemos 1996, caption to pl. 21).

[59] See Karageorghis 1967 and 1973; Crouwel 1985 and 1987 (with references in n. 15 to such burials at Amathus, Tamassos and Palaepaphos).

[60] See p. 34, note 166 (Balıkesir-Üçpınar and Sardes). There are vehicle burials of much earlier date (third millennium), involving wagons and carts with disk wheels, from Mesopotamia and Iran (Zarins 1986; Littauer and Crouwel 1979a, 16f.). Chariot burials are well well-known from the Egyptian New Kingdom, the tomb of Tut'ankhamun containing no less than six such vehicles (Littauer and Crouwel 1985).

[61] Stary 1994, 60–5, 164–75; 1989; Nebelsick 1992, 92–7.

[62] See especially Pare 1987b; 1987d; 1992; Schönfelder 2002; Van Endert 1987.

[63] Stary 1989, 157, 172, 177.

[64] See, for instance, Dennis 1999 (discussing the important role of transport by cart in Africa, in the present as well as the future).

In addition, Y-poled carts in central and northern Italy display a distinctly Italic feature, the so-called 'poggiaredini' – a complex metal pole-end fitting that is first attested in tombs of the later eighth century (Pls 76a–b, 80a). Yet other features, such as the suspended footboard of some of the Y-poled carts, and the often illustrated railwork siding, have parallels among the central-poled carts in the Greek colonies in southern Italy and among those of mainland Greece (Pls 115, 149). Similarities like these may or may not be accidental.

The figured documents of the seventh century and later usually illustrate the use of mule- or horse-drawn carts carrying seated people in wedding or other processions, thereby reflecting the interest of the artists and their patrons. The passengers, mainly but not exclusively women, are shown seated or reclining, and are sometimes protected by a parasol or an arched tilt.

The use of carts for personal transport is confirmed by the funerary evidence. The actual carts, like the buried chariots and wagons, may be decorated to varying degrees. Such vehicles were surely a means of transport of the local elite, as well as a symbol of their social status.

Written sources bearing on Roman Republican and earlier times refer to the transport of women, priests or grandees by vehicle, either a cart or a wagon. Such journeys took place in and around Rome and other cities, but also between one city and another.[65]

Wagons are far less well attested than carts (or chariots) in the material record and by figured documents of first millennium Italy (Chapter IV). One highly ornate four-wheeler, from the Tomba del Carro at Como, Ca'Morta in the north and dating to the earlier fifth century, has close counterparts, in respect of both its construction and bronze decoration, in wagons found in various tombs of the Hallstatt culture north of the Alps (Pls 117, 159). These costly vehicles were clearly not suited to travel or carrying farm produce or other bulky materials, but must have been used for special, ceremonial purposes. At the same time, the wagons were symbols of the elevated social position of their owners. These were mostly men, but sometimes women, as in the case of the wagons from Como, Ca'Morta and the famous tomb at Vix in Burgundy.[66]

How are we to explain the close links between the wagons from Como, Ca'Morta and Hallstatt burial sites? They clearly have a common origin, which may perhaps be sought north rather than south of the Alps. The use of ceremonial four-wheelers goes back to the time of the Urnfield culture (*c.* 1300–800) in western, central and eastern Europe.[67] At the same time, the technology of wheelmaking shared by the wagons and other vehicles in Italy and the wagons of Hallstatt Europe, apparent in the metal axle caps, nave fittings, felloe clamps and nailed-on tyres, quite probably ultimately derives from the Near East.[68]

Remains of two other ceremonial four-wheelers come from 'Tombe Principesche' of the seventh century at Cerveteri and Veii in central Italy. The vehicles' siding is very low and decorated in bronze, recalling the wagon from the Tomba del Carro at Como, Ca'Morta and its Hallstatt counterparts. There is evidence to show that the four-wheeler from Veii, and possibly also the hand-pulled one from Cerveteri, were last used as hearses, unlike the Como' Ca'Morto and Halstatt wagons.

The few four-wheelers depicted on figured documents from Italy dating before the Roman Imperial period again carry people at special occasions.

Apart from carrying people, two-wheeled carts and four-wheeled wagons in Italy surely played an

---

[65] See pp. 87–88.

[66] For the Hallstatt vehicles and similarities to the wagon from Como, Ca'Morta, see pp. 90 and 96.

[67] See a.o. Pare 1992, 194, 214f. For connections between Italy and regions north of the Alps at the time of the Urnfield and Halstatt cultures, see contributions to *Etrusker nördlich von Etruria* (1992), *Archäologische Untersuchungen zu den Beziehungen zwischen Altitalien und der Zone nordwärts der Alpen* (1998) and *Gli Etruschi a nord del Po* (2000).

[68] See Kossack 1971; Piggott 1983, 168–70; Pare 1987d, 192–5; 1992, 165–9; Von Hase 1992, 261f.; Frey 1998, 271; Emiliozzi 2001b; Cf. Egg 1998, 271.; Koch, J. K. 2006, 247, 249. See also our p. 34 and note 168.

important role in the transport of goods which were too heavy and/or bulky to be carried by human porters or pack animals. This was particularly useful in the case of agricultural commodities and building materials. Support for this view is provided by a bronze model from Bolsena in Toscana (Pl. 88), by textual sources and by the evidence for vehicular roads, which will have facilitated the vehicles' role in civilian transport, and as part of a military baggage train.[69]

It may briefly be noted here that Roman textual sources of the later Republican and Imperial periods also testify to the use of another means of transport for important individuals – the open or close litter carried by human porters. The first illustrations of such conveyances may be seen on second–first century Etruscan cinerary urns from Volterra.[70] The litters are closed and thus recall the carts with arched tilts depicted on other urns (Pl. 112).

As we have seen, faster, horse-drawn *chariots* with two-spoked wheels are first attested in the eleventh–tenth centuries (by miniature bronze models from Lazio in central Italy)[71] and, more firmly, from the eighth century onwards (by remains of actual vehicles from central and northern Italy). Two-dimensional figured documents showing chariots first appear in the seventh century, with many more dating to later centuries.

Unlike carts and wagons, chariots are not designed for transporting of goods or seated or reclining people, but for carrying one or more standing occupant(s). In Italy, there were no prototypes for this kind of two-wheeled vehicle, and the conclusion must be that the earliest chariots in Italy were not locally developed but were indebted to foreign models. As noted in Chapter II, there is good reason to assume influences from the eastern Mediterranean, where chariots had been known for a long time. What may be called the true chariot was developed out of earlier types of vehicle in the early second millennium in the Near East.[72] From there it spread to Egypt and the Aegean before the middle of that century.[73] The relatively late appearance of the chariot in Italy may be due to the considerable geographical distance, the low intensity of trade contacts, as well as the less advanced socio-political development. The chariot – a vehicle requiring considerable skill, and costly to manufacture and maintain, with a team of horses and a crew needing extensive training – would of necessity have been confined to fairly complex societies. The craft of the wheelwright (who made not spoked, but disk and cross-bar types of wheel) and the concomitant use of paired animals in draught (not horses, but oxen, asses or mules) were, however, already known in parts of Italy. This is demonstrated by the early actual wheels from sites in the north. In addition, the keeping of horses, quite probably for riding rather than as draught animals, is documented in the later part of the second millennium in northern Italy by the presence of antler-tine cheekpieces of bridle bits.

As was noted above, in central and northern Italy, there is evidence – particularly from tombs of the ninth–seventh centuries – for the rise of élite groups. Striking, if as yet not fully understood, features of this process are the massed wealth of the elite and their close ties with the eastern Mediterranean, at first especially with the Levant and then increasingly with mainland and East Greece. These leaders had a great interest in weaponry and luxury craft goods, and the chariot would have fitted in very well with their lifestyle, becoming a symbol of their superior standing.[74]

---

[69] See pp. 1–3 and 88.

[70] See Alföldi 1970, 103–6; De Azevedo 1938, 19–21; Pisani Sartorio 1988, 103–6; Cateni and Fiaschi 1984, pl. 38.

[71] See pp. 52–53.

[72] Littauer and Crouwel 1979a, especially 68–71; more recently, Crouwel 2004a, 78–82. For the view that the chariot was first developed in the Eurasian steppe, see especially Anthony 1995 and 2007, especially 397–408, 459–63. For criticism, see Littauer and Crouwel 1996b (= 2002, 145–52); Jones-Bley 2000.

[73] For Egypt, see Herold 2004; Raulwing and Clutton-Brock 2009. For the Aegean, see Crouwel 1991, especially 148f.; 2004, 341–3; 2005. For the long-standing view that the chariot was introduced to Greece from the north, see a.o. Messerschmidt 1988; Penner 1998 (criticallly reviewed by Kaiser 2001; Crouwel 2001); cf. Kristiansen 2005, 685–7.

[74] See especially Guidi 1998; Putz 1998; De Santis 1998; Pacciarelli 2000; Riva 2001–3 and 2010; Drago Troccoli 2005; Torelli 2006; Seubers

Indeed, chariots were considered an enviable possession by many peoples at various times and places. Apart from their military possibilities, the vehicles were, with their teams of horses, an exciting and impressive sight. Both the chariot and its team of horses were suitable for lavish decoration, thus catering to the love of ostentation of an elite. Chariots lent prestige to their owners, raising them literally above their fellows. Moreover, the possession of chariots contributed to the development of a privileged group within society.

According to a long held view, the chariot was introduced in central and northern Italy from the Near East, together with other 'orientalizing' features, in the course of increasing trade contacts conducted mainly by the Phoenicians.[75] Indeed, certain elements, such as bronze or iron felloe clamps and nailed-on iron tyres, commonly found among the actual remains of chariots and other wheeled vehicles in tombs in central and northern Italy, along with the cheekpiece designs of some of the metal horse bits, probably derive from the Near East (see above). However, when taken together, the five types of chariot which can be distinguished in the material record and figured documents from central and northern Italy are very different from those seen on ninth–seventh century Assyrian reliefs and other contemporary or later figured documents from different parts of the Near East (Pls 125–129). So there is no question of a wholesale adoption in Italy of Near Eastern models.[76] Chariots in Italy also differ markedly from the actual vehicles and their two-and three-dimensional representations of the eighth–sixth centuries and later from Cyprus (Pls 130–131).[77]

One type of chariot in Italy (our Type III) has much in common with the High-front chariot which became standard in mainland Greece in the eighth century and is later represented in the Greek colonies in southern Italy and Sicily.[78]

Chariot Type I, which is the best documented in the material as well as in the artistic record of central Italy, shares a number of features with East Greek chariots, i.e. those illustrated in figured documents of the sixth–early fifth centuries from the Greek cities on the west coast of Anatolia. The similarities include a preference for draught teams of two horses, harnessed under a neck yoke. (In contrast, the High-front chariots of mainland Greece were usually drawn by teams of four horses of which two were under a dorsal yoke.) A note of caution is necessary here: features in common illustrated in Italian-made figured documents quite often seem to be iconographic rather than real, deriving from Greek artistic models.[79]

Chariots and horse gear in Italy also appear to have some elements in common with Europe north of the Alps, as regards vehicle construction (the so-called angle-sockets of chariot Type III which are first attested in the seventh century), certain types of bits and other horse gear (particularly in northern Italy).[80]

It is often difficult to distinguish between the role of foreign influences, which are especially apparent in wheel construction, and local invention.[81] Indeed, it should be stressed that from the eighth century onwards Italic chariots had their own structural peculiarities, including the narrow U-shaped floor of Type I and its later variant Type II. Such a floor could accommodate a passenger standing behind and

---

2008; also Cornell , C. J. 1995, ch. 4; Barker and Rasmussen 1998, 60–84.

[75] Stary 1979, 190; 1980; 1981a, especially 193f.; Nebelsick 1992, 97–110; Emiliozzi 2001b.

[76] See Littauer and Crouwel 1979a, chs 9 and 10. Of particular relevance here are the box-like chariots on Phoenician coins minted at Sidon (Studniczka 1907, 189–92; Hill 1910, pls 17–21; Franke and Hirmer 1964, pl. 195 = our Pl. 129).

[77] Crouwel 1987.

[78] See also Nebelsick 1992, 11. Pare (1987d, 222, 227, 230; 1992, 211, 212) – unconvincingly – proposed that the metal element with spiraliform ending of our type IV chariot derives from the mainland Greek Rail chariot.

[79] See also pp. 23, 57–58. For the question as to whether what is represented reflects local contemporary realities, see also Barker and Rassmussen 1998, 218, 260. In spite of the strong criticism by Ridgway and Serra Ridgway (1999, 450–2), this book has been of great use to me.

[80] See pp. 20–21, 46, 48–49.

[81] See Burmeister 1999.

not beside the driver. The form and construction of the vehicles' siding are also characteristic of Italic chariots.

It has been assumed that once arrived in Italy chariots were also actively used in warfare, as they were in the Near East. In Italy such a use would have lasted until the introduction of Greek hoplite weaponry in the second half of the seventh century.[82] However, the available evidence does not support this view. For instance, in Italy many vehicles were too narrow for an archer to stand beside the driver, and they lacked bowcases and quivers of arrows attached to their siding. The chariot's military function in Italy, if it had one at all, must have been the same as that firmly documented for Greece in the second millennium and possibly lasting until the eighth century, namely as an élite means of transport. However, the Italian sources of the eighth–sixth centuries are ambiguous on this point.

Chariots in central and northern Italy should, in fact, be regarded as status symbols rather than as instruments of war. What is well documented, in the material record and among the figured documents, is the use of chariots for ceremonial purposes. Indeed, some of the surviving vehicles are so highly decorated in bronze, and therefore so heavy and cumbersome, that they clearly could not be put to more strenuous use. The famous Monteleone chariot, from a sixth century tomb in Umbria, is the prime example of this.

From the fifth century onwards, chariots in Italy certainly had no military function but were solely used for civil purposes, including religious or funerary ceremonies and racing. The latter use, which is first documented in the sixth century, was almost certainly adopted from mainland or East Greece – either directly or via the Greek colonies in southern Italy. However, there are also typical Italic features in chariot racing, such as the protective caps and corsets worn by the drivers, and the reins tied around their hips.

No clear structural development of chariots in Italy can be traced. At times, different types existed side by side. This is well illustrated by the presence of chariots of Types I, II and III on terracotta revetment plaques of the late sixth century (Pl. 71a–b).[83] One type (our Type I) seems to predominate from the eighth century onwards and later became the prototype of the Roman racing chariot.

This study concludes with a few words on chariots in Italy during the period of the Roman Empire. Roman chariots were clearly much indebted to the earlier ones, in their types and aspects of their construction, in the ways the harness teams were harnassed and controlled, and in the use to which the equipages were put. The Roman chariots did not serve for warlike purposes, although it should be remembered that the use of a *quadriga* in the Triumph may well reflect a traditional function as a means of elite military transport. Instead, these vehicles served civil purposes, as conveyances for the Imperial family and, at times, other grandees. Their use in racing, while going back to earlier times in Italy, lasted into the Byzantine era.

---

[82] See p. 56 and note 315.
[83] See pp. 18, and p. 10, note 17.

Appendices

A survey of wheeled transport in Italy before the Roman Empire is incomplete without briefly considering the horse-drawn vehicles that appear in certain representations from northern Italy.

Appendix 1. Wheeled vehicles in Situla Art

Chariots, carts and wagons are depicted on a distinctive class of bronzework often called Situla Art. The name derives from the characteristic bronze buckets, or situlae, with elaborate repoussé decoration arranged in friezes.[1]

Examples of Situla Art, which must have been made in only a few workshops, are known from sites in northern Italy, the Italian-Austrian Alpine region, the Ljubliana area of present-day Slovenia, but also at Kuffarn on the Danube in Austria. The chronology of Situla Art is rather controversial, with most scholars opting for a wide time span, from the sixth to the fourth century, making it contemporary with the late Hallstatt and early La Tène periods in Europe north of the Alps. Other scholars attribute this class of bronzework entirely to the sixth century, even if some examples have been found in later (mostly funerary) contexts.

Chariots are quite often illustrated in Situla Art, including two complete examples found in Italy – the so-called Arnoaldi Situla from Bologna and the Benvenuti Situla from Este (Pls 164–165).[2] Here the vehicles are shown carrying only a driver. There are also representations showing two occupants, with one standing behind the other. The approximately hip-high siding usually corresponds with that of our Type IV chariot. Its hoop-shaped rail is entirely or partly filled-in with screening material, sometimes with thongs running down from the top, or in other cases is left entirely open. Another feature in common with chariots of Type IV is the inward-curving element at the upper front corner, which has been linked with metal scroll-type terminals found in several central Italian vehicle tombs of the later eighth and seventh centuries, as well as in burials of the early sixth century at Sesto Calende in northern Italy (Pls 15–16).[3] On the Arnoaldi Situla from Bologna such a chariot, carrying two occupants, is depicted

---

[1] See especially Frey 1962 and 1992; Lucke and Frey 1962; Boardman 1971; Bonfante 1981, 14–91; Torbrügge 1992; Cassola Guida 1997 (with bibliography); Teržan 1997; Koch, L. C. 2002; 2006. For the scenes with vehicles, see also Kromer 1980, 227–36; Piggott 1983, 178–82; Camerin 1997, 42f. and figs 9–10; Schönfelder 2002, 283–7 with figs 179–80 and table 50; Zaghetto 2006.

[2] **Situla from Bologna**, Arnoaldi tomb 96: see a.o. Lucke and Frey 1962, no. 3 and pls 13, 15, 63; Piggott 1983, 179f. and fig. 111: above; Schönfelder 2002, fig. 180:2; Macellari 2002, 202 and pls 16, 121–3. **Situla from Este**, Benvenuti tomb 126 (formerly tomb 73): see a.o. Lucke and Frey 1992, no. 7 and pls 23, 65; Frey 1969, 101f. no. 4; *Gli Etruschi* cat. no. 569; Schönfelder 2002, fig. 180: 4; Pare 1987d, 220 and fig. 23: 1; 1992, 210 and fig. 151: 1. The other chariot illustrations occur on situlae, or fragments thereof, from Vače (our Pl. 166; see Lucke and Frey 1962, no. 33 and pls 48, 73; Schönfelder 2002, fig. 179:6), Rovereto (see Lucke and Frey 1962, no. 12 and pl. 32; Piggott 1983, 189 and fig. 111: below; Schönfelder 2002, fig. 179: 8), Pillerhöhe (see Schönfelder 2002, fig. 179: 9), Moritzing/San Maurizio (see Lucke and Frey 1962, no. 13 with fig. 12 and pls 29, 66; Schönfelder 2002, fig. 179: 10), Kuffarn (see Lucke and Frey 1962, no. 40 and pls 52, 57, 75; Schönfelder 2002, fig. 179: 9) and Dolenjske, Topliče (see Lucke and Frey 1962, no. 32 and pls 46, 72; Schönfelder 2002, fig. 180: 3; Egg and Eibner 2005). There are also two examples from Visače/Nesactium (see Schönfelder 2002, fig. 180: 5 and 6; for the first of these, see also Lucke and Frey 1962, no. 30a and pl. 45).

[3] See p. 22 and note 82.

moving slowly, along with speeding one-man chariots; the latter vehicles have an open rail siding of rather triangular form (Pl. 164).

The wheels have 4–10 spokes, mostly six, and are mounted on central axles. The traction system includes a brace dropping obliquely from the top of the front breastwork to the pole, often with a knob-like swelling about halfway along.[4] An oblique pole brace, restricting the tendency of the floor frame and pole to pull apart particularly in rough going, is not otherwise documented on contemporary chariots in Italy, or in mainland or East Greece. It is, however, shown on Near Eastern chariots.[5] The knob-swelling of the pole brace is unique and unexplained (Pls 164, 166).

The harness teams consist of no more than two horses, apparently under a neck yoke. Control is by bitted bridle, identifiable by the crescent-shaped or prominent U-shaped cheekpieces. Both of these cheekpiece designs occur among actual bits from Italy and further north. For instance, pairs of bronze bits with prominent U-shaped cheekpieces have been found, together with scroll-type terminals and other metal remains of a two-wheeled vehicle, in the Tomba di Guerriero B at Sesto Calende, and also in late Hallstatt and early La Tène contexts beyond the Alps (Pl. 26).[6] Goads of varying length are illustrated, but no whips.

The chariots may be depicted moving slowly, as if in procession, accompanied by people on foot, on horseback or, in one case, seated in a cart (Pl. 166).[7] Other scenes illustrate fast-moving chariots engaged in a race, the drivers leaning forward and sometimes having the reins tied around their waist (Pl. 164).[8] The latter practice is well known from sixth–fifth and later, Roman representations of chariot racing in Italy (Pls 34–36, 41–42, 45).[9] There is no evidence of a role for chariots in warfare.[10]

Illustrations of two-wheeled carts and four-wheeled wagons are less frequent than those of chariots in Situla Art, and none have been found in Italy (Pls 166–167).[11] The vehicles are horse-drawn, moving slowly as in procession, and carry two to four passengers. These are seated and not standing as in chariots. When four occupants are shown one behind the other, they presumably are meant to be seated two abreast. The siding of some carts and wagons are depicted as raised high on vertical and oblique posts over the six- or eight-spoked wheels. The siding itself is low, and sometimes has bird-headed finials at either end. A Y-pole appears to be indicated on one of the carts,[12] recalling the Y-poled carts that are attested by figured documents and actual remains from different parts of Italy (see Chapter III.1). The Y-perch that is rendered in plan view with two wagons,[13] in turn recalls the actual four-wheelers with undercarriages from Como, Ca'Morta in northern Italy and from Hallstatt tombs.[14] The teams of two horses, like those of chariots, are controlled by bitted bridles, again indicated by crescent- or U-shaped cheekpieces. Goads are also in evidence.

Situla Art poses the problem of deciding to what extent it reflects actual elements and activities in the

---

[4] Called 'Brüstungsanker' by Nebelsick (1992, 105, 107) and Schönfelder (2002, 298); see also Piggott 1983, 179.

[5] Littauer and Crouwel 1979a, 110, 148; see also seventh century Cypro-Phoenician silver bowls, some of which have been found in central Italy (our p. 26 and note 111).

[6] See p. 46 and note 251.

[7] See p. 109, note 2 (Vače situla).

[8] See p. 109, note 2 (the Arnoaldi Situla from Bologna and the situla from Kuffarn).

[9] See pp. 67–68.

[10] For weaponry and military activities illustrated in Situla Art, see especially Frey 1973.

[11] **Carts**: situla from Vače (Pl. 166), probably a fragment from Sanzeno (Lucke and Frey 1992, no. 15 and pl. 67; Schönfelder 2002, fig. 179: 7), possibly also a fragment from Mechel (Lucke and Frey 1992, no. 8e and pl. 27). **Wagons**: situlae from Mechel (Lucke and Frey 1962, no. 11 and pl. 28; Piggott 1983, 182 and fig. 112: below; Schönfelder 2002, fig. 179: 1), from Moritzing/San Maurizio (Lucke and Frey 1982, no. 14 with fig. 13 and pl. 30; Schönfelder 2002, fig. 179: 2), from Novo mesto (our Pl. 167; Schönfelder 2002, fig. 179: 3 and 4), from Pfatten/Vadena (Schönfelder 2002, fig. 179: 5) and probably one from Waisenberg (Schönfelder 2002, fig. 179: 4).

[12] The Vače situla, see p. 109, note 2.

[13] The Mechel and Novo mesto situlae, see p. 109, note 2.

[14] See pp. 91–92.

areas where this class of bronzework was made, as opposed to reflecting external artistic influences.[15] The scenes showing chariot racing are a case in point. On the one hand, they hark back to Etruscan models, one of the situlae showing drivers with the reins tied around their hips and another with the driver looking back at his fellow competitors – details well-known from tomb and vase paintings and terracotta revetment plaques in central Italy. On the other hand, there are many undoubtedly local elements, such as the pointed cap worn by the same drivers, the chariots' oblique pole brace with its knob-like swelling and the U-shaped cheekpieces of several of their harness teams.

Appendix 2. The 'Celtic chariot'

Horse-drawn two-wheelers appear on several of the so-called Palaeovenetic funerary stelae from Padua in north-eastern Italy.[16] Some of these carved stone monuments, which are thought to date to the first century, illustrate chariots with a scroll-type terminal at the upper front of the closed body (Pl. 62).[17] The vehicles depicted on two other such stelae, however, are very different and have often been linked with the much discussed 'Celtic chariot' of pre-Roman and Roman times in western Europe.

The first of these stelae shows a man and a woman(?), seated behind each other but perhaps meant to be side by side. The man is holding the reins and a two-lashed whip, the pointed stock of which probably indicates that it was also used as a goad (Pl. 168).[18] The vehicle has a low, double-hooped side railing and was almost certainly open at the front and rear. The floor frame, hoops and the Y-shaped element shown inside the hoops are all decorated with a circle-and-dot design. An oval shield rests on its side inside the railing. This type of shield with its spindle-shaped boss is well-known and long-lived in different parts of Europe, its first representations going back to the sixth century in central Italy.[19] A spear projects obliquely backwards. The wheel is shown with seven spokes and a T-shaped linch pin to help secure it on to the central axle. The thickening of the spokes near the nave may suggest a metal casing; the wheel rim is in two parts, the outer one of which is either made of wood or represents an iron tyre. The pole rises steeply to the neck yoke. The two-horse team is shown with decorated neck- or breaststrap and girth, and a bitted bridle, the curved cheekpiece held by a bifurcated cheekstrap.

The second stele illustrates a similar vehicle but in much less detail.[20] The two-man crew consists of a standing warrior with a similar oval shield and brandishing a sword or other short-range weapon, with a driver beside him. The two horses are rearing.

The same type of light, two-wheeled vehicle, in which the occupants could be either seated or standing, can be seen on some Roman bronze coins and on others minted by the Remi tribe in the region of Rheims in northern France, all dating from around the middle of the first century.[21] Here, the low,

---

[15] For recent discussion, see a.o. Torbrügge 1992; Teržan 1997; Koch, L. C. 2002 and 2006.

[16] See p. 22.

[17] See p. 22, note 79, *s.v.* chariot Type IV.

[18] The so-called Stele Albinasego, from a cemetery at the Via Ognissanti in Padua. See especially Frey 1968; Harbison 1969, 46f.; Stead 1971, 171 and pl. 25; Fogolari 1975, 134 and pl. 75; *Padova preromana* no. 71; Piggott 1983, 210 and fig. 128; Zampieri 1994, no. 151; Egg and Pare 1997, 49 and fig. 3; Schönfelder 2002, 288 and fig. 181.

[19] See a.o. Stary 1977, 104–6; 1981c, 287–306; Piggott 1983, 196. Such shields are also shown on other Padovan funerary stelae where they are carried by warriors on horseback; see *Padova preromana* nos 72–3. An oval shield and a spear are held by the driver of Celtic appearance in a two-horse, spoke-wheeled vehicle, depicted on a second century Etruscan stone sarcophagus from Chiusi; the (damaged) vehicle siding is not of the type with two hoops; see Herbig 1952, no. 14 and pl. 48; Stead 1965, 264f. with fig. 5 and pls 54, 55b; Höckmann 1991, 225f. no. 7 and pl. 48; Egg and Pare 1993, 214 and fig. 182; Schönfelder 2002, 288f. and fig. 182.

[20] Frey 1968, 319 and pl. 40: 1; *Padova preromana* no. 68; Piggott 1983, 210.

[21] For these coins, see especially Piggott 1952; 1983, 209f. and fig. 127: A–B, D; Harbison 1969, 47–9; Schönfelder 2002, 290, 292 and fig. 183: 7–8, 10–11.

double hoop-shaped siding may have had forked wooden braces or straps inside, like the vehicle on the first Padua stela discussed above (Pl. 169). A *denarius* of L. Hostilius Saserna illustrates a warrior thus armed standing with widespread legs in his vehicle and facing backwards, while his driver is seated at the front and is whipping the galloping team (Pl. 169).[22] On a later coin, minted for Julius Caesar, an unharnessed vehicle of this type, along with a shield and spears, appears among the trophies of his Gallic Wars.[23]

These vehicles and particularly their apparent military function have often been linked with the 'Celtic chariots' referred to in Greek and Roman literary sources of the second century and later. According to these sources, wheeled vehicles were used in war and peace by Celtic tribes not only in France and Britain but also in Italy, where they are mentioned in the battles at Sentinum (in 295), Telamon (in 225) and Clastidium (in 222), as well as in a raid on Delphi in Greece (in 279).[24]

The vehicles depicted on the coins and funerary stelae from France and Italy have also been used in various attempts to reconstruct the actual two-wheeled vehicles that were buried in numerous La Tène tombs. Most of these tombs date to the fifth–fourth centuries and their distribution ranges from Romania to Britain.[25] All that was left of these prestige vehicles are impressions in the soil and a variety of metal fittings, such as linch pins, felloe clamps, 'sweated-on' iron tyres, yoke terminals and horse bits. According to a recent reconstruction, based on the vehicle remains from a tomb at Wentwang in Yorkshire, the rectangular floor with meshed-thong flooring was suspended from Y-shaped straps which were fastened to the double-hooped side rails. The suspension system, when tested in practical experiments in the field, proved to greatly facilitate driving at speed over uneven ground (Pl. 170).[26]

Caution is needed in linking these different sources – figured, textual and material. All we can say is that a distinct type of horse-drawn two-wheeler is first attested by figured documents among Venetic-speaking people in north-eastern Italy (the Padua stelae bear inscriptions in the Venetic language) and then among local tribes in France.[27] This light vehicle, with its low double-hooped breastwork along the sides was clearly multi-functional. Whereas the driver is always seated, the passenger is either standing or seated, depending on whether the vehicle is used in battle or for travel. The carriage may therefore be described as both chariot and cart.

---

[22] A coin of Scaurus, probably minted at Narbo in southern France around the end of the second century, shows a similar warrior standing in a vehicle without any siding. See Piggott 1952, pl. 1a; 1983, fig. 127D; Schönfelder 2002, fig. 183: 4–5.

[23] Piggott 1983, fig. 127C and Schönfelder 2002, fig. 183: 9.

[24] See p. 57 and note 323. For discussion of the literary sources bearing on the vehicles and their military and other use by Celtic tribes, see especially Droyson 1886, 135 n. 29; D'Arbois de Jubainville 1888; Anderson 1965, 349f.; 1975, 177; Greenhalgh 1973, 14f.; Piggott 1983, 231–5; Schönfelder 2002, 293–7. For relevant information in Old Irish literature, see especially Greene 1972; Harbison 1969, 49–54; 1971; Piggott 1983, 235–8; Kaul 2007. The Celtic raid on Delphi is sometimes thought to be shown in the terracotta pedimental sculptures of the later second–first century from Civitalbà in Umbria; see Andrén 1939–40, 297–308 nos II: 1–15 and pl. 101: 360–65; Stead 1965, 263f. and fig. 4; Von Freytag gen Löringhoff 1986, 93; Sprenger and Bartoloni 1990, pls 280–1; Höckmann 1991, 212–19. Among these sculptures is a two-horse chariot with a Celtic-looking driver. The vehicle's siding, with fabric draped between vertical posts at the front and sides, is very different from those seen on the stelae and coins considered above, but somewhat resembles the chariot of Adrastus among the pedimental terracotta sculptures from Talamone (ancient Telamon) (see our Pl. 69a; p. 26 and note 110) and more closely the vehicles in a mythological setting on a marble frieze from Pergamum (see Winter, F. 1908, no. 387; Froning 1881, pl. 37: 2).

[25] For the vehicle burials, see especially Harbison 1969; Piggott 1983, 199–225; various contributions to *Keltski Voz* (1984); Van Endert 1987; Duval 1988, especially 311–15; Schönfelder 2002, 320–7. See also Stead 1965; Frey 1976; Egg and Pare 1993, 214–18 and figs 183, 186 (distribution map); 1997, 48–51; Diepenveen-Jansen 2001, especially 199–201; Carter and Hunter 2003 (the first such burial discovered in Scotland).

[26] Personal information R. Hurford. See also Hurford and Spence 2005 (the full-scale reconstruction and experiments with its use featured in the BBC documentary film *Chariot Queen* which was shown on TV on 19 February 2002 as part of the Series *Meet the Ancestors*); for the find context, see Dent 1985. For earlier reconstructions of 'Celtic chariots', see especially Fox 1946, 25–7 and fig. 13; Frey 1976; Cahen-Delhaye 1980, 25; Piggott 1983, 210f.; Metzler and Kunter 1986, 164–74; Furger-Gunti 1991 and 1993; Cahen-Delhaye and Hurt 1994; Müller, F. 1995 (arguing for a different suspension system); Schönfelder 2002, 275–82; Karl 2003.

[27] Unfortunately, nothing is known about the construction of the actual vehicle that was buried with its harness team at Adria in north-eastern Italy in the third century, apart from its two wheels having had metal nave hoops and iron tyres; see p. 5 and note 36, p. 33, note 161.

Bibliography

Abaecherli, A. L. 1935–36. 'Fercula, carpenta and tensae in the Roman procession', Bollettino dell'associazione internazionale degli studi mediterranei 6, 1–20.

Achse, Rad und Wagen. Fünftausend Jahre Kultur- und Technikgeschichte. Treue, W. (ed.) 2nd edn). Göttingen 1986.

Adam, A.-M. 1980. 'Bronzes campaniens du Ve siècle avant J.-C.', Mélanges de l'École française de Rome 92, 641–679.

Adam, A.-M. 1984. Bronzes étrusques et italiques (Bibliothèque Nationale. Département de monnais, médailles et antiquités). Paris.

Adam, A.-M. 1990. 'Les cités étrusques et la guerre au Ve siècle avant notre ère'. In Crise et transformation 327–356.

Adam, A.-M. 1993. 'Les jeux, la chasse et la guerre. La Tomba Querciola de Tarquinia'. In Spectacles sportifs 69–95.

Adam, A.-M. and Rouveret, A. 1995a. 'Cavaleries et aristocraties cavalières en Italie entre la fin du VIe siècle et le premier tiers du IIIe siècle avant notre ère', Mélanges de l'École française de Rome 107, 7–12.

Adam, A.-M. and Rouveret, A. 1995b. 'Aspects de l'iconographie des cavaliers en Étrurie du VIe au IVe siècle avant notre ère: représentation et idéologie', Mélanges de l'École française de Rome 107, 71–96.

Adam, J.-P. and Varène, P. 1970. L'attività archeologica in Basilicata'. In La Magna Grecia nel mondo ellenistico (Atti del convegno di studi sulla Magna Grecia, Taranto 1969). Napoli, 215–237.

Adam, J.-P. and Varène, P. 1974. La Basilicata antica. Storia e monumenti. Salerno.

Adam, J.-P. and Varène, P. 1980. 'Une peinture romaine représentant une scène de chantier, Revue archéologique, 213–238.

Adamesteanu and Dilthey, H. 1992. Macchia di Rossano. Il santuario della Mefitis. Rapporto preliminare. Galatina.

Adams, C. 2007. Land Transport in Roman Egypt. A Study of Economics and Administration in a Roman Province. Oxford.

Adams, J. N. 1993. 'The generic use of Mula and the status and employment of female mules in the Roman world', Rheinisches Museum für Philologie (Neue Folge) 136, 352–361.

Adams, J.-P. 1994. Roman Building, Materials and Techniques. London.

Adornato, G. 2008. 'Delphic enigmas? The Γέλας ανάσσων, Polyzalos, and the charioteer statue', American Journal of Archaeology 112, 29–55.

ΑΕΙΜΝΗΣΤΟΣ. Miscellanea di studi per Mauro Cristofani. 2006. Adembri, B. (ed.) I–II. Prospettiva, Supplemento 2. Florence.

Åkerström, Å. 1951. Architektonische Terrakottaplatten in Stockholm. Lund.

Åkerström, Å. 1954. 'Untersuchungen über die figürlichen Terrakottenfriese aus Etrurien und Latium', Opusucula romana 1, 191–231.

Åkerström, Å.1966. Die architektonischen Terrakottenplatten Kleinasiens. Lund.

Akten des Kolloquiums zum Thema "Der Orient und Etrurien". Zum Phänomenon des "Orientalisierens" im westlichen Mittelmeerraum (10.–6. Jh. v.Chr.). Prayon, Fr. and Röllig, W. (eds). Tübingen 1997. Pisa–Rome 2000.

Alberti-Parronchi, G. and Piccard, G. 1950–1951. 'Sui bronzi sacri del Bagno di Selene (Terma di Chianciano)', Studi etruschi 21, 249–260.

Albizzati, C. 1918–19. 'Una fabbrica vulcente di vasi a figure rosso', Mélanges d'archéologie et d'histoire 38, 107–178.

Alföldi, A. 1970. Die monarchische Repräsentation im römischen Kaiserreich. Darmstadt (first published in Römische Mitteilungen 49 (1934), 1–118, and 50 (1935) 1–158; reprinted in 1977).

Amann, P. 2000. Die Etruskerin. Geschlechtverhältnis und Stellung der Frau im frühen Etrurien (9.–5. Jh. v.Chr.). Österreichische Akademie der Wissenschaften. Philosophisch-historische Klasse. Denkschriften, 289 Band. Archäologische Forschungen 5. Vienna.

Ambrosch, I. A. 1837. De Charonte etrusco. Bratislawa.

Amyx, D. A. 1988. Corinthian Vase-Painting of the Archaic Period I–II. Berkeley–Los Angeles–London.

Anati, E. 1982. Valcamonica: 10.000 anni di storia. Studi Camuni 8 (2nd edn). Capo di Monte (Brescia).

Ancient Italy in its Mediterranean Setting. Studies in Honour of E. Macnamara. Ridgway, D., Serra Ridgway, F. R., Pearce, M., Whitehouse, R. and Wilkins, J. B. (eds). Accordia Specialist Studies in the Mediterranean 4. London 2000.

Anderson, J. K. 1961. Ancient Greek Horsemanship. Berkeley–Los Angeles.

Anderson, J. K. 1965. 'Homeric, British and Cyrenaic chariots', American Journal of Archaeology 69, 349–352.

Anderson, J. K. 1975. 'Greek chariot-borne and mounted infantry', *American Journal of Archaeology* 79, 175–187.

Anderson, J. K. 1991. 'Hoplite weapons and offensive arms'. In Hanson, V. D. (ed.), *Hoplites. The Classical Greek Battle Experience*. London, 15–62.

Andrén, J. K. 1939–1940. *Architectural Terracottas from Etrusco-Italic Temples*. Lund–Leipzig.

Andrén, J. K. 1948. 'Oreficeria e plastica etrusche', *Opuscula archeologica* 5, 91–112.

Andrén, J. K. 1974. 'Osservazioni sulle terracotte architettoniche etrusco-italiche', *Opusucula romana* 8, 1–16 (first published in *Lectiones Boëthianae* 1 (1971).

Annibaldi, G. 1960. 'Grozzalina (Ascoli Piceno) – Rinvenimento di tombe picene', *Notizie degli scavi di antichità* (Serie 8), 14, 366–392.

Anthony, D. W. 1995. 'Horse, wagon and chariot: Indo-European languages and archaeology', *Antiquity* 69, 554–565.

Anthony, D. W. 2007. *The Horse, the Wheel and Language. How Bronze Age Riders from the Eurasian Steppes Shaped the Modern World*. Princeton NJ.

Antiche genti d'Italia (exhibition catalogue, Rome 1994). Guzzo, P. G., Moscati, S. and Susini, G. (eds). Rome 1994.

Antichità dall'Umbria a New York (exhibition catalogue, New York 1991). *Gens Antiquissima Italiae*. Perugia 1991.

Archäologische Untersuchungen zu den Beziehungen zwischen Altitalien und der Zone nordwärts der Alpen während der frühen Eisenzeit. Ergebnisse eines Kolloquiums in Regensburg 1994. Regensburger Beiträge zur prähistorischen Archäologie 4. Bonn 1998.

L'archeologia racconta. Lo sport nell'antichità (exhibition catalogue, Florence 1988). Florence 1988.

Arietti, A. and Martellotta, B. 1998. *La tomba principesca di Vivaro di Rocca di Papa*. Città di Castello.

Armi. Gli instrumenti di guerra in Lucania antico (exhibition catalogue, Melfi 1993). Bottini, A. (ed.). Bari 1994.

Art of the Classical World in the Metropolitan Museum of Art. Greece – Cyprus – Etruria – Rome. New Haven–London 2007.

Un artista etrusco e il suo mondo. Il pittore di Micali (exhibition catalogue) Rome 1988. Rizzo, M. A. and Cristofani, M. (eds). Rome 1988.

Atkinson, F. and Ward, A. 1965. 'A pair of "clog" wheels from northern England (of the early 19th century)', *Transactions of the Yorkshire Dialect Society* XI, Part 64, 33–40.

Azzaroli, A 1972. 'Il cavallo domestico in Italia dell'età del bronzo agli Etruschi', *Studi etruschi* 40, 274–308.

Azzaroli, A 1975. *Il cavallo nella storia antica*. Milan.

Azzaroli, A 1979. 'Su alcuni resti di cavalli protohistorici dell'Italia centrale', *Studi etruschi* 47, 231–236.

Azzaroli, A 1980. 'Venetic horses from Iron Age burials at Padova', *Rivista di scienze preistoriche* 35, 281–307.

Azzaroli, A 1989. 'L'arte equestre degli Etruschi'. In *Secondo congresso internazionale etrusco* II, 1429–1443.

Bakker, J. A. 2004. 'Die neolithische Wagen in nördlichen Mitteleuropa'. In *Rad und Wagen* 283–294.

Bakker, J. A., Kruk, J., Lanting, A. E. and Milisauskas, S. 1999. 'The earliest evidence of wheeled vehicles in Europe and the Near East', *Antiquity* 73, 778–790.

Balkwill, C. J. 1973. 'The earliest horse-bits of western Europe', *Proceedings of the Prehistoric Society* 39, 425–452.

Barfield, L. 1971. *Northern Italy*. London.

Barfield, L. 1994. 'The Bronze Age of northern Italy: recent work and social interpretation'. In Mathers, C. and Stoddart, S. (eds), *Development and Decline in the Mediterranean Bronze Age. Sheffield Archaeological Monographs* 129–144.

Barker, G. 1976. 'Animal husbandry at Narce'. In Potter, T. W. (ed.), *A Faliscan Town in South Etruria. Excavations at Narce 1966–71*. London, 295–307.

Barker, G. and Rassmussen, T. B. 1998. *The Etruscans*. Oxford.

Barnett, R. D. and Lorenzini, A. 1975. *Assyrian Sculpture in the British Museum*. Toronto.

Bartoccini, R., Lerici, C.M. and Moretti, M. 1959. *Tarquinia. La Tomba delle Olimpiadi*. Milan.

Bartoloni, G. 1981. *Archeologia classica* 33, 386–391 (review of Rassmussen, T. B., *Bucchero Pottery from Southern Etruria*. Cambridge 1979).

Bartoloni, G. 1992. 'Palazzo o tempio? A proposito dell'edificio arcaico di Poggio Buco', *Annali del Seminario di studi del mondo classico: sezione di archeologia e storia antica* 14, 9–31.

Bartoloni, G. 1993. 'Documentazione figurata e deposizioni funerarie : le tombe con carro', *Archeologia classica* 45, 271–291.

Bartoloni, G. 2003. *Le società dell'Italia primitiva. Lo studio delle necropoli e la nascità delle aristocrazie*. Rome.

Bartoloni, G. 2006. 'Frammenti di un carro da Perugia alla Bibliothèque Nationale di Parigi'. In *ΑΕΙΜΝΗΣΤΟΣ* I, 424–431.

Bartoloni, G. and Grottanelli, C. 1984. 'I carri a due ruote nelle tombe femminili del Lazio e dell'Etruria', *Opus* 3, 383–410 (reprinted in *Le donne in Etruria* 55–73).

Bartoloni, G., Cataldi, M. and Zevi, F. 1982. 'Aspetti dell'ideologia funeraria nella necropoli di Castel di Decima'. In Gnoli, G. and Vernant, J.-P. (eds), *La mort, les morts dans les sociétés anciennes*. Cambridge, 257–273.

Baserga, G. 1929. 'Tomba con carro ed altre scoperte alla Ca'Morta', *Rivista archeologica dell' antica provincia e diocesi di Como* 96–98, 25–44.

Basileis. Antichi re in Basilicata (exhibition catalogue, Rome 1995). Bottini, A. and Setari, E. (eds). Naples 1995.

Bassi, G. and Forno, G. 1988. *Gli strumenti di lavoro. Tradizionali lodigiani e la loro storia* I. *L'aratro e il carro lodigiani nel contesto storico padano*. Milan.

Bastianelli, S. 1940. 'Monumenti etruschi del Museo Communale di Civitavecchia', *Studi etruschi* 14, 359–366.

Bastien, J.-L. 2007. *Le triomphe romain et son utilisation politique à Rome aux trois derniers siècles de la République. Collection de l'École française de Rome* 392. Rome.

Beazley, J. D. 1947. *Etruscan Vase-Painting.* Oxford.

Bedini, A. 1977. 'L'ottavo secolo nel Lazio e l'inizio dell'orientalizzante antico. Alla luce di recenti scoperte nelle necropoli di Castel di Decima. Lazio arcaico e mondo greco – III. Castel di Decima', *La Parola del passato* 32, 274–309.

Beijer, A. J. 1993. 'Una lastra architettonica figurata di terracotta dall'abitato arcaico a Borgo le Ferriere ("Satricum")'. In *Deliciae Fictiles* I, 287–289.

Bellelli, V. 1997. 'Il contesto del Carro Dutuit: Storia degli studi'. In *Carri da guerra* 301–303.

Bender, H. 1978. *Römischer Reiseverkehr. Cursus Publicus und Privatreisen. Kleine Schriften zur Kenntnis der römischen Besetzungsgeschichte Südwestdeutschlands* 20. Stuttgart–Aalen.

Berger, E. 1982. *Antike Kunstwerke aus der Sammlung Ludwig* II. *Terrakotten und Bronzen.* Mainz am Rhein.

Bermond-Montanari, G. 1962. 'Nuova stele villanoviana rinvenuto a Bologna', *Arte antica e moderna* 17, 41–54.

Bermond-Montanari, G. 1965. 'Tomba ad incinerazione da Via Tofana (Bologna)'. In *Studi in honore di Luisa Banti* 51–57.

Bertoldi, M. A. 1968. 'Un monumento commemmorativo sul Campidogliou', *Quaderni dell'instituto di topografia antica della università di Roma* 5, 39–53.

Bertolone, M. 1956–1957. 'Tomba della prima età del ferro, con carretino, scoperta alla Cà'Morta di Como', *Sibrium* 3, 37–40.

Bevan, L. 2006. *Worshippers and Warriors. Reconstructing Gender and Gender Relations in the Prehistoric Rock Art of Naquane National Park, Valcamonica, Brescia, Northern Italy.* BAR International Series 1485. Oxford.

Bianco Peroni, B. 1970. *Die Schwerter in Italien. Prähistorische Bronzefunde* IV.1. Munich.

Biel, J. 1987. 'Der Wagen aus dem Fürstengrabhügel von Hochdorf'. In *Vierrädrige Wagen* 121–128.

Bietti Sestieri, A. M. and De Santis, A. 2000. *The Protohistory of the Latium Peoples* (exhibition catalogue, Rome 2000). Milan.

Bishop, M. C. 1988. 'Roman cavalry equipment in the first century AD'. In Coulston, J. C. (ed.), *Military Equipment and the Identity of Roman Soldiers.* BAR International Series 394. Oxford, 67–195.

Black, E. 1995. *Cursus Publicus. The Infrastructure of Government in Roman Britain.* BAR British Series 241. Oxford.

Blasques-Martinez, J. M. 1957–1958. 'Caballos en el infierno etrusco', *Ampurias* 19–20, 31–68.

Blasques-Martinez, J. M. 1965. 'La Tomba del Cardinale y la influencia orfico-pitagórica en las creencias etruscas de ultratumba', *Latomus* 24, 3–39.

Blegen, C. W. 1952. 'Two Athenian grave groups of about 900 BC', *Hesperia* 21, 279–294.

Bloch, R. 1950. 'Vases et intailles originaires d'Étrurie' *Collection Latomus* 9, 141–148.

Boardman, J. 1967. 'Archaic finger rings', *Antike Kunst* 10, 3–31.

Boardman, J. 1971. 'A southern view of Situla Art'. In *The European Community in Later Prehistory* 123–140.

Boardman, J. and Vollenweider, M.-L. 1978. *Catalogue of the Engraved Gems and Finger Rings* I. *Greek and Etruscan* (Ashmolean Museum). Oxford.

Bocci, P. 1960. 'Il sarcofago tarquiniese delle Amazzoni al Museo Archeologico di Firenze', *Studi etruschi* 28, 109–125.

Boehmer, R. M. 1983. *Boğazköy-Hattuša* XIII. *Die Reliefkeramik.* Berlin.

Bökönyi, S. 1991. 'The earliest occurrence of domestic asses in Italy'. In Meadow, R. H. and Ürpmann, H.-P. (eds), *Equids in the Ancient World* II. *Beihefte zum Tübinger Atlas des Vorderen Orients.* Wiesbaden, 217–225.

Boitani, F. 1983. 'Veio: la tomba "principesca" della necropoli di Monte Michele', *Studi etruschi* 51, 535–556.

Boitani, F. 1985. 'La biga di Ischia di Castro'. In *Strade degli Etruschi* 217–232 (p. 233: note on restauration by P. Aureli).

Boitani, F. 1987. 'La biga etrusca di Castro', *Antiqua* 12:5–6, 84–91.

Boitani, F. 1997. 'Il carro di Castro della tomba della biga (Reg. 100)'. In *Carri da guerra* 203–206.

Boitani, F. 2001. 'I.G.8. La tomba principesca n. 5 di Monte Michele'. In *Veio, Cerveteri, Vulci. Città d'Etruria a confronto* (exhibition catalogue, Rome 2001). Moretti Sgubini, A. M. (ed.). Rome, 113–118.

Boitani, F. and Aureli, P. 1988. 'Conservazione sullo scavo e restauro in laboratorio: alcuni recenti interventi'. In Colonna, G., Bettine, C. and Staccione, R. (eds), *Etruria meridionale. Conoscenza, conservazione, fruizione* (*Atti del convegno,* Viterbo 1985). Rome, 127–140.

Bonami, M. 2006. 'Dalla vita alla morte tra Vanth e Turms Aitas'. In *ΛΕΙΜΝΗΣΤΟΣ* II, 522–538.

Bonamici, M. 1974. *I buccheri con figurazioni graffite. Biblioteca di "Studi etruschi"* 8. Florence.

Bonauda, R. 2002–2003. 'Trasmissioni iconografiche e construzioni immaginere: riformulazione di modelli attici su alcune stele felsinee', *Annali dell'Instituto universitario orientali di Napoli* (Nuove Serie) 9–10, 103–113.

Bonfante, L. 1975. *Etruscan Dress.* Baltimore–London.

Bonfante, L. 1981. *Out of Etruria. Etruscan Influence North and South.* BAR International Series 103. Oxford.

Bonfante, L. 2005. 'The Verucchio Throne and the Corsini

Chair: two status symbols of ancient Italy'. In Pollini, J. (ed.) *Terra Marique. Studies in Art History and Marine Archaeology in Honour of Anna Marguerita McCann on the Receipt of the Gold Medal of the Archaeological Institute of America*. Oxford, 3–11.

Bonfante, L. and Emiliozzi, A. 1991. 'Rethinking a parade chariot', *Archaeology* 44, 50–53.

Bonfante Warren, L. 1964. 'A Latin triumph on a Praenestine cista', *AJA* 68, 35–42.

Bonfante Warren, L. 1970. 'Roman triumphs and Etruscan kings: the changing face of the triumph', *Journal of Roman Studies* 60, 49–66.

Bonomi Ponzi, L. 1970. 'Il ripostiglio di Contigliano', *Bollettino di paletnologia Italiana* 21, 95–156.

Bordenache Battaglia, G. and Emiliozzi, A. 1979. *Le ciste prenestine* I.1. Rome.

Bordenache Battaglia, G. and Emiliozzi, A. 1990. *Le ciste prenestine* I.2. Rome.

Borghini, L. 1984. 'La "scena" del carro e la donna divina: Gordio, Pisistrato e Tarquinio Prisco', *Materiali e discussioni per l'analisi dei testi classici* 12, 61–115.

Boroffka, N. 1998. 'Bronze- und früheisenzeitliche Geweih-trensenknebel aus Rumänien und ihre Beziehungen', *Eurasia Antiqua (Zeitschrift für Archäologie Eurasiens)* 4, 81–135.

Bottini, A. 2007. 'Il sarcofago tarquiniese delle Amazzoni', *Ostraka* 16, 11–22.

Braun, K. 1998. *Katalog der Antikensammlung des Instituts für klassische Archäologie der Universität des Saarlandes.* Bibliopolis (Möhnensee).

Breitenstein, N. 1941. *Catalogue of Terracottas* (Danish National Museum). Copenhagen.

Brendel, O. J. 1995. *Etruscan Art* (2nd edn). New Haven–London.

Briquet. M. F. 1968. 'Urnes archaïques étrusques', *Revue archéologique*, 49–72.

Brize, P. 1985. 'Samos und Stesichoros. Zu einem früharchaischen Bronzeblech', *Athenische Mitteilungen* 100, 53–90.

Brizio, E. 1899. 'Il sepolcreto gallico di Montefortino presso Arcervia', *Monumenti antichi* 9, 617–791.

Brodie, N. 2008. 'The donkey: an appropriate technology for Early Bronze Age land transport and traction'. In Brodie, N., Doole, J., Gavalas, G. and Renfrew, C. (eds), *Horizon. A Colloquium on the Prehistory of the Cyclades.* Cambridge, 299–304.

Bronson, C. 1965. 'Chariot racing in Etruria'. In *Studi in honore di Luisa Banti* 89–106.

Bronson, C. 1966. 'Three master-pieces of Etruscan black-figure vase-painting', *Archeologia classica* 18, 21–40.

Brouwers, J. J. 2007. 'From horsemen to hoplites. Some remarks on Archaic Greek warfare', *Bulletin Antieke Beschaving* 82, 305–319.

Brown, A. C. 1974. 'Etrusco-Italic architectural terracottas in the Ashmolean Museum', *Archaeological Reports* 1973–1974, 60–65.

Brown, W. L. 1960. *The Etruscan Lion.* Oxford.

Bruni, S. 2002. 'I carri perugini: nuove proposte di ricostruzione'. In Della Fina, M. (ed.) *Atti del IX convegno di studi sulla storia e l'archeologia dell'Etruria. Annali della Fondazione per il Museo "Claudio Faina"* 9. Perugia, 21–47.

Brunn, G. and Körte, G. 1916. *I rilievi delle urne etrusche* III. Rome–Berlin.

Buchholz, H.-G. and von Wangenheim, C. 1984. 'Flügel-pferde", *Archäologische Anzeiger*, 237–262.

Bugh, G. R. 1988. *The Horsemen of Athens.* Princeton.

Buranelli, F. 1983. *La necropoli villanoviana "Le Rose" di Tarquinia. Quaderni del centro di studio per l'archeologia etrusco-italica* 6. Rome.

Burford, A. 1993. *Land and Labour in the Greek World.* Baltimore–London.

Burmeister, S. 1999. 'Innovation, ein semiologisches Abenteuer – Das Beispiel der Hallstattzeit in südwest Deutschland', *Archäologische Informationen* 22/2, 241–260.

Burmeister, S. 2004a. 'Der Wagen im Neolithikum und in der Bronzezeit: Erfindung, Ausbreitung und Funktion der ersten Fahrzeuge'. In *Rad und Wagen* 13–40.

Burmeister, S. 2004b. 'Neolithische und bronzezeitliche Moorfunde aus den Niederlanden, Nordwestdeutschland und Dänemark'. In *Rad und Wagen* 321–340.

El caballo en la antigua Iberia. Quesada Sanz, F. and Zamora Merchán, M. (eds). *Bibliotheca archaeologica hispana* 19. Madrid 2003.

Cahen-Delahaye, A. 1980. 'Sépultures à char de l'âge du fer dans l'Ardenne belge', *Archéologie* (August), 20–27.

Cahen-Delahaye, A. and Hurt, V. 1994. 'Reconstruction d'un char à deux roues de La Tène', *Lunula. Archaeologia Protohistorica* 2, 47–50.

Cahn, D. 1989. *Waffen und Zaumzeug* (Basel, Antikenmuseum und Sammlung Ludwig). Basel.

Cahn, H. A., Mildenberg, L., Russo, R. and Voegtli, H. 1988. *Griechische Münze aus Grossgriechenland und Sizilien.* (Basel, Antikenmuseum und Sammlung Ludwig). Basel.

The Cambridge History of Greek and Roman Warfare I–II. 2007. Sabin, P., Van Wees, H. and Whitby, M. (eds). Cambridge.

Camerin, N. 1997a. 'L'Italia antica: Italia settentrionale'. In *Carri da guerra* 33–44.

Camerin, N. 1997b. 'La ricostruzione dei carri nella storia dei ritrovamenti'. In *Carri da guerra* 87–93.

Cameron, A. 1973. *Porphyrius the Charioteer.* Oxford.

Cameron, A. 1976. *Circus Factions. Blues and Greens at Rome and Byzantium.* Oxford.

Camporeale, G. 1967a. *La Tomba del Duce.* Florence.

Camporeale, G. 1967b. 'Su due placche bronzee da Marsiliana', *Studi etruschi* 35, 31–40.

Camporeale, G. 1972. *Buccheri e cilindretto di fabbrica orvietana.* Florence.

Camporeale, G. 1984. *La caccia in Etruria. Archaeologia* 50. Rome.

Camporeale, G. 1989. 'La mitologia figurata nella cultura etrusca arcaica'. In *Secondo congresso internazionale etrusca* II, 905–924.

Camporeale, G. 1991. *La collezione C.A. Impasti e buccheri* I. Rome.

Camporeale, G. 1993. 'Sull'origine della corsa armata in Etruria'. In *Spectacles sportifs* 7–19.

Canciani, F. 1980. 'Eine neue Amphora aus Vulci und das Problem der pseudochalkidischen Vasen', *Jahrbuch des Deutschen Archäologischen Instituts* 95, 140–162.

Canciani, F. and Von Hase, F. W. 1979. *La Tomba Bernardini di Palestrina. Latium Vetus* 2. Rome.

Capelletti, M. 1992. *Museo Claudio Faina di Orvieto. Ceramica etrusca figurata.* Perugia.

Capuis, L. 1993. *I Veneti. Società e cultura di un popolo dell'Italia preromana e romana.* Milan.

Carafi, P. 2000. 'I documenti figurati relativi al rito dell'aratura'. In *Roma. Romolo, Remo* 271–272.

Carandini, A., Ricci, A. and de Vos, M. 1982. *Filosofiana. La villa di Piazza Armerina.* Palermo.

Cardarelli, A. 1993. 'Le età dei metalli nell'Italia settentrionale in Italia preistorica'. In Guidi, A. and Piperno, M. (eds), *Italia preistorica* (2nd edn). Rome–Bari, 366–419.

Carpenter, T. H. 1984. 'The Tyrrhenian group: problems of provenance', *Oxford Journal of Archaeology* 3, 45–56.

Carpenter, T. H. 1986. *Dionysian Imagery in Archaic Greek Art. Its Development in Attic Black-figure Vase Painting.* Oxford.

Carri da guerra e principi etruschi (exhibition catalogue, Viterbo 1997–1998). Emiliozzi, A. (ed.). Rome 1997 (reprinted in 1999 and 2000).

I carri etruschi di Castel San Mariano. Perugia (Museo Archeologico Nazionale dell'Umbria) 2002.

Carter, J. T. 1998. 'Horse burial and horsemanship in Magna Grecia'. In *Man and the Animal World*, 131–146.

Carter, S. and Hunter, F. 2003. 'An Iron Age chariot burial from Scotland', *Antiquity* 77, 531–535.

Caruso, I. and Emiliozzzi, A. 1997. 'San Giuliano (Barbarano Romana). I carri dal Tumulo del Caiolo: Tomba B (Rep. 130–131)'. In *Carri da guerra* 275–283.

Caselli, G. 1994. *Guida alle antiche strade romane.* Novara.

Cassola Guida, P. 1977. 'Spunti sull'interpretazione dell' "arte delle situle": la situla della Tomba Benvenuti 126', *Ostraka* 6, 201–213.

Casson, L. 1974. *Travel in the Ancient World.* London (reprinted, Baltimore and London 1994).

Castritius, H. 1971. 'Zum höfischen Protokoll in der Tetrarchie', *Chiron* 1, 365–376.

Cataldi Dini, M. 1993. 'Terrecotte arcaiche e tardo-arcaiche da Tarquinia'. In *Deliciae Fictiles* I, 207–219.

Catalli, F. 1990. *Monete etrusche.* Rome.

Cateni, G. and Fiaschi, F. 1984. *Le urne di Volterra e l'artigianato artistico degli Etruschi.* Florence.

La ceramica degli Etruschi: la pittura vascolare. Martelli, M. (ed.). Novara 1987.

Catling, H. W. 1996. 'The Dark Age and later bronzes', In *Knossos North Cemetery* II, 543–574.

The Celts (exhibition catalogue, Venice 1991). Moscati, S. *et al.* (eds). Milan 1991.

Cerchiai, L. 1984. 'Nuova "tomba principesca" da Pontecagnano'. In *Opus* 3, 411–413.

Cerchiai, L. 1985. 'Una tomba principesca del periodo orientalizzante antico a Pontecagnano', *Studi etruschi* 53, 27–49.

Cerchiai, L. 1988. 'Le stele villanoviane', *Annali dell'Instituto universitario orientali di Napoli* 9, 227–238.

Cerchiai, L. 1995. 'Il programma figurativo dell'Hydria Ricci', *Antike Kunst* 38, 81–91.

Cerchiai, L. 2009. 'La Tomba delle Olimpiadi di Tarquinia'. In *Etruria e Italia preromana* I, 215–222.

Cerchiai, L., Colucci Pescatori, C. and D'Henry, G. 1997. 'L'Italia antica: Italia meridionale'. In *Carri da guerra* 25–32.

Chamoux, F. 1955. *L'aurige de Delphes.* Paris.

Chandezon, C. 2005. '"Il est le fils de l'âne ...". Remarques sur les mulets dans le monde grec'. In Gardeisen, A. (ed.), *Les équidés dans le monde méditerranéen antique* (*Actes du colloque organisé par l'École française d'Athènes, le Centre Camille Jullian, et l'UMR 5140 du CNRS,* Athens 2003). Lattes, 207–217.

Chateigner, C. 1989. 'Cortèges en armes en Étrurie. Une étude iconographique de plaques de revêtement architectonique étrusque du VIe siècle', *Revue belge de philologie et d'histoire* 67, 122–138.

Cherici, A. 2005. 'Armi e armati nella società visentina: note sul carrello e sul cinerario dell'Olmo Bello'. In Della Fina, G. M. (ed.), *Orvieto, l'Etruria meridionale interna e l'Agro Falisco* (*Atti del XII convegno internazionale di studi sulla storia e l'archeologia dell'Etruria,* Orvieto 2004). *Annali della fondazioni per il Museo "Claudio Faina"* 12, 125–172.

Chevallier, R. 1976. *Roman Roads.* London.

Civiltà degli Etruschi (exhibition, Florence 1985). Cristofani, M. (ed). Milan, 1985.

Christiansen, J. and Winter, N. A. 2010. *Architectural Terracottas and Painted Wall Plaques, Pinakes, c. 625–200 BC. Ny Carlsberg Glyptotek. Catalogue Etruria* I. Copenhagen.

Civiltà del Lazio primitivo (exhibition catalogue, Rome 1976). Colonna, G. (ed.). Rome, 1976.

La civiltà picena nelle Marche. Studi in onore di Giovanni Annibaldi (conference, Ancona 1988). Ripratransone 1992.

Clark, J. 1995. 'Horseshoes'. In *The Medieval Horse and*

its Equipment c. 1150–c. 1450. Medieval Finds from Excavations in London 5. London, 75–123.

Clausing, C. 2000. 'Untersuchungen zur gesellschaftlichen Schichtung in der jüngeren Bronzezeit Mitteleuropas'. In *Eliten in der Bronzezeit*, 319–420.

Coarelli, F. 1981. 'Sul separatore di cavalli scoperto a Decima', *La Parola del passato* 36, 23–24.

Coarelli, F. 1988. *Il Foro Boario. Dalle origini alla fine della Republica*. Rome.

Coldstream, J. N. 2003. *Geometric Greece* (2nd edn). London.

Coldstream, J. N. 2008. *Greek Geometric Pottery* (2nd edn). Exeter.

Colonna, G. 1993a. 'Brandelli di una gigantomachia tardo-arcaica da un tempio etrusco'. In *Deliciae Fictiles* I, 147–152.

Colonna, G. 1993b. 'Strutture teatriformi in Etruria'. In *Spectacles sportifs* 321–347.

Colonna, G. 1996. 'Roma arcaica e i suoi sepolcreti e le vie per i Colli Albani'. In Pasquali, A. (ed.), *Alba Longa. Mito, storia, archeologia* (*Atti dell'incontro di studio*, Albano Laziale 1994). *Studi pubblicati dall'instituto italiano per la storia antica* 60. Rome, 335–354.

Colonna, G. 1997. 'L'Italia antica: Italia centrale'. In *Carri da guerra* 15–23.

Colonna, G. and Di Paolo, E. 1997. 'Il lette vuoto, la datazione del corredo el la "finestra" dell Tomba Regolini-Galassi'. In Nardi, G. and Pandolfini, G., Drago, L. and Berardinetti, A. (eds), *Etrusca et Italica* 1. *Scritti in ricordo di M. Pallottino*. Pisa–Rome, 131–172.

A Companion to the Roman Army. Erdkamp, P. (ed.). Oxford 2007.

Comstock, M. B. and Vermeule, C. C. 1976. *Sculpture in Stone. The Greek, Roman and Etruscan Collections of the Museum of Fine Arts, Boston*. Boston.

Connolly, P. 1988. 'The Roman saddle'. In Coulston, J. C. (ed.)*Roman Military Equipment. The Accoutrements of War*. BAR International Series 336. Oxford, 7–27.

Connolly, P. and van Driel-Murray, C. 1991. 'The Roman cavalry saddle', *Brittania* 22, 33–50.

Cook, R. M. 1952. 'Dogs in battle'. In *Festschrift A. Rumpf*. Krefeld, 38–42.

Cook, R. M. 1981. 'The Swallow Painter and the Bearded Sphinx Painter', *Archäologischer Anzeiger*, 454–461.

Cook, R. M. 1981. *Clazomenian Sarcophagi. Kerameus* 3. Mainz.

Cordano, F. 1994. 'Carro: Etruria, Italia centrale e Roma, Carro cultuale'. In *Enciclopedia dell'arte antica, classica e orientale. Secondo Supplemento 1971–1994*, vol. I. Rome, 901–903.

Cornaggia Castiglioni, O. and Calegari, G. 1978. 'Le ruote preistoriche italiane a disco ligneo', *Rivista archeologica dell'antica provincia e diocesi di Como* 160, 5–50.

Cornell, T. J. 1995. *The Beginnings of Rome. Italy and Rome from the Bronze Age to the Punic Wars (c. 1000–264 BC)*. London–New York.

Corpus delle urne etrusche di età ellenistica 2. *Urne volterrane* 2. *Il Museo Guarnacci* 1. Cristofani, M. (ed.). Florence 1977.

Cotterell, B. and Kamminga, J. 1990. *The Mechanics of Pre-industrial Technology*. Cambridge.

Coulston, J. C. N. 2001. 'Transport and travel on the Column of Trajan'. In Adams, C. E. P. and Laurence, R. (eds), *Travel and Geography in the Roman Empire*. London, 106–137.

Cozza, A. and Pasqui, A. 1897. 'Cività Castellana (antica Valeria). Scavi della necropoli falisca in contrada "Valsiarosa", *Notizie degli scavi di antichità*, 307–319.

Crawford, M. 1974. *Roman Republican Coinage* I–II. Cambridge.

Crielaard, J. P. 1996. *The Euboeans Overseas. Long-distance Contacts and Colonization as Status Activities in Early Iron Age Greece* (doctoral thesis, University of Amsterdam).

Crielaard, J. P. 2007. 'Eretria's West Cemetery revisited: burial plots, social structure and settlement organisation during the 8th and 7th centuries BC'. In Mazarakis Ainian, A. (ed.), *Oropos and Euboea in the Early Iron Age* (*Acts of the International Round Table*, University of Thessaly, 2004). Volos, 169–194.

Crise et transformation des sociétés archaïques de l'Italie antique au Ve siècle av. J.-C. (Acts de la table ronde organisée par l'École française de Rome et l'Unité de recherches étrusco-italique associée au CNRS (UA 1132), Rome 1987). Adam, A.-M. and Rouveret, A. (eds). *Collection de l'École française der Rome* 137. Rome 1990.

Cristofani, M. 1971. 'Per una nova letture delle pisside della Pania', *Studi etruschi* 39, 63–89.

Cristofani, M. 1979. *The Etruscans. A New Investigation*. London.

Cristofani, M. 1985a. *I bronzi degli Etruschi* I. *La plastica votiva*. Novara.

Cristofani, M. 1985b. 'Itinerari terrestre e marittimi' and 'Veicoli terrestri ed imbarcazioni'. In *Strade degli Etruschi* 13–47, 48–87.

Cristofani, M. and Michelucci, M. 1981. 'La valle dell'Albegna'. In Cristofani, M. (ed.), *Gli Etruschi in Maremma*. Milan, 97–113.

Crouwel, J. H. 1981. *Chariots and Other Means of Land Transport in Bronze Age Greece. Allard Pierson Series* 3. Amsterdam.

Crouwel, J. H. 1985. 'Carts in Iron Age Cyprus', *Report of the Department of Antiquities, Cyprus*, 203–221.

Crouwel, J. H. 1987. 'Chariots in Iron Age Cyprus', *Report of the Department of Antiquities, Cyprus*, 101–118.

Crouwel, J. H. 1990. 'A chariot from Salamis newly restored', *Report of the Department of Antiquities, Cyprus*, 101–105.

Crouwel, J. H. 1991. 'A group of terracotta chariot models:

Cypriot or Phoenician?' In *Cypriote Terracottas (Proceedings of the First International Conference of Cypriote Studies*, Brussels, Liège and Amsterdam 1989; Vandenabeele, F. and Laffineur, R. eds). Brussels and Liège, 115–129.

Crouwel, J. H. 1992. *Chariots and Other Wheeled Vehicles in Iron Age Greece. Allard Pierson Series* 9. Amsterdam.

Crouwel, J. H. 1997. 'Il mondo greco'. In *Carri da guerra* 11–13.

Crouwel, J. H. 2001. Review of Penner, S. 1998. In *American Journal of Archaeology* 105, 545–546.

Crouwel, J. H. 2004a. 'Der alte Orient und seine Rolle in der Entwicklung von Fahrzeugen'. In *Rad und Wagen* 69–86.

Crouwel, J. H. 2004b. 'Bronzezeitliche Wagen in Griechenland'. In *Rad und Wagen* 341–346.

Crouwel, J. H. 2005. 'Early chariots in the Aegean and their eastern connections'. In *Emporia. Aegeans in the Central and Eastern Mediterranean (Proceedings of the 10th International Aegean Conference*, Athens 2004). Laffineur, R. and Greco, E. (eds). *Aegaeum* 25, 39–44.

Crouwel, J. H. 2006. 'Chariot depictions – from Mycenaean to Geometric Greece and Etruria'. In *Pictorial Pursuits*, 165–170.

Crouwel, J. H. 2010. 'The chariots'. In *Il tempio arcaico di Cisterna di Torrechia* 123–131.

Cucini, C. 1983. 'Un finimento equino dall'area vetuloniese (Scarlino – GR)', *Archeologia classica* 35, 212–218.

Cunliffe, B. 1992. *The Celtic World*. London.

Curci, A. and Tagliacozzo, A. 1995. 'Il pozzetto rituale con scheletro di cavallo dell'abitato eneolitico di Le Cerquete-Fianello (Maccarese-RM)', *Origini. Preistoria e protostoria delle civiltà antiche* 18, 297–350.

Curci, A. and Tagliacozzo, A. 1998. 'The most ancient ritual burial of domestic horse in Italy from the Eneolithic site of Le Cerquete-Fianello (Maccarese, Rome)'. In *The Iron Age in Europe* 6.I, 107–112.

Curtis, C. D. 1919. 'The Bernardini Tomb', *Memoirs of the American Academy in Rome* 3, 9–90.

Curtis, C. D. 1925. 'The Barberini Tomb', *Mempoirs of the American Academy in Rome* 5, 9–52.

Cygielman, M. 1997. 'La tomba del Littore di Vetulonia ed i suoi carri'. In *Carri da guerra* 263–273.

Cygielman, M. and Pagnoni, L. 2006. *La Tomba del Tridente a Vetulonia. Monumenti etruschi* 9. Pisa–Rome.

d'Agostino, B. 1990. 'Military organization and social structure in Archaic Etruria'. In Murray, O. and Price, S. (eds), *The Greek City. From Homer to Alexander*. Oxford, 59–82.

d'Agostino, B. 1991. 'Dal palazzo alla tomba. Percorsi della *imagerie* etrusca arcaica'. In *Miscellanea etrusca e italica in onore di M. Pallottini. Archeologia Classica* 43, 223–235.

d'Agostino, B. 1996. 'La "stipe dei cavalli" di Pitecusa'. In *Atti e memorie della Società Magna Grecia* (Serie 3), 9–108.

Dall'Orso, I. 1915. *Guida illustrata del Museo Nazionale di Ancona*. Ancona.

Dahm, M. K. 2007. 'Not twins at all: the Agora oinochoe reinterpreted', *Hesperia* 76, 717–730.

Damarato. Studi di antichità classica offerti a Paola Pelegatti. 2000. Berlingò, I. *et al.* (eds). Milan.

D'Arbois de Joubainville, H. 1888. 'Le char de guerre dans quelques textes historiques', *Revue celtique* 9, 387–393.

DarSag = Dictionnaire des antiquités grecques et romaines 1–5. (Daremberg, Ch. and Saglio, E. eds). Paris 1877–1919.

David, W. 2001. Review of Penner, S. 1998. In *Germania* 79, 443–448.

De Agostino, A. 1957. 'Populonia. Scoperte archeologiche nella necropoli negli anni 1954–1956', *Notizie degli scavi di antichità* (Serie 8) 11, 1–52.

De Azevedo, M. C. 1938. *Civiltà romana. I trasporti e il traffico*. Rome.

De Caro, S. 1994. *La villa rustica in località Villa Regina a Boscoreale*. Rome.

Decker, W. 1984. 'Bemerkungen zur Konstruktion des ägyptischen Rades in der 18. Dynastie. In Altenmüller, H. and Wildung, D. (eds), *Festschrift Wolfgang Helck zu seinem 70. Geburtstag. Studies zur altägyptischen Kultur* 11. Hamburg, 475–488.

Decker, W. 1991. 'Wagenrennen bei den Etruskern – Ein Beitrag zur Anwendungsgeschichte des Wagens'. *Achse, Rad und Wagen. Beiträge zur Geschichte der Landfahrzeuge* 1, 3–13 (with a contribution by H. Hayen, 10–11).

Decker, W. 1992. 'Zum Wagenrennen in Olympia – Probleme der Forschung'. In Coulson, W. and Kyrieleis, H. (eds), *Proceedings of an International Symposium on the Olympic Games* (Athens 1988). Athens, 129–139.

De Grossi Mazzorin, J. 1994. 'I resti faunistici provenienti dalle Terramare esposti nel Museo Civico di Modena: alcune considerazioni', *Quaderni del Museo Archeologico Etnologico di Modena* 1, 145–152.

De Grossi Mazzorin, J. 1995. 'Economie di alleramento in Italia centrale dall' età del bronze alle fine dell'età del ferro'. In Christie, N. (ed.), *Settlement and Economy in Italy 1500 BC–AD 1500 (Papers of the Fifth Conference of Italian Archaeology*, Oxford 1992). *Oxbow Monographs* 41. Oxford, 167–177.

De Grossi Mazzorin, J. 1996. 'Archeozoologia delle "ossa bruti" provienti dagli scavi della stazione preistorica sul Monte Castelluccio presso Imola'. In Pacciarelli, M. (ed), *Musei Civici di Imola. La collezione Scavabelli* 2. *Preistoria*. Imola, 181–218.

De Grossi Mazzorin, J. and Riedel, A. 1997. 'Le faune della Terramare'. In *Terramare* 475–480.

De Grossi Mazzorin, J., Riedel, A. and Tagliacozzo, A. 1998. 'Horse remains in Italy from the Eneolithic to the Roman period'. In *The Iron Age in Europe* 6.I, 87–92.

Dehn, W. 1980. 'Einige Bemerkungen zu hallstattzeitlichen Trensen Sloweniens'. *Situla* 20–21, 325–332.

Dei, A. 1996. 'Alcuni finimenti equini del circolo vetuloniese degli Acquastrini: osservazioni e problemi', *Rassegna di archeologia* 13, 199–220.

Deliciae Fictiles I (*Proceedings of the First International Conference on Central Italic Architectural Terracottas*, Rome 1990. Rystedt, E., Wikander, C. and Wikander, Ö. (eds). Stockholm 1993.

Deliciae Fictiles II (*Proceedings of the Second International Conference on Archaic Architectural Terracottas from Italy*, Rome 1996. Lulof, P. S. and Moormann, E. M. (eds). *Scrinium* 12. Amsterdam 1997.

Deliciae Fictiles III. *Architectural Terracottas in Ancient Italy. New Discoveries and Interpretations* (Rome 2002). Edlund-Berry, I., Greco, G. and Kenfield, J. (eds). Oxford 2006.

Deloche, J. 1983. *Contribution à l'histoire de la voiture en Inde*. Paris.

De Marinis, G. and Palermo, L. 2008. 'Il principi della tomba 182 in località Crocifissa a Matelica. Il currus e il calesse'. In *Potere e splendore gli antichi Piceni a Matelica* (exhibition catalogue, Matelica 2008). Silvestrini, M. and Sabbatini, T. (eds). Rome, 234–244.

De Marinis, R. C. 1975. 'Le tombe di guerriero de Sesto Calende e le spade e i pugnali halstattiani scoperti nell'Italia nord-occidentale'. In *Archaeologica. Scritti in onore di A. Neppi Modena*. Firenze, 213–269.

De Marinis, R. C. 1988a. 'I commerci dell'Etruria con i paesi a nord del Po dal IX al VI secolo a.C.' In *Gli Etruschi a nord del Po* I (exhibition catalogue, Mantua 1987). De Marinis, R. C. (ed.). Udine, 52–102.

De Marinis, R. C. 1988b. 'Liguri e Celti-liguri'. In *Italia omnium terrarum alumna* 159–259.

De Marinis, R. C. 1991. 'Golasecca culture and its links with Celts beyond the Alps. In *The Celts* 93–102.

De Marinis, R. C. 1997. 'Golasecca: I più antichi Celti d'Italia'. In *Popoli italici e culture regionali. Popoli dell'Italia antica*. Antico Gallina, M. (ed.). n.p., 10–41.

De Marinis, R. C. and Gambari, F. M. 2005. 'La cultura di Golasecca dal X agli inizi del VII secolo a.C.: cronologia relativa e correlazioni con altre aree'. In *Oriente e occidente* 197–225.

De Marinis, R. C. and Premoli Silva, D. 1968–1969. 'Revisione di vecchi scavi nella necropoli de Ca'Morta', *Rivista archeologica dell'antica provincia e diocesi di Como* 150–151, 99–172.

Dent, J. 1985. 'Three cart burials from Wentwang, Yorkshire', *Antiquity* 59, 85–92.

Dentzer, J.-M. 1982. *Le motif du banquet couché dans le Proche-Orient et le monde grec du VIIe au IVe siècle avant J.-C.* Rome.

D'Ercole, V. and Martellone, A. 2006. 'Necropoli di Campovalano a Campli'. In *Museo Civico Archeologico ("F. Savini")* (exhibition catalogue, Teramo 2006). Di Felice, P. and Torrieri, V. (eds). Teramo, 77–84.

D'Ercole, V. and Trucco, F. 1992. 'Canino (Viterbo), località Banditella. Un luogo di culto all'aperto presso Vulci', *Bollettino di archeologia* 13–15, 77–85.

De Reuver, M. 1997. 'Archaic frieze plaques from central Italy in the Ashmolean Museum in Oxford'. In *Deliciae Fictiles* II, 63–69.

De Ruyt, F. 1934. *Charun. Démon étrusque de la mort.* Bruxelles.

De Santis, A. 2005. 'Da capi guerrieri a principi: la strutturazione del potere politico nell'Etruria protourbana. In *Dinamiche di Sviluppo* II, 615–631.

De Santis, A. 2009. 'La definizione delle figure sociali ricognoscibili in relazione alla nascità e allo sviluppo della cultura laziale'. In *Scienze dell'antichità. Storia archeologia antropologia* 15, 359–370.

De Simone, C. 1978. 'I Galli in Italia: testimonianze linguistiche'. In *Galli e l'Italia* (exhibition catalogue, Rome 1978). Santoro, P. (ed.). Rome, 261–269.

Dickinson, O. 1999. 'Robert Drews's theories about the nature of warfare in the Late Bronze Age'. In Laffineur, R. (ed.), *Polemos. Le contexte guerrier en Égée à l'âge du bronze* (*Actes de la 7e Rencontre égéenne internationale*, Liège 1998) I. *Aegaeum* 19. Liège and Austin, 21–27.

Diehl, E. 1964. *Die Hydria*. Mainz am Rhein.

Diepeveen-Jansen, M. 2001. *People, Ideas and Goods. Amsterdam Archaeological Studies* 7. Amsterdam.

Dietz, U. 1998. *Spätbronze- und früheisenzeitliche Trensen im Nordschwarzmeergebiet und im Nordkaukasus. Prähistorische Bronzefunde* XVI.5. Munich.

Dinamiche di sviluppo delle città nell'Etruria meridionale. Veio, Caere, Tarquinia, Vulci (*Atti del XXII convegno d studi etruschi ed italici*, I–II, Viterbo 2001). Camporeale, G. (ed.). Pisa–Rome 2005.

Di Paolo, L. 1999. *Viaggi, trasporti e itinerazioni. Studi sul cursus publicus*. Messina.

Dixon, K. R. and Southern, P. 1997. *The Roman Cavalry*. London.

Dohrn, T. 1937. *Die schwarzfigürlichen etruskischen Vasen aus der zweiten Hälfte der sechsten Jahrhunderts*. Berlin.

Dohrn, T. 1938. 'Die etruskischen schwarzfigürlichen Vasen', *Studi etruschi* 12, 279–290.

Dohrn, T. 1966. 'Originale etruskische Vasenbilder?', *Bonner Jahrbücher der rheinischen Landesmuseums in Bonn und des Vereins von Altertumsfreunden im Rheinlande* 166, 113–145.

Donder, H. 1980. *Zaumzeug in Griechenland und Zypern. Prähistorische Bronzefunde* XVI.3. Munich.

Le donne in Etruria. Rallo, A. (ed.). *Studia archeologica* 52. Rome, 1989.

Dragendorf, H. 1928. 'Amphora strengen Stils in Freiburg am Breisau', *Jarhbuch des Deutschen Archäologischen Instituts* 43, 331–359.

Drago Troccoli, L. 2005. 'Una coppia di principi nella

necropoli di Cassale del Fosso a Veio'. *Dinamiche di sviluppo* I, 87–124.

Drenth, E. and Bakker, J. A. 2005/2006. 'In memoriam Albert Lanting. 10 April 1941–13 December 2004', *Palaeohistoria* 47/48, 3–37.

Drews, R. 2004. *Early Riders. The Beginnings of Mounted Troops in Asia and Europe*. New York–London.

Droysen, H. 1885. 'Die Balustradenreliefs'. In Bohn, R., *Das Heiligtum der Athena Polias Nikephoros. Altertümer aus Pergamon* 2. Berlin, 95–138.

Drukker, A. A. 1988. 'Dansers en fladderaars', *Mededelingenblad Vereniging van Vrienden van het Allard Pierson Museum Amsterdam* 43, 24–27.

Ducati, P. 1910. 'Le pietre funerarie felsinee', *Monumenti antichi* 20, 357–727.

Ducati, P. 1932. *Pontische Vasen*. Berlin.

Ducati, P. 1943. 'Nuove stele funerarie felsinee', *Monumenti antichi* 39, 373–446.

Dular, J. 2007. 'Pferdegräber und Pferdebestattungen in der hallstattzeitlichen Dolenjsko-Gruppe'. In *Scripta Preistorica* 737–752.

Dunbabin, K. M. D. 1982. 'The victorious charioteer on mosaics and related monuments', *American Journal of Archaeology* 86, 65–89.

Dunbabin, K. M. D 1999. *Mosaics of the Greek and Roman World*. Cambridge.

Dunst, G. 1972. 'Archaische Inschriften und Dokumente der Pentekontaetie aus Samos', *Athenische Mitteilungen* 87, 98–163.

Duval, A. 1988. 'Des chars processionels aux chars de combat'. In Mohen, J. P., Duval, A. and Elmère, Ch.(eds), *Les princes celtes et la Mediterranée*. Paris, 303–319.

Egg, M. 1986a. 'Zum "Fürstengrab" von Radkersburg (Südsteiermark)', *Jahrbuch des Römisch-germanischen Zentralmuseums, Mainz* 33, 199–214.

Egg, M. 1986b. 'Zu den hallstattzeitlichen "Tüllenaufsätzen"', *Jahrbuch des Römisch-germanischen Zentralmuseums, Mainz* 33, 215–220.

Egg, M. 1987. 'Das Wagengrab von Ohnenheim im Elsass'. In *Vierrädrige Wagen* 77–102.

Egg, M. 1991. 'Ein neuer Kesselwagen aus Etrurien', *Jahrbuch des Römisch-germanischen Zentralmuseums, Mainz* 38, 191–220.

Egg, M. and Eibner, A. 2005. 'Einige Anmerkungen zur figural verzierter Bronzesitula aus Dolenjske, Toplice in Slowenien', *Archaeologisches Korrespondenzblatt* 35, 191–204.

Egg, M. and France-Lanord, A. 1987. 'Der Wagen aus dem Fürstengrab von Vix, Dép. Côte-d'Or, Frankreich'. In *Vierrädrige Wagen* 145–179.

Egg, M. and France-Lanord, A. 2003. 'Le char. Nouvelle reconstruction'. In *La tombe princière de Vix* 58–75.

Egg, M. and Lehnert, R. 2000a. 'Der hallstattzeitliche Wagen aus Hügel 7, Grab 1 von Diarville'. In *Zeremonialwagen* 26–

44 (first published in *Jahrbuch des Römisch-germanischen Zentralmuseums, Mainz* 46 (1999), 26–44).

Egg, M. and Lehnert, R. 2000b. 'Die vierrädrige Wagen aus Grabhügel 7, Grab 1 von Diarville "Devant Giblot" (Dép. Meurthe e Moselle)', *Jahrbuch des Römisch-germanischen Zentralmuseums, Mainz* 47, 301–327.

Egg, M. and Pare, C. 1993. 'Keltische Wagen und ihre Vorläufer'. In *Das keltische Jahrtausend*. Dannheimer, H. and Gebhard, R. (eds). Mainz am Rhein, 209–218.

Egg, M. and Pare, C. 1995. *Die Metallzeiten in Europa und in Vorderen Orient. Kataloge vor- und frühgeschichtlichen Altertümer 26. Römisch-germanisches Zentralmuseum Monographien 26*. Mainz am Rhein.

Egg, M. and Pare, C. 1997. 'Il mondo celtico'. In *Carri da guerra* 45–51.

Eibner, A. 2007. 'Thron – Schemel – Zepter. Zeichen der Herrschaft und Würde'. In *Scripta Prehistorica* 435–451.

Eisenberg, J. M. 2007. 'The Monteleone chariot forgery', *Minerva* 18:4, 49–60.

Eliten in der Bronzezeit. Ergebnisse zweier Kolloquien in Mainz und Athen. Römisch-germanisches Zentralmuseum Monographien 43.2. Bonn 2000.

Emiliozzi, A. 1988. 'Nuovi documenti d'archivio per la Tomba Bernardini di Palestrina'. In *Archeologia Laziale 9. Qaderni del centro di studio per l'archeologia etrusco-italica* 16, 288–311.

Emiliozzi, A. 1991. 'The Monteleone chariot: from discovery to restauration'. In *Antichità dall'Umbria a New York* 103–120 (in Italian and English).

Emiliozzi, A. 1992. 'I resti del Carro Bernardini nel quadro delle attestazioni coeve dell'area medio-italica'. In *La necropoli di Praeneste. "Periodi orientalizzante e medio repubblicano"* (*Atti del 2o convegno di studi archeologici sull'antica Praeneste*, Palestrina 1990). Palestrina, 85–108.

Emiliozzi, A. 1996a. 'Sull'origine del carro da Monteleone di Spoleto: una nuova impostazione del problema'. In *Identità e civiltà dei Sabini* (*Atti del XVIII convegno di studi etruschi ed italici*, Rieti and Magliano Sabina 1993). Florence, 333–337.

Emiliozzi, A. 1996b. 'Il carro'. In *Memorie dal sottosuolo. Una prima pagina di scavo dalla necropoli di Castel di Decima* (exhibition catalogue, Rome EUR 1996–1997). Bedello Tata, M. (ed.). Rome.

Emiliozzi, A. 1997. 'La ricerca moderna: i primi risultati'. In *Carri da guerra*, 95–103.

Emiliozzi, A. 2000. 'Zur Restaurierung des Wagens aus dem etruskischen Grabhügel bei Castellina in Chianti'. In *Zeremonialwagen* 17–20 first published in *Jahrbuch des Römisch-germanischen Zentralmuseums, Mainz* 46, 1999, 17–20).

Emiliozzi, A. 2001a. 'La sepoltura del carro nell'Italia antica. I carri dalla Tomba A di Casale Marittimo'. In *Principi guerrieri. La necropoli etrusca di Casale Marittima* (exhibition catalogue, Florence 2001). Esposito, A. M. (ed.). Milan, 43–47.

Emiliozzi, A. 2001b. 'Technical problems concerning orientalizing vehicles in Cyprus and Etruria'. In *Italy and Cyprus in Antiquity: 1500–45 BC* (*Proceedings of an International Symposium*, New York 2000). Bonfante, L. and Karageorghis, V. (eds). Nicosia, 315–334.

Emiliozzi, A. 2004. 'I principi etruschi di Trevignano'. In *La voce del Lago. Mensile di informazione e cultura del territorio del Lago di Bracciano* 26, 8–9.

Emiliozzi, A. 2004–2005. 'Nuovi spunti per una lettura del calesse dalla tomba 928 di Pontecagnano'. In Cerchiai, L. and Gastaldi, P. (eds), *Pontecagnano: la città, il paesaggio e la dimensione simbolica. Annali del'Instituto universitario orientali di Napoli* (Nuova Serie) 11–12, 139–144.

Emiliozzi, A. 2006. 'Ipotesi di riconstruzione del Carro Dutuit'. In Bellelli, V. *La tomba "principesca" dei Quattordici Ponti nel contesto di Capua arcaica. Studia archeologica* 142. Rome, 131–148.

Emiliozzi, A., Moscati, P. and Santoro, P. 2007. 'The princely cart from Eretum'. In Moscati, P. (ed.), *Virtual Museums and Archaeology. The Contribution of the Italian National Research Council. Archeologia e calcolatori*, Supplemento 1, 143–162.

Emiliozzi, A., Romualdi, A. and Cecchi, F. 2000. 'Der currus aus dem "Tumulo dei Carri" von Vetulonia'. In *Zeremonialwagen* 5–16 (first published in *Jahrbuch des Römisch-germanischen Zentralmuseums, Mainz* 46, 1999, 5–16).

Equids from the Ancient World I–II. Meadows, R. and Ürpmann, H. P. (eds). *Beihefte zum Tübinger Atlas des Vorderen Orients* A. Wiesbaden 1986.

Erdkamp, P. 1998. *Hunger and the Sword. Warfare and Food in Roman Republican Wars (264–30 BC)*. Amsterdam.

Erdkamp, P. 2007. 'War and state formation in the Roman Republic'. In *A Companion to the Roman Army*, 96–113.

Eroi e regine. Piceni popolo d'Europa (exhibition catalogue, Rome 2001). Rome, 2001.

Esch, A. 1997. *Römische Strassen in ihrer Landschaft*. Mainz.

Etruria e Italia preromana. Studi in onore di Giovannangelo Camporeale I–II. Bruni, S. (ed.). *Studi erudita* 4. Pisa 2009.

Etruschi. Le antiche metropoli del Lazio (exhibition catalogue Rome 2008–2009). Torelli, M. and Moretti Sgubini, A. M. (eds). Rome 2008.

Etrusker in der Toskana. Etruskische Gräber der Frühzeit (exhibition catalogue, Hamburg 1987). Cygielman, M. and Bruni, S. (eds). Florence 1987.

Etrusker nördlich von Etrurien. Etruskische Präsenz in Norditalien und nördlichen Alpen sowie ihre Einflüsse auf einheimischen Kulturen (Akten des Symposions von Wien-Schloss Neuwald, 1989). Aigner-Foresti, L. (ed.). Wien 1992.

Gli Etruschi (exhibition catalogue, Venice 2000). Torelli, M. (ed.). Milan 2001.

Gli Etruschi di Tarquinia (exhibition catalogue, Milan 1986). Bonghi Jovino, M. (ed.). Modena 1986.

Les Étrusques et l'Europe (exhibition catalogue, Paris 1992). Milan, 1992.

The European Community in Later Prehistory. Studies in Honour of C. F. C. Hawkes. Boardman, J., Brown, M. A. and Powell, T. G. E. (eds). London.

Fabbricotti, E. 1977–79. 'Fregi fittili arcaici in Magna Grecia', *Attie e memorie della Società Magna Grecia* (Nuova Serie) 18–20. Rome, 149–170.

Fairbanks, A. 1928. *Catalogue of the Greek and Etruscan Vases* I. *Early Vases, Preceding Athenian Black-figured Ware* (Boston, Museum of Fine Arts). Cambridge, MA.

Falchi, I. 1891. *Vetulonia e la sua necropoli antichissima*. Florence.

Falchi, I. 1895. 'Vetulonia – Scavi dell'anno 1984', *Notizie degli scavi di antichità*, 272–317.

Falconi Amorelli, M. T. 1968. 'Materiali di Ischia di Castro conservati nel Museo di Villa Giulia', *Studi etruschi* 36, 169–177.

Fehr, B. 1971. *Orientalische und griechische Gelage*. Bonn.

Fenton, A. 1973. ' Transport with pack-horse and slide-car in Scotland'. In Fenton, A., Podolàk, J. and Rassmussen, H. (eds), *Land Transport in Europe*. Copenhagen, 121–127.

Fernández-Miranda, M. and Olmos, R. 1986. *Las ruedas de Toya y el origen del carro en la peninsula Iberica. Museo Arqueologico Nacional, Catálogos y Monografías* 9. Madrid.

Festschrift zum 50 jährigen Bestehen des Institutes für Ur- und Frühgeschichte der Leopold-Franzes-Universität Innsbruck. Lippert, A. and Spindler, K. (eds). *Universitätsforschungen zur prähistorischen Archäologie* 8. Bonn 1992.

Feugère, M. 2002. *Weapons of the Romans*. Stroud.

Fields, N. 2006. *Bronze Age War Chariots*. Oxford.

Fiore, I., Salerno, R. and Tagliacozzo, A. 2003. 'I cavalli paleoveneti del santuario di Altino – località "Fornace"'. In *Produzioni, merci e commerci in Altino preromana e romana* 115–141.

Foerst, G. 1978. *Die Gravierungen der pränestischen Cisten*. Roma.

Fogolari, G. 1940. 'Scavi di una necropoli preromana e romana presso Adria', *Studi etruschi* 14, 431–442.

Fogolari, G. 1975. 'La proistoria delle Venezie'. In *Popoli e civiltà dell'Italia antica* 4, 63–222.

Fogolari, G. and Prodoscimi, A. L. 1988. *I Veneti antichi. Lingua e cultura*. Padua.

Fogolari, G. and Scarfí, B. M. 1970. *Adria Antica*. Milan.

Forbes, R. J. 1934. *Notes on the History of Ancient Roads and their Construction. Allard Pierson Stichting Archeologisch-Historische Bijdragen* 3. Amsterdam.

La formazione della città in Emilia Romagna II. *Prima esperienze urbane attraverso le nuove scoperte archeologiche* (exhibition catalogue, Bologna 1987–1988). Bermond Montanari, G. (ed.). Bologna 1987.

Fortenberry, C. D. 1990. *Elements of Mycenaean Warfare* (doctoral thesis, University of Cincinnati).

Fortunati, F. R. 1989. 'Il tempio delle Stimmate'. In *Museo Civico di Velletri. Itinerario dei musei, gallerie, scavi e monumenti d'Italia* (Nuove Serie 53). Rome, 57–87.

Fortunati, F. R. 1993. 'Il tempio delle Stimmate di Velletri: il rivestimento arcaico e considerazioni sul sistema decorativo'. In *Deliciae Fictiles* I, 255–265.

Fox, C. 1946. *A Find of the Early Iron Age from Llyn Cerrig Bach, Anglesey*. Cardiff.

Franke, P. R. and Hirmer, M. 1964. *Die griechischen Münzen*. Munich.

Frederiksen, M. W. and Ward-Perkins, J. B. 1957. 'The ancient road systems of the central and northern *Ager Faliscus*', *Papers of the British School at Rome* 25, 67–208.

French, D. H. 1993. 'A road problem: Roman or Byzantine', *Istanbuler Mitteilungen* 43, 445–454.

Frey, O.-H. 1968. 'Eine neue Grabstele aus Padua', *Germania* 46, 317–320.

Frey, O.-H. 1969. *Die Entstehung der Situlenkunst. Studien zur figürlich verzierten Toreutik von Este. Römisch-germanische Forschungen* 31. Berlin.

Frey, O.-H. 1976. 'The chariot tomb from Adria: some notes on Celtic horsemanship and chariotry'. In *To Illustrate the Monuments. Essays on Archaeology Presented to Stuart Piggott* (Megaw, J. V. S. ed.). London–New York, 172–179.

Frey, O.-H. 1984. 'Ein seltenes Zaumzeug aus Caporetto/Kobarid'. In "Preistoria del Caput Adriae". (*Atti del convegno internazionale*, Triest 1983). Trieste, 119–129.

Frey, O.-H. 1992. 'Beziehungen der Situlenkunst zum Kunstschaffen Etruriens'. In *Etrusken nördlich von Etrurien*, 93–101.

Frey, O.-H. 1998. 'Hallstatt und Italien. Zur Bedeutung des mediterranen Imports'. In *Archäologische Untersuchungen zu den Beziehungen zwischen Altitalien und der Zone nordwärts der Alpen während der frühen Eisenzeit*, 265–284.

Froning, H. 1981. *Marmor-Schmuckreliefs mit griechischen Mythen im 1. Jahrhundert v.Chr.* Mainz am Rhein.

Fulminante, F. 2003. *Le "sepolture principesche" nel Latium Vetus tra la fine della prima età del ferro e l'inizio dell'età orientalizzante*. Rome.

Fulminante, F. 2009. 'Landscapes of power and proto-urban developments toward urbanisation in Bronze Age and Early Iron Age *Latium vetus*'. In Bachuber, C. and Gareth Roberts, R. (eds), *Forces of Transformation. The End of the Bronze Age in the Mediterranean*. Themes from the Ancient Near East. BANEA Publication Series 1. Oxford, 119–130.

Furger-Gunti, A. 1991. 'The Celtic war chariot: the experimental reconstruction in the Schweizerische Landesmuseum'. In *The Celts*, 356–359.

Furger-Gunti, A. 1993. 'Der keltische Streitwagen im Experiment. Nachbau eines *essedum* im schweizerischen Landesmuseum', *Zeitschrift für schweizerische Archäologie und Kunstgeschichte* 50, 213–221.

Gabelmann, H. 1980. 'Circusspiele in der spätantiken Repräsentationskunst', *Antike Welt* 11:4, 25–38.

Gàbrici, E. 1913. 'Cuma I–II', *Monumenti antichi* 22.

Gagé, J. 1963a. *Matronalia. Essai sur les dévotions et les organisations cultuelles des femmes dans l'ancienne Rome*. Brussels.

Gagé, J. 1963b. 'La mort de Servius Tullius et le char de Tullia', *Revue belge de philologie et d'histoire* 41, 25–62 (also *Enquêtes sur les structures sociales et religeuses de la Rome primitive. Collection Latomus* 152. Brussels, 1977, 36–68).

Gail, A. J. 1986. 'Der Wagen in Indien'. In *Achse, Rad und Wagen*, 153–167.

Galeotti, L. 1986–88. 'Considerazioni sul carro a due ruote nell'Etruria e nel Latium Vetus', *Archeologia classica* 38–40, 94–104.

Galhano, F. 1973. *O carro de bois en Portugal*. Lisbon.

Galli, E. 1912. 'I sepolcreto visentino delle "Bucacce"', *Monumenti antichi* 21, 409–498.

Gambacurta, G. 2003. 'Le sepolture equini nelle necropoli di Altino'. In *Produzione, merci e commerci in Altino preromana e romana*, 89–113.

Gambacurta, G. and Tirelli, M. 1996. 'Le sepolture di cavallo nella necropoli "Le Brustolade". In *La protostoria tra Sile e Tagliamento. Antiche gente tra Veneto e Frinli* (exhibition catalogue, Concordia Sagittaria and Pordenone 1996–1997). Padua, 71–74.

Gamber, O. 1978. *Waffe und Rüstung Eurasiens*. Braunschweig.

Games of the Gods. The Greek Athlete and the Olympic Spirit (Boston Museum of Fine Arts). Boston.

Gantz, T. N. 1974. 'The procession frieze from the Etruscan sanctuary at Poggio Civitate', *Römische Mitteilungen* 81, 1–14.

Garbsch, J. 1978. *Römische Pferderüstungen* (exhibition catalogue, Nürnberg and Munich 1978–1979). Munich.

Garbsch, J. 1986. *Man und Ross und Wagen. Transport und Verkehr im antiken Bayern* (exhibition catalogue, Munich 1986). Munich.

Garrido Roiz, J. P. and Orta García, E. M. 1978. *Excavaciones en la necrópolis de "La Joya" (Huelva) 2. Excavaciones arqueologicas en España* 96. Madrid.

Gegeschidse, M. 1956. *Georgischer Volkstransport* I. *Landsbeforderungsmittel*. Tblisi.

Gejvall, N.-G. 1967. 'Esame del materiale osteologico'. In Östenberg, C. E. *et al.*, *Luni sul Mignone e problemi della preistoria d'Italia* II.1. Lund, 261–276.

Gejvall, N.-G. 1982. 'Animal remains from Zone A in Acqarosso'. In Lundgren, M.-B. and Wendt, L., *Acquarossa* III. Stockholm, 68–70.

Gentili, G. V. 1957. 'Le gare del circo nel mosaico di Piazza Armerina', *Bollettino d'arte* 42, 7–27.

Gentili, G. V. 1959. *La villa erculia di Piazza Armerina. I mosaici figurati.* Rome.

Gentili, G. V. 1978. 'Coperchietto d'avorio con quadriga dell'orientalizzante recente di Marzabotto', *Il Carrobbio* 4, 255–262.

Gentili, G. V. 1987. 'Verucchio.' In *La formazione della città in Emilia Romagna* II, 207–263.

Gentili, G. V. 2003. *Verucchio villanoviana. Il sepolcreto in località Le Regge e la necropoli al piede della Rocca Malastiana* I–II. Rome.

Georganas, I. 2002. 'Constructing identities in Early Iron Age Thessaly: the case of the Halos tumuli', *Oxford Journal of Archaeology* 21, 289–298.

Ghedini, F. 2009. *l carro dei Musei Capitolini. Antenor Quaderni* 13. Rome.

Ghini, G. 1987. 'Il corredo'. In 'Recupero di una tomba orientalizzante presso Rocco di Papa', *Archeologia Laziale* 8. *Quaderni del Centro di studio per l'archeologia etrusco-italica* 14, 213–217.

Ghislanzoni, E. 1930. 'Il carro di bronzo della Camorta', *Rivista archeologico dell'antica provincia e diocesi di Como* 99–101, 3–25.

Ghislanzoni, E. 1939. 'Il sepolcreto di Vadena (Bolzano)', *Monumenti antichi* 38, 315–530.

Ghislanzoni, E. 1944. 'Una nuova tomba di guerriero scoperta a Sesto Calende'. In *Munera. Raccolta di scritti in onore di Antonio Giussani.* Milan, 1–56.

Giatti, C. 2007. 'Il sepolcro CD. 'Arieti' sull'Esquilino: nuove proposte di letture del monumento', *Archeologia classica* 58, 75–107.

Giebel, M. 1999. *Reisen in der Antike.* Düsseldorf–Zürich.

Giglioni, G. Q. 1921. 'Cratere etrusco del museo di Trieste', *Ausonia* 10, 88–108.

Giglioni, G. Q. 1929. 'La tomba chiusiana di Fontecucchiaia ora al Museo Nazionale di Copenhagen', *Studi etruschi* 3, 473–475.

Giglioni, G. Q. 1935. *L'arte etrusca.* Milan.

Giuliano, A. 1963. 'Un pittore a Vulci nella seconda metà del VII sec. A.C.', *Jahrbuch des Deutschen Archäologischen Insitituts* 78, 183–199.

Giuliano, A. 1964. 'Il pittore delle rondini', *Prospettiva* 3, 4–8.

Gleba, M. 2008. *Textile Production in Pre-Roman Italy.* Oxbow Books, Ancient Textiles Series 4. Oxford.

Gleba, M. 2009. 'Archaeology in Etruria 2003–2009'. In *Archaeological Reports* 2008–2009, 103–121.

Gnade, M. 1997. 'Satricum. Preliminary report on the 1996 excavations by the University of Amsterdam, *Bulletin Antieke Beschaving* 72, 93–103.

Gnade, M. 2002. *Satricum in the Post-Archaic Period. A Case Study of the Interpretation of Archaeological Remains as Indicators of Ethno-Cultural Identity.* Leuven.

Gnade, M. 2006. ' La ventottesima campagna di ricerce a Satricum dell'Università di Amsterdam nel 2004,' *Lazio e Sabina* 3, 255–260.

Gnade, M. 2007. 'I risultati della campagna di scavi 2005 e 2006 a *Satricum*', *Lazio e Sabina* 4, 191–200.

Goldscheider, L. 1941. *Etruscan Sculpture.* London.

Goldsworthy, A. K. 1996. *The Roman Army at War 100 BC–AD 200.* Oxford.

Govi, E, 2009. 'Aspetti oscuri del rituale funerario nelle stele felsinee'. In *Etruria e Italia preromana* II, 455–463.

Gran-Aymerich, J. 1999. 'Images et mythes sur les vases noirs d'Étrurie'. In *Le mythe grec en l'Italie antique* 383–404.

La grande Roma dei Tarquini (exhibition catalogue, Rome 1990). Cristofani, M. (ed.). Rome 1990.

Greci, Enotri e Lucani nella Basilicata meridionale. I Greci in occidente (exhibition catalogue, Policorno 1996). Bianco, S., *et al.* (eds). Naples 1996.

I Greci in occidente (exhibition catalogue, Venice 1996). Pugliese Carratelli, G. *et al.* (eds). Milan 1996.

Greene, D. 1972. 'The chariot as described in Irish literature'. In Thomas, C. (ed.), *The Iron Age in the Irish Sea Province. Council for British Archaeology, Research Report* 9. London, 59–73.

Greenhalgh, P. A. L. 1973. *Early Greek Warfare. Horsemen and Chariots in the Homeric and Archaic Ages.* Cambridge.

Grottanelli, C. 1987. 'Servio Tullio, fortuna e l'oriente', *Dialoghi di archeologia* (Serie 3), 5, 71–110.

Grünhagen, W. 1948. *Antike Originalarbeiten der Kunstsammlung des Instituts* (Archäologisches Institut der Universität Erlangen). Nurenburg.

Gualandi, M. L. 1990. 'Strade, viaggi, trasporti en servizi postali'. In Settis, S. (ed.), *La civiltà dei Romani. La città, il territorio, l'impero.* Milan, 199–214.

Guerriero e sacerdote. Autorità e comunità nell'età del ferro a Verucchio. La Tomba del Trono. Von Eles, P. (ed.). *Quaderni di archeologia dell'Emilia Romagna* 6. Florence 2002.

Guidi, A. 1983. *Scambi tra la cerchia hallstattiana orientale e il mondo a sud delle Alpi nel VII secolo a.C. Kleine Schriften aus dem vorgeschichtlichen Seminar Marburg* 13. Marburg.

Guidi, A. 1993. *La necropoli veiente dei Quattro Fontanili nel quadro della fase recente della prima età del ferro italiana. Biblioteca di Studie etruschi* 26. Florence.

Guidi, A. 1998. 'The emergence of the state in central and northern Italy', *Acta Archaeologica* (Copenhagen) 69, 139–161.

Güntner, W. 2000. *Figürlich bemalte mykenische Keramik aus Tiryns. Tiryns* XII. Mainz am Rhein.

Guzzo, P. G. 2000. 'La tomba 104 Artiaco di Cuma o sia dell'ambiguità del segno'. In *Damarato* 135–147.

Hague Sinos, R. 1994. 'Godlike men: A discussion of the Murlo procession frieze'. In De Puma, R. and Small, J. P. (eds), *Murlo and the Etruscans. Art and Society in Ancient Etruria. Essays in Memory of K. M. Phillips.* Madison, 100–117.

Hanblin, E. J. 1975. *The Etruscans*. New York (Time-Life Book).

Hampe, R. 1941. 'Der Wagenlenker von Delphi'. In Brunn, H. and Bruckmann, F. (eds), *Denkmäler griechischer and römischer Skulptur*. München, 1–43, *s.v.* pls 786–790.

Hampe, R. and Simon, E. 1964. *Griechische Sagen in der frühen etruskischen Kunst*. Mainz am Rhein.

Hampe, R. and Simon, E. 1967. 'Gefälsschte etruskische Vasenbilder?', *Jahrbuch des Römisch-germanischen Zentralmuseums, Mainz* 14, 68–98.

Hampe, R. and Simon, E. 1971. '"Pontische" Amphora des Paris-Malers'. In Hampe, R. *et al.*, *Neuerwerbungen 1957–1970. Katalog der Sammlung antiker Kleinkunst des Archäologischen Instituts der Universität Heidelberg* 2. Mainz am Rhein, 42–43.

Hanfmann, G. M. A. 1937. 'Studies in Etruscan bronze reliefs. The gigantomachy', *Art Bulletin* 19, 463–484.

Hannestad, L. 1974. *The Paris Painter. An Etruscan Vase-painter*. Copenhagen.

Hannestad, L. 1976. *The Followers of the Paris Painter*. Copenhagen.

Harbison, P. 1969. 'The chariot of Celtic funerary tradition'. In Frey, O.-H. (ed.), *Marburger Beiträge zur Archäologie der Kelten. Festschrift für Wolfgang Dehn zum 60. Geburtstag. Fundberichte aus Hessen*, Beiheft 1. Bonn, 34–58.

Harbison, P. 1971. 'The old Irish chariot', *Antiquity* 45, 171–177.

Harris, H. A. 1972. *Sport in Greece and Rome*. London.

Hayen, H. 1980–1981. 'Zwei in Holz erhalten gebliebene Reste von Wagenräder aus Olympia', *Die Kunde* (Neue Folge) 31–32, 135–191.

Hayen, H. 1983. 'Handwerklich-technische Lösungen im vor- und frühgeschichtlichen Wagenbau'. In *Das Handwerk in vor- und frühgeschichtlicher Zeit* II (Jahnkuhn, H., Janssen, W., Schmidt-Wiegand, R. and Tiefenbach, H. eds). Göttingen, 415–470.

Hayen, H. 1986. 'Der Wagen in europäischer Frühzeit'. In *Achse, Rad und Wagen* 109–138.

Hayen, H. 1991. 'Zu Bauweise und Anschirrung der dargestellten Rennwagen'. In Decker, W. 1991, 10–11.

Haynes, S. 1965a. 'Zwei archaisch-etruskische Bildwerke aus dem "Isis-Grab" von Vulci'. In *Antike Plastik* IV. Berlin, 13–25.

Haynes, S. 1965b. *Etruscan Bronze Utensils* (British Museum). London.

Haynes, S. 1977. 'The Isis-tomb'. In *La civiltà arcaica di Vulci e la sua espansione* (Atti del X convegno di studi etruschi e italica, Grossetto, Roselle and Vulci 1975). Florence, 17–29.

Haynes, S. 1985. *Etruscan Bronzes*. London–New York.

Haynes, S. 2000. *Etruscan Civilization. A Cultural History*. London.

Heilmeyer, W.-D. 1994. 'Frühe olympische Bronzefiguren. Die Wagenvotive'. In *IX. Bericht über die Ausgrabungen in Olympia*. Berlin–New York, 172–208.

Helbig, W. 1963. *Führer durch die öffentlichen Sammlungen klassischer Altertümer in Rom* I. *Die päpstlichen Sammlungen in Vatikan und Lateran* (4th edn). Tübingen.

Helbig, W. 1966. *Führer durch die öffentlichen Sammlungen klassischer Altertümer in Rome* II. *Die städtliche Sammlungen, die staatliche Sammlungen*. Munich.

Hemelrijk, J. M. 1984. *Caeretan Hydriae*. Kerameus 5. Mainz am Rhein.

Hemelrijk, J. M. 2009. *More about Caeretan Hydrae. Addenda et Clarificanda*. Allard Pierson Series 17. Amsterdam.

Hencken, H. 1957. 'Horse tripods of Etruria', *American Journal of Archaeology* 61, 1–4.

Hencken, H. 1968. *Tarquinia, Villanovans and Early Etruscans* I–II. *American School of Prehistoric Research, Peabody Museum*, Bulletin 23. Cambridge, MA.

Herbig, R. 1952. *Die jüngeretruskischen Steinsarkophage*. Berlin.

Heres, G. 1975. 'Beiträge zur antiken Bronzekunst I. Stirnschmuck eines Rennpferdes', *Forschungen und Berichte* (Staatliche Museen, Berlin) 16, 217–221.

Herold, A. 2004. 'Funde und Funktionen – Streitwagen-technologie im Alten Ägypten'. In *Rad und Wagen*, 123–142.

Herold, A. 2006. 'Auf Biegen und Brechen... Zum Nachbau eines altägyptischen Streitwagens', *Achse, Rad und Wagen. Beiträge zur Geschichte der Landfahrzeuge* 14, 5–19.

Herrmann, G. 1989. 'Parthian and Sasanian saddlery. New light from the Roman West'. In De Meyer, L. and Haerinck, E. (eds), *Archaeologia Iranica et Orientalia. Miscellanea in Honorem Louis Vanden Berghe*. II. Gent, 757–809.

Herrmann, H.-V. 1968. 'Frühgriechische Pferdeschmuck vom Luristantypes', *Jahrbuch des Deutschen Archäologischen Instituts* 83, 1–38.

Herrmann, H.-V. 1983. 'Altitalisches und Etruskisches in Olympia', *Annuario della Scuola archaeologica di Atene e delle Missione italiane in oriente* 61, 271–294.

Hill, G. F. 1910. *Catalogue of the Greek Coins of Phoenicia in the British Museum*. London.

Höckmann, U. 1977. 'Zur Darstellung auf einer "tyrrhenischen" Amphora in Leipzig'. In Höckmann, U. and Krug, A. (eds), *Festschrift für Frank Brommer*. Mainz, 181–185.

Höckmann, U. 1991. 'Gallierdarstellungen in der etruskischen Grabkunst der 2. Jahrhunderts v.Chr.', *Jahrbuch des Deutschen Archäologischen Instituts* 106, 199–230.

Höckmann, U. 1992. *Die Bronzen aus dem Fürstengrab von Castel Mariano. Staatliche Antikensammlungen München. Katalog der Bronzen* I. Munich.

Höckmann, U. 2006. 'Die Entwicklung des figürlichen Treibrelief in Griechenland und Etrurien in archaischer Zeit'. In *ΑΕΙΜΝΗΣΤΟΣ* I, 311–316.

Hoffmann, U. 2004. 'Kulturgeschichte des Fahrens im Ägypten des Neuen Reiches'. In *Rad und Wagen*, 121–156.

Holliday, P. J. 1990. 'Processional imagery in late Etruscan funerary art', *American Journal of Archaeology* 94, 73–93.

Holliday, P. J. 2002. *The Origins of Rome. Historical Commemoration in the Visual Arts*. Cambridge.

Hoplites. The Classical Greek Battle Experience. Hanson, V. D. (ed.). London 1991.

Hüttel, H.-G. 1981. *Bronzezeitliche Trensen in Mittel- und Osteuropa. Prähistorische Bronzefunde* XVI.2. Munich.

Huls, Y. 1957. *Ivoire d'Étrurie. Études de philologie, d'archéologie et d'histoire ancienne publiées par l'Institut historique belge de Rome* 5. Brussels–Rome.

Humphrey, J. H. 1986. *Roman Circuses. Arenas for Chariot Racing*. Berkeley–Los Angeles.

Humphrey, J. W., Olesen, J. P. and Sherwood, A. N. 1998. *Greek and Roman Technology. A Sourcebook*. London–New York.

Hurford, R. and Spence, N. 2005. *Building a British Iron Age Chariot* (British Museum). London.

Hurwit, J. M. 2002, 'Reading the Chigi Vase', *Hesperia* 71, 1–22.

Hurwit, J. M. 2011. 'The shipwreck of Odysseus: strong and weak imagery in Late Geometric art', *American Journal of Archaeology* 115, 1–18.

Hyland, A. 1990. *Equus: the Horse in the Roman World*. London.

Iaia, C. 1999. *Simbolismo funerario e ideologia alle origini di una civiltà urbana. Forme rituali nelle sepolture "villanoviane" a Tarquinia e Vulci, e nel loro entroterra. Grande contesti e problemi della protostoria italiana* 3. Florence.

The Iron Age in Europe (The Colloquia of the XIII International Conference of Prehistoric and Protohistoric Sciences, Forlí 1996) 6.I. Forlí, 1998.

Italia omnium terrarum alumna I. *La civiltà dei Veneti, Reti, Liguri, Piceni, Umbri, Latini, Campani e Iapigi*. Chiego Bianchi, A. M. (ed.). Milano 1998.

Italian Iron Age Artefacts in the British Museum. (Papers of the Sixth British Museum Classical Colloquium) London 1982. Swaddling, J. (ed.). London 1986.

Italy of the Etruscans (exhibition catalogue, Jerusalem 1991). Jucker, E. (ed.). Mainz am Rhein, 1991.

Jacobs, B. 2005. Review of *Rad und Wagen*. In *Orientalistische Literaturzeitung* 100, 429–438.

Jacopi, G. 1974. *Werkzeug und Gerät aus dem Oppidum von Manching*. Römisch-germanische Kommission des Deutschen Archäologischen Instituts. Wiesbaden.

Jacobsthal, P. 1944. *Early Celtic Art*. Oxford.

Jaeckel, P. 1965. 'Pergamenische Waffenreliefs'. In *Waffen und Kostümkunde* 7:2, 94–122.

Jannot, J.-R. 1984. *Les reliefs archaïques de Chiusi. Collection de 'École française de Rome* 71. Rome.

Jannot, J.-R. 1985. 'Les cités étrusques et la guerre. Remarques sur la fonction militaire dans le cite étrusque', *Ktema* 10, 127–141.

Jannot, J.-R. 1986a. 'Les cavaliers étrusques. Armement, mode de combat, fonction. VIIe au VIe siècle ', *Römische Mitteilungen* 93, 109–133.

Jannot, J.-R. 1986b. 'La tombe clusienne de Poggio al Moro ou le programme des jeux clusiens', *Ktema* 11, 189–197.

Jannot, J.-R. 1987. 'Les "Amazones" de Capoue et les "jockeys" de Murlo', *Latomus* 48, 693–703.

Jannot, J.-R. 1989. 'À propos des cavaliers étrusques' In *Secondo congresso internazionale Etrusco* III, 1549–1556.

Jannot, J.-R. 1991. 'Armement. Tactique et société. Réflexions sur l'example de l'Étrurie archaïque'. In Santillo Frizell, B. (ed.), *Arte militare e architettura nuragica. Nuragic Architecture in its Military, Territorial and Socio-economic Context*. Stockholm, 73–81.

Jannot, J.-R. 1995. 'À propos des cavaliers de la Tombe Querciola', *Mélanges de l'École française de Rome* 107, 13–31.

Jantzen, U. 1937. *Bronzewerkstätten in Grossgriechenland und Sizilien*. Berlin.

Jensen, J. 1998. *Prehistory of Denmark. Guides to the National Museum*. Copenhagen.

Jerem, E. 1998. 'Iron Age horse burial at Spron-Krantacker (NW Hungary). Aspects of trade and religion'. In *Man and the Animal World*, 319–334.

Jettmar, K. 1967. *Art of the Steppes*. London.

Johansen, F. 1979. 'Etruskische Bronzereliefter in Glyptoteket', *Meddedelser fra Ny Carlsberg Glyptotek* 36, 67–89.

Johner, A. 1992. 'Mythe et theâtre: le motif de la dame au char dans la légende royale de Rome', *Ktema* 17, 29–37.

Jones-Blay, K. 2000. 'The Sintashta "Chariots". In Dans-Kimball, J., Murphey, E., Koryakova, L. and Yablonsky, L. (eds), *Kurgans, Ritual Sites and Settlements. Eurasian Bronze and Iron Age*. BAR International Series 890. Oxford, 135–140.

Junkelmann, M. 1990. *Die Reiter Roms* I. *Reise, Jagd, Triumph und Circusrennen. Kulturgeschichte der antiken Welt* 45. Mainz am Rhein.

Junkelmann, M. 1991. *Die Reiter Roms* II. *Reitweise und militärischer Einsatz. Kulturgeschichte der antiken Welt* 49. Mainz am Rhein.

Junkelmann, M. 1992. *Die Reiter Roms* III. *Zubehör, Reitweise, Bewaffnung. Kulturgeschichte der antiken Welt* 53. Mainz am Rhein.

Junkelmann, M. 1996. *Reiter wie Statuen aus Erz. Antike Welt* Sonderheft. Mainz am Rhein.

Jurgeit, F. 1986. *Le ciste prenestine* II.1. *"Cistenfüsse". Etruskische und praenestiner Bronzewerkstätten*. Rome.

Jurgeit, F. 1999. *Die etruskischen und italischen Bronzen sowie Gegenstände aus Eisen, Blei und Leder im Badischen Landesmuseum Karlsruhe* I–II. Pisa–Rome.

Kähler, H. 1958. *Rom und seine Welt*. Munich.

Kaiser, E. 2002. Review of Penner, S. 1998. In *Prähistorische Zeitschrift* 75, 239–241.

Kästner, V. 1988. 'Architektonische Terrakotten aus Kampanien,

Latium and Etrurien der Berliner Antikensammlung'. In *Die Welt der Etrusker. Internationales Kolloquium*, 281–285.

Kästner, V. 2006. 'Ikonographisch bemerkenswerte Fragmente von spätarchaischen Terrakottafriesen aus Cerveteri in der Berliner Antikensammlung'. In *Deliciae Fictiles* III, 77–82.

Kästner, V. 1968. *Excavations in the Necropolis of Salamis* I. Nicosia

Kästner, V. 1973. *Excavations in the Necropolis of Salamis* III. Nicosia.

Kästner, V. 1995. *The Coroplastic Art of Ancient Cyprus* IV. *The Cypro-Archaic Period. Small Male Figurines*. Nicosia.

Karageorghis, V. 1968. *Excavations in the Necropolis of Salamis* I. Nicosia

Karageorghis, V. 1973. *Excavations in the Necropolis of Salamis* III. Nicosia.

Karageorghis, V. 1995. *The Coroplastic Art of Ancient Cyprus* IV. *The Cypro-Archaic Period. Small Male Figurines*. Nicosia.

Karl, R. 2003. 'Iron Age chariots and medieval texts: a step too far in "breaking down boundaries"?', *e-Keltoi* (*Journal of Interdisplinary Celtic Studies*) 5. *Warfare*, 1–29.

Kaul, F. 1991. 'The Dejbjerg carts'. In *The Celts*, 536–537.

Keltski Voz. Guštin, M. and Pauli, L. (eds). *Posavski Muzej Brežice, Knjiga* 6. Brežice 1984.

Kemble, I. M. 1855. 'On some remarkable sepulchral objects from Italy, Styria and Mecklenburg', *Archaeologia* 36, 349–369.

Kilian, K. 1974. 'Zu den früheisenzeitlichen Schwertformen der Apenninhalbinsel'. In Müller-Karpe, H. (ed.), *Beiträge an italischen und griechischen Bronzefunde. Prähistorische Bronzefunde* XX.1. Munich, 33–80.

Kilian, K. 1975. *Fibeln aus Thessalien. Prähistorische Bronzefunde* XIV.2. Munich.

Kilian, K. 1977a. 'Das Kriegergrab von Tarquinia. Beigaben aus Metall und Holz', *Jahrbuch des Deutschen Archäologischen Instituts* 92, 24–98.

Kilian, K. 1977b. 'Zwei italische Neufunde der frühen Eisenzeit aus Olympia', *Archäologisches Korrepondenzblatt* 7, 121–126.

Kilian-Dirlmeier, I. 1985. 'Fremde Weihungen in griechischen Heiligtümer vom 8. bis zum Beginn des 7. Jahrhunderts v.Chr.', *Jahrbuch des Römisch-germanischen Zentralmuseums, Mainz* 32, 215–254.

Kjellberg, L. 1940. *Larisa am Hermos* II. *Die architektonischen Terrakotten*. Stockholm.

Kluiver, J. 1992. 'The "Tyrrhenian" group: its origins and the neck-amphorae in The Netherlands and Belgium', *Bulletin Antieke Beschaving* 67, 73–91.

Knoop, R. R. 1987. *Antefixa Satricana. Sixth-century Architectural Terracottas from the Sanctuary of Mater Matuta at Satricum (Le Ferriere). Satricum* I. Assen–Maastricht.

Knossos North Cemetery. Early Greek Tombs I–IV. Coldstream, J. N. and Catling, H. W. (eds). Annual of the British School at Athens Supplementary volume 28. London.

Koch, J. K. 2006. *Hochdorf* V. *Der Wagen und das Pferdegeschirr aus dem späthallsttattzeitlichen Fürstengrab von Eberdingen-Hochdorf (Kr. Ludwigsburg). Forschungen und Berichte zur Vor- und Frühgeschichte in Baden-Württenberg* 89. Stuttgart.

Koch, L. C. 2002. 'Notizen zu zwei Bilder der Situlenkunst'. *Archäologisches Korrespondenzblatt* 32, 67–79.

Koch, L. C. 2006. 'Zu den Deutungsmöglichkeiten der Situlenkust', In Veit, U., Kienlin, T. L., Kümmel, C. and Schmidt, S. (eds), *Spuren und Botschaften: Interpretationen materieller Kultur*. Münster–New York–Munich–Berlin, 347–367.

Kohler, E. L. 1980. 'Cremations of the Middle Phrygian period at Gordion'. In *From Athens to Gordion. The Papers of a Memorial Symposium for R. S. Young* (De Vries, K. ed.). *University Museum Papers* 1. Philadelphia, 65–89.

Kohler, E. L. 1995. *The Lesser Phrygian Tumuli* I. *The Inhumations The Gordion Excavations (1950–1973). Final Reports* II. *University Museum Monographs* 88. Philadelphia.

Kökten Ersoy, H. 1998a. 'Conservation and reconstruction of Phrygian chariot wheels from Mysia'. In Tuna, N., Aktüre, Z. and Lynch, M. (eds), *Thracians and Phrygian. Problems and Parallelism*. Ankara, 131–146.

Kökten Ersoy, H. 1998b. 'Two wheeled vehicles from Lydia and Mysia', *Istanbuler Mitteilungen* 48, 107–133.

Kolb, A. 2000. *Transport und Nachrichtentransfer im römischen Reich. Klio*, Beiheft (Neue Folge) 2. Berlin.

Kolendo, J. 1980. *L'agricultura nell'Italia romana*. Rome.

Kopcke, G. 1968. 'Heraion von Samos: die Kampagnen 1961/65 im Südtemenos (8.–6 Jahrhundert)', *Athenische Mitteilungen* 83, 250–314.

Koşay, H. Z. 1951. *Alaca-Hoyük. Das Dorf Alaca-Hoyük. Materialien zur Ethnographie und Volkskunde von Anatolien*. Ankara.

Kossack, G. 1954. 'Pferdegeschirr aus Gräbern der älteren Hallstattzeit Bayers', *Jahrbuch des Römisch-germanischen Zentralmuseums, Mainz* 1, 111–178.

Kossack, G. 1956–1957. 'Zu den Metallbeigaben des Wagengrabes von Ca'Morta (Como)', *Sibrium* 3, 41–54.

Kossack, G. 1971. 'The construction of the felloe in Iron Age spoked wheels'. In *The European Community in Later Prehistory* 143–163.

Kossack, G. 1992. 'Lebensbilder, mythische Bildererzählung und Kultfestbilder. Bemerkungen zu Bildszenen aus einer Thronlehne von Verucchio'. In *Festschrift zum 50 jährigen Bestehen des Institutes für Vor- und Frühgeschichte der Leopold-Franzens-Universität Innsbrück* 231–246.

Krämer, W. 1964. 'La Tènezeitliche Trensenanhänger in Omegaform', *Germania* 42, 250–257.

Kraus, Th. and von Matt, L. 1973. *Pompeji und Herculaneum*. Cologne.

Krauskopf, I. 1974. *Der thebanische Sagenkreis und andere griechische Sagen in der etruskischen Kunst*. Mainz am Rhein.

Krauskopf, I. 1984. 'Die Ausfahrt des Amphiaraus auf Amphoren der tyrrhenischen Gruppe'. In Cahn, H. A. and Simon, E. (eds), *Tainia. Roland Hampe zum 70. Geburtstag am 2. December 1978*. Mainz am Rhein, 105–116.

Krausse, D. 1992. 'Treibstachel und Peitsche. Bemerkungen zur Funktion hallstattzeitlicher Stockbewehrungen', *Archäologisches Korrespondenzblatt* 22, 515–523.

Krentz, P. 2002. 'Fighting by the rules. The invention of the hoplite agôn', *Hesperia* 71, 23–39.

Krentz, P. 2007. 'Warfare and hoplites'. In Shapiro, H. A. (ed.), *The Cambridge Companion to Archaic Greece*. Cambridge, 61–84.

Kristiansen, K. 2004. 'Kontakte und Reisen im 2. Jahrtausend v.Chr.' In *Rad und Wagen*, 443–454.

Kromer, K. 1980. 'Das Situlenfest. Versuch einer Interpretation der Darstellungen auf figural verzierten Situlen', *Situla* 20–21, 225–240.

Kübler, K. 1954. *Kerameikos* V.1. *Die Nekropole des 10. bis 8. Jahrhunderts*. Berlin.

Kübler, K. 1970. *Kerameikos* VI.2. *Die Nekropole des späten 8. bis frühen 6. Jahrhunderts*. Berlin.

Künzl, E. 1988. *Der römische Triumph. Siegesfeiern im antiken Rom*. Munich.

Kunze, E. 1967. 'Prometopidia'. In *8. Bericht über die Ausgrabungen in Olympia 1958–1962*. Berlin, 184–195.

Kyrieleis, H. and Röllig, W. 1988. 'Ein altorientalischer Pferdeschmuck aus dem Heraion von Samos', *Athenische Mitteilungen* 103, 37–75.

Lacroix, L. 1974. *Études d'archéologie numismatique*. Paris.

Lambrechts, R. 1959. *Essai sur les magistratures des républiques étrusques*. Rome.

Landels, J. G. 1978. *Engineering in the Ancient World*. London.

Landolfi, M. 2001. 'La Tomba della Regina nella necropoli picena "I Pini" di Sirolo-Numana'. In *Eroi e regine*, 350–354.

Larsson, T. B. 2004. 'Streitwagen, Karren und Wagen in der bronzezeitlichen Felskunst Skandinaviens'. In *Rad und Wagen*, 381–398.

Latacz, J. 1977. *Kampfparänese, Kampfdarstellungen und Kampfwircklichheit in der Ilias, bei Kallinos und Tyrtaios*. Zetemata 66. Munich.

Lauffer, S. 1971. *Diokletians Preisedikt*. Berlin.

Laubscher, H.-P. 1975. *Der Reliefschmuck des Galeriusbogen in Thessaloniki. Archäologische Forschungen* 1. Berlin.

Laurence, R. 1998. 'Land transport in Roman Italy: costs, practice and the economy'. In Parkins, H. and Smith, C. (eds), *Trade, Traders and the Ancient City*. New York, 129–148.

Laurence, R. 1999. *The Roads of Roman Italy. Mobility and Cultural Change*. London–New York.

Laurens, A.-F. 1986. 'Pour une "systématique" iconografique: lecture du vase de Ricci de la Villa Giulia'. In *Iconographie et identités regionales. Bulletin de correspondence helléniques* Supplement 14, 45–56.

Lawson, A. K. 1978. 'Studien zur römischen Pferdegeschirr', *Jahrbuch des Römisch-germanischen Zentralmuseums, Mainz* 25, 131–172.

Lepiksaar, J. 1975. 'Animal remains'. In Hellström, P., *Luni sul Mignone* II.2. *The Zone of the Large Iron Age Building*. Stockholm, 77–86.

Leppert, F. and Frere, S. 1988. *Trajan's Column*. Gloucester.

Leprévost, R. 1977. 'Vases villanoviens du Musée du Louvre', *Revue de Louvre* 5–11.

Letzner, W. 2009. *Der römische Circus. Massenunterhaltung im römischen Reich*. Mainz am Rhein.

Lewis, C. T. and Short, C. *A Latin Dictionary*. Oxford (1966 edn).

Lippold, G. 1956. *Die Skulpturen des vaticanischen Museums* III.2. Berlin.

Littauer, M. A. 1977. 'Rock-carvings of chariots of Transcaucasia, Central Asia and Outer Mongolia', *Proceedings of the Prehistoric Society* 43, 243–262.

Littauer, M. A. 1981. 'Early stirrups', *Antiquity* 55, 99–105.

Littauer, M. A. and Crouwel, J. H. 1973. 'Early metal models of wagons from the Levant', *Levant* 5, 102–126.

Littauer, M. A. and Crouwel, J. H. 1976. 'A bronze chariot group from the Levant in Paris', *Levant* 8, 71–81.

Littauer, M. A. and Crouwel, J. H. 1977a. 'The origin and diffusion of the cross-bar wheel?', *Antiquity* 51, 95–105.

Littauer, M. A. and Crouwel, J. H. 1977b. 'Chariots with Y-poles in the ancient Near East', *Archäologischer Anzeiger*, 1–8.

Littauer, M. A. and Crouwel, J. H. 1979a. *Wheeled Vehicles and Ridden Animals in the Ancient Near East*. Leiden–Köln.

Littauer, M. A. and Crouwel, J. H. 1979b. 'An Egyptian wheel in Brooklyn', *Journal of Egyptian Archaeology* 65, 107–120.

Littauer, M. A. and Crouwel, J. H. 1983. 'Chariots in Late Bronze Age Greece', *Antiquity* 57, 187–192.

Littauer, M. A. and Crouwel, J. H. 1985. *Chariots and Related Equipment from the Tomb of Tut'ankhamun. Tut'ankhamun Tomb Series* 8. Oxford.

Littauer, M. A. and Crouwel, J. H. 1988a. 'New light on Priam's wagon?', *Journal of Hellenic Studies* 108, 194–196.

Littauer, M. A. and Crouwel, J. H. 1988b. 'New type of bit from Iran?', *Iranica antiqua* 23, 323–327.

Littauer, M. A. and Crouwel, J. H. 1996a. 'Robert Drews and the role of chariots in Bronze Age Greece', *Oxford Journal of Archaeology* 15, 297–305.

Littauer, M. A. and Crouwel, J. H. 1996b. 'The origin of the true chariot', *Antiquity* 70, 934–939.

Littauer, M. A. and Crouwel, J. H. 1997. 'Antefatti nell'Oriente Mediterraneo: Vicino Oriente, Egitto e Cipro'. In *Carri da guerra* 5–10.

Littauer, M. A. and Crouwel, J. H. 2001. 'The earliest evidence for metal bits', *Oxford Journal of Archaeology* 20, 329–338.

Littauer, M. A. and Crouwel, J. H.. 2002. *Selected Writings on Chariots and Other Early Vehicles, Riding and Harness* (Raulwing, P. ed.). *Culture and History of the Ancient Near East* 6. Leiden–Boston–Cologne.

Littauer, M. A., Crouwel, J. H. and Hauptmann, H. 1991. 'Ein spätbronzezeitliches Speichenrad vom Lidar Höyük in der Südost-Turkei', *Archäologischer Anzeiger*, 349–358.

Lorimer, H. L. 1903. 'The country cart of ancient Greece', *Journal of Hellenic Studies* 23, 132–151.

Loukomski, G.-K. 1930. *Art étrusque*. Paris.

Lubtchansky, N. 2005. *Le cavalier tyrrhénien. Représentations équestres dans l'Italie archaïque. Bibliothèque des Écoles françaises d'Athènes et de Rome* 320. Rome.

Lubtchansky, N. 2006. 'Triomfo e coroplastica nel *Latium Vetus*. Il condottieri di *Pometia*, l'*Octavius* di *Velitrae* e il Napoleone d'Ingres (sotto lo sguardo di Baudelaire)', *Archeologia classica* 57, 536–545.

Lubtchansky, N. 2010. 'Les petits chevaux de Pometia. Les significations du programme iconographique des frises de Caprifico'. In *Il tempio arcaico di Caprifico di Torrechia*, 133–171. Rome.

Lucas, A. T. 1972. 'Prehistoric block-wheels from Doogarymore, Co. Roscommon, and Timahoe East, Co. Kildare', *Journal of the Royal Society of Antiquaries of Ireland* 102, 19–48.

Lucas Pellicer, M. R. 2004. 'Narigón y ronzal *versus* locado de caballo: el arrastre de los équidos', *Gladius* 24, 99–108.

Lucassen, M. 1995. *De reis per wagen op Etruskische steles uit Bologna* (MA thesis, University of Leiden).

Lucchi, G. 1968. 'Sul significato del *carpentum* nella monetazione romana imperiale', *Rivista italiana numismatica* 70, 131–141.

Lucke, W. and Frey, O. H. 1962. *Die Situla in Providence (Rhode Island). Ein Beitrag zur Situlenkunst des Osthallstattzeit. Römisch-germanische Forschungen* 26. Berlin.

Lulof, P. S. 1997. 'Myths from Greece. The representation of power on the reliefs of Satricum', *Mededeelingen van het Nederlands Historisch Instituut te Rome* 56, 85–114.

Lulof, P. S. 2006. 'La riconstruzione di un tetto perduto', *Archeologia classica* 57, 516–529.

Lulof, P. S. 2010a. 'The architectural terracottas from Caprifico'. In *Il tempio arcaico di Caprifico di Torrecchia* 25–78.

Lulof, P. S. 2010b. 'Manufacture and reconstruction'. In *Il tempio arcaico di Caprifico d Torrecchia* 79–111.

McGowan, E. P. 1995. 'Tomb marker and turning post. Funerary columns in the Archaic period', *American Journal of Archaeology* 99, 615–632.

Maaskant-Kleibrink, M. 1992. *Settlement Excavations at Borgo Le Ferriere "Satricum"* II. *The Campaigns 1983, 1985 and 1987*. Groningen.

Maaskant-Kleibrink, M. 1993. 'Religious activity on the "Timone della Motta", Francavilla Marittima, and the identification of Lagaría', *Bulletin Antieke Beschaving* 68, 1–47.

MacCall, J. B. 2002. *The Cavalry of the Roman Republic*. London–New York.

Macellari, R. 2002. *Il sepolocreto etrusco nel terreno Arnoaldi di Bologna (550–350 a.C.)*. Bologna.

MackIntosh, J. 1974. 'Representations of furniture on the frieze plaques from Poggio Civitate (Murlo)', *Römische Mitteilungen* 81, 15–40.

MacIntosch Turfa, J. 2005. *Catalogue of the Etruscan Gallery of the University of Pennsylvania Museum of Archaeology and Anthropology*. Philadelphia.

Macnamara, E. 1990. *The Etruscans* (British Museum). London.

Maggiani, A. 1976. 'La "bottega dell'urna Guarnacci 621": osservazioni su una fabbrica volterrana nel I secolo a.C.', *Studi etruschi* 44, 111–146.

Maggiani, A. 2003. 'Il cavallo (alato e aggiogato) in Etruria'. In *Produzioni, merci e commerci in Altino preromana e romana*, 161–178.

Maggiani, A. and Bellelli, V. 2006. 'Terrecotte architettoniche a Cerveteri (Vigna Parrochiale): nuove acquisizioni'. In *Deliciae Fictiles* III, 83–96.

Maiuri, A., 1922. *La Casa del Menandro e il suo tesoro di argenteria*. Rome.

Malerei der Etrusker in Zeichnungen des 19. Jahrhunderts (exhibition catalogue, Cologne 1987). Mainz 1987.

Man and the Animal Word. Studies in Memoriam Sandor Bökönyi. Archaeozoology, Archaeology, Athropology. Anreiter, P., Bartosiewicz, L., Jerem, E. and Meid, M. (eds). *Archaeolingua* 8. Budapest 1998.

Manakidou, E. P. 1994. *Παραστάσεις με άρματα (8ος–5ος αι. π.Χ.) Παρατηρήσεις στην εικονογραφία τους*. Thessalonika.

Mangani, E. and Emiliozzi, A. 1997. 'Capena, necropoli di San Martino. Il carro dalla Tomba XV'. In *Carri da guerra*, 285–289.

Maran, J. 2004a. 'Die Badener Kultur und ihre Räderfahrzeuge'. In *Rad und Wagen*, 265–282.

Maran, J. 2004b. 'Kulturkontakte und Wege der Ausbreitung der Wagen Technologie'. In *Rad und Wagen*, 429–442.

Marchesetti, C. 1993. *Scritti sulla necropoli di S.Lucia di Tolmino (scavi 1884–1902)*. Trieste.

Mari, Z. 1996. 'Insidiamenti arcaici nella Sabina meridionale'. In *Identità e civiltà dei Sabini (Atti del XVIII convegno di studi etruschi*, Rieti and Magliano Sabina 1993). Florence, 299–309.

Marinetti, A. 2003. 'Il "signore del cavallo" e i riflessi istituzionali dei dati di lingua. Venetico *ekupetaris*'. In *Produzioni, merci e commerci in Altino preromana e romana*, 142–160.

Markoe, G. 1985. *Phoenician Bronze and Silver Bowls from Cyprus and the Mediterranean*. Berkeley–Los Angeles–London.

Martelli, M. 1984a. 'Prima di Aristonothos', *Prospettiva* 38, 2–15.

Martelli, M. 1984b. 'Avant Aristonothos (à propos d'un vase peint de Caere, MA 297)'. In Brijder, H. A. G. (ed.), *Ancient Greek and Related Pottery. Allard Pierson Series* 5. Amsterdam, 193–197.

Martelli, M. 1988. 'Un'anfora orientalizzante ceretana a Würzburg ovverro il Pittore dell'Eptacordo', *Archäologischer Anzeiger*, 285–296.

Martelli, M. 2000. 'Un plachetta eburnea etrusca e 'l'Intagliatore di New York'. In *Damarato* 167–170.

Martelli, M. 2001. 'Nuove proposte per i Pittori dell'Eptacordo e delle Gru', *Prospettiva* 101, 2–18.

Martelli, M. 2005. 'Rivisitazione delle lamine di rivestimento di carri nella Ny Carlsberg Glyptotek di Copenaghen', *Prospettiva* 117–118, 122–130.

Martha, J. 1889. *L'art étrusque*. Paris.

Massa-Pairault, F.-H. 1985. *Recherches sur l'art et l'artisanat étrusco-italiques à l'époque hellénistique. Bibliothèque des Écoles françaises d'Athènes et de Rome* 257. Rome.

Massa-Pairault, F.-H. 1986. 'Les jeux équestres de Poggio Civitate. Représentation et société', *Ktema* 11, 179–187.

Massa-Pairault, F.-H. 1993. 'Aspects idéologiques des *Ludi*'. In *Spectacles sportifs*, 247–279.

Massa-Pairault, F.-H. 1996. *La cité des Étrusques*. Paris.

Mattingly, H. 1953. 'Some new studies on the Roman Republican coinage', *Proceedings of the British Academy*, 281–285.

Mayer, W. 1978. 'Gedanken zum Einsatz von Streitwagen und Reitern in neuassyrischer Zeit', *Ugarit-Forschungen* 10, 175–186.

Melis, F. 1986. 'Considerazioni e ricerche antiquarie su un gruppo di lastre fittile ceretane'. In *Italian Iron Age Artefacts*, 159–169.

Memorie dal Sottosuolo. Una pagina di scavo dalla necropoli di Castel di Decima (exhibition, Rome 1996–1997). Rome 1997.

Menichetti, M. 1994. *Archeologia del potere. Re, immagini e miti a Roma e in Etruria in età arcaica. Biblioteca di Archeologia* 21. Milan.

Mertens-Horn, M. 1992. 'Die archaischen Baufriese aus Metapont', *Römische Mitteilungen* 99, 1–122.

Mertens-Horn, M. 2005/2006. 'Initiation und Mädschenraub am Fest der lokrischen Persephone', *Römische Mitteilungen*, 112, 7–75.

Mesado Oliver, N. 2003. 'El caballo ibérico de la Regenta (Burriana, Castellón)'. In *El caballo en la antigua iberica*, 179–186.

Messerschmidt, W. 1988. 'Der ägäische Streitwagen und seine Beziehungen zum nordeurasisch-vorderasiatischen Raum', *Acta Archaeologica et Praehistorica* 20, 31–44.

Messerschmidt, W. 1994. 'Der römische Circus', *Achse, Rad und Wagen. Beiträge zur Geschichte der Landfahrzeuge* 3, 11–17.

Messerschmidt, W. 2000. 'Die Entwicklung des vierrädrigen Wagens in der griechisch-römischen Antike', *Achse Rad und Wagen. Beiträge zur Geschichte der Landfahrzeuge* 8, 4–11.

Metzler, J. and Kunter, M. 1986. 'Ein frühlatènezeitliches Gräberfeld mit Wagenbestattung bei Grosbous-Vichten', *Archäologisches Korrespondenzblatt* 16, 161–177.

Milani, L. A. 1894. 'Capodimonte – Nuovi scavi nella necropoli visentina nel comune di Capodimonte sul lago di Bolsena', *Notizie degli scavi di antichità*, 123–141.

Milani, L. A. 1908. 'Populonia -Relazione preliminare sulla prima campagna degli scavi governati di Populonia nel comune di Piombino', *Notizie degli scavi di antichità*, 199–231.

Miller, M. C. 1992. 'The parasol: an oriental status-symbol in late Archaic and Classical Athens', *Journal of Hellenic Studies* 112, 91–105.

Milsent, P. Y. 2003. 'Status et fonctions d'un personnage féminin hors norme'. In *La tombe princière de Vix* 312–366.

Minetti, A. 2005. 'La Tomba della Quadriga Infernale di Sarteamo', *Studi etruschi* 70, 137–159.

Minetti, A. 2006. *La Tomba della Quadriga Infernale nella necropoli delle Pinaccedi di Sarteano*. Rome.

Minetti, A. 2007. 'La tomba dipinta di Sarteano', *Ostraka* 6, 79–91.

Mingazzini, P. 1938. 'Il santuario della dea Marica alle foci del Garigliano', *Monumenti antichi* 37, 693–984.

Mingazzini, P. 1973. 'Über die Echtheit dreier pontischen Amphoren', *Bonner Jahrbücher des rheinischen Landesmuseums in Bonn und des Vereins von Altertumsfreunden im Rheinlande* 173, 112–116.

Miniero, P. 1987. 'Studi di un carro romano dalla Villa C.D. di Arianna a Stabia', *Mélanges de l'École française de Rome* 99, 171–209.

Miniero, P. 1991–1992. 'Stabiae. Attività dell'ufficio scavi: 1991', *Rivista di studi pompeiani* 5, 221–228.

Minto, A. 1914. 'Populonia', *Notizie degli scavi di antichità*, 411–463.

Minto, A. 1921. *Marsiliana d'Albegna*. Florence.

Minto, A. 1943. *Populonia*. Florence.

Mitchell, S. 1976. 'Requisitioned transport in the Roman Empire. A new inscription from Pisidia', *Journal of Roman Studies* 66, 106–131.

Molin, M. 1984. 'Quelques considérations sur le chariot des vendages de Langres', *Gallia* 42, 97–114.

Moltesen, M. 1982. 'Til vaeddeløb i Etrurien', *Meddelelser fra Ny Carlsberg Glyptotek* 38, 53–72.

Moltesen, M. and Nielsen, M. 1996. *Etruria and Central Italy Ny Carlsberg Glyptotek*. Copenhagen.

Montelius, O. 1904. *La civilisation primitive en Italie depuis l'introduction des métaux* II. Stockholm.

Moore, M. B. 1971. *Horses on Black-figure Greek Vases of the Archaic Period: ca. 620–480 BC.* (doctoral thesis, New York University).

Moore, M. B. 1975. 'The Cottenham relief', *Getty Museum Journal* 2, 37–50.

Moore, M. B. 2006. Hoplites and a comic chorus', *Journal of the Metropolitan Museum of Art* 41, 33–57.

Moretti, L. 1953. *Iscrizione agonistiche greche*. Rome.

Moretti, L. 1957. *Olympionikai. I vincitori negli antichi agoni olimpici*. Rome.

Moorey, P. R. S. 1971. *Ancient Persian Bronzes in the Ashmolean Museum*. Oxford.

Morigi Govi, C. 1970. 'Persistenze orientalizzanti nelle stele felsinee', *Studi etruschi* 38, 67–89.

Morigi Govi, C. 2000. 'L'orientalizzante settentrionale'. In *Principi Etruschi*, 329–336.

Morigi Govi, C. and Sassatelli, G. 1993. 'Il sepolcreto etrusco del Polisportivo di Bologna: nuove stele funerarie', *Ocnus (Quaderni della Scuola di specializzazione in archeologia*, Bologna) 1, 103–124.

Moscati, P. 1997. 'Un gruppo di urne volterrane con rappresentazione del "viaggio agli inferni in *carpentum*"'. In *Etrusca et Italica. Scritti in ricordo di M. Pallottino* II. Pisa–Rome, 403–423.

Moscati, S. 1987. *L'Italia prima di Roma*. Rome.

Müller, F. 1975. 'Keltische Wagen mit elastischer Aufhängung: eine Reise von Castel di Decima nach Clonmacnoise'. In Schmid-Sikimič, B. and Della Casa, P. (eds), *Trans Europam. Festschrift für Margarita Primas. Beiträge zur Bronze- und Eisenzeit zwischen Atlantik und Italien*. Bonn, 265–275.

Müller, S. 1996. 'Herrlicher Ruhm im Sport oder im Krieg – Der *Apobates* und die Funktion der Sport in der griechischen Polis', *Nikephoros* 9, 41–69.

Müller-Karpe, H. 1962. 'Metalbeigaben der Kerameikos-Gräber', *Jahrbuch des Deutschen Archäologischen Instituts* 77, 59–129.

Müller-Karpe, H. 1974. 'Das Grab 871 von Veji, Grotta Gramiccia'. In Müller-Karpe, H. (ed.), *Beiträge zu italienischen und griechischen Bronzefunde. Prähistorische Bronzefunde* XX.1. Munich, 89–97.

Mura Sommella, A. 2004–2005. 'Aspetti dell'orientalizzante antico a Capena', *Atti della Pontificia Accademia romana di archeologia. Rendicondi* 77, 219–287.

Muscarella, O. W. 1988. *Bronze and Iron. Ancient Near Eastern Artifacts in the Metropolitan Museum of Art*. New York.

Il Museo Civico Archeologico di Bologna. Realità regionale. Musei Guide 2. Morigi Govi, C. and Vitali, D. (eds). Bologna 1982.

Mutti, A., Provenzano, N., Rossi, M. G. and Rottoli, M. 1988. *La Terramare di Castione dei Marchese. Studi e documenti di archeologia* 5. Bologna.

Muzzolini, A. 1991. 'The technogical evolution from biga to quadriga in the eastern Mediterranean, the Maghreb and the Sahara: when and why?' In Waldren, W. H., Ensenyat, J. A. and Kennard, R. C. (eds), *IInd Deià Conference of Prehistory* II. *Archeological Technology and Theory*. BAR International Series 574. Oxford, 307–320.

Le myth grec dans l'Italie antique. Fonction et image (Actes du colloque international organisé par l'École française de Rome, l'Instituto italiano per gli studi filosofici (Naples) *et l'UMR 126 du CNRS Archéologies d'Orient et d'Occident,* Rome 1996). Massa-Pairault, F.-H. (ed.). Rome, 1999.

Nachod, H. 1909. *Der Rennwagen der Italiker und ihre Nachbarn*. Leipzig.

Nardi, G. 1989. 'Nuovi dati dalla ricognizione a Caere e nelle aree adiacenti: principali vie etrusche dell'entroterra'. In *Secondo congresso internazionale etrusco* II, 517–523.

Naso, A. 2000a. 'Etruscan and Italic artefacts from the Aegean'. In *Ancient Italy in its Mediterranean Setting* 193–207.

Naso, A. 2000b. 'Etruskische und italische Weihungen in griechischen Heiligtümer und neue Funde. In Krinzinger, F. (ed.), *Die Ägäis und das westliche Mittelmeer. Beziehungen und Wechselwirkungen 8. bis 5. Jh. v.Chr.* Vienna, 157–163.

Naso, A. 2003. I *bronzi etruschi e italici del Römisch-germanisches Zentralmuseum. Kataloge vor- und frühgeschichtlicher Altertümer* 33. Mainz am Rhein.

Nava, M. L. 1979. *Stele daunie. Vita, culti e miti nella Puglia protohistorica*. n.p.

Nebelsick, L. D. 1992. 'Orientalische Streitwagen in der zentral- und westmediterranen Welt', *Acta Praehistorica et Archaeologica* 24, 85–110.

Neppi Modona, A. 1925. *Cortona etrusca e romana nella storie e nell'arte*. Florence.

Nielsen, M. 1990. 'Sacerdotesse e associazioni cultuali femminili in Etruria: testimonianze epigrafiche e iconografiche', *Analecta Romana Instituti Danici* 19, 45–67.

Nijboer, A. J. 2005. 'La cronologia dell'età del ferro nel Mediterraneo, dibattito sui metodi e sui risultati'. In *Oriente e occidente* 527–556.

Norman, C. 2009. 'Warriors and weavers: sex and gender in Daunian stelae'. In *Gender Identities in Italy in the First Millennium BC*. BAR International Series 1983. Oxford, 37–54.

Nunzio, A. 1984. 'Scavi e scoperte. Necropoli samnitica in loc. Curti (prop. Colorizio'), *Studi etruschi* 52, 514.

Oakley, H. J. H. and Hague Sinos, R. 1993. *The Wedding in Ancient Greece*. Munich.

Ohler, N. 1993. *Reisen im Mittelalter* (3rd edn). Munich.

Özgen, E. 1984. 'The Urartian chariot reconsidered II. Archaeological evidence, 9th–7th centuries BC', *Anatolica*, 91–154.

Olbrich, G. 1986. 'Friese und Pinakes aus Magna Graecia', *La Parola del passato* 41, 122–152.

Oliver A., Jr. 1968. *The Reconstruction of two Apulian Tomb Groups. Antike Kunst*, Beiheft 5. Bern.

Oriente e occidente. Metodi e discipline a confronto. Riflessioni sulla cronologia dell'età del ferro in Italia (*Atti dell'incontro di studi*, Rome 2003). Bartoloni, G. and Delpino, F. (eds). *Mediterranea* 1. Pisa–Rome.

Ornella Acanfore, M. 1970. 'Manufatti di legno di Polada e Barche di Solferino', *Bolletino di paletnologia italiana* (Nuove Serie) 79, 157–244.

Osborne, R. 2001. 'Why did Athenian pots appeal to the Etruscans?', *World Archaeology* 33, 277–295.

Pacciarelli, M. 2000. *Dal villaggio alla città. La svolta protourbana del 1000 a.C. nell'Italia tirrenica. Grandi contesti e problemi della preistoria italiana* 4. Florence.

Pacciarelli, M. 2002. 'Raffigurazioni di miti e riti su manufatti metallici di Bisenzio e Vulci tra il e il 650 a.C.' In Carandini, A. (ed.), *Archeologia del mito. Emozione e ragione fra primitivi e moderni*. Rome, 301–332.

Padova preromana (exhibition catalogue, Padova 1976). Padua.

Pagnotta, M. A. 1977–1978. '*Carpentum*: privilegio del carro e ruole sociale della matrona romana', *Annali della facoltà di lettere e filosofia. Università degli studi di Perugia* (Nuove Serie) 15, 159–170.

Pairault Massa, F.-H. (see also Massa Pairault) 1992. *Iconologia e politica nell'Italia antiqua. Roma, Lazio, Etruria dal VII al I secolo a.C. Biblioteca di archeologia* 18. Milan.

Pallottino, M. 1952. *Etruscan Painting*. New York.

Pallottino, M. 1991. *A History of Earliest Italy*. London (originally *Storia della prima Italia*. Milan, 1984).

Palm, J. 1952. 'Veiian tomb groups in the Museo Preistorico, Rome', *Opuscula archaeologica* 7, 50–86.

Panicelli, S. 1990. 'Sepolture bolognesi dell'VIII secolo a.C.'. In Carancini, G. L. (ed.), *Miscellanea protostorica. Archeologia Perusina* 2, 189–391.

Pare, C. F. E. 1987a. 'Wheels with thickened spokes, and the problem of cultural contact between the Aegean world and Europe in the Late Bronze Age', *Oxford Journal of Archaeology* 6, 43–61.

Pare, C. F. E. 1987b. 'Der Zeremonialwagen der Bronze- und Urnenfelderzeit: seine Entstehung, Form und Verbreitung'. In *Vierrädrige Wagen*, 25–67.

Pare, C. F. E. 1987c. 'Bemerkungen zum Wagen von Hochdorf'. In *Vierrädrige Wagen*, 128–133.

Pare, C. F. E. 1987d. 'Der Zeremonialwagen der Hallstattzeit: Untersuchungen zu Konstruktion, Typologie und Kulturbeziehungen'. In *Vierrädrige Wagen*, 189–248.

Pare, C. F. E. 1989. 'From Dupljana to Delphi: the ceremonial use of the wagon in later prehistory', *Antiquity* 63, 80–100.

Pare, C. F. E. 1992. *Wagons and Wagon-graves of the Early Iron Age in Central Europe. Oxford University Committee for Archaeology Monograph* 35. Oxford.

Pareti, L. 1947. *La Tomba Regolini-Galassi del Museo Gregoriano Etrusco e la civiltà dell'Italia centrale nel secolo VII a.C.* Vatican City.

Paribeni, E. 1905. 'Civitella S.Paolo. Scavi nella necropoli capenate', *Notizie degli scavi di antichità*, 301–362.

Paribeni, E. 1906. 'Necropoli del territorio capenate', *Monumenti antichi* 16, 277–490.

Paribeni, E. 1928. 'Bolsena – Ritrovamento di bronzi', *Notizie degli scavi di antichità* (Serie 6) 4, 339–343.

Paribeni, E. 1938. 'I rilievi chiusini arcaici', *Studi etruschi* 12, 57–139.

Parrot, A. 1961. *Assur*. Paris.

Paturik, N. 1985. *A Second Paradise. Indian Court Life 1590–1947* (exhibition catalogue) New York 1985. New York.

Pearce, M. 1998. 'New research on the *terramare* of northern Italy', *Antiquity* 72, 743–746.

Pekáry, Th. 1968. *Untersuchungen zu den römischen Reichsstrassen*. Bonn.

Pellegrini, G. 1903a. 'Pitigliano. Nuove scoperte di antichità nella necropoli', *Notizie degli scavi di antichità*, 267–279.

Pellegrini, G. 1903b. 'Tombe greche arcaiche e tomba greco-samnitica a tholos della necropoli di Cuma'. *Monumenti antichi* 13, 201–294.

Penner, S. 1998. *Schliemanns Schachtgräberrund und der europäische Nordosten. Saarbrücker Beiträge zur Altertumskunde* 60. Bonn.

Percossi Serenelli, E. 1992. 'La tomba di S. Egidio di Tolentino nella problematica dell'orientalizzante piceno'. In *La civiltà picena nelle Marche* 140–177.

Peroni, R. 1983. 'Die frühbronzezeitliche Pflug von Lavagnone', *Archäologisches Korrespondenzblatt* 13, 187–195.

Peroni, R. 1987. *Scavi archeologici nella zona palaefitticola di Fiavé-Carera* II. *Campagne 1969–1976. Resti della cultura materiale: metallo – osso – litica – legno. Patrimonio storico e artistico del Trentino* 9. Trento.

Peroni, R. 1997. 'Il potere e i suoi simboli'. In *Le Terramare* 661–676.

Peroni, R. *et al.* 1975. *Studi sulla cronologia delle civiltà di Este e Golasecca*. Florence.

Pertlwieser, M. 1988. 'Frühhallstattliche Wagenbestattungen in Mittelkirchen'. In *Prunkwagen*, 55–70.

Petersen, E. 1894. 'Bronzen von Perugia', *Römische Mitteilungen* 9, 253–319.

Pfrommer, M. 1993. *Metalwork from the Hellenized East* (J. Paul Getty Museum) Malibu.

Phillips, K. M., Jr. 1993. *In the Hills of Tuscany. Recent Excavations at the Etruscan Site of Poggio Civitate (Murlo, Siena)*. Philadelphia.

Picard, C. 1941. 'Une cimaise thasienne archaïque', *Monuments et mémoirs. Fondation E. Piot* 38, 55–92.

Pictorial Pursuits. Figurative Painting on Mycenaean and Geometric Pottery. Papers from two Seminars at the Swedish Institute at Athens in 1999 and 2001. Rystedt, E. and B. Wells (eds). Stockholm 2006.

Piggott, S. 1952. 'Chariots on Roman coins', *Antiquity* 26, 87–88.

Piggott, S. 1983. *The Earliest Wheeled Transport. From the Atlantic Coast to the Caspian Sea.* London.

Piggott, S. 1992. *Wagon, Chariot and Carriage.* London.

Pincelli, R. and Morigi Govi, C. 1975. *La necropoli villanoviana di San Vitale. Fonti per la storia di Bologna. Cataloghi* 1. Bologna.

Pinza, G. 1907. 'La Tomba Regolini-Galassi e le altre rinvenute al "Sorbo" in territorio di Cerveteri', *Römische Mitteilungen* 22, 35–186.

Pinza, G. 1935. *La civiltà latina* I–II. Rome.

Pisani Sartorio, G. 1988. *Mezzi di trasporto e traffico. Vita e costumi dei Romani antichi* 6 (Museo della Civiltà Romana). Rome.

Placidi, C. 1978. 'Fauna'. In Puglisi, S. M. *et al.,* 'Torrionaccio', *Notizie degli scavi di antichità* (Serie 8) 23, 270.

Poehler, E. E. 2006. 'The circulation of traffic in Pompeii's *Regio VI*', *Journal of Roman Studies* 19, 53–74.

Pontrandolfo, A. and Rouveret, A. 1992. *Le tombe dipinte di Paestum.* Modena.

Ponzi Bonomi, L. 1970. 'Il ripostiglio di Contigliano', *Bollettino di paleontologia italiana* (Nuove Serie) 21, 95–156.

Popham, M. R. 1993. 'The main excavation of the building (1981–3)'. In Popham, M. R., Calligas, P. G. and Sackett, L. H. (eds), *Lefkandi* II.2. *The Protogeometric Building at Toumba. The Excavation, Architecture and Finds.* British School at Athens Supplementary volume 23. London, 7–31.

Popham, M. R., Calligas, P. G. and Sackett, L. H. 1989. 'Further excavation of the Toumba cemetery at Lefkandi, 1984 and 1986. Preliminary report'. In *Archaeological Reports* 1988–1989, 117–129.

Popham, M. R. and Lemos, I. 1996. *Lefkandi* III. *The Early Iron Age.* British School at Athens Supplementary volume 29. London.

Popoli e civiltà dell'Italia antica 1–9. Rome, 1974–1989.

Postgate, J. N. 2000. 'The Assyrian army in Zamua', *Iraq* 62, 89–108.

Potere e splendore. Gli antichi Piceni a Matelica (exhibition catalogue, Matelica 2008). Silvestrini, M. and Sabbatini, T. (eds). Rome 2008.

Potratz, J. A. H. 1966. *Pferdetrensen des Alten Orient.* Rome.

Powell, T. E. G. 1963. 'Some implications of chariotry'. In Foster, J. Ll., and Alcock, L. (eds), *Culture and Environment. Essays in Honour of Sir Cyril Fox.* London, 153–169.

Powell, T. E. G. 1980. *The Celts* (2nd edn). London.

Prayon, F. 1975. *Frühetruskische Grab- und Hausarchitektur. Römische Mitteilungen*, Ergänzungsheft 22. Heidelberg.

Principi etruschi tra Mediterraneo ed Europa (exhibition catalogue, Bologna 2000–2001). Bartoloni, G., Delpini, F., Morigi Govi, C. and Sassatelli, G. (eds). Venice 2000.

Produzioni, merci e commerci in Altino preromana e romana. (*Atti del convegno.* Venice 2001). Cresci Marrone, G. and Tirelli, M. (eds). *Studi e richerche sulla Gallia Cisalpina* 17. *Studi di archeologia, epigrafia e storia* 3. Rome 2003.

Provenzano, N. 1997. 'Produzione in osso e corno della terramare emiliane'. In *Le Terramare* 524–544.

Prückner, H. 1968. *Die lokrischen Tonreliefs.* Mainz.

Prunkwagen und Hügelgrab. Kultur der frühen Eisenzeit von Hallstatt bis Mitterkirchen (exhibition catalogue, Linz 1988). *Kataloge des Ö. Landesmuseums* (Neue Folge) 13. Linz 1988.

Pryce, F. N. 1931. *Catalogue of Sculpture in the Department of Greek and Roman Antiquities of the British Museum* I.2. *Cypriot and Etruscan.* London.

Putz, U. 1998. 'Gesellschaftlicher Wandel in Mittelitalien im Spiegel villanovazeitlicher Prunkgräber'. In *Archäologische Untersuchungen zu den Beziehungen zwischen Altitalien und der Zone nordwärts der Alpen,* 49–68.

Quesada Sanz, F. 1997. 'La penisola iberica'. In *Carri da guerra,* 53–59.

Quesada Sanz, F. 2003. 'El caballo en la antigua Iberia'. In *El caballo en la antigua Iberia,* 9–19.

Quilici, L. 1989. 'Le antiche vie dell'Etruria'. In *Secondo congresso internazionale etrusco* I, 451–506.

Quilici, L. 1992. 'Evoluzione della tecnica stradale nell'Italia centrale'. In Quilici, L. and Quilici Gigli, S. (eds), *Tecnica stradale romana. Atlante tematico di topografia antica* 1. Rome, 19–32.

Quilici, L. 1997. 'Le strade carraie nell'Italia arcaica'. In *Carri di guerra,* 73–82.

Rad und Wagen. Der Ursprung einer Innovation im Vorderen Orient und Europa. Fansa, M. and Burmeister, S. (eds). Mainz am Rhein 2004.

Radnóti, A. 1961. 'Ein Jochbeschlag der römischen Kaiserzeit', *Saalburg Jahrbuch* 19, 18–36.

Radke, G. 1981. *Viae publicae romanae.* Bologna.

Raepsaet, G. 2002. *Attelages et techniques de transport dans le monde gréco-romain.* Brussels.

Randsborg, K. 1991. 'Gallemose. A chariot from the early second millennium BC in Denmark?', *Acta Archaeologica* (Copenhagen) 62, 109–122.

Rathje, A. 1986. 'Five ostrich eggs from Vulci'. In *Italian Iron Age Artefacts,* 397–404.

Rathje, A. 1989. 'Alcuni considerazioni sulle lastre da Poggio Civitate con figure femminile'. In *Le donne in Etruria,* 75–84.

Rathje, A. 1993. 'Il fregio di Murlo: status sulle considerazioni'. In *Deliciae Fictiles* I, 135–138.

Rathje, A. 2000. '"Princesses" in Etruria and *Latium Vetus?*'. In *Ancient Italy in its Mediterranean Setting*, 295–300.

Raubitschek, I. 1998. *Isthmia* VII. *The Metal Objects (1952–1989)*. Princeton.

Rauwling, P. and Clutton-Brock, J. 2009. 'The Buhen horse: fifty years after its discovery', *Journal of Egyptian History* 2, 1–106.

Rawlings, L. 2007. 'Army and battle during the conquest of Italy (350–264 BC)'. In *A Companion to the Roman Army*, 45–62.

Rawson, E. 1981. 'Chariot-racing in the Roman Republic', *Papers of the British School at Rome* 49, 1–16.

RE = Pauly-Wissowa, *Real-Encyclopädie der classischen Altertumswissenschaft*. Stuttgart (later München) 1893– .

Reber, K. 1999. 'Apobaten auf einem geometrischen Amphorenhals', *Antike Kunst* 42, 126–141.

Rebuffat, M. R. 1962. 'Une pyxis d'ivoire de la Tomba Regolini-Galassi', *Mélanges de l'École française de Rome* 74, 369–431.

Rega, L. 1991–1992. 'Progetto di ricostruzione del carro della villa di Arianna', *Rivista di studi pompeiani* 5, 228.

Regter, W. 2003. *Imitation and Creation. Development of Early Bucchero Design at Cerveteri in the Seventh Century BC. Allard Pierson Series* 15. Amsterdam.

Reusser, C. *et al.* 1988. *Etruskische Kunst* (Basel, Antikenmuseum und Sammlung Ludwig). Basel.

Ricci, G. 1946–48. 'Una hydria ionica da Caere', *Annuario della Scuola archaeologica di Atene e delle Missione italiane in Oriente* 24–26, 49–57.

Rich, J. 2007. 'Warfare and the army in early Rome'. In *A Companion to the Roman Army*, 7–23.

Richardson, E. 1953. 'The Etruscan origins of early Roman sculpture', *Memoirs of the American Academy in Rome* 21, 77–124.

Richardson, E. 1964. *The Etruscans. Their Art and Civilization*. Chicago–London.

Richardson, E. 1968. *Engraved Gems of the Greeks and the Etruscans*. London.

Richter, G. M. A. 1915. *Greek, Etruscan and Roman Bronzes in the Metropolitan Museum of Art*. New York.

Richter, G. M. A. 1939. 'Fittings from an Etruscan chariot', *Studi etruschi* 13, 433–435.

Richter, G. M. A. 1968. *Engraved Gems of the Greeks and the Etruscans*. London.

Ridgway, D. and Serra Ridgway, F. R. 1999. 'Early Rome and Latium again: typology and chronology', *Journal of Roman Archaeology* 12, 436–452.

Ridgway, F. R. 1986. 'Impasto ceretano stampigliato: gli esemplari del British Museum: origine e affinità'. In *Italian Iron Age Artefacts*, 283–292.

Riedel, A. 1982. 'The Paleovenitian horse of Le Brustolade (Altino)', *Studi etruschi* 50, 227–256.

Riva, C. 1999. 'Funerary ritual, cultural identity and memory in Orientalizing south Etruria'. In *Proceedings of the XVth International Congress of Classical Archaeology. Towards the Third Millennium* (Amsterdam 1998). Docter, R. F. and Moormann, E. M. (eds). *Allard Pierson Series* 12. Amsterdam, 331–335.

Riva, C. 2001–2003. 'Keeping up with the Etruscans? Picene élites in central Italy during the Orientalising period'. In *Accordia Research Papers* 9, 69–91.

Riva, C. 2010. *The Urbanisation of Etruria. Funerary Practices and Social Change, 700–600 BC*. Cambridge.

Rizzo, M. A. and Martelli, M. 1988–1989. 'Un incunabolo del mito greco in Etruria', *Annuario della Scuola archaeologica di Atene e delle Missone italiane in Oriente* 66–67, 7–56.

Robb, J. E. 1996. 'New directions in Italian burial studies: a disorganized renaissance?', *American Journal of Archaeology* 100, 773–776.

Röring, Chr. W. 1983. *Untersuchungen zu römische Reisewagen*. Koblenz.

Roller, L. E. 1981a. 'Funeral games in Greek art', *American Journal of Archaeology* 85, 107–119.

Roller, L. E. 1981b. 'Funeral games for historical persons', *Stadion* 7, 1–18.

Rolley, C. 1990. 'En regardant l'aurige', *Bulletin de correspondance hellénique* 114, 285–297.

Roma. Romolo, Remo e la fondazione della città (exhibition catalogue, Rome 2000). Carandini, A. and Cappelli, R. (eds). Milan, 2000.

Root, M. C. 1973. 'An Etruscan horse race from Poggio Civitate', *American Journal of Archaeology* 77, 121–137.

Rostovtzeff, M. 1957. *The Social and Economic History of the Roman Empire* (2nd edn; revised by P. M. Fraser). Oxford.

Roth, J. P. 1999. *The Logistics of the Roman Army at War (264 BC–AD 235)*. Leiden–Boston–Köln.

Roth, J. P. 2009. *Roman Warfare*. Cambridge.

Rottoli, M. 1997. 'I legni della terramare di Castione Marchesi'. In *Le Terramare*, 481–486.

Rouveret, A. and Pontrandolfo, A. G. 1983. 'Pittura funeraria in Lucania e Campania. Puntualizzazioni cronologiche e proposte di lettura', *Dialoghi di archeologia* (Serie 3) 1, 91–130.

Rumpf, E. 1928. *Katalog der etruskischen Skulpturen*. (Berlin, Staatliche Museen). Berlin.

Sage, M. M. 2008. *The Republican Roman Army. A Sourcebook*. New York–London.

Salmon, J. 1977. 'Political hoplites', *Jorunal of Hellenic Studies* 91, 84–101.

Sandor, B. I. 2004. 'The rise and decline of the Tutankhamun-class chariot', *Oxford Journal of Archaeology* 23, 153–175.

Sannibale, M. 1998. *Le armi della collezione Gorga al Museo Nazionale Romano. Studia archaeologica* 92. Rome.

Santoro, P. 2006. 'Tomba XI di Colle del Forno: simbologie

funerarie nella decorazione di una lamina di bronzo'. In *ΑΕΙΜΝΗΣΤΟΣ* I, 267–273.

Il sarcofago delle Amazzoni. Bottini, A. and Setari, E. (eds). Milan 2007.

Saronio, P. 1968–69. 'Revisione e presentazione dei corredi di alcune tombe dell'età del ferro dalla necropoli della Ca'Morta', *Rivista archeologica dell'antica provincia e diocese di Como*, 150–151, 47–98.

Sassatelli, G. 1989. 'Problemi cronologici delle stele felsinee alla luce dei rispettivi corredi tombali'. In *Secondo congresso internazionale etrusco* II, 927–949.

Sassatelli, G. 1993. 'Rappresentazioni di giochi atletici in monumenti funerari di area padana'. In *Spectacles sportifs*, 45–67.

Sassatelli, G. 1996. 'Verucchio, centro etrusco "di frontiera"', *Ocnus* (*Quaderni della Scuola di specializzazione in archeologia*, Bologna) 4, 249–271.

Sassatelli, G. and Govi, E. 2007. 'Ideologia funeraria e celebrazione del defunto nelle stele etrusche di Bologna', *Studi etruschi* 73, 67–92.

Saulnier, C. 1980. *L'armée et la guerre dans le monde étrusco-romain (VIIIe–IVe s.)*. Paris.

Scalia, F. 1968. 'I cilindretti di tipo chiusino con figure umane', *Studi etruschi* 36, 357–401.

Scanlon, T. F. 1984. *Greek and Roman Athletics. A Bibliography*. Chicago.

Scarfi, B. M. and Tombolani, M. 1985. *Altino preromana e romana*. Piave.

Scavo nello scavo. Gli Etruschi non visti. Ricerche e "riscoperte" nei depositi dei musei archeologici dell'Etruria meridionale (exhibition catalogue, Viterbo 2004). Moretti Sgubini, A. M. (ed.). Rome 2004.

Schäfer, T. 1989. *Imperii Insignia. Sella Curulis und Fasces. Zur Repräsentation römischer Magistrate*. Mainz am Rhein.

Schauenburg, K. 1957. 'Zu Darstellungen aus der Sage des Admet und des Kadmos', *Gymnasium* 64, 210–230.

Schauer, P. 1987. 'Der vierrädrige Wagen in Zeremonialgeschehen und Bestattungsgebrauch der orientalisch-ägäischen Hochkulturen und ihre Randgebiete'. In *Vierrädrige Wagen* 1–23.

Scheffer, C. 2003. 'Dangerous driving: an Etruscan motif against the Greek and Roman background', *Opusucula romana* 28, 47–72.

Schefold, K. 1993. *Götter- und Heldensagen in der früh- und hocharchaischen Kunst*. München.

Schenal Pileggi, R. 2003. In Lissi Caronna, E., Sabbione, C. and Vlad Borelli, L. (eds), *I pinakes di Locri Epizefiri. Musei di Reggio Calabria e di Locri* II. *Atti e memorie della Società Magna Grecia* (Quarta Serie) II, 764–786.

Sciacca, F. and Di Blassi, L. 2003. *La Tomba Calabresi e la Tomba del Tripode di Cerveteri* (Musei Vaticani. Museo Gregoriano Etrusco). Vatican City 2003.

Schlichtherle, H. 2004. 'Wagenfunde aus den Seeufersiedlungen im zirkumalpinen Raum'. In *Rad und Wagen*, 295–314.

Schönfelder, M. 2000. 'Der spätkeltische Wagen von Boé'. In *Zeremonialwagen* 44–58 (first published in *Jahrbuch des Römisch-germanischen Zentralmuseums, Mainz* 46 (1999), 44–58).

Schönfelder, M. 2002. *Das spätkeltische Wagengrab von Boé. Studien zu Wagen und Wagengräber der jüngeren Latènezeit. Römisch-germanisches Zentralmuseum Mainz Monographien* 54. Mainz am Rhein.

Schulman, A. R. 1979. 'Chariots, chariotry, and the Hyksos', *Journal for the Study of Egyptian Antiquities* (Toronto) 10:2, 105–153.

Schumacher, E. 1983. 'Zur Datierung, Einordnung und Gliederung der Felsbilder der Valcamonica', *Prähistorische Zeitschrift* 58, 61–88.

Scripta prehistorica in honorem Biba Teržan. Blečič, V. M. *et al.* (eds). *Situla* 44. Ljubliana.

Schwartz, A. 2009. *Reinstating the Hoplite. Arms, Armour and Phalanx Fighting in Archaic and Classical Greece*. Berlin.

Secondo congresso internazionale etrusco (Florence 1985) I–III. *Supplemento di Studi etruschi*. Rome, 1989.

Sestieri, P. C. 1958. 'Tomba a camera d'età lucana', *Bollettino d'arte* 43(Serie 4), 46–63.

Sestieri, P. C. 1959. 'A new painted tomb at Paestum', *Archaeology* 12, 33–37.

Seubers, J. F. 2008. 'A key to the coffin. A model to assess social change in Villanovan tombs from Veii, Tarquinia and Verucchio (950 to 700 BC)', *Bulletin Antieke Beschaving* 83, 1–16.

Sgubini Moretti, A. M. 1992. 'Pitino. Necropoli di Monte Penna: tomba 31'. In *La civiltà picena nelle Marche*, 178–203.

Sgubini Moretti, A. M. and Ricciardi, L. 1993. 'Le terrecotte architettoniche di Tuscania'. In *Deliciae Fictiles* I, 163–181.

Sherratt, A. 2004. 'Wagen, Plug, Rind: ihre Ausbreitung und Nutzung – Probleme der Quelleninterpretation'. In *Rad und Wagen* 409–428.

Sherratt, A. 2006. 'Animal traction and the transformation of Europe'. In Arbogast, M., Ptrequin, A.-M., van Willegen, S. and Bailly, M. (eds), *La traction animale et la transformation de l'Europe néolitique*. Paris, 329–360.

Signori di Maremma (exhibition catalogue, Firenze 2010). Celuzza, M. and Cianferoni, G. C. (eds). Florence 2010.

Simon, E. 2006. 'Stele eines daunischen Kriegers in Kioto'. In *ΑΕΙΜΝΗΣΤΟΣ* I, 240–245.

Singor, H. W. 1998. *Oorsprong en betekenis van de hoplietenphalanx in het Archaïsche Griekenland* (doctoral thesis, Leiden).

Sion, J. 1935. 'Quelques problèmes de transport dans l'antiquité: le point de vue d'un géographe mediterranéen', *Annales d'histoire économique et sociale* 7, 628–633.

Sirano, F. 1995. 'Il sostegno bronzeo della tomba 104 del Fondo Artiaco di Cuma e il "problema" dell'origine dell'holmos'. In *Studie sulla Campania preromama* 1–50.

Smith, C. 1894. 'Polledrara ware', *Journal of Hellenic Studies* 14, 206–223.

Smith, C. J. 1996. *Early Rome and Latium*. Oxford.

Snead, S. 1989. *Animals in Four Worlds. Sculptures from India*. Chicago–London.

Snodgrass, A. 1996. 'Iron'. In *Knossos North Cemetery* II, 575–597.

Sommella, P. 1971–1972. 'Heroon di Enea a Lavinium. Recenti scavi a Pratica di Mare'. In *Atti della Pontificia Academia romana di archeologia. Rendiconti* 44, 47–74.

Sommella Mura, A. 1997–1998. 'Le recenti scoperti sul Campodoglio e la fondazione del tempio di Giove Capitolino', *Atti della Pontificia Academia romana di archeologia, Rendiconti* 70, 59–79.

Spadea, R. 1994. 'Il tesoro di Hera', *Bollettino d'arte* 88, 1–34.

Spadea, R. 1997. 'Santuari di Hera a Crotone'. In de la Genière, J. (ed.), *Héra. Images, espaces, cultus. Collection du Centre Jean Bérard* 15. Naples, 235–251.

Spectacles sportifs et scéniques dans le monde étrusco-italique. Collection de l'École française de Rome 172. Rome 1993.

Spence, I. G. 1993. *The Cavalry of Classical Greece. A Social and Military History with Particular Reference to Athens*. Oxford.

Spivey, N. J. 1987. *The Micali Painter and his Followers*. Oxford Monographs in Classical Archaeology. Oxford.

Spivey, N. J. and Stoddart, S. 1990. *Etruscan Italy. An Archaeological History*. London.

Sprenger, M. and Bartoloni, G. 1990. *Die Etrusker. Kunst und Geschichte* (photographs by Hirmer, M. and A.). Munich.

Spruytte, J. 1978. 'L'attelage sportif. Quadrige de course'. *Plaisirs équestres* 102 (novembre-décembre), 418–424.

Spruytte, J. 1983a. *Early Harness Systems. Experimental Studies. A Contribution to the History of the Horse*. London.

Spruytte, J. 1983b. 'La conduite du cheval chez l'archer assyrien', *Plaisirs équestres* 129 (mai–juin), 66–71.

Spruytte, J. 1993. 'Le trige de guerre assyrien au IXe siècle avant J.C.', *Préhistoire anthropologie méditerranéenne* 2, 193–200.

Spruytte, J. 1994. Étude technologique. La roue du char royal assyrien', *Revue d'Assyriologie* 88, 37–48.

Spruytte, J. 1996. *Attelages antiques libyens. Archéologie saharienne expérimentale. Collection archéologie expérimentale et ethnographie des techniques* 2. Paris.

Spruytte, J. 1997. L'aggiogamento degli equini nel mondo antico. Aspetti tecnici generali'. In *Carri da guerra*, 69–72.

Staccioli, R. 2003. *Strade romane*. Rome.

Stary, P. F. 1977. 'Keltische Waffen auf der Apennin-Halbinsel', *Germania* 57, 99–110.

Stary, P. F. 1979. 'Foreign elements in Etruscan arms and armour: 8th to 3rd centuries BC', *Proceeedings of the Prehistoric Society* 45, 179–206.

Stary, P. F. 1980. 'Zur Bedeutung und Funktion zweirädrigen Wagen während der Eisenzeit in Mittelitalien', *Hamburger Beiträge zur Archäologie* 7, 7–21.

Stary, P. F. 1981a. *Zur eisenzeitlichen Bewaffnung und Kampfesweise in Mittelitalien, ca. 9. bis 6. Jh. v.Chr. Marburger Studien zur Vor- und Frühgeschichte* 3. Mainz am Rhein.

Stary, P. F. 1981b. 'Ursprung und Ausbreitung der eisenzeitlichen Ovalbuckelschilde mit Spindelbuckel', *Germania* 59, 287–306.

Stary, P. F. 1981c. 'Orientalische und griechische Einflüsse in der etruskischen Bewaffnung und Kampfweise'. In *Die Aufnahme fremder Kultureinflüsse in Etrurien und das Problem des Retardierens in der etruskischen Kunst. Schriften der deutschen Archäologen-Verbandes* 5. Mannheim, 25–40.

Stary, P. F. 1986–1987. 'Die militärischen Rückwirkungen der keltischen Invasion auf die Apennin-Halbinsel', *Hamburger Beiträge zur Archäologie* 13/14, 65–117.

Stary, P. F. 1989. 'Eisenzeitliche Wagengräber auf der iberischen Halbinsel', *Madrider Mitteilungen* 30, 151–183.

Stary, P. F. 1990. 'Keltische Einflüsse im Kampfwesen der Etrusker und benachbarter Völker'. In *Die Welt der Etrusker. Internationales Kolloquium*, 59–66.

Stary, P. F. 1994. *Zur Eisenzeitlichen Bewaffnung und Kampfesweise der Iberischen Halbinsel*. Berlin–New York.

Stary, P. F. 2000. 'Early Iron Age armament and warfare'. In *Ancient Italy in its Mediterranean Setting*, 209–220.

Stary-Rimpau, J. 1988. *Die Bologneser Stelen des 7. bis 4. Jh. v.Chr. Kleine Schriften aus dem vorgeschichtlichen Seminar der Phillips-Universität Marburg* 24. Marburg.

Stead, I. M. 1965. 'The Celtic chariot', *Antiquity* 39, 259–265.

Stead, I. M. 1984. 'Cart burials in Britain'. In *Keltski Voz*, 31–40.

Stead, I. M. 1991. *Iron Age Cemeteries in East Yorkshire. Excavations at Burton Fleming, Rudston, Garton-on-the-Wolds, and Kirkburn. English Heritage Archaeological Report* 22. London.

Steingräber, S. 1979. *Etruskische Möbel. Archaeologica* 9. Rome.

Steingräber, S. 1985. *Etruskische Wandmalerei*. Stuttgart–Zürich.

Steingräber, S. 2006. *Abundance of Life. Etruscan Wall Painting* (J. Paul Getty Museum). Los Angeles.

Steinhart, M. 1990. 'Eine Kleeblattkanne der Memnon-Gruppe', *Archäologischer Anzeiger*, 487–494.

Stenico, A. 1963. *Roman and Etruscan Painting*. New York.

Stewart, A. 1990. *Greek Sculpture. An Exploration*. New Haven–London.

Stibbe-Twiest, A. G. E. 1977. 'The Moon-goddess from Chianciano Terme', *Mededeelingen van het Nederlands Historisch Instituut te Rome* 39, 19–28.

Stoop, M. W. 1970–1971. 'Santuario di Athena sul Timpone

della Motta. I – Bronzi, II – Terrecotte e ceramica'. In *Atti e memorie della Società Magna Grecia* (Nuove Serie) 11–12, 37–66.

Strade degli Etruschi. Vie e mezzie di communicazione nell'antica Etruria. Cristofani, M. (ed.). Milan 1985.

Strandberg Olofsson, M. 2006. 'Herakles rivisited. On the interpretation of the mould-made architectural terracottas from Acquarossa'. In *Deliciae Fictiles* III, 122–129.

Strøm, I. 1971. *Problems Concerning the Origin and Early Development of the Etruscan Orientalizing Style. Odense University Classical Studies* 2. Odense.

Studi in onore di L. Banti. Rome.

Studniczka, F. 1907. 'Der Rennwagen im syrisch-phönikischen Gebiet', *Jahrbuch des Deutschen Archäologischen Instituts* 22, 147–196.

Szilágyi, J. G. 1981. 'Impletae modis saurae', *Prospettiva* 24, 2–23.

Szilágyi, J. G. 1992. *Ceramica etrusco-corinzia figurata* I. *630–580 a.C. Monumenti etruschi* 7. Florence.

Tagliente, M. 1994. 'Brocchetta indigena'. In *Armi*, 79–81.

Talocchini, A. 1963. 'La città e la necropoli di Vetulonia secondo i nuovo scavi (1959–62), *Studi etruschi* 31, 435–451.

Tassi Scandone, E. 2001. *Verghe, scuri e fasci littori in Etruria. Contributi allo studio degli Insignia Imperii.* Pisa–Rome.

Il tempio arcaico di Caprifico di Torrecchia (Cisterna Latina) i materiali e il contesto. Palombi, D. (ed.). Rome 2010.

Le Terramare. La più antica civiltà padana (exhibition catalogue, Modena, 1997). Bernabò Brea, M., Cardarelli, A. and Cremaschi, M. (eds). Milan 1997.

Teržan, B. 1997. 'Heros der Hallstattzeit. Beobachtungen zum Status an Gräbern aus das Caput Adriae'. In Becker, C., Dunkelmann, M.-L., Metzner-Nebelsick, C., Peter-Röcher, H., Roeder, M. and Teržan, B. (eds), *ΧΡΟΝΟΣ. Beiträge zur prähistorischen Archäologie zwischen Nord- und Südeuropa. Festschrift für Bernard Hänsel.* Espelkamp, 653–669.

Il tesoro di Hera. Scoperte nel santuario di Hera Lacinia a Capo Colonna di Crotone (exhibition catalogue, Rome 1996). Spadea, R. (ed.). Milan 1996.

Thiermann, E. 2009. *Capua – Grab und Gemeinschaft. Eine kontextuelle Analyse der Nekropole Fornaci (570–400 v.Chr.)* (doctoral thesis, University of Amsterdam).

Thuillier, J. P. 1975. 'Denys d'Halicarnasse et les jeux romains (*Antiquités romaines* VII, 72–73)', *Mélanges de l'École française de Rome* 87, 563–581.

Thuillier, J. P. 1976. 'La frise gravée du lébès Barone de Capoue'. In *L'Italie préromaine et la Rome républicaine. Mélanges offerts à J. Heurgon. Collection de l'École française de Rome* 27. Rome, 981–990.

Thuillier, J. P. 1985. *Les jeux athlétiques dans la civilisation étrusque. Bibliothèque des l'École françaises d'Athènes et de Rome* 256. Rome.

Thuillier, J. P. 1987. 'Le programme hippique des jeux romains: une curieuse absence', *Revue des études latines* 65, 53–73.

Thuillier, J. P. 1990. 'L'organisation et le financement des *ludi circenses* au début de la République: modèle grec ou modèle étrusque?'. In *Crise et transformation*, 358–372.

Thuillier, J. P. 1992. 'L'aurige Ratumena: histoire et légende'. In *La Rome des premiers siècles. Légende et histoire* (Actes de la Table Ronde en l'honneur de M. Pallottino, Paris 1990). Florence, 247–255.

Thuillier, J. P. 1993. 'Les représentations sportifs dans l'oeuvre du Peintre de Micali'. In *Spectacles sportifs*, 21–44.

Thuillier, J. P. 1997a. 'Un relief archaïque inédit de Chiusi', *Revue archéologique*, 243–260.

Thuillier, J. P. 1997b. 'Le Tombe des Olympiades de Tarquinia ou les jeux étrusques ne sont pas les concours grecs', *Nikephoros* 10, 257–264.

Das Tier in der Antike (exhibition catalogue, Zürich 1974). Zürich 1974.

La Tomba François di Vulci (exhibition catalogue, Vatican City 1987). Buranelli, F. (ed.). *Monumenti Musei e Gallerie Pontifice.* Rome 1987.

La tombe princière de Vix. Rolley, C. (ed.). Paris 2003.

Tomei, M. A. 1997. *Museo Palatino* (Soprindendenza archeologica di Roma). Milan.

Toms, J. 1998. 'The construction of gender in Early Iron Age Etruria'. In Whitehouse, R. D. (ed.), *Gender and Italian Archaeology. Challenging the Stereotypes. Accordia Specialist Studies on Italy* 7. London, 157–179.

Torbrügge, W. 1992. 'Bemerkungen zur Kunst, die Situlenkunst zu deuten'. In Metzger, I. R. and Gleirscher, P. (eds), *Die Räter – I Reti.* Bolzano, 581–609.

Torelli, M. 1988. *Die Etrusker.* Frankfurt–New York.

Torelli, M. 1992. 'I fregi figurati delle "*regiae*" latine ed etrusche. Imaginario del potere arcaico', *Ostraka* 1, 249–274 (reprinted in Torelli 1997, 87–121).

Torelli, M. 1996. 'Rango e ritualità nell'iconografia italica più antica', *Ostraka* 5, 333–368 (reprinted in Torelli 1997, 13–51).

Torelli, M. 1997. *Il rango, il mito e l'immagine. Alle origini della rappresentazione storica romana.* Milan.

Torelli, M. 2001. '*Lares, maiores, summi viri.* Percorsi dell'imagine eroica a Roma e nell'Italia antica'. In Couday, M. and Späth, T. (eds), *L'invention des grands hommes dans la Rome antique.* Paris, 309–320.

Torelli, M. 2002. 'Ideologia e paesaggi delle morte in Etruria tra arcaismo ed età ellenistica'. In Colpo, I., Favaretto, I. and Ghedini, F. (eds), *Iconografia 2001. Studi sull'imagine* (Atti del convegno, Padua 2001). *Antenor Quaderni* 1. Rome.

Torelli, M. 2006. '*Insignia Imperii.* La genesi dei simboli del potere nel mondo etrusco e romano', *Ostraka* 15, 407–430.

Tovoli, S. 1989. *Il sepolcreto villanoviano Benacci Caprara di Bologna.* Bologna.

Toynbee, J. M. C. 1973. *Animals in Roman Life and Art.* London.

Tsujimura, S. 1991. 'Ruts in Pompeii – The traffic system in the Roman city', *Opuscula Pompeiana* 1, 58–86.

Tziafalias, A. 1978. 'Ἀνασκαφικὲς ερεύνες στον Ἁγιον Γεόργιο Λάρισας', *Athens Annals of Archaeology* 11, 156–182.

Tziafalias, A. 1994. 'Ἅγιος Γεόργιος Λάρισας'. In *Thessalia* II. Athens, 179–188.

Vallarino, G. 2006. 'Le indagini nel portico orientale del santuario repubblicano a *Trebula Mutuesca* (*Terzo incontro di studi sul Lazio e la Sabina*, Rome 2004), *Lazio e Sabina* 3, 85–92.

Van Berg-Osterrieth, M. 1972. *Les chars préhistoriques du Val Camonica. Centro Camuno di studi preistoriche, Archivi* 3. Capo di Ponte (Brescia).

Van Buren, E. D. 1921. *Figurative Revetments in Etruria and Latium in the VI. and V. Centuries.* London.

Van Endert, D. 1987. *Die Wagenbestattungen der späten Hallstattzeit und der La Tènezeit im Gebiet westlich des Rheins.* BAR International Series 355. Oxford.

Van Hoorn, G. 1951. *Choes and Anthesteria.* Leiden.

Van Leusen, M. 1989. *Roman Vehicles* (MA thesis, University of Amsterdam).

Van Tilburg, C. 2005. *Romeins verkeer. Weggebruik en verkeersdrukte in het Romeinse rijk.* Amsterdam.

Van Tilburg, C. 2007. *Traffic and Congestion in the Roman Empire.* London.

Van Wees, H. 1994. 'The Homeric way of war: The *Iliad* and the hoplite phalanx (I–II)', *Greece and Rome* 41, 1–18, 131–155.

Van Wees, H. 2000. 'The development of the hoplite phalanx: iconography and reality in the seventh century'. In Van Wees, H. (ed.), *War and Violence in Ancient Greece.* London and Swansea, 125–166.

Van Wees, H. 2004. *Greek Warfare. Myths and Realities.* London.

Van der Meer, L. B. 1986. 'Greek and local elements in a sporting scene by the Micali Painter'. In *Italian Iron Age Artefacts*, 439–446.

Van der Meer, L. B. 2004. *Myths and More. On Etruscan Stone Sarcophagi.* Leuven.

Verger, S. 1996. 'Une tombe à char oubliée dans l'ancienne collection Poinchy de Richebourg'. *Mélanges de l'École française de Rome* 108, 641–669.

Versnel, H. S. 1970. *Triumphus. An Inquiry into the Origin, Development and Meaning of the Roman Triumph.* Leiden.

Vierrädrige Wagen der Hallstattzeit. Untersuchungen zu Geschichte und Technik. Römisch-germanisches Zentralmuseum Monographien 12. Mainz am Rhein 1987.

Vighi, R. 1931–39. 'Le terracotte templari di Caere', *Studi etruschi* 5, 105–146.

Vighi, R. and Minissi, F. 1955. *Il nuove Museo di Villa Giulia.* Rome.

Vigneron, P. 1968. *Le cheval dans l'antiquité gréco-romaine* I–II. Nancy.

Villa, C. 1995. *Le strade consolari di Roma.* Rome.

Vinattieri, V. 1948–49. 'Per la forma, la tecnicà e la destinazione dei cosidetti "incensieri di tipo vetuloniese"', *Studi etruschi* 20, 199–214.

Vogel, L. 1969, 'Circus race scenes in the early Roman empire', *Art Bulletin* 51, 156–159.

Von Bothmer, D. 1985. *The Amasis Painter and his World.* Malibu–New York–London.

Von Freytag gen. Löringhoff, B. 1986. *Das Giebelrelief von Telamon und seine Stellung innerhalb der Ikonographie der "Sieben gegen Theben". Römische Mitteilungen*, Ergänzungsheft 27. Mainz

Von Hagen, V. 1978. *Le grandi strade di Roma del mondo* (2nd edn). Rome.

Von Hase, F. W. 1969. *Die Trensen der Früheisenzeit in Italien. Prähistorische Bronzefunde* XVI.1. Munich.

Von Hase, F. W. 1989. 'Etrurien und das Gebiet nordwärts der Alpen in der ausgehenden Urnenfelder- und frühen Hallstattzeit'. In *Secondo congresso internazionale etrusco* II, 1031–1061.

Von Hase, F. W. 1992. 'Etrurien und Mitteleuropa -zur Bedeutung der ersten italisch-etruskischen Funde der späten Urnenfelder- und frühen Hallstattzeit in Zentraleuropa'. In *Etrusker nördlich von Etrurien*, 235–266.

Von Hase, F. W. 1995. 'Ägäische, griechische und vorderorientalische Einflüsse auf das tyrrhenische Mittelitalien'. In *Beiträge zur Urnenfelderzeit nordlich und südlich der Alpen. Römisch-germanisches Zentralmuseum Monographien* 35. Bonn, 239–286.

Von Mehren, M. 1993. 'The Murlo frieze plaques. Considerations of their distribution and number'. In *Deliciae Fictiles* I, 139–145.

Von Mehren, M. 1997. 'Composite motifs on Etruscan frieze plaques – a local and foreign phenomenon'. In *Deliciae Fictiles* II, 219–227.

Von Mercklin, E. 1916. 'New representations of chariots on Attic Geometric vases', *American Journal of Archaeology* 20, 397–406.

Von Mercklin, E. 1933. 'Wagenschmuck aus der römischen Kaiserzeit', *Jahrbuch des Deutschen Archäologischen Instituts* 48, 84–177.

Waarsenburg, D. J. 1995. *The Northwest Necropolis of Satricum. An Iron Age Cemetery in Latium Vetus. Satricum* III. *Scrinium* VIII. Amsterdam.

Walde-Psenner, E. 1982. 'Das Wagenrelief von Maria Saal'. In *Festschrift zum 50 jährigen Bestehen des Institutes für Ur- und Frühgeschichte der Leopold-Franzes-Universität Innsbruck*, 623–627.

Walters, H. B. 1899. *Catalogue of the Bronzes (Greek, Roman and Etruscan) in the Department of Greek and Roman Antiquities of in the British Museum.* London.

Walters, H. B. 1903. *Catalogue of Terracottas in the British Museum.* London.

Ward Perkins, J. B. 1957. 'Etruscan and Roman roads in southern Etruria', *Journal of Roman Studies* 47, 139–143.

Ward Perkins, J. B. 1962. 'Etruscan engineering: road-building, water-supply and drainage'. In Renard, M. (ed.), *Hommages à Albert Grenier* 1. *Collection Latomus* 58. Brussels–Berchem, 1636–1643.

Warden, P. G. 1977. 'A decorated terracotta stand from Poggio Civitate (Murlo)', *Römische Mitteilungen* 84, 199–210.

Weber, W. 1978. *Die Darstellungen einer Wagenfahrt auf römischen Sarkophagdeckeln und Loculusplatten der 3. und 4. Jahrhunderts n.Chr.* Rome.

Weber, W. 1979. 'Die Reliquienprozession auf der Elfenbeintafel des Trierer Domschatz und das kaiserliche Hofzeremoniell', *Trierer Zeitschrift* 42, 135–151.

Weber, W. 1983. 'Das Ehrenrecht des Wagenfahrens in römischen Städten'. In *Spätantike und frühes Christentum* (exhibition catalogue, Frankfurt 1983–1984). Frankfurt, 308–311.

Weber, W. 1986. 'Der Wagen in Italien und in den römischen Provinzen'. In *Achse, Rad und Wagen*, 85–108.

Weber, W. 1991. 'Die Wagen in der spätantiken Repräsentation', *Achse, Rad und Wagen. Beiträge zur Geschichte der Landfahrzeuge* 1, 14–20.

Weege, F. 1909. 'Oskische Grabmalerei', *Jahrbuch des Deutschen Archäologischen Instituts* 24, 99–162.

Wegener Sleeswyk, A. 1987a. 'Pre-stressed wheels in ancient Egypt', *Antiquity* 61, 90–96.

Wegener Sleeswyk, A. 1987b. 'A Scandinavian wagon construction', *Antiquity* 61, 416–423.

Wegener Sleeswyk, A. 1992a. *Wielen, wagens en koetsen.* Leeuwarden.

Wegener Sleeswyk, A. 1992b. 'The development of the earliest wheels: a viewpoint', *Polhem. Tidskrift für Teknikhistoria* 10, 109–130.

Die Welt der Etrusker. Archäologische Denkmäler aus Museen der sozialistischen Länder (exhibition catalogue, East Berlin). Schade, S. (ed.). Berlin 1988.

Die Welt der Etrusker. Internationales Kolloquium. Heres, H. and Kunze, M. (eds). Berlin 1990.

Werner, W. M. 1988. *Eisenzeitliche Trensen an der unteren und mittleren Donau. Prähistorische Bronzefunde* XVI.4. Munich.

Wheeling the Challenges of Animal Traction. Starkey, P. and Kaumbutho, P. (eds). London.

White, K. D. 1970. *Roman Farming.* London.

White, K. D. 1984. *Greek and Roman Technology.* London.

Whitley, J. 2005. 'Archaeology in Greece 2004–2005'. In *Archaeological Reports* 2004–2005, 1–118.

Whitley, J. 2006. 'Archaeology in Greece 2005–2006'. In *Archaeological Reports* 2005–2006, 1–112.

Wiesner, J. 1968. *Fahren und Reiten. Archäologia Homerica* I, F. Göttingen.

Wildhaber, R. 1979. 'Bauerliche Bremsenvorrichtungen an Wagen und Schlitten'. In Fenton, A., Podolàk, J. and Rassmussen, H. (eds), *Land Transport in Europe.* Copenhagen, 488–513.

Winghart, S. 1999. 'Die Wagengräber von Poing und Hart a.d. Alz. Evidenz und Ursachen spätbronzezeitlicher Elitenbildung in der Zone nordwärts der Alpen'. In *Eliten in der Bronzezeit* 533–563.

Winter, F. 1908. *Altertümer von Pergamon* VII.2. *Die Skulpturen mit Ausnahme des Altarreliefs.* Berlin.

Winter, N. A. 1993. *Greek Architectural Terracottas from the Prehistoric to the Archaic Period.* Oxford.

Winter, N. A. 2005. 'Gods walking on the roof: the evolution of terracotta statuary in Archaic Etruscan architecture in light of the kings of Rome', *Journal of Roman Archaeology* 18, 241–251.

Winter, N. A. 2006. 'Il tetto di Caprifico a confronto', *Archeologia classica* 57, 530–535.

Winter, N. A. 2009. *Symbols of Wealth and Power. Architectural Terracotta Decoration in Etruria and Central Italy, 640–510 BC. Memoirs of the American Academy in Rome* Supplement 9. Ann Arbor.

Winter, N. A. 2010. 'The Caprifico roof in its wider context.' In *Il tempio arcaico di Caprifico di Torrecchia*, 113–131.

Winther, H. C. 1997. 'Princely tombs of the Orientalizing Period in Etruria and Latium Vetus'. In Damgaard Andersen, H., Hornæs, H., Houby-Nielsen, S. and Rathje, A. (eds), *Urbanisation in the Mediterranean in the 9th to 6th Centuries BC. Acta Hyberborea* 7, 423–446.

Woytowitsch, E. 1978. *Die Wagen der Bronze- und frühen Eisenzeit in Italien. Prähistorische Bronzefunde* XVII.1. Munich.

Wrede, W. 1916. 'Kriegers Ausfahrt in der archaisch-griechischen Kunst, *Athenische Mitteilungen* 41, 221–374.

Yalouri, A. 1971. 'A hero's departure', *American Journal of Archaeology* 75, 269–275.

Yalouri, A. 1972. 'Χάλκα ελάσματα μετα φυτικῶν κοςμίματων', *Archaiologiki Ephemeris*, 113–126.

Zaccagnino, C. 2006. 'Una tomba con carro nell'Apennnino tosco-emiliano. Recupero di un rinvenimento settecentesco', *Mélanges de l'École française de Rome* 118, 215–236.

Zaghetto, L. 2006. 'La ritualità nella prima arte delle situle'. In Von Eles, P. (ed.), *La ritualità funeraria tra età del ferro e orientalizzante in Italia.* Pisa-Rome, 41–55.

Zampieri, G. 1983. Nuova stele paleoveneta patavina di epoca romana', *Bollettino del Museo Civico di Padova* 72, 23–154.

Zampieri, G. 1988. 'Un'altra stele paleoveneta patavina ritrovato presso Camin'. In *Atti e memorie dell' Academia patavina di scienze, lettere ed arti* 99 (1986–1987). Parte II. *Classe di scienze morali, lettere ed arti.* Padua, 133–155.

Zampieri, G. 1994. *Il Museo Archeologico di Padova. Dal*

Palazzo della Ragione al Museo agli Eremitani. Storia della formazione del Museo Civico Archeologico di Padova e guida alle collezioni. Milan.

Zampieri, G. 1999. 'La stele 608 del Museo Maffeiano di Verona'. In *Protostoria e storia del "Venetorum angulus". Atti del XX convegno di studie etruschi ed italici* (Porgnano–Quanto d'Altino–Este–Adria 1996). Pisa–Rome, 267–285.

Zancani Montuoro, P. 1955. 'La teogamia di Locri Epizefiri', *Archivio storico per la Calabria e la Lucania* 24, 283–308.

Zancani Montuoro, P. 1996. 'I pinakes di Lokri'. In *Atti e memorie della Società Magna Grecia* (Terza Serie III, 1994–1995), 153–261.

Zeremonialwagen. Statussymbole eisenzeitlicher Eliten. Mainz am Rhein 2000 (reprinted from *Jahrbuch des Römisch-germanischen Zentralmuseums, Mainz* 46 (1999), 3–59).

Zaphiropoulou, P. N. 2006. 'Geometric battle scenes on vases from Paros'. In *Pictorial Pursuits* 271–277.

Zarins, J. 1986. 'Equids associated with human burials in third millennium BC Mesoptamia: two complementary facts'. In *Equids from the Ancient Word* I, 164–193.

Zevi, F. 1969. 'Nuovi vasi del Pittore della Sfinge Bardatuta', *Studi etruschi* 38, 39–58.

Zevi, F. 1975. 'Tomba a fossa n. 15'. In 'Castel di Decima (Roma). La necropoli arcaica', *Notizie degli scavi di antichità* (Serie 8), 29, 251–294.

Zevi, F. 1995. 'Demarato e i re "corinzi" di Roma'. In *L'incidenza dell'antico. Studi in memoria di Ettore Lepore* 1. (*Atti del convegno internazionale*, Anacapri 1991). Storchi Marino, A. (ed.). Naples, 291–314.

Züchner, Ch. 2004. 'Frühbronzezeitliche Wagen und Transportmittel in der Felskunst Süd- und Südwesteuropas'. In *Rad und Wagen*, 399–408.

Zweierlei-Diehl, E. (see also Diehl, E.) 1969. *Antike Gemmen in Deutschen Sammlungen* II. *Berlin*. Munich.

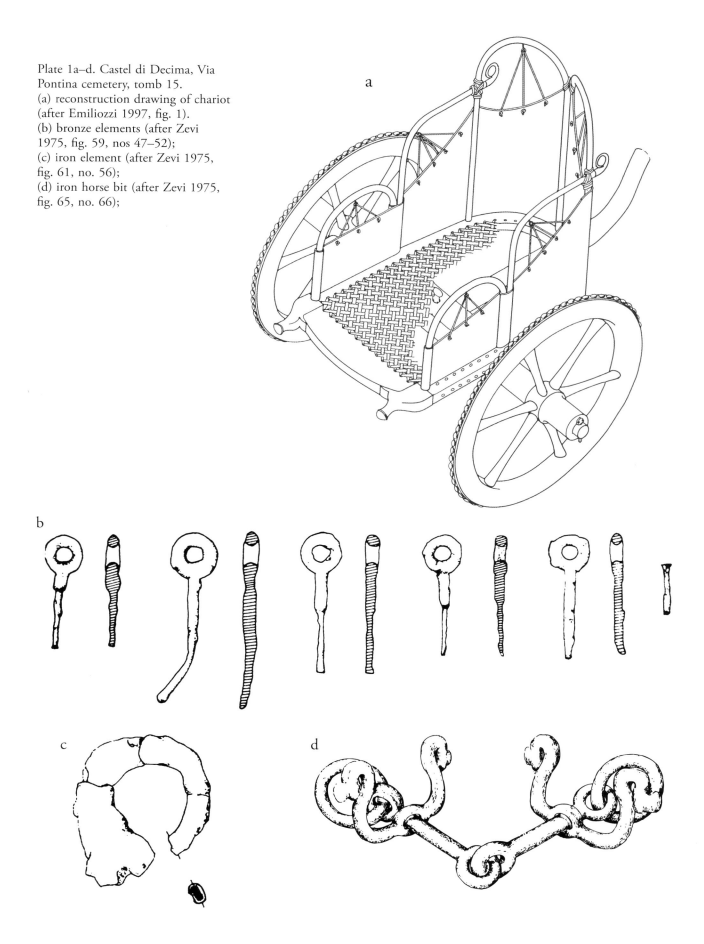

Plate 1a–d. Castel di Decima, Via Pontina cemetery, tomb 15.
(a) reconstruction drawing of chariot (after Emiliozzi 1997, fig. 1).
(b) bronze elements (after Zevi 1975, fig. 59, nos 47–52);
(c) iron element (after Zevi 1975, fig. 61, no. 56);
(d) iron horse bit (after Zevi 1975, fig. 65, no. 66);

a

b

c

d

Plate 2a–c. Chariot, as reconstructed, from Vulci, Osteria cemetery, Tomba del Carro. Rome, Museo Nazionale di Villa Giulia 84877 (after *Carri da guerra* 149f., figs 16, 13, 15).

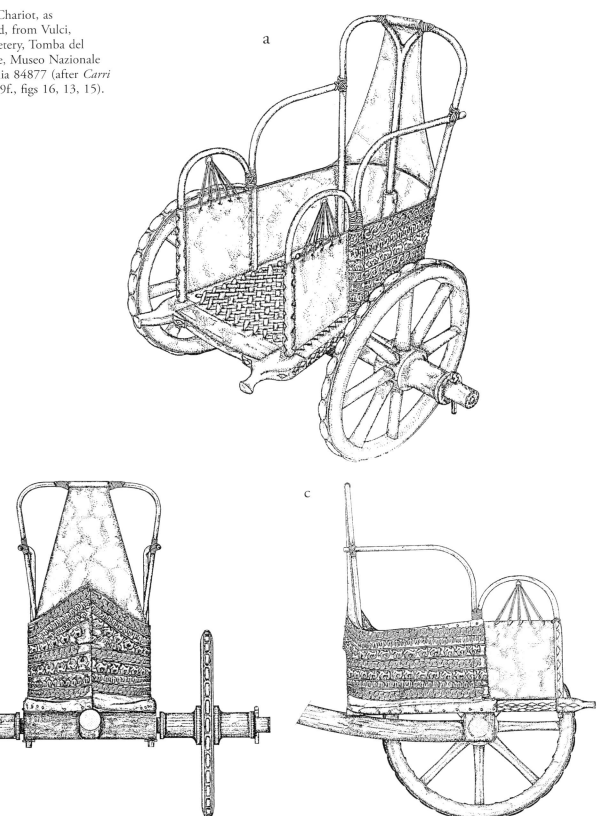

a

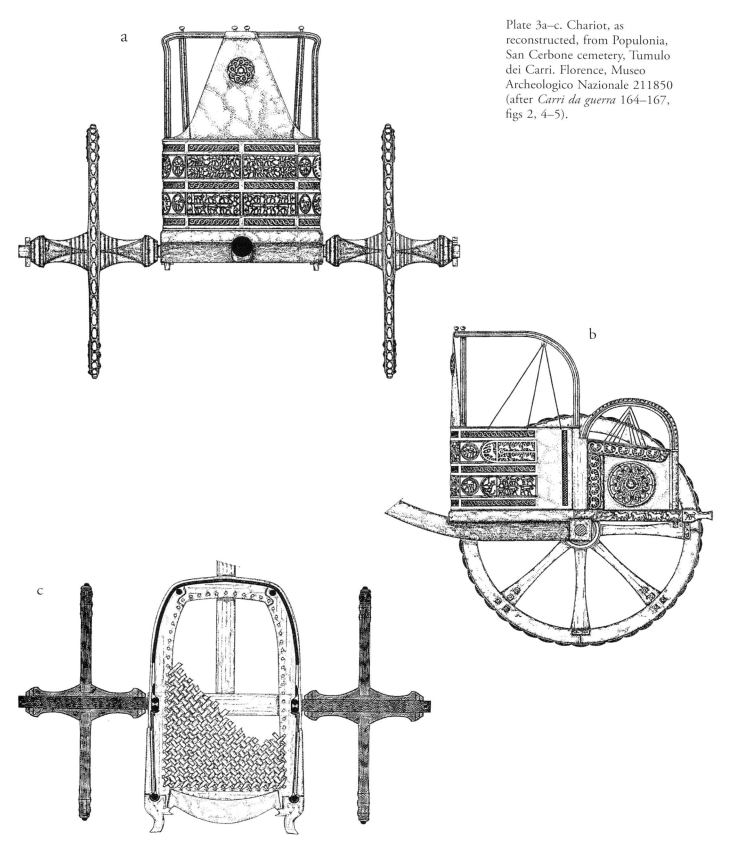

Plate 3a–c. Chariot, as reconstructed, from Populonia, San Cerbone cemetery, Tumulo dei Carri. Florence, Museo Archeologico Nazionale 211850 (after *Carri da guerra* 164–167, figs 2, 4–5).

b

c

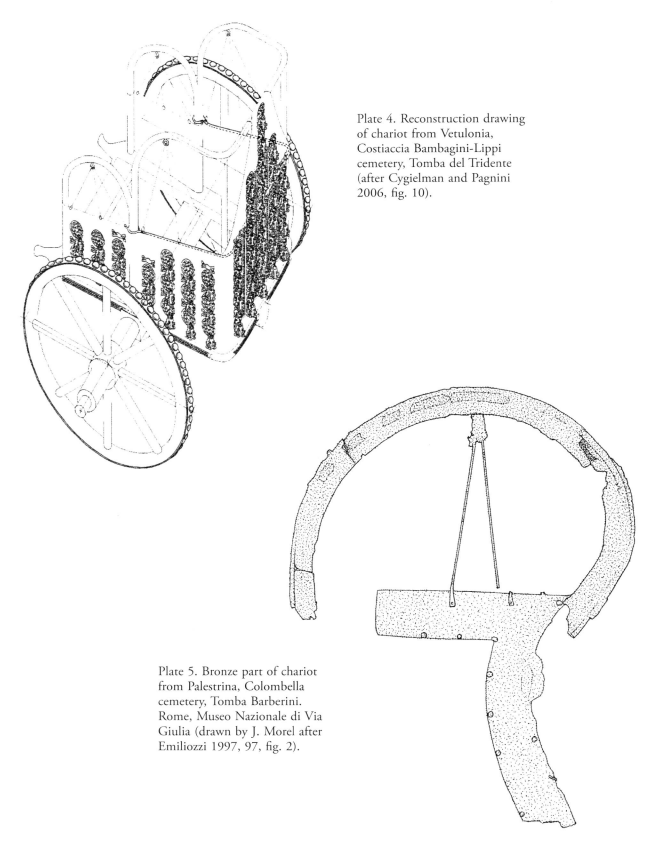

Plate 4. Reconstruction drawing of chariot from Vetulonia, Costiaccia Bambagini-Lippi cemetery, Tomba del Tridente (after Cygielman and Pagnini 2006, fig. 10).

Plate 5. Bronze part of chariot from Palestrina, Colombella cemetery, Tomba Barberini. Rome, Museo Nazionale di Via Giulia (drawn by J. Morel after Emiliozzi 1997, 97, fig. 2).

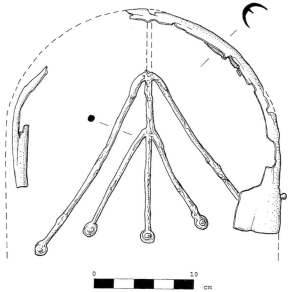

Plate 6. Iron parts of chariot from Matelica, Crocifisso cemetery, tomb 182 (drawn by J. Morel after *Potere e splendore* ill. of cat. no. 316).

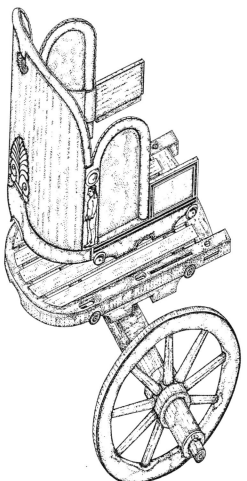

Plate 7. Chariot, as restored, from Ischia di Castro, Poggi di Castro cemetery, Tomba della Biga. Rome, Museo Nazionale di Villa Giulia (after *Carri da guerra* 204, fig. 1).

a

Plate 8a–c. Chariot from Monteleone di Spoleto, Colle del
Capitano cemetery, Tomba del Carro. New York, Metropolitan
Museum of Art, Rogers Fund, 1903, 03.23.1.
(a) as presently restored (museum photograph);
(b–c) reconstruction drawings (after *Carri da guerra* 184f.,
figs 3, 4, right).

b

c

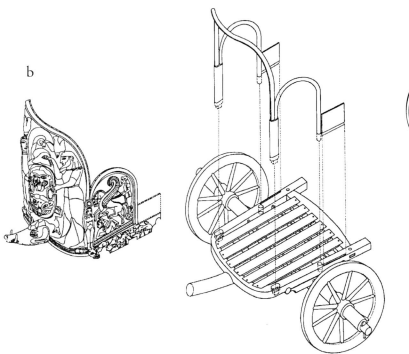

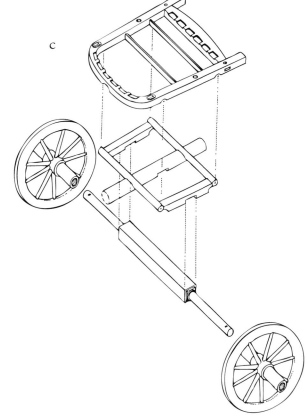

a

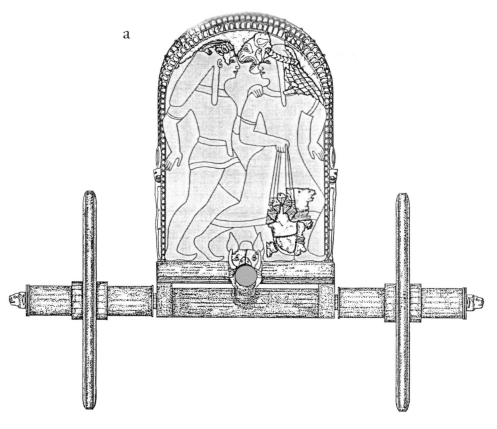

b

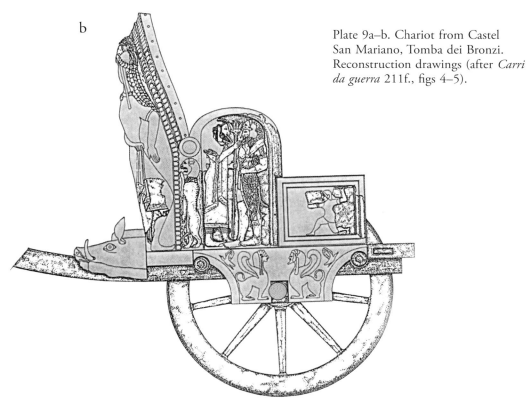

Plate 9a–b. Chariot from Castel San Mariano, Tomba dei Bronzi. Reconstruction drawings (after *Carri da guerra* 211f., figs 4–5).

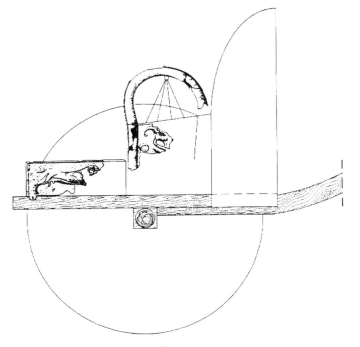

0   50 cm

Plate 10. Bronze part of chariot
(the Dutuit chariot) from Capua,
Quattordici Ponti cemetery, Tomba
Dutuit. Paris, Petit Palais ADUT00157
(after Emiliozzi 2006, pl. 26).

Plate 11. Chariot, as restored, from
Cerveteri, Sorbo cemetery, Tomba
Regolini Galassi. Vatican, Museo
Gregoriano Etrusco 15037 (museum
photograph).

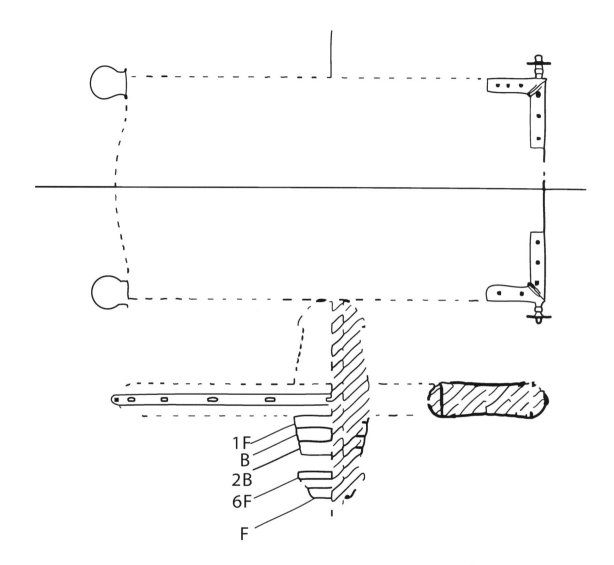

1F
B
2B
6F

F

Plate 12. Reconstruction drawing of parts of chariot from Vetulonia, Acquastrini cemetery, Tomba del Littore. Florence, Museo Archeologico Nazionale 8597–8598 (after *Carri da guerra* 268, fig. 5).

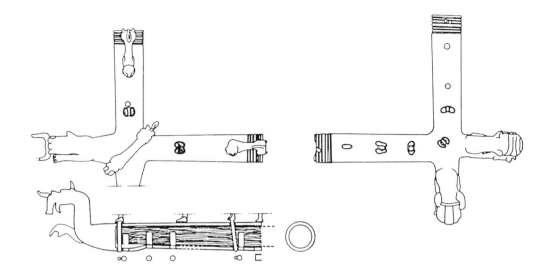

Plate 13. Bronze angle-socket from Palestrina, Chiesa di San Rocco cemetery, Tomba Bernardini
(after Emiliozzi 1997, fig. 5, above).

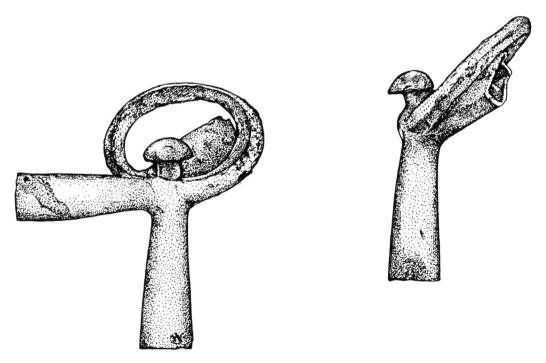

Plate 14. One of pair of bronze element with spiraliform end from Narce, Contrada Morgi cemetery, tomb tomb 8 (LVI)
(after Emilozzi 1997, fig. 4, above).

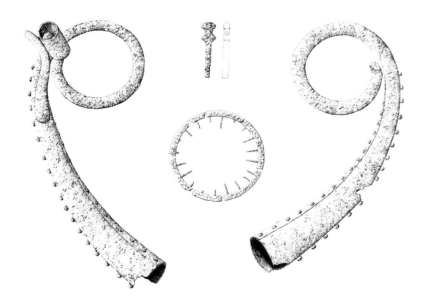

Plate 15. Parts of chariot from Sesto Calende, Castiona cemetery, Tomba di Guerriero A. Milan, Museo Castello Sforzesco (after Woytowitsch 1978, pl. 19, no. 109).

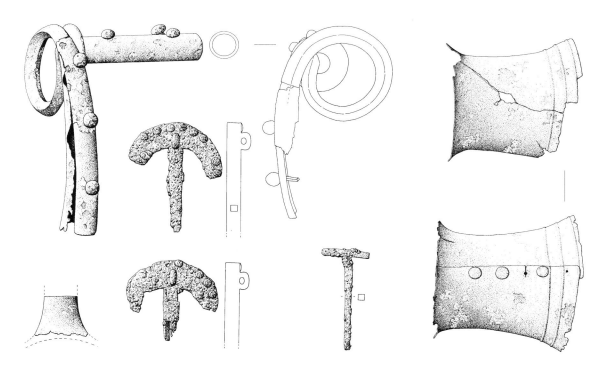

Plate 16. Parts of chariot from Sesto Calende, Carrera cemetery, Tomba di Guerriero B. Varese, Museo Civico Archeologico (after Woytowitsch 1978, pl. 19, no. 110).

a

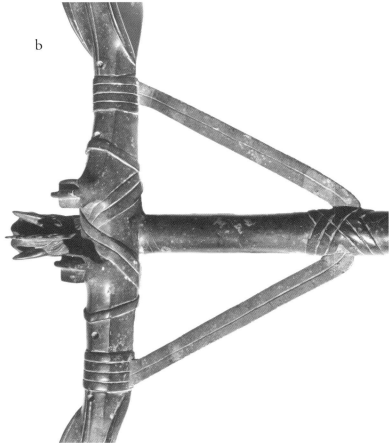

b

Plate 17a–b. Remains of bronze chariot group from Chianciano, sanctuary of Moon goddess. Florence, Museo Archeologico 76525 (photographs Alinari and Soprintendenza alle Antichità di Etruria).

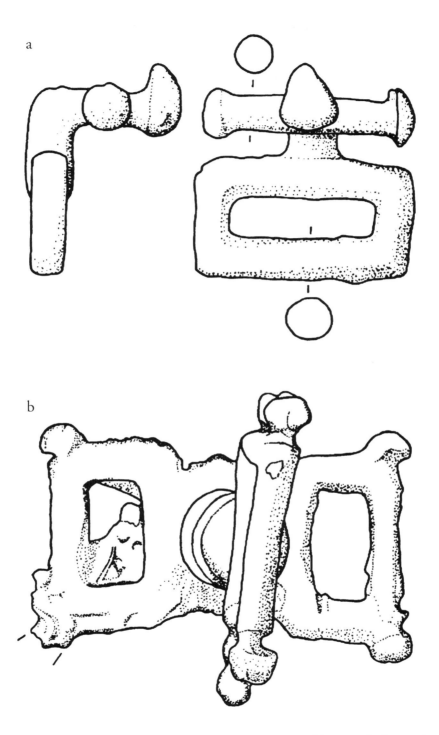

Plate 18a–b. Bronze harness elements from Verucchio, Lippi cemetery, tomb 89 (Tomba del Trono) (after *Guerriero e sacerdote* pl. 67, nos 141, 142a).

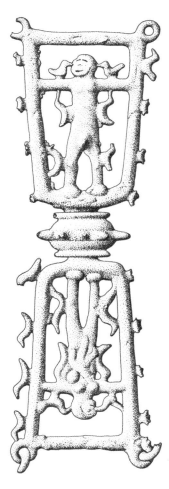

Plate 19. Bronze harness element from Civiltà Castellana, Madonna della Rosa cemetery, tomb 2 (after Woytowitsch 1978, pl. 43, no. 29).

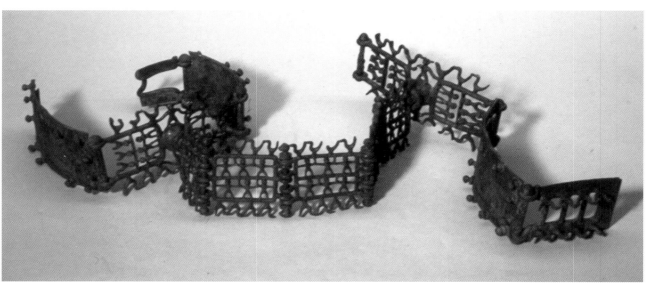

Plate 20. Bronze harness element(?). London, British Museum 1851.8–13.139 (museum photograph).

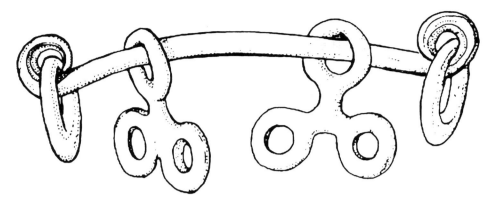

Plate 21. Bronze horse bit of Type 1 from Veii, Quattro Fontanili cemetery, tomb DE 12–13
(after *Notizie degli scavi di antichità* (Serie 8) 29 (1975), 89, fig. 16, no. 4.

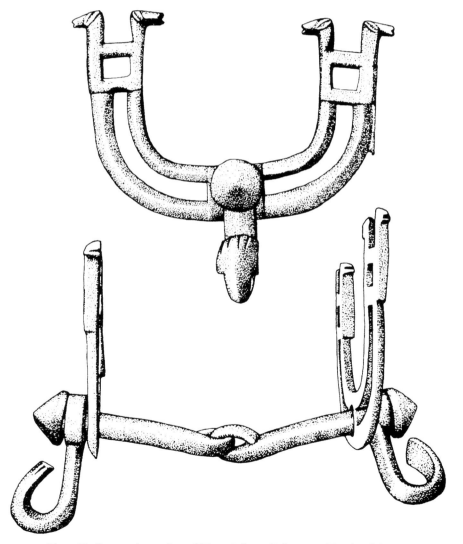

Plate 22. Bronze horse bit of Type 2 from Belmonte, Tomba del Duce
(after von Hase 1969, pl. 21, no. 269).

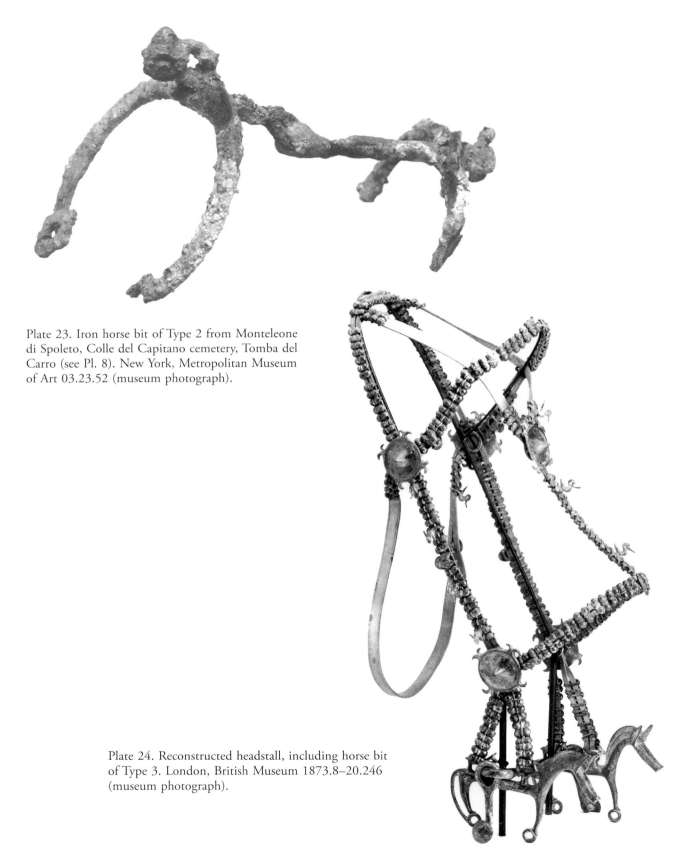

Plate 23. Iron horse bit of Type 2 from Monteleone di Spoleto, Colle del Capitano cemetery, Tomba del Carro (see Pl. 8). New York, Metropolitan Museum of Art 03.23.52 (museum photograph).

Plate 24. Reconstructed headstall, including horse bit of Type 3. London, British Museum 1873.8–20.246 (museum photograph).

Plate 25. Iron horse bit of type 4 from Como, Ca'Morta cemetery, Tomba del Carrettino. Como, Museo Civico Archeologico Giovio (drawn by J. Morel after De Marinis 1988b, fig. 151).

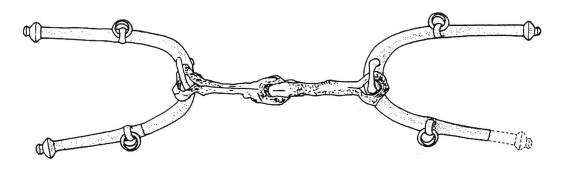

Plate 26. Iron and bronze horse bit of type 4 from Sesto Calende, Carrera cemetery, Tomba Guerriero B (see Pl. 16) (after De Marinis 1975, pl. 7:1).

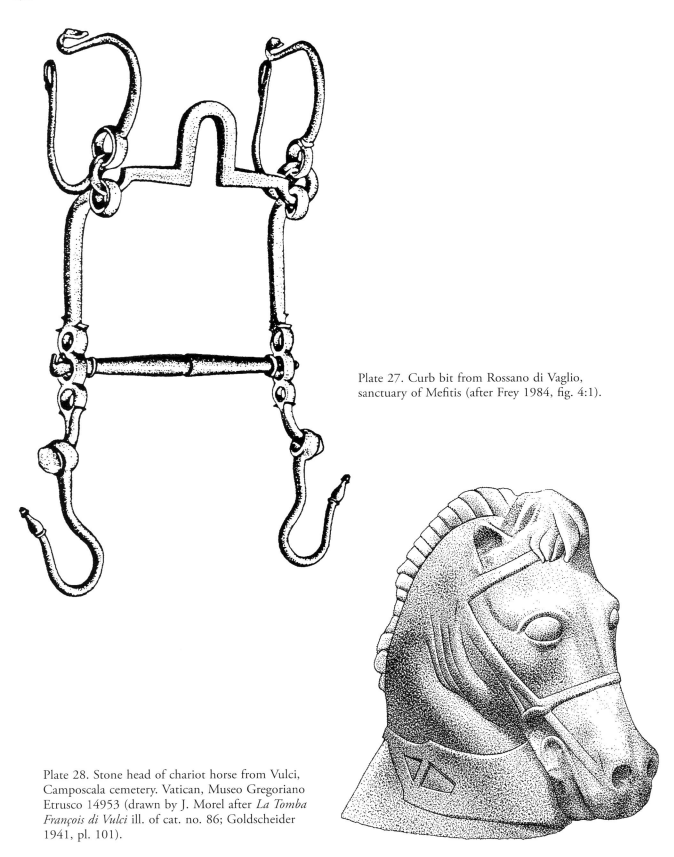

Plate 27. Curb bit from Rossano di Vaglio, sanctuary of Mefitis (after Frey 1984, fig. 4:1).

Plate 28. Stone head of chariot horse from Vulci, Camposcala cemetery. Vatican, Museo Gregoriano Etrusco 14953 (drawn by J. Morel after *La Tomba François di Vulci* ill. of cat. no. 86; Goldscheider 1941, pl. 101).

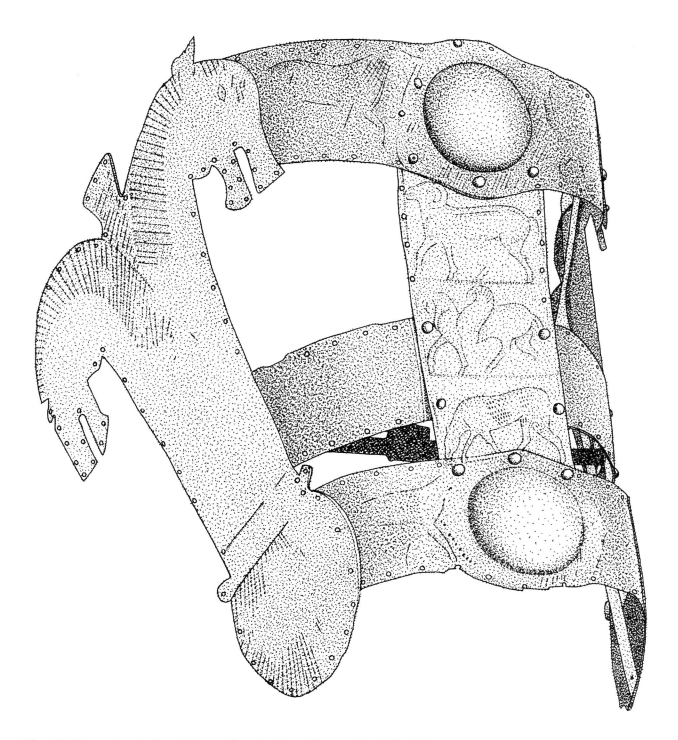

Plate 29. Bronze headstall, including a frontlet, from Sferrecavallo, Colle del Forno cemetery, tomb XI. Copenhagen, Ny Carlsberg Glyptotek (drawn by J. Morel after *Carri de guerra* 295, fig. 22).

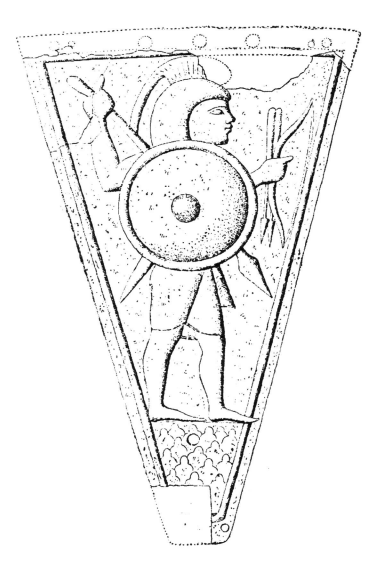

Plate 30. One of pair of bronze frontlets from Marsiliana d'Albegna, Circolo di Perazetta. Florence, Museo Archeologico Nazionale (after Minto 1921, fig. 29).

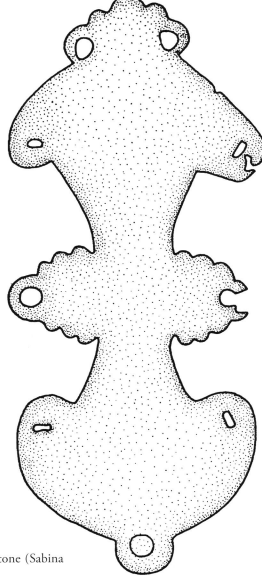

Plate 31. One of pair of bronze frontlets(?) from Cretone (Sabina Tibertina) (after Colonna 1997, fig. 7).

Plate 32. One of pair of bronze frontlets from
Pontecagnano, Corso Italia cemetery, tomb 4461.
Pontecagnano, Museo Nazionale dell'Agro Picentino
91979 (after Cerchiai 1985, fig. 2).

Plate 33. Chariot model on ivory pyxis lid from Marzabotto. Marzabotta, Museo Etrusco Pompeo Aria 1201
(after Gentili 1978, figs 6–11).

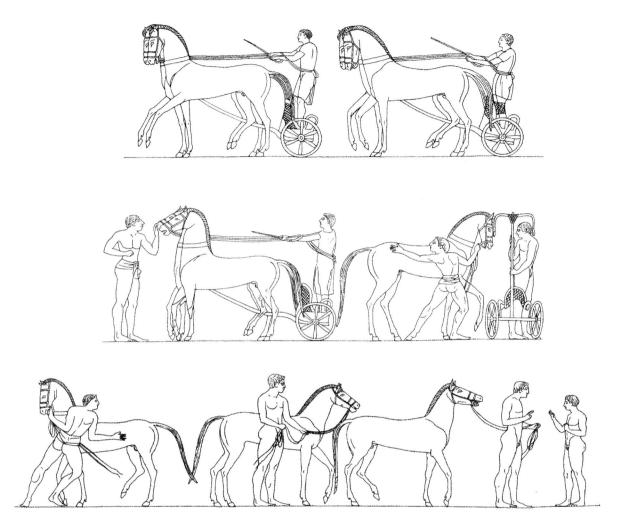

Plate 34. Wall painting from Tarquinia, Tomba delle Bighe. Tarquinia, Museo Nazionale Archeologico
(drawn by J. Morel after Steingräber 1985, fig. 83).

Plate 35. Wall painting from Tarquinia, Tomba delle Olimpiadi. Tarquinia, Museo Nazionale Archeologico
(drawn by J. Morel after Bartoccini, Lerici and Moretti 1959, figs 4, above; 5–9).

Plate 36. Wall painting from Chiusi, Tomba di Poggio al Moro (after Steingräber 1985, pl. 192, above).

Plate 37. Wall painting from Orvieto, Tomba degli Hescanas. Florence, Museo Archeologico Nazionale (photograph Alinari).

Plate 38. Wall painting from Tarquinia, Tomba Querciola I (after *Malerei der Etrusker* no. XI).

Plate 39. Wall painting from Orvieto, Tomba Golini I (after Steingräber 1985, fig. 43, below, right).

a

b

Plate 40a–b. Details of neck and belly of Etruscan black-figure neck-amphora by the Amphiaraus Painter, from Vulci. Munich, Staatliche Antikensammlungen 838. (a) after Åkerström 1954, fig. 11; (b) museum photograph).

Plate 41. Detail of Etruscan black-figure neck-amphora by the Painter of the Berlin Amphora F 2154, from Vulci. Berlin, Staatliche Museen, Antikensammlung F 2154 (museum photograph).

Plate 42. Detail of Etruscan black-figure neck-amphora by the Painter of Vatican 238. Amsterdam, Allard Pierson Museum 1806 (museum photograph).

Plate 43. Detail of Etruscan black-figure neck-amphora by the Paris Painter. Heidelberg, Archäologisches Institut der Universität 59/5 (drawn by J. Morel after from Hampe and Simon 1971, pl. 47).

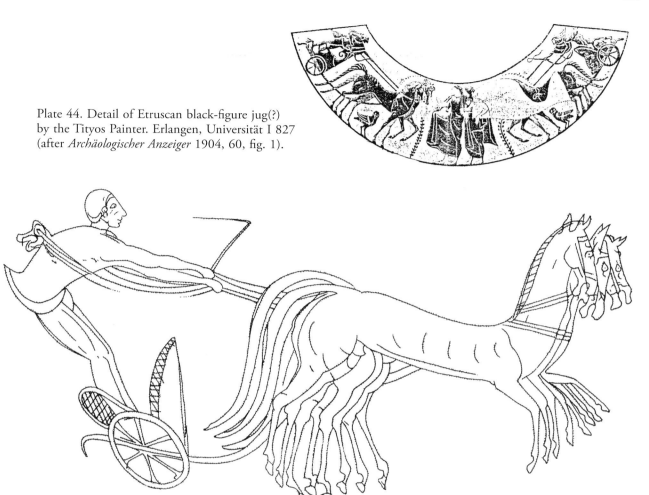

Plate 44. Detail of Etruscan black-figure jug(?)
by the Tityos Painter. Erlangen, Universität I 827
(after *Archäologischer Anzeiger* 1904, 60, fig. 1).

Plate 45. Etruscan black-figure neck-amphora by the Micali Painter. Copenhagen, Ny Carlsberg Glyptotek H.I.N. 676
(drawn by J. Morel after *Un artisto etrusco* ill. no. 18).

Plate 46. Detail of neck-amphora by the Painter of the Heptachord (drawing J. Morel; Crouwel 2006, fig. 8).

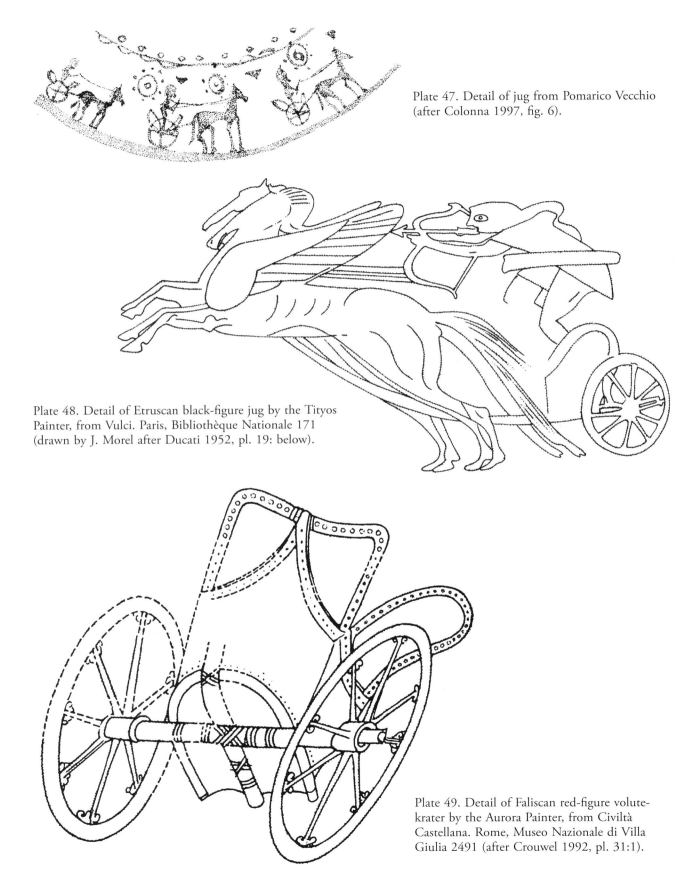

Plate 47. Detail of jug from Pomarico Vecchio (after Colonna 1997, fig. 6).

Plate 48. Detail of Etruscan black-figure jug by the Tityos Painter, from Vulci. Paris, Bibliothèque Nationale 171 (drawn by J. Morel after Ducati 1952, pl. 19: below).

Plate 49. Detail of Faliscan red-figure volute-krater by the Aurora Painter, from Civiltà Castellana. Rome, Museo Nazionale di Villa Giulia 2491 (after Crouwel 1992, pl. 31:1).

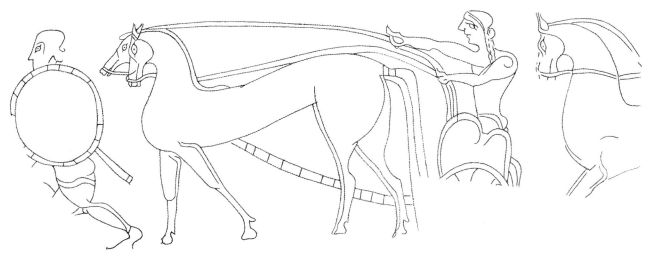

Plate 50. Fragments of Bucchero jug. Geneva, Collection C.A. (drawn by J. Morel after Camporeale 1993, fig. 1a–b).

Plate 51. Detail of Bucchero jug, perhaps from Vulci rather than Ischia di Castro. Rome, Museo Nazionale di Villa Giulia 64578 (after Jannot 1986, fig. 1).

Plate 52. Detail of terracotta stand from Poggio Civitate near Murlo (drawn by J. Morel after Warden 1977, pls 101:1 and 107:1–2).

Plate 53. Impasto tripod vessel from Bisenzio, Palazetta cemetery. Florence, Museo Archeologico Nazionale 75412 (after Woytowitsch 1978, pl. 44, no. 157).

Plate 54. Detail of bronze sheathing from Vulci, Polledrara cemetery, probably Isis Tomb. London, British Museum GR 1850.2–27.15B*bis* (drawn by J. Morel after Colonna 1997, fig. 4).

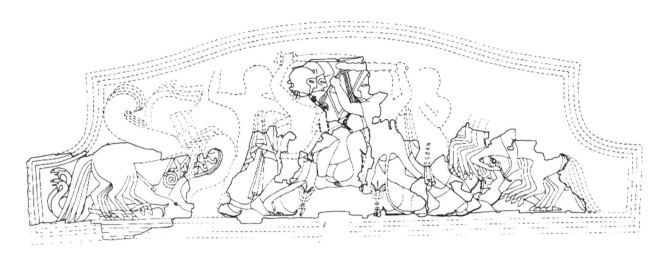

Plate 55. Bronze sheathing of chariot from Castel San Mariano, Tomba di Bronzi. Perugia, Museo Archeologico Nazionale dell'Umbria (after Höckmann 1982, fig. 25).

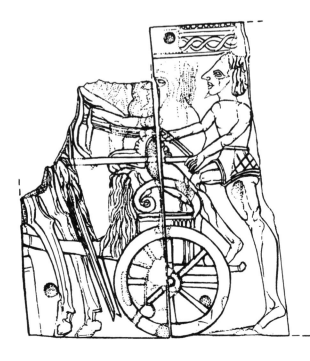

Plate 56. Incomplete ivory plaque from Montefortini, Comeana di Carmignano, tomb. Florence, Museo Archeologico 224109 (after *Carri da guerra* p. 62, no. S.4).

Plate 57. Detail of ivory pyxis from Chiusi, Tomba della Pania. Florence, Museo Archeologico Nazionale 73846 (after Cristofani 1971, fig. 9).

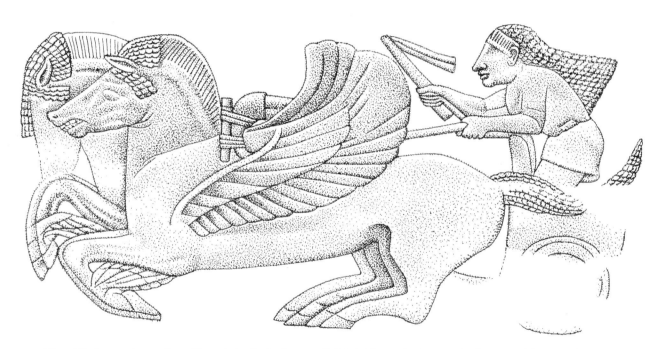

Plate 58. Ivory plaque from Tarquinia. Paris, Louvre S 2028 (drawn by J. Morel after Brendel 1995, fig. 117).

Plate 59. Detail of carved ostrich egg from Vulci, Polledrara cemetery, probably Isis Tomb. London, British Museum GR 1850.2–27.8 (after Rathje 1986, fig. 4).

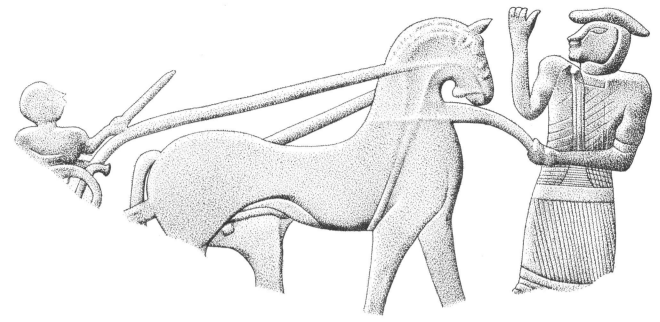

Plate 60. Detail of stone funerary stele (the Stele Zannoni or Pietra Zannoni) from Bologna. Bologna, Museo Civico Archeologico 21999 (drawn by J. Morel after *Principi etruschi* 328, ill. of cat. no. 444).

Plate 61. Detail of stone funerary stele no. 168 from Bologna. Bologna, Museo Civico Archeologico (museum photograph).

Plate 62. Detail of stone funerary stele of Ostiala Gallenia from Padua. Padua, Museo Civico Archeologico 813 (drawn by J. Morel after De Marinis 1988, ill. p. 84).

Plate 63. Detail of stone sarcophagus from Cerveteri, Banditaccia cemetery. Vatican, Museo Gregoriano Etrusco 14949 (drawn by J. Morel after Herbig 1952, pl. 1, no. 83).

Plate 64. Detail of alabaster cinerary urn from Volterra. Florence, Museo Archeologico Nazionale 5513
(photograph Deutsches Archäologisches Institut, Rome).

Plate 65. Detail of stone sarcophagus of Ramtha Viśnai from Vulci. Boston, Museum of Fine Arts 1975.799
(museum photograph).

Plate 66. Stone sarcophagus from Vulci. Copenhagen, Ny Carlsberg Glyptotek H.I.N. 57
(drawn by J. Morel after Moltesen and Nielsen 1996, ill. no. 7).

Plate 67. Detail of stone sarcophagus from Tuscania. Vatican, Museo Gregoriano Etrusco 14950 (museum photograph).

Plate 68. Pair of terracotta chariot horses
from Tarquinia, Ara della Regina. Tarquinia,
Museo Nazionale Archeologico 2726 (museum
photograph).

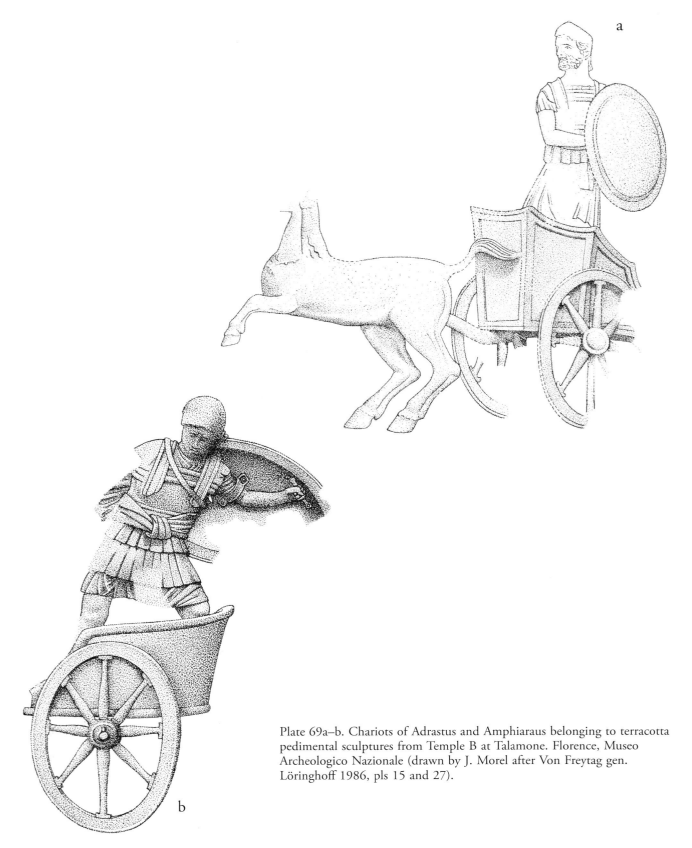

Plate 69a–b. Chariots of Adrastus and Amphiaraus belonging to terracotta pedimental sculptures from Temple B at Talamone. Florence, Museo Archeologico Nazionale (drawn by J. Morel after Von Freytag gen. Löringhoff 1986, pls 15 and 27).

Plate 70. Terracotta revetment plaques from Velletri. Velletri, Museo Communale 518–519
(after Fortunati 1983, figs 3–4 and 11).

Plate 71a. Terracotta revetment plaques of Roma-Caprifico type (drawings L. Opgenhaften and P. Lulof).

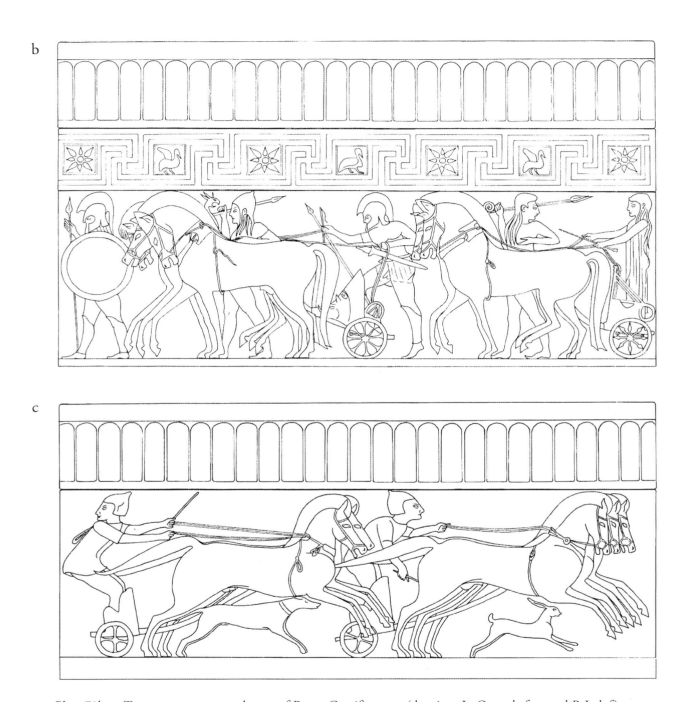

Plate 71b–c. Terracotta revetment plaques of Roma-Caprifico type (drawings L. Opgenhaften and P. Lulof).

Plate 72. Reconstruction drawing of terracotta revetment plaques from Cerveteri (after Kästner 1988, pl. 54:1)

Plate 73. Terracotta revetment plaque from Palestrina. Rome, Museo Nazionale di Villa Giulia 27038 (drawn by J. Morel after *La grande Roma* pl. 17, no. 7.4.1. 28).

Plate 74. Terracotta revetment plaque from Acquarossa (after Winter, N. A. 2009, ill. 4.8.2, no. 4.D.4.b).

Plate 75. Reconstruction drawing of Frieze I of terracotta revetment plaques from Metaponto, San Biagio, Temple C (after Mertens-Horn 1992, fig. 1).

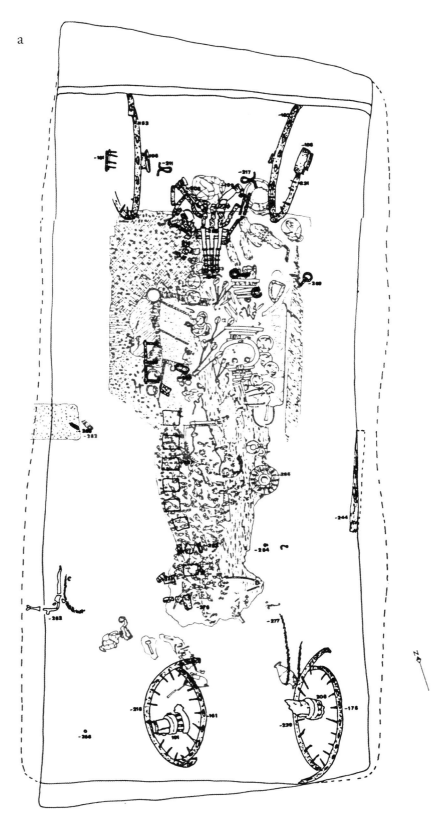

Plate 76a. Sirolo, I Pini cemetery, Circolo 1, tomb 4 (Tomba della Principessa): tomb plan with remains of cart, chariot and other finds (after *Carri da guerra* 253, fig. 1).

b

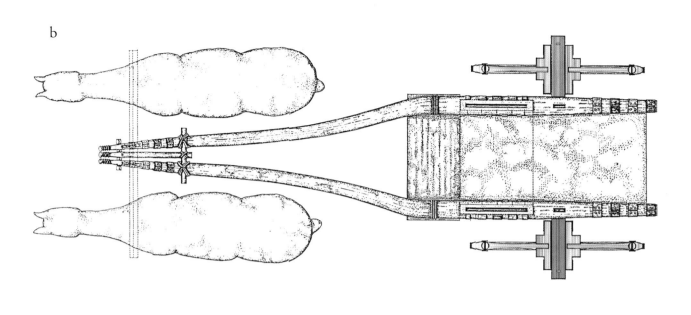

c

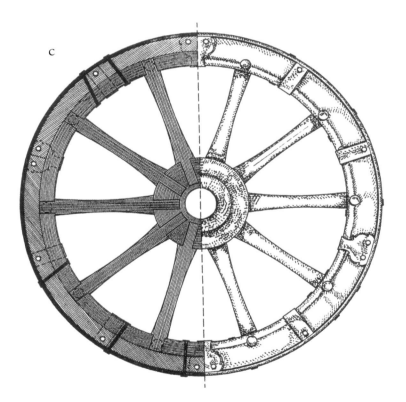

Plate 76b–c. Sirolo, I Pini cemetery, Circolo 1, tomb 4 (Tomba della Principessa): (b) reconstruction drawing of cart; (c) reconstruction of cart wheel (after *Carri da guerra* 250–252, figs 19–20).

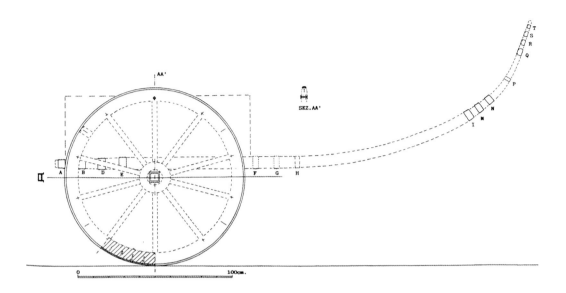

Plate 77. Reconstruction drawing of cart from Vetulonia, Acquastrini cemetery, Tomba del Littore (see Pl. 12)
(after *Carri da guerra* 265 fig. 2, below).

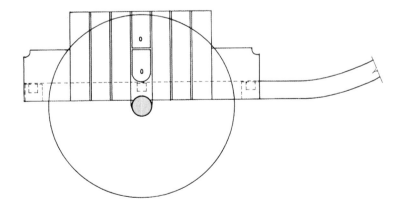

Plate 78. Reconstruction drawing of cart from Sferracavallo, Colle del Forno cemetery, tomb XI (see Pl. 29)
(after *Carri da guerra* 300, fig. 33 (reconstruction drawing).

a

b

c

Plate 79a–c. Reconstruction of cart from
Castel San Mariano, Tomba dei Bronzi
(see Pl. 9) (after Bruni 2002, figs 11–14).

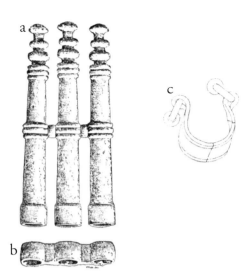

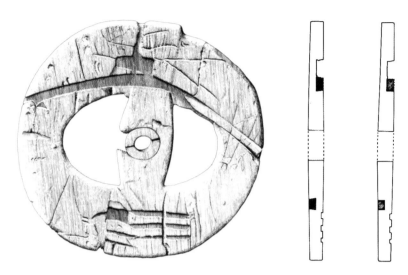

Plate 80a–c.
(a) Bronze 'poggiaredini';
(b) bronze triple ring;
(c) iron 'stirrup' from Verucchio, Fornace
 cemetery, tomb VIII (after Camerin 1997a, fig. 6).

Plate 81. Fragmentary disk wheel from Castioni dei Marchese. Parma, Museo Nazionale di Antichità (after Woytowitsch 1978, pl. 2, no. 1).

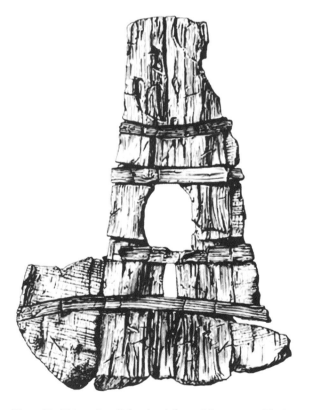

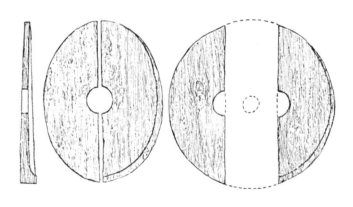

Plate 82. Tripartite disk wheel from Mercurago. Turin, Museo di Antichità (cast only) (after Woytowitsch 1978, pl. 1, no. 2).

Plate 83. Fragmentary disk wheel from Mercurago. Turin, Museo di Antichità (now lost) (after from Cornaggia Castiglioni and Calagari 1978, pl. VIB–C).

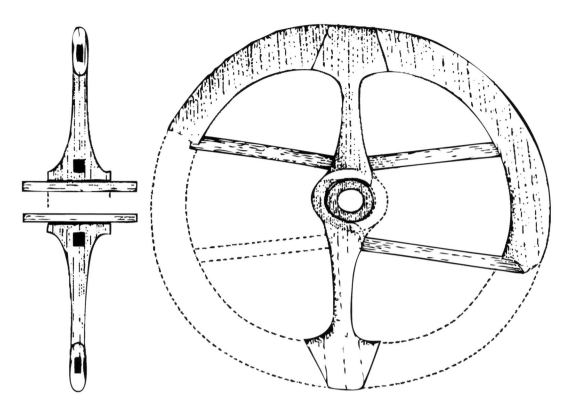

Plate 84. Incomplete cross-bar wheel
from Mercurago. Turin, Museo di
Antichità (cast only)
(after Crouwel 1992, pl. 36:4).

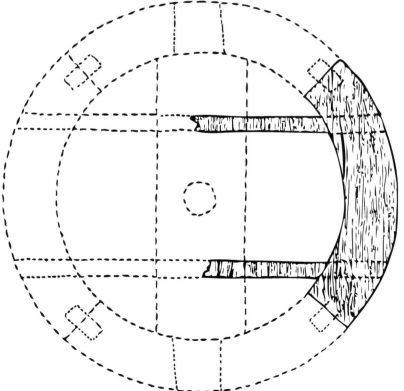

Plate 85. Incomplete cross-bar wheel
from Mercurago. Turin, Museo di
Antichità (after Cornaggia Castigioni
and Calagari 1978, pl. VIA).

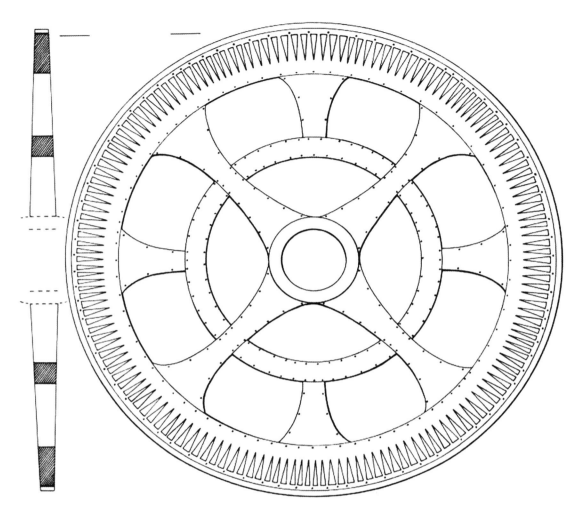

Plate 86. Bronze sheathing of wheel from Populonia, San Cerbone cemetery, Tumulo dei Carri. Florence, Museo Archeologico 116485 (after Woytowitsch 1978, pl. 9, no. 66).

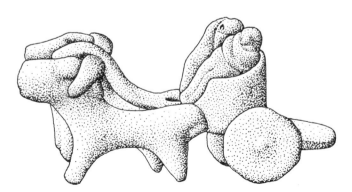

Plate 87. Bronze model from Vetulonia, Poggio alla Guardia cemetery. Florence, Museo Archeologico Nazionale 8264 (after Woytowitsch 1978, pl. 31, no. 165).

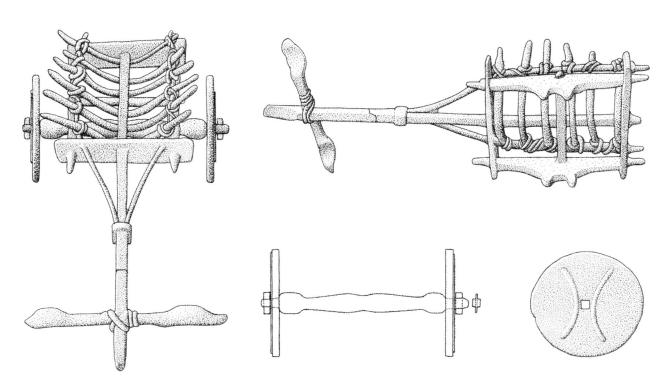

Plate 88. Bronze model from Bolsena. Rome, Museo Nazionale di Villa Giulia 56097 (after Crouwel 1992, pl. 33:1).

Plate 89. Bronze model from Civiltà Castellana. New York, Metropolitan Museum of Art 09.221.20A (museum photograph).

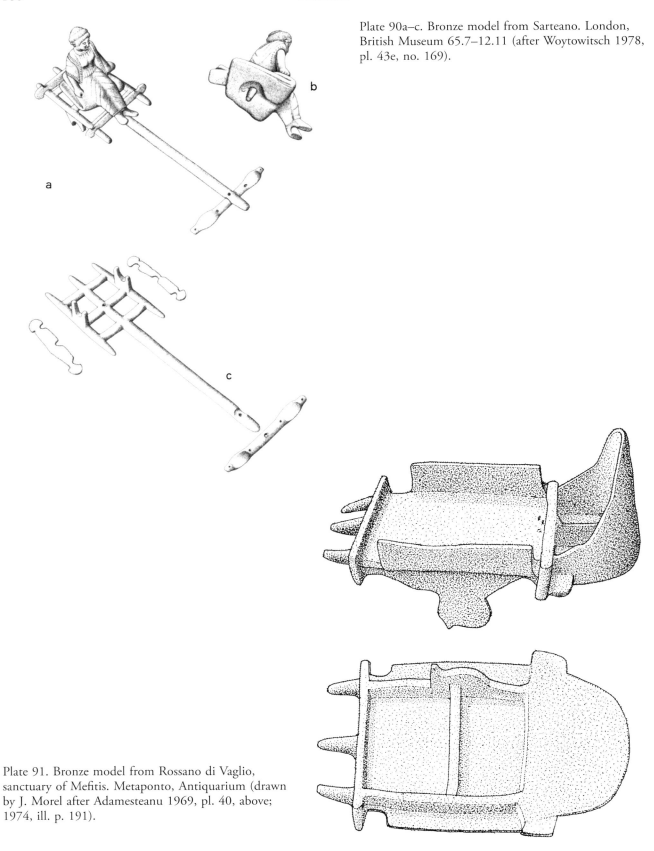

Plate 90a–c. Bronze model from Sarteano. London, British Museum 65.7–12.11 (after Woytowitsch 1978, pl. 43e, no. 169).

a

b

c

Plate 91. Bronze model from Rossano di Vaglio, sanctuary of Mefitis. Metaponto, Antiquarium (drawn by J. Morel after Adamesteanu 1969, pl. 40, above; 1974, ill. p. 191).

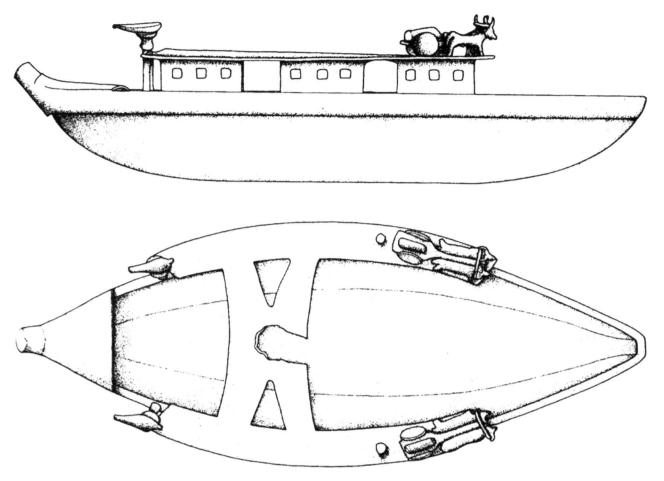

Plate 92. Bronze boat model with two carts from Crotone, sanctuary of Hera. Crotone, Museo Archeologico Nazional 59366 (after Spadea 1997, 249, fig. 15b and d).

Plate 93. Incomplete terracotta model from Pithecusae (on Ischia) (after Crouwel 1992, pl. 33:3).

Plate 94. Detail of tomb painting from Paestum, Gaudo, tomb 2 (after Sestieri 1959, ill. p. 39).

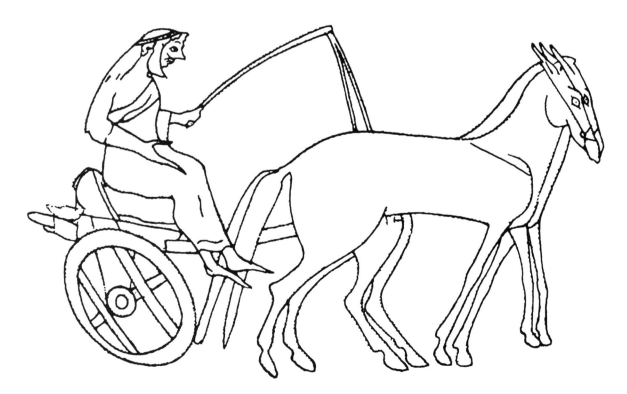

Plate 95. Detail of Pseudo-Chalcidian black-figure neck-amphora of the Memnon Group. London, British Museum 1772.3–20.5* (after Crouwel 1992, pl. 28:1).

Plate 96. Detail of Etruscan red-figure neck-amphora of the Praxias Group, from Vulci. Munich, Staatliche Antikensammlungen F3185 (museum photograph).

Plate 97. Detail of Etruscan red-figure stamnos from Vulci. Berlin, Staatliche Museen, Antikensammlung F2954 (drawn by J. Morel after Albizzati 1918–19, fig. 4).

Plate 98. Detail of (now lost) Apulian red-figure vase from Ruvo (after Crouwel 1992, pl. 34:3).

Plate 99. Detail of Paestan red-figure bell-krater by Python. New York, Metropolitan Museum of Art 1989.144 (drawn by J. Morel after museum photograph).

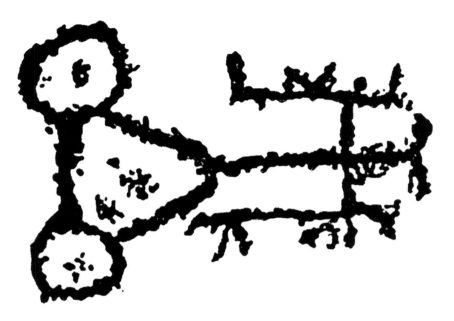

Plate 100. Rock carving from Val Camonica (after Züchner 2004, fig. 8:10).

Plate 101. Detail of sard gem. Boston, Museum of Fine Arts 27.663 (museum photograph).

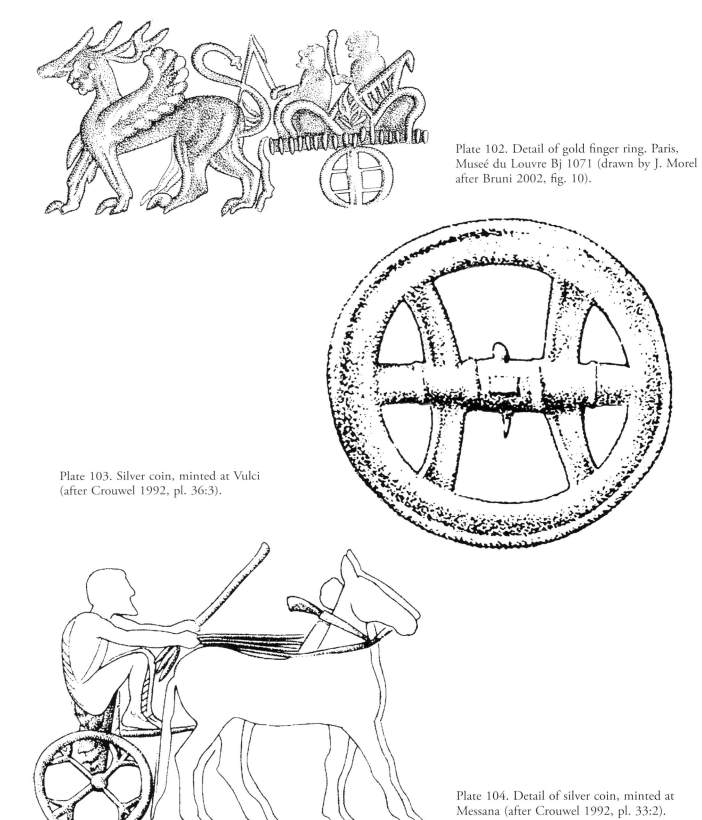

Plate 102. Detail of gold finger ring. Paris, Museé du Louvre Bj 1071 (drawn by J. Morel after Bruni 2002, fig. 10).

Plate 103. Silver coin, minted at Vulci (after Crouwel 1992, pl. 36:3).

Plate 104. Detail of silver coin, minted at Messana (after Crouwel 1992, pl. 33:2).

Plate 105. Detail of stone funerary stele (Stele di Via Tofana) from Bologna. Bologna, Museo Civico Archeologico 67495 (after Bermond-Montanari 1962, fig. 4).

Plate 106. Detail of stone funerary stele no. 164 from Bologna. Bologna, Museo Civico Archeologico (museum photograph).

Plate 107. Detail of stone funerary stele no. 169 (side A) from Bologna. Bologna, Museo Civico Archeologico (museum photograph).

Plate 108. Detail of stone funerary stele no. 63 from Bologna. Bologna, Museo Civico Archeologico (museum photograph).

Plate 109. Detail of stone sarcophagus of Ramta Viśnai from Vulci (see also Pl. 65). Boston, Museum of Fine Arts 1975.799 (museum photograph).

Plate 110. Detail of stone sarcophagus from Tarquinia. Tarquinia, Museo Nazionale Archeologico 3062
(drawn by J. Morel after *EAA* Supplement II, 365, fig. 527).

Plate 111. Detail of stone sarcophagus from Sulmona, Church of Santa Maria Pietraluna. Sulmona, Museo Civico
(drawn by J. Morel after *Antiche gente d'Italia* ill. of cat. no. 733).

Plate 112. Detail of alabaster cinerary urn from
Volterra. Florence, Museo Archeologico Nazionale 5513
(photograph Deutsches Archäologisches Institut, Rome).

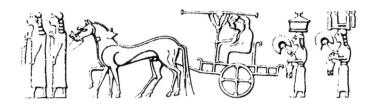

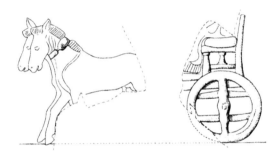

Plate 113. Terracotta revetment plaque from Poggio Civitate (Murlo). Murlo, Antiquarium di Poggio Civitate SAT nos. 112603(A) and 112598(B) (after *Carri da guerra* 65, ill. of no. s.10).

Plate 114. Detail of terracotta plaque from Locri Epizephyrii. Reggio di Calabria, Museo Nazionale (after Crouwel 1992, pl. 34:2).

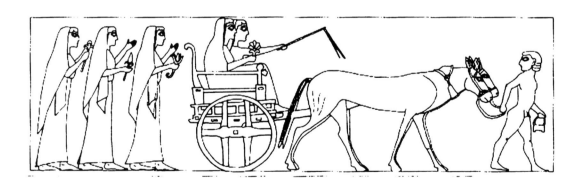

Plate 115. Frieze II of terracotta revetment plaques from Metaponto, San Biagio, Temple C (see Pl. 75). Metaponto, Antiquarium (after Mertens-Horn 1992, fig. 2).

a

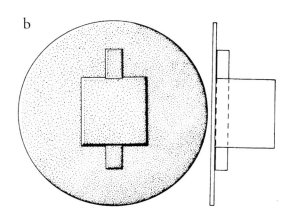

b

Plate 116a–b. Reconstruction and bronze axle cap of four-wheeler from Cerveteri, Sorbo cemetery, Tomba Regolini-Galassi (see Pl. 11). Vatican, Museo Gregoriano Etrusco 15037.
(a) museum photograph;
(b) after Woytowitsch 1978, pl. 12, no. 31a.

a

b

c

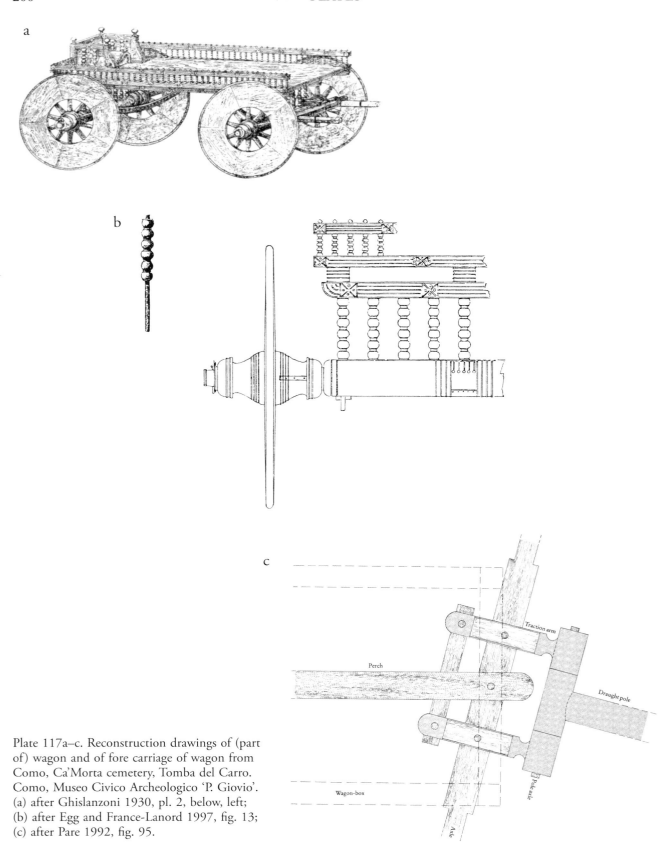

Plate 117a–c. Reconstruction drawings of (part of) wagon and of fore carriage of wagon from Como, Ca'Morta cemetery, Tomba del Carro. Como, Museo Civico Archeologico 'P. Giovio'. (a) after Ghislanzoni 1930, pl. 2, below, left; (b) after Egg and France-Lanord 1997, fig. 13; (c) after Pare 1992, fig. 95.

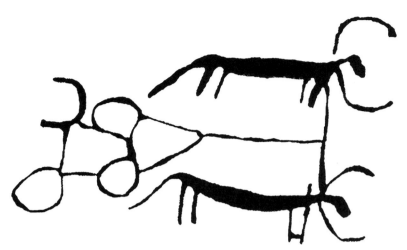

Plate 118. Rock engravings from Val
Camonica, Cemmo rock II (after Züchner
2004, fig. 8:1).

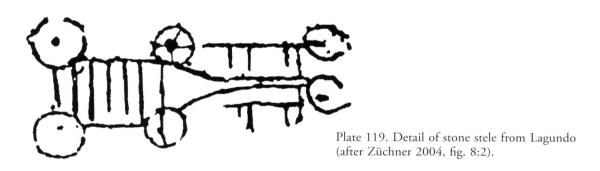

Plate 119. Detail of stone stele from Lagundo
(after Züchner 2004, fig. 8:2).

Plate 120. Detail of stone cippus, quite probably from Chiusi. Berlin, Staatliche Museen, Antikensammlung 1227
(drawn by J. Morel after Rumpf 1928, pl. 20, no. E 30).

Plate 121. Detail of stone urn from Vulci (now lost) (after Pare 1992, fig. 147:1).

Plate 122. Detail of the wooden chair (the Verucchio Throne), from Verucchio, Lippi cemetery, tomb 89 (Tomba del Trono).
Verucchio, Museo Civico Archeologico 13539 (after *Guerriero and sacerdote* fig. 129).

Plate 123. Detail of stone cinerary urn from Volterra. Firenze, Palazzo Aldobrandini (after Nielsen 1990, figs 9 and 9a).

Plate 124. Terracotta model from Frattesima di Fratta Polesine (after Woytowitsch 1978, no. 143a, pl. 29).

Plate 125. Detail of Assyrian stone relief of Ashurnasirpal II, from Nimrud. Berlin. Vorderasiatisches Museum VA 959 (after Littauer and Crouwel 1979a, fig. 53).

Plate 126. Detail of Assyrian stone relief of Ashurbanipal from Niniveh. Berlin, Vorderasiatisches Museum VA 961 (after Littauer and Crouwel 1979a, fig. 56).

Plate 127. Detail of Neo-Hittite
stone relief from Sakçagözü.
Berlin, Vorderasiatisches Museum
VA 971 (after Littauer and
Crouwel 1979a, fig. 58).

Plate 128. Detail of Achaemenid
stone relief from Persepolis (after
from Littauer and Crouwel 1979a,
fig. 80).

Plate 129. Silver coin, minted at
Sidon (drawn by J. Morel after
Franke and Hirmer 1964, pl. 195,
middle of third row).

Plate 130. Chariot D and its harness team, as found in the dromos of Salamis (Cyprus), tomb 79 (after Karageorghis 1973, pl. 251).

Plate 131. Detail of stone sarcophagus from Amathus. New York, Metropolitan Museum of Art 74.51.2453 (museum photograph).

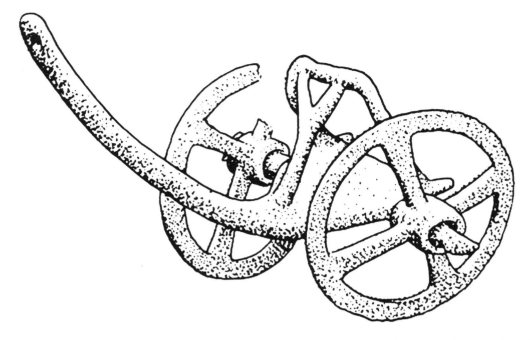

Plate 132. Bronze model from Olympia. Athens, National Museum 6128 (after Crouwel 1992, pl. 3:1).

Plate 133. Bronze model from
Olympia. Olympia Museum B
1670 (after Crouwel 1992, pl. 3:2).

Plate 134. Bronze model from Olympia. Olympia Museum B 1671
(after Crouwel 1992, pl. 3:3).

Plate 135. Detail of Attic Late Geometric jug from Athens, Agora tomb XIII. Athens, Agora Museum P 4885 (after Crouwel 1992, pl. 7:3).

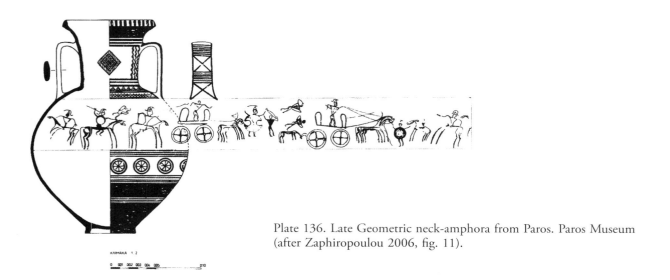

Plate 136. Late Geometric neck-amphora from Paros. Paros Museum (after Zaphiropoulou 2006, fig. 11).

Plate 137. Detail of Attic black-figure pyxis by Exekias, from Myrrhinous (in Attica). Brauron Museum (after Crouwel 1992, pl. 10:1).

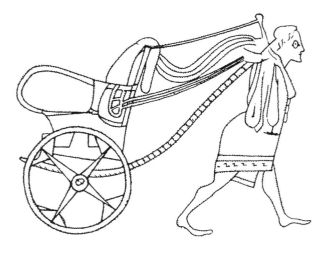

Plate 138. Terracotta model from Tanagra. Athens, National Museum 4082 (after Crouwel 1992, pl. 5:2).

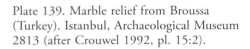

Plate 139. Marble relief from Broussa (Turkey). Istanbul, Archaeological Museum 2813 (after Crouwel 1992, pl. 15:2).

Plate 140. Terracotta revetment plaque. Paris, Cabinet des Médailles (after Crouwel 1992, pl. 16:1).

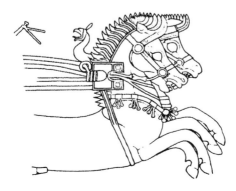

Plate 141. Incomplete terracotta revetment plaque. Copenhagen, Ny Carlsberg Glyptotek I.N.3426 (after Crouwel 1992, pl. 16:2a–b).

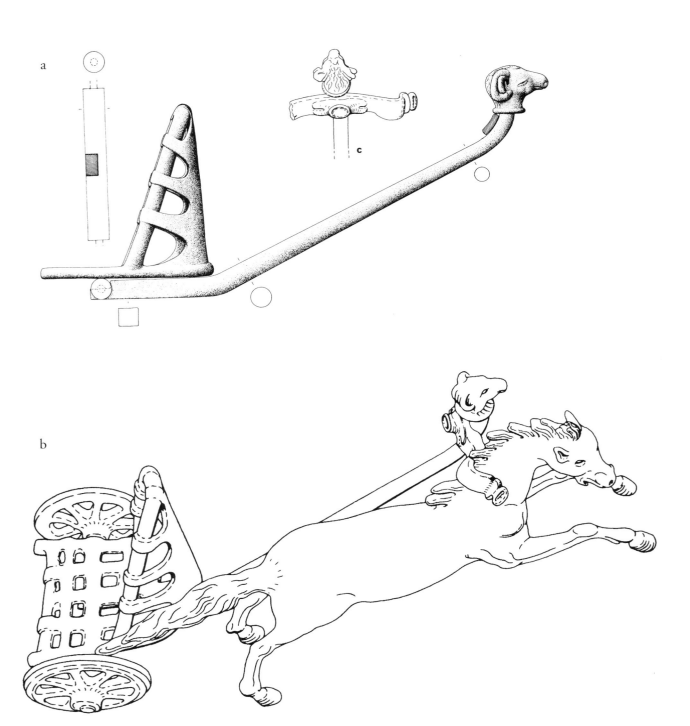

Plate 142a–c. Bronze model, reportedly from the River Tiber. London, British Museum 1894.10–30.1
(after Woytowitsch 1978, pl. 41, no. 175a, b, d).

Plate 143. Terracotta Campana relief. Vienna, Kunsthistorisches Museum, Antikensammlung V 49 (museum photograph).

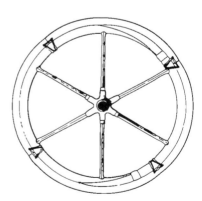

Plate 144. Detail of wheel of chariot A 5 from Thebes (Egypt), Valley of the Kings, tomb of Tut'ankhamun (after Littauer and Crouwel 1985, pl. 55).

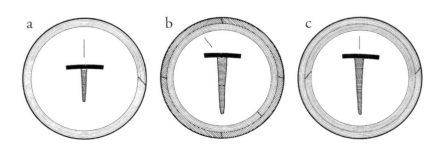

Plate 145a–c. Felloe types: (a) Gottesberg; (b) Grosseibstadt; (c) Bruck (after Pare 1992, fig. 53:1–3).

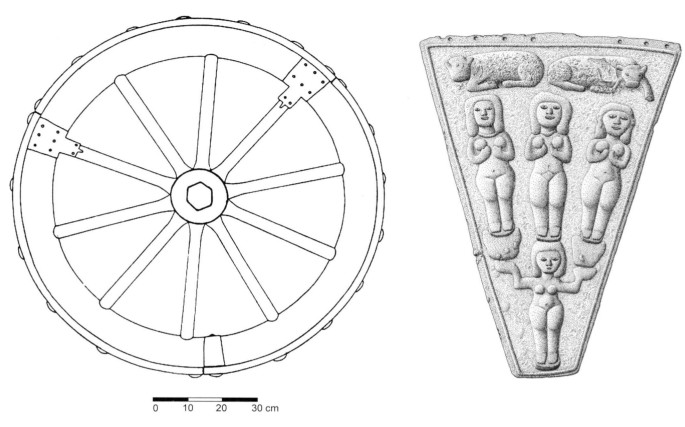

Plate 146. Reconstruction drawing of wheel from Balıkesir-Üçpinar, tomb (after Kökten Ersoy 1998, fig. 5).

Plate 147. Bronze frontlet from Samos, Heraeum. Samos Museum B 1123 (after Donder 1980, pl. 20, no. 201).

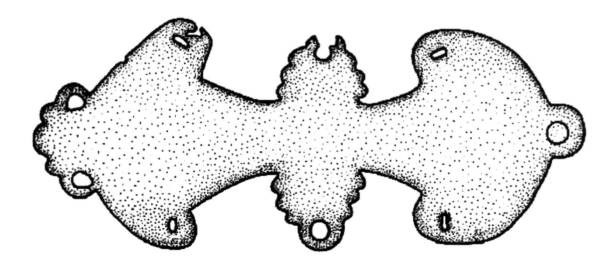

Plate 148. One of pair of bronze frontlets from Balıkesir-Üçpinar, tomb (after Kökten Ersoy 1998, fig. 1f).

Plate 149. Detail of Attic black-figure lekythos by the Amasis Painter. New York, Metropolian Museum of Art 56.11.1 (museum photograph).

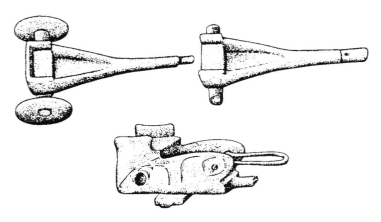

Plate 150. Bronze model from Collado de los Jardines (Despeñaperros, Jaén in southern Spain) (after Weber 1986, ill. p. 128, above, left).

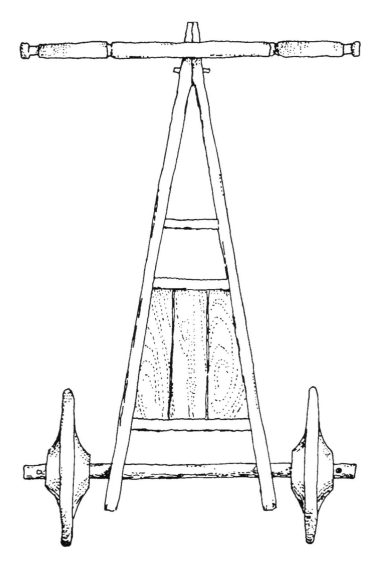

Plate 151. A-frame cart from Lchaschen (Armenia), tomb (after Littauer and Crouwel 1977a, fig. 8).

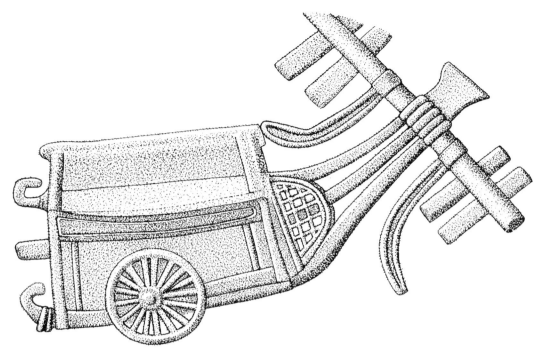

Plate 152. Detail of stone relief from Bharhut (India). Calcutta, Indian Museum
(drawn by J. Morel after Gail 1986, ill. p. 157; Snead 1989, pl. 73).

Plate 153. Bronze model from Kolhapur (India) (drawn by J. Morel after Gail 1986, ill. p. 159).

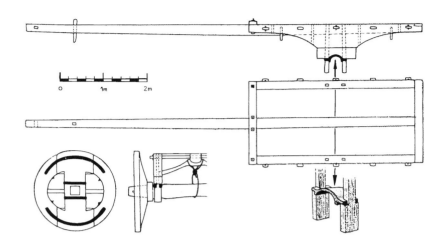

Plate 154. Portugese cart (after Crouwel 1992, pl 35:3).

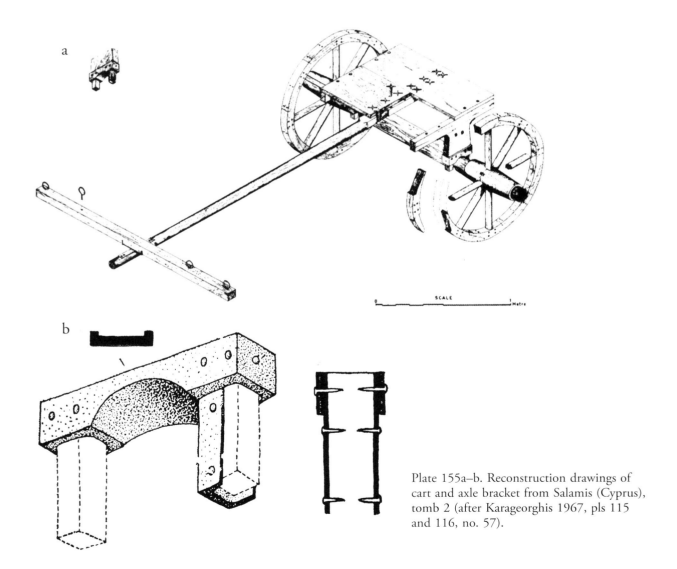

a

b

Plate 155a–b. Reconstruction drawings of cart and axle bracket from Salamis (Cyprus), tomb 2 (after Karageorghis 1967, pls 115 and 116, no. 57).

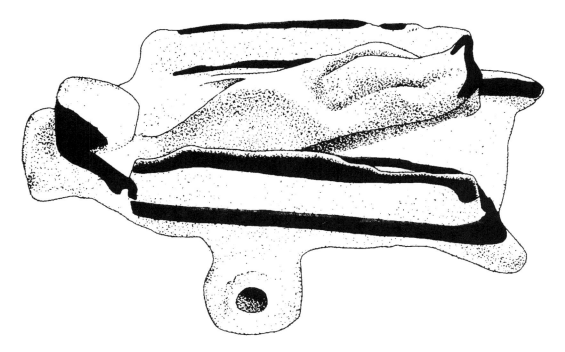

Plate 156. Terracotta model from Cyprus. Nicosia, Cyprus Museum C 48 (after Crouwel 1992, pl. 35:1).

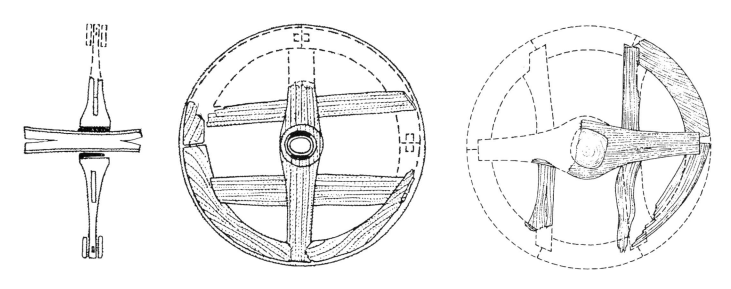

Plate 157. Incomplete cross-bar wheel from Olympia, Well 17, Olympia Museum (after from Crouwel 1992, pl. 17:1).

Plate 158. Incomplete cross-bar wheel from Küçük Hüyük, Gordion (after Crouwel 1992, pl. 36:3).

a

b

c

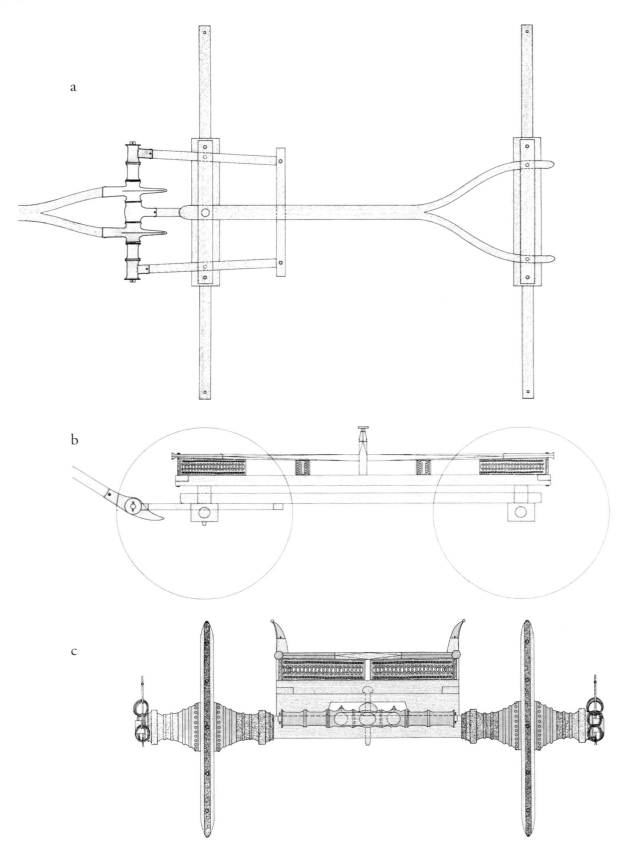

Plate 159a–c. Reconstruction drawings of wagon from Ohnenheim, tomb. Strassburg, Musée Rohan
(after Egg 1987, figs 22–4).

a

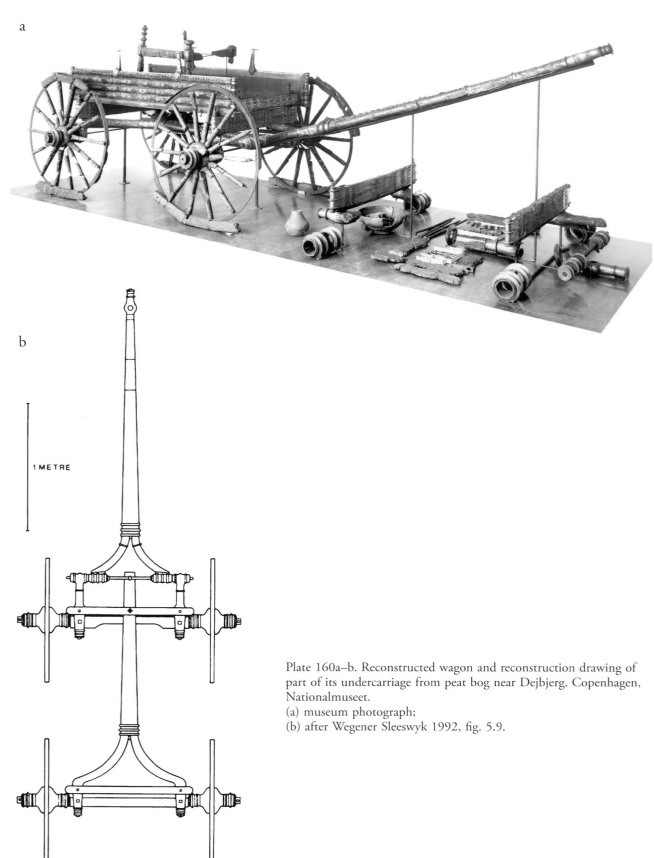

b

1 METRE

Plate 160a–b. Reconstructed wagon and reconstruction drawing of part of its undercarriage from peat bog near Dejbjerg. Copenhagen, Nationalmuseet.
(a) museum photograph;
(b) after Wegener Sleeswyk 1992, fig. 5.9.

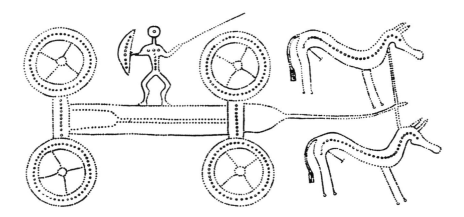

Plate 161. Detail of bronze couch from Eberdingen-Hochdorf, tomb. Stuttgart, Württenberger Landesmuseum V 86, 3
(after Pare 1992, fig. 142).

Plate 162. Detail of stone sarcophagus. Stockholm, Medelhavsmuseet Sk 0185 (photograph Ove Kaneberg).

Plate 163. Terracotta revetment plaques of Rome-Caprifico type from Caprifico near Cisterna di Latina
(drawing L. Opgenhaften and P. Lulof).

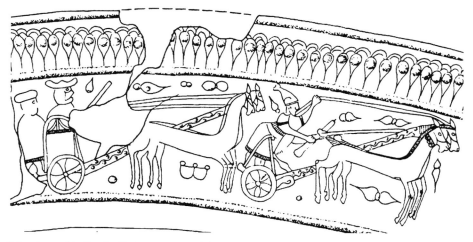

Plate 164. Detail of the Arnoaldi Situla. Bologna, Arnoaldi cemetery, tomb 96. Bologna, Museo Civico Archeologico 17960
(after Lucke and Frey 1962, pl. 63).

Plate 165. Detail of the
Benvenuti Situla. Este,
Benvenuti cemetery, tomb 126.
Este, Museo Nazionale Atestino
I.G. 4667 (after Lucke and Frey
1962, pl. 65).

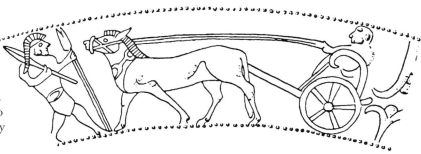

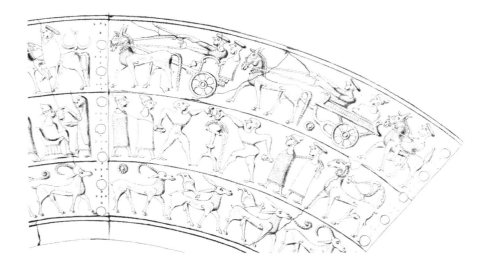

Plate 166. Detail of situla from
Vače. Ljubljana, Narodni Muzej
P 581 (after Lucke and Frey
1962, pl. 73).

Plate 167. Fragment of situla
from Novo mesto, Kapiteljska
njiva, tomb III/12 (after
Schönfelder 2002, fig. 179:3).

Plate 168. Detail of relief decoration on stone funerary
stele from Padua. Padua, Museo Civico Archeologico
(museum photograph).

Plate 169. Detail of bronze coin (*denarius*), minted for L. Hostilius Saserna
(drawn by J. Morel after Cunliffe 1992, ill. p. 56: above).

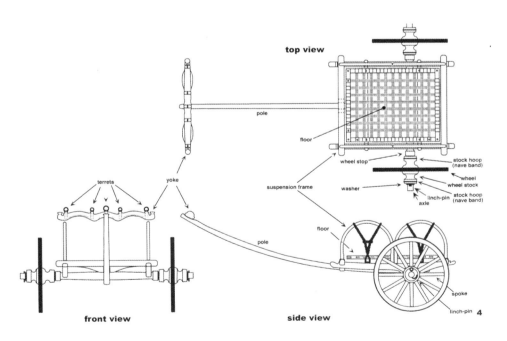

Plate 170. Reconstruction of 'Celtic chariot' (Trustees of the British Museum, London.
Illustrations drawn by Stephen Crummy).

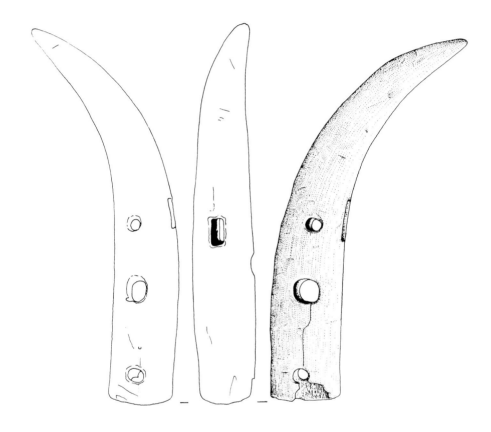

Plate 171. Antler-tine cheekpiece of horse bit from Castioni dei Marchese (after Woytowitsch 1978, pl. 52, no. 5).

Index

Note. Greek words are included in transliteration. Modern authors' names only appear when their views are specifically mentioned in the text. The contents of individual plates have not been indexed in detail but see text for cross-references; n = footnote